# Science & Service

# Science & Service

## A History of the Land-Grant University and Agriculture in California

ANN FOLEY SCHEURING

WITH

CHESTER O. McCORKLE

AND

JAMES LYONS

**FOR INFORMATION ABOUT ORDERING THIS BOOK, WRITE TO**

**ANR PUBLICATIONS**
**UNIVERSITY OF CALIFORNIA**
**6701 SAN PABLO AVENUE**
**OAKLAND, CALIFORNIA 94608-1239**

**TELEPHONE (510) 642-2431**
**1-800-994-8849 WITHIN CALIFORNIA**
**FAX (510) 643-5470**

ISBN 1-879906-17-1
Library of Congress Catalog Card Number: 94-60131

**PHOTO CREDITS**

11, 24, 27, 44–45, 55, 58, 59, 62, 63, 79, 92, 109, 111, 132, from the Bancroft Library Archives, UC Berkeley. 38, 126, 138, 139, 140, 162, photographs by Ansel Adams for the University of California, Davis. © 1967, Regents of the University of California. All rights reserved. 167, 178, 188, 194, 202, 206, 208, 210, 222, 223, 225, 227, 229, 230, 234, 235, Jack Kelly Clark. 2, 6, 8, 33, 34, 39, 52, 60, 67, 68, 69, 70, 81, 82, 83, 97, 104, 107, 115, 117, 133, 136, 142, 147, 165, 166, 171, 172, 173, 174, 175, 177, 179, 180, 181, 182, 185, 186, 191, 220, from the Special Archives Collection, Shields Library, UC Davis. 7, by permission of the Huntington Library, San Marino, California. 19, John Muir papers, Holt-Atherton Department of Special Collections, University of the Pacific libraries. © 1984, Muir-Hanna Trust. 41, reproduced from the 1892–93 Report of the California Experiment Station. 72, 73, 134, 189, UC Riverside. 100, 105, 116, reproduced from the 1923 Report of the California Agricultural Experiment Station. 130, Dorothea Lange/Library of Congress, Farm Security Administration collection. 183, courtesy of Roger Garrett, Department of Agricultural Engineering, UC Davis. 216, College of Agricultural History. 218, SAREP. 226, John Stumbos. 228, Alfred Smith. 231, courtesy of Gail McGranahan.

1m-pr-1/95-PE/FB

# Contents

# Foreword

In the years since passage of the Morrill Act in 1862, the world, the nation, and the State of California have changed in unprecedented ways. Less than a century old in 1862, the United States was what we now call a developing country, its far frontiers not fully explored and its potential clearly not realized. The transcontinental railroad was yet to be completed, and California was still an outpost on the Pacific, its population only a few hundred thousands scattered across an immensely exciting but often forbidding territory. With an economy based largely on mining and other such enterprises that simply wrenched the most obvious wealth from the earth without trying to protect resources, Californians had much to learn about the land's problems and capacities.

Wars, depressions, population movements, and technological change all have altered the nation and state beyond the wildest dreams of the mid-nineteenth-century Congressional visionaries who enacted the Agricultural Colleges Land-Grant Act. But the land-grant universities begun in the wake of that pathbreaking legislation have helped shape history, too. This volume recounts some of the ways in which the University of California has both led and adapted to change and, in the process, contributed to the evolution of California's multibillion-dollar agricultural industry.

The immediate purpose of UC agricultural research and extension, of course, is to help California agriculture maintain and increase its productivity and efficiency, while conserving and maintaining the quality of the state's natural resource base. But the benefits of research, resident instruction, and extension extend far beyond the farm gate.

In the early part of this century and well into the post–World War II era, rising productivity in agriculture made it possible not only to feed a growing population but to release large amounts of labor and land to the nation's industrializing economy. Throughout much of this century, agriculture has been one of the leading net export sectors of the economy, thereby contributing to growth in employment and income and to the nation's balance of payments. Whole new industries have sprung up to service the needs of agriculture for manufactured production inputs and to process and market food and fiber in the myriad forms that today we take for granted.

The ultimate beneficiaries of the growth in agricultural productivity and efficiency, however, have been consumers of food and fiber here and abroad. At no time in the history of any nation have consumers had access to such a broad array of dependable, high-quality food and fiber products, and at such low costs relative to disposable income, as in the United States today. This simple, indisputable fact is often overlooked.

The leaders trained at the University—teachers, scientists, engineers, journalists, legislators, and businesspersons—have been key to the state's political and economic progress. The research discoveries made in University laboratories have helped develop the technological innovations that have brought California worldwide fame. And the active extension of research findings into California businesses and communities has helped develop a quality of life (here and elsewhere) for the average citizen that was beyond the grasp of even the wealthy in centuries gone by.

A study completed by the Agricultural Issues Center at the University of California examined the relationships between agricultural research and extension and the growth in output and productivity of California. It also estimated returns on public investment from 1949 to 1985—years chosen because they could be documented and analyzed, though they actually reveal only a small part of the picture since 1875, the year in which the California Agricultural Experiment Station was established at the University. The results of the study are dramatic.

In 1985 California farmers were producing nearly three times their total output of 1949 with only 1.6 times the inputs (feed, seed, fertilizer, electricity, machinery, fuels, and so on). The difference was primarily due to improved and new technology, much of it emanating from UC agricultural research and extension investments. In investment terms, public financial support of UC's agricultural research and exten-

sion yielded an average annual rate of return of about 20 percent during the 36 years studied—a very handsome return by any investor's standards!

A closer look at just three of California's many specialized agricultural industries: dairy, viticulture and winemaking, and strawberries—will illustrate these impressive contributions..

In recent decades the productivity of California's dairy industry, the state's top farm income producer, has grown at a rate substantially faster than that of the rest of the nation. By 1991 California dairies produced more than 14 percent of total U.S. dairy output, compared with about 6 percent in 1960, and the average California cow produced 3,756 pounds (or 25 percent) more milk than the national average. Particular dairy research successes of recent years include the development of a vaccine for *E. coli* mastitis, used on about 300,000 cows by 1993 with an estimated annual savings to California dairy producers of $17 million.

California's renowned wine industry has benefited enormously from UC research. UC Davis has trained many of the state's grape growers, winemakers, and private-sector researchers. Since the 1958 initiation of the California Registration of Grapevines Program, UC has distributed more than 70 million certified disease-free grape plants to the California grape industry. Chardonnay production has grown by leaps and bounds in California largely because of UC investigations that identified and propagated superior varieties of the Chardonnay grape.

The multimillion-dollar California strawberry industry accounts for about 80 percent of all U. S. fresh and processed strawberry production. Average California yields per acre are the highest in the world, partly because of the extended bearing season that in this state now lasts nearly 11 months of the year. Almost 90 percent of California's acreage is planted to UC-developed varieties (a succession of about 40 varieties since 1945), which since 1945 have increased average yields from 3.1 to 26.8 tons per acre.

There are many such success stories to be told, and many of them are recounted in this volume authored by Ann Foley Scheuring. But UC agricultural research and extension have made contributions to other fields as well: animal research has aided developments in human medicine; biological "systems" investigations have contributed to better environmental management; agricultural engineering projects have had applications beyond farm fields; and extension education programs have contributed greatly to an improved quality of life in many communities throughout the state.

Now, as we approach the twenty-first century, UC research and extension and California agriculture face new challenges and opportunities. Advances in communication and transportation technologies have inextricably linked California agriculture with world markets for food and fiber. The North American Free Trade Agreement and its ultimate extension to other countries of the Americas portends an economically seamless market for agricultural products across many national boundaries. And California agriculture is well positioned to take advantage of rising demand for high-value food and fiber products in the world's most rapidly growing countries around the Pacific Rim. Retaining competitiveness in the globally interdependent markets of the twenty-first century will necessitate a continuing emphasis on science and education and increased investments in research to maintain growth in productivity of California agriculture.

In several respects, however, maintaining that growth into the next century will be even more complex and difficult than in the past. Enhancement of on-farm productivity, for example, will have to reckon explicitly with societal goals for envi-

ronmental quality and the plethora of state, national, and international regulations still evolving to advance those goals. Agricultural production and agricultural research and extension will need to be cast in a broader, more holistic ecological and social framework that balances often-competing goals such as those related to natural resource sustainability, environmental quality, food safety, and the welfare of consumers and communities at the agricultural-urban interface as well as producers. The old goal of research—"to make two blades of grass grow where one grew before"—will no longer suffice. Advances in the basic biological and information sciences have laid the foundations of a potentially new agricultural "revolution," one that may ultimately eclipse those of the past century associated with engineering and chemistry.

Like any human institution, the University of California has experienced its ups and downs, but its commitment to agricultural education, research, and extension has been unwavering. The tripartite system of research, resident instruction, and extension has proved itself over and over again to be a model of effectiveness in service to Californians, increasing the quantity and quality of the urban food supply and improving rural communities. Dedicated faculty and staff continue to make discoveries for today and tomorrow, putting their creative efforts into the search for solutions to complex problems. The system is resilient and adaptable, able to meet new challenges. As the twenty-first century begins to dawn, the University of California still stands ready to provide both science and service.

KENNETH R. FARRELL

VICE PRESIDENT,
AGRICULTURE AND NATURAL RESOURCES

# Preface

The University of California was created through the union of two widely disparate educational philosophies: on one hand, advocates of higher education in the classical tradition as exemplified by eastern private schools (such as Yale, Harvard, and Dartmouth); on the other, advocates of practical training as espoused by the populists (a common man-oriented political movement), the Grange (a secret society concerned with rural issues), and many if not most farmers. In his 1968 centennial history of the University, Verne Stadtman gave us a detailed account of the formation of the institution, and it seems appropriate to review the highlights of that story here.

The story begins with a group of classicists wishing to found an institute of higher learning in the fledgling state. (This was actually the second group to establish a college in early California; the first was Mills College, in Oakland.) The leading proponents of the new institution, at first a church-sponsored high school, were Henry Durant, a Yale graduate, and Samuel H. Willey, a Dartmouth graduate. With the support of leading businessmen, clergymen, and politicians, they established the Contra Costa Academy in Oakland in 1853, its curriculum devoted largely to Greek and Latin literature and philosophy. Two years later the Academy formally became the College of California, a tiny private school dependent on fund-raising.

At about the same time, the cause of public higher education was winning growing national support. Interest was rising in the formation of colleges and universities open to all, in which instruction of a practical nature would be offered. A very early expression of that interest had appeared in the Congressional Ordinance of 1787, which provided for the creation of states in the Northwest Territory (then comprising the upper Midwest); this led to federal land grants in support of public education, the first of which went to Ohio. The practice continued as new states were formed west of the Mississippi River. California, too, received such land grants: in 1853, Congress allotted 72 sections (about 46,000 acres) for a "seminary of learning" to be established from the proceeds of their sale.

In 1857 continuing national agitation for state universities and colleges that would prepare students for careers in business, industry, and practical professions led to the submission of a congressional bill, approved by Congress but vetoed by President Buchanan. The bill was resubmitted in

1862, passed by Congress, and signed into law by President Lincoln. This Land-Grant College Act (the Morrill Act) gave each state 30,000 acres of public land for each Senator and Representative in Congress. It specified that the money from the sale of these lands was to be held in a perpetual fund, never to be diminished, with interest earned on it used for "the endowment, support and maintenance of at least one College" whose leading objective would be to teach branches of learning related to agriculture and the mechanic arts, in a manner designated by each legislature. Military instruction was also required, and other scientific and classical studies were not excluded.

In California, official response to the Morrill Act was delayed until 1866, when the legislature acted to establish a state Agricultural, Mining and Mechanical Arts College. A surprisingly broad curriculum was specified. The act placed at the disposal of the College all the federal land grants to California made for higher education since 1853, but little real progress was made until the following year.

A crucial event took place at the little College of California's commencement on June 6, 1867. Reacting to a statement made by its principal speaker, Dr. Benjamin Silliman of Yale University, that the proposed state college was inadequately conceived and could not serve as a basis for a state university, Governor Frederick Low said at the meeting of the College of California Alumni, "You have here in your College, scholarship, organization, enthusiasm, and reputation, but not money: we in undertaking the state institution, have none of these things, but we have money. What a pity they could not be joined together."

Some months later, the trustees of the College of California decided to pursue Governor Low's suggestion, passing a formal resolution to merge with the state school. This was duly accepted by the directors of the Agricultural, Mining, and Mechanical Arts College on November 7, 1867. A draft bill, crafted to protect the college from political interference, was drawn up, deftly balancing the considerations of both practical and classical studies. The University bill passed the legislature and was signed by Governor Haight on March 23, 1868. In the fall of 1869 instruction in the new University of California began at the Oakland site of the College of California. After the first University buildings were completed, administration and classes moved to a site in Berkeley previously acquired by the College of California (now the site of the Berkeley campus).

Controversy soon arose over the adequacy of the University's instruction in agriculture. Farm and populist supporters of the formation of the University had had it firmly in mind that the curriculum would emphasize practical agriculture, including hands-on experience in farming, but the school was ill prepared to offer competent instruction in agriculture. The first Professor of Agriculture, Ezra Carr, was a proponent of practical training (as recounted in chapter 1 of this volume), but his career at the University was short and accomplished relatively little.

Though the College of Agriculture was supposed to offer one of the University's leading programs, in its early years it suffered from a serious handicap—a paucity of students. The low registration was regarded so seriously by University President Gilman that he had instructed Professor Carr to make the University better known throughout the state, through lectures "in all the agricultural counties and centers of population . . . and in every convenient neighborhood where accommodations can be obtained." Gilman further stated in 1873 that "the University domain is being developed, with a view to illustrate the ability of the state for special cultures, whether of forests, fruits, or field crops, and the most economic methods of production. It will be the station where new plants and processes will be tested and the results be made known to the public." But Carr's efforts—and his emphasis on practical training—did nothing to increase college enrollments.

It was Eugene Hilgard, Carr's successor and the true father of the University's College of Agriculture, who eventually proved the worth of scientific study for agricultural students. Hilgard considered the University's failure to attract many students in agriculture to be a natural condition of most American colleges. (A dearth of students was in fact not surprising, given the low enrollments in college preparatory curricula in the state's school system—in 1851, total public school enrollment in California was only 1,846; and in 1888, 20 years after the formation of the University, high school students numbered only 2,938.)

During Hilgard's early career, national debate continued over whether agricultural education should be conducted in a separate, "applied" college or in conjunction with a university that also offered the liberal arts. The former view attracted some support, then lost ground. In Hilgard's view, "This grave error, so diametrically opposed to the letter and spirit of the Morrill Act, has served long and well to sharpen the arrows of satire against the agricultural colleges and to deter ambitious young men from entering them, even where a different system prevailed."

In a two-part article in the *Atlantic Monthly* (April and May, 1882), Hilgard expressed his views on a "rational" approach to agriculture and on low enrollments in the agricultural colleges. A main concern of the colleges, he argued, should be the consequences of the exploitive, soil-depleting cultural practices in use throughout the country, and the need for scientific investigation into means of maintaining or increasing soil fertility and agricultural productivity. He found the popular emphasis on practical, as opposed to scientific, training to be a primary obstacle to adequate student enrollments. He also thought that agricultural education was severely handicapped by a shortage of qualified teachers.

To establish a scientific basis for instruction in agriculture was in part the motive of Hilgard's strong interest in agricultural research. He saw the agricultural experiment station as a necessary platform for the promotion of rational agriculture. He described these stations as places where "questions of local and general importance are systematically and thoroughly investigated under the light that science can give, and whence reliable results are directly and promptly communicated to those interested." This experimental enterprise he thought entirely consistent with the intent of the Morrill Act.

Hilgard's attitude was reflected in a national movement in support of associating experiment stations with colleges of agriculture. The culmination of this movement was the passage of the Hatch Act in 1887. Intended to foster the establishment of state agricultural experiment stations by contributing federal funds toward their support, the act was broadly framed to provide wide latitude in the selection of issues to be investigated. In a 1955 amendment, the objectives of the original Hatch Act were restructured and broadened in these terms:

> To conduct original and other researches, investigations and experiments bearing directly on and contributing to the establishment of a permanent and effective agricultural industry in the United States, including research basic to the problems of agriculture in its broadest aspects, and such experiments as have as their purpose the development and improvement of the rural home and life and the maximum contribution to the welfare of the consumer, as may be advisable, having due regard for the varying needs of the respective states.

The extent of Hilgard's influence on the development of the entire University is not measurable in specific terms, but it undoubtedly was very large. Recognition of Hilgard's achievements in agriculture by the state legislature undoubtedly led to more generous funding of the University than *xiv* would otherwise have been possible—a consequence of general benefit to other fields of learning as well.

Some of the fundamental accomplishments in the formative years of the University of California included its establishment through constitutional and legislative enactments as an institution of higher education that would forever be free from outside political interference; its responsiveness to the views of individual citizens and organizations; and the creation of a university in which purely academic Letters and Science could cooperate with the Applied Sciences. Even today, these many years after the formation of the University (now comprising nine campuses), there are many different interpretations of its founding principles, reflected in its funding mandates and in its administrations. While we are still making changes in our goals and procedures, in this ever changing world that is perhaps not a bad thing. Striving to meet the needs of the state, and its people, is what keeps the University a living institution.

LOY L. SAMMET

PROFESSOR EMERITUS,
AGRICULTURAL AND RESOURCE ECONOMICS
UNIVERSITY OF CALIFORNIA, BERKELEY

# Author's Preface and Acknowledgments

This volume is not a history of agriculture in California, the definitive account of which remains to be written. It is rather a history of the land-grant University of California's long association with the state's agriculture, from the earliest days of the Grange movement in the nineteenth century to recent lawsuits and hotly debated policy issues. As an institutional history it describes significant periods in the development of the agricultural sciences and some of the leaders who helped shape the institution. While the narrative primarily follows the activities of the University's College of Agriculture, it also covers the general evolution of California farming as well as some of the historical relations of farmers with the state and federal governments. Thus, as a recapitulation of agricultural history, it touches on the broad socioeconomic and political concerns of successive periods. Our hope is that the effort to integrate these several lines of narrative will help shed light on the nature—and dilemmas—of the land-grant university in its role as provider of public service.

This project began in 1988 when, as an individual researcher encouraged by the interest of newly appointed Vice President Kenneth Farrell, I undertook the task of writing the history of the College of Agriculture. It took nearly three years to complete the first six chapters, covering 100 years. I expected others to write the history of the next 25 years; but in 1992, with no prospect of that in sight, I began a collaboration with Chester O. McCorkle and James Lyons to complete the project. In this day of telephone conferencing, computer mailboxes, and fax machines, the meticulous sequential record of earlier times is no more, and expanding information networks actually exert a kind of centrifugal force on details; but between the three of us we were able to identify the many strands of recent institutional history and to retrieve significant portions of widely scattered relevant material. McCorkle and Lyons brought to the project an intimate knowledge of recent Division history based on many years of teaching, research, and administrative experience. Both have also taken a long-range, thoughtful view of divisional activities. Their contributions to the last chapter have thus provided both insight and balance, though they are not to be held liable for errors or misinterpretations that may have crept into the text.

It is impossible to acknowledge all the people who contributed toward the completion of this long project, but foremost among them must be those kindly librarians who took a genuine interest in helping: William Roberts of the Bancroft Library and Norma Kobzina of the Biosciences Library at UC Berkeley; Don Kunitz, John Skarstad, Axel Borg, and Ted Sibia of Shields Library at UC Davis; and other cooperative staff in several smaller, specialized libraries. I am also greatly indebted to those patient readers who made comments on earlier drafts of several chapters: especially Elmer Learn, Alex McCalla, Robert Peyton, and James Shideler, but also Carroll Brentano, Harold Carter, Ray Coppock, Constance Delwiche, Roger Garrett, the late Hans Jenny, Grace Larson, Harry Lawton, Peter Lindert, Robert Loomis, Chancellor Emeritus James Meyer, Morton Rothstein, and Wilson Smith. Their knowledge and insights helped me avoid numerous mistakes and oversights, though they are in no way responsible for any that may remain.

A special tribute goes to Loy L. Sammet, Professor Emeritus in Agricultural Economics and longtime administrative officer in the Division, whose "velvet glove" helped start the ball rolling on a division history. After his retirement Professor Sammet took an interest in documenting the accomplishments of the College of Agriculture, writing up copious notes based on his reading in the Bancroft Library. While this volume has taken shape independently and in fact reflects a view of history different from his, without his gentle prodding and active encouragement this project might never have begun.

To Kenneth Farrell, Vice President of the Division of Agriculture and Natural Resources, goes another special thankyou. Without his steadfast interest and financial support the project would never have been completed. Nor could the work have been completed without the tolerance and affection of my husband David, to whom I owe most of my personal knowledge about agriculture. If I have neglected to mention any of the many other persons who assisted this project in ways both large and small, it is only because of the length of the list of persons who helped the work along.

Some of the material in this volume will be new to most readers; some will be familiar to those who have followed various issues in recent years. Selecting what to write about was not always easy, because of the wealth of information to be found in archival deposits. Because of sheer volume, I decided early that the project could be saved from foundering under the weight of names and details only by staying with broad themes and key figures. Some readers may be disappointed because not all the accomplishments of the College have been covered, or because they cannot find specific names of friends, relatives, or popular figures from the past; their disappointment should be tempered by the realization that opportunities yet remain for others to make significant contributions to the history of the institution in the form of campus histories, department histories, and biographies of outstanding scientists and leaders. With this volume the work has really only begun.

I am grateful to have had the opportunity to explore the past in this project: the interplay of land-grant activities against the larger backdrop of state and national events; the educational, social, and philosophical debates about the role of the University; the evolution of scientific work over time, and the resultant revolutionary changes in agriculture and society. I hope that readers too will find these explorations thought-provoking, and may more fully appreciate the contributions of the land-grant University to the state and to the nation.

If the past is prologue, there will yet be many years of rich institutional achievement ahead, and our world will be the better for it.

ANN FOLEY SCHEURING

# 1

# The Beginnings of a College

## 1869–1874

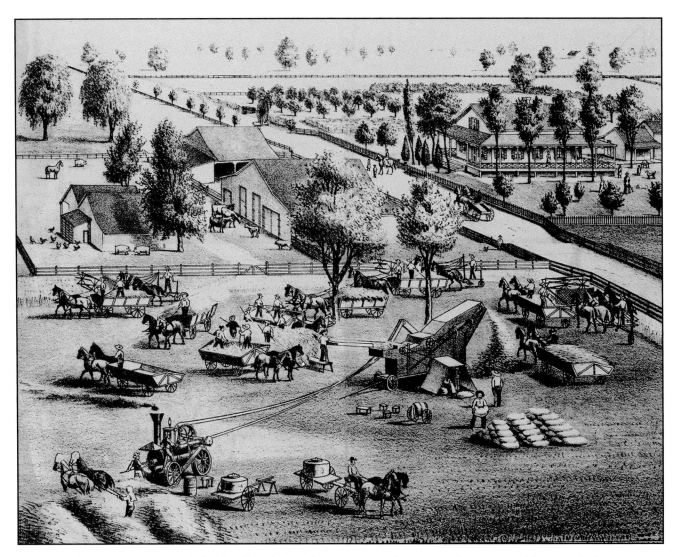

*Lithograph depicting an idealized early California farm, laid out with geometrical precision and boasting the latest steam-operated threshing machinery.*

THE YEARS BETWEEN 1850 AND 1875 WERE A CRUCIAL ERA IN THE UNITED STATES AND IN CALIFORNIA. DRIVEN IN PART BY DEMANDS OF THE CIVIL WAR, THE NATION MOVED RAPIDLY TOWARD INDUSTRIALIZATION, AND IN 1862 CONGRESS PASSED AN ACT ESTABLISHING PUBLIC INSTITUTIONS OF HIGHER EDUCATION TO SUPPORT THE NATION'S INDUSTRIAL PROGRESS. WESTWARD EXPANSION ACROSS THE CONTINENT BROUGHT HUGE NEW TERRITORIES INTO THE UNION. ON THE WESTERN SHORE, THE NEW STATE OF CALIFORNIA GROPED TOWARD A CIVIL LIFE THAT INCLUDED AN EMERGING AGRICULTURE AND A LAND-GRANT UNIVERSITY. DURING THIS TUMULTUOUS PERIOD OF GROWTH AND SOCIAL CHANGE, THE UNIVERSITY OF CALIFORNIA SURVIVED ITS FIRST TRIAL BY FIRE, INSTIGATED BY A RESTIVE FARM ORGANIZATION.

# 1

# The Beginnings of a College  1869–1874

## A NATION IN TRANSITION

In the middle of the turmoil of the Civil War, a beleaguered U.S. Congress passed three pieces of legislation that, though pending for some time, had previously been waylaid by representatives of the South. With secession from the Union, Southerners were no longer present to object on the basis of states' rights, and the bills moved forward. Compared with the events of the war, the bills were not particularly dramatic, but they would eventually have profound impacts on the nation's agriculture and the subsequent course of American history. Between May and July 1862 Congress established the U.S. Department of Agriculture, enacted the Homestead Act, and passed the Agricultural Colleges Land Grant Act.

All three acts were aimed at developing a stronger and more productive American agriculture. The Department of Agriculture was empowered to collect and disseminate all kinds of useful information on agricultural subjects, and to "procure, propagate, and distribute among the people new and valuable seeds and plants." The Homestead Act liberalized previous land laws, offering parts of the public domain to settlers and thus encouraging the spread of population into remoter areas of the West. Perhaps most far-reaching of all, however, was the legislation that is usually called the Morrill Act after its chief sponsor in Congress. By using some of the nation's capital assets in land for endowments, this law enabled states to establish public institutions of higher education. The "land-grant colleges," unlike the proprietary "classical" and denominational colleges already functioning in the nineteenth century, would offer instruction in agriculture, the mechanic and practical arts, military training, and other industrial vocational fields to a democratically broad range of students at public expense. The ramifications of this idea were enormous: a century after the Morrill Act, the institutions so established could claim credit for having educated millions in the practical professions that supported America's technological advancement, while contributing to much of the truly revolutionary change in American farming.[1]

By the mid-nineteenth century American agriculture was already commercial in most major aspects, from the early tobacco and cotton exports of the South to the milk and meat products supplied by regional farmers to eastern seaboard cities. Still, many American farms—particularly in the West—were primarily self-sustaining units supporting a family but contributing relatively little to the larger world. Although the United States was rapidly industrializing well before the

Civil War, more than half of the American population was still employed in agriculture at the time of that conflict.

Nevertheless, some farmers were dissatisfied. Yankee inventiveness and a growing number of agricultural associations and newspapers were changing traditional ways of producing crops and doing business, but disparity between rural and urban living standards was becoming ever more obvious. While thousands of families from less prosperous agricultural areas sought better farming opportunities in the West from the 1840s and 1850s onward, many bright young men and women left their rural homes for more economically and socially rewarding occupations in town, their exodus from rural areas enlarging the urban work force.

Industrial expansion, however, required increasing amounts of food for off-farm consumption. The draining North-South struggle created a still greater temporary demand for food and fiber. As factory and town building proceeded on a wider scale, fueled by waves of European immigration both before and after the war, the nation's economic growth was contingent on a dependable national commerce in agriculture—a surplus beyond local needs that might be poured into industrializing cities.[2] What farmers needed in order to provide that surplus, beyond the old triumvirate of land, tools, and sweat, was an organized system for gathering or discovering useful information and encouraging greater productivity. The landmark laws of 1862 would begin to meet those needs.

## CALIFORNIA ON THE THRESHOLD

By 1862 California had already been a state for twelve years, but the vast distances and intimidating geographical barriers separating the Pacific coast from the rest of the continent still prevented its easy integration into the Union. News from the East came slowly; even the fastest of the mail services, the short-lived Pony Express, took ten days to reach Sacramento from Missouri. Not until the transcontinental railroad was completed in 1869 would this isolation be broken.

While California's isolation was not unique among western states, the character of many of its early residents was. Extraordinary human as well as geographical determinants helped shape its eventual development, for in the national saga of westward expansion California was from its beginnings an anomaly. Most other western states, including California's northern neighbor, Oregon, were settled incrementally, but California woke suddenly to statehood. After quiet decades under Spanish and Mexican rule, California experienced the Gold Rush as a veritable paroxysm. Hordes of fortune hunters and adventurers from all over the world swept across California in 1849 and the years immediately thereafter. Only a handful of these early argonauts were ready to make a lifetime commitment; many simply hoped to get rich quick and get out. Though the state was admitted to the Union in 1850, permanent settlers were few. Speculators, however, were many.

There were reasons for this. In its early years California was not, by and large, a prepossessing place. The state's topography—the great bulwark of the Sierra Nevada on one side, the Pacific Ocean on the other—made it almost literally an island, reachable only by long ocean voyage around Cape Horn, by way of the fever-ridden Isthmus of Panama, or by exhausting treks across the Great American Desert. To be sure, new arrivals generally found the scenery arresting and the climate pleasing, but much of the state was mountain or desert, and even on the broad plains of the Central Valley the pattern of winter rains and summer drought did not encourage them to think in terms of conventional farming as they might have known it elsewhere. Waterways swollen by mountain snowmelt might burst out of their banks in winter and spring, flooding great areas, then dry up completely under three to five months of blazing sun. Soils were extraordinarily

6 variable, ranging from near-sand in some areas to adobe clay that cracked into huge rock-hard chunks in midsummer. There were astonishing differences between regions, from the rough lava rock districts of the northeast to the "goose-lands" of the Sacramento Valley—so called because the winter's accumulation of water on heavy soils attracted great flocks of migrating geese; from the "tuleland" peat soils of the Sacramento River delta to the dusty alkali flats of the central San Joaquin Valley; from the red mesa-lands of the southern basin to the pale and desolate dunes of the Imperial trough just above the Mexican border. Rainfall too was radically variable, diminishing with the latitude from more than 100 inches along the Humboldt County coast to less than 5 inches in the southern deserts.

All of these factors posed enormous challenges for any kind of agriculture, especially for Yankees accustomed to farming in the humid East and Midwest. The great Mexican latifundia of California grazed cattle and sheep "on a thousand hills" but produced little food beyond that sufficient for their own needs. Though the possibilities of irrigation were clearly present, it would take decades to accumulate the capital and expertise necessary to begin effective systems on a broad scale. Great stretches of the Central Valley and southern California lay barely touched for many years, populated

EARLY RANCH SCENE NEAR CAMBRIA, CALIFORNIA. HACKING FARMSTEADS OUT OF THE WILDERNESS WAS HARD, DIRTY WORK.

only by roving bands of elk or antelope and huge flocks of migratory birds during the wet winter months.

Thus the population first attracted to California—a mob of gold-seekers spurred on by tales of nuggets to be found lying in streams or by easy digging—was often an amalgam of wanderers and outcasts from many corners of the globe. Though a magnet for opportunists, California was not a hospitable place for the average American farmer. Its shabby, brawling early towns in no way resembled the neat, neighborly family enclaves of New England or the Midwest, and would-be settlers were frequently frustrated by the legacy of clouded land titles from the Mexican era. Shady manipulations of laxly enforced U.S. land laws and shrewd purchases by clever capitalists concentrated holdings of hundreds of thousands of acres in relatively few hands.[3]

Until about 1900 California accounted for less than 2 percent of the total U.S. population, but less than 1 percent of U.S. farms and farm population. The 1870 census found that of California's 582,000 people the proportion engaged in agricultural occupations was only about 20 percent, whereas in the nation as a whole it was about 47 percent and in the rural South up to 80 percent. Most Californians lived in the northern half of the state and tended to cluster in towns. The seaport of San Francisco was far and away the leading city, followed by Sacramento. Los Angeles was little more than a dusty pueblo, its streets populated with almost as many dogs as human residents.

## A POLYGLOT POPULATION

The first Californians were the native Indians, then the colonizers of Spanish heritage from Mexico. In the swirl of various midcentury world upheavals after the Gold Rush, however, many ethnic national groups joined the Americans coming to California. Some came from Europe, either directly or after way-stops in other states. Many thousands of Chinese arrived from their strife-torn country after 1850. In the 1860 census the three largest foreign-born groups in California were the Germans, the Irish, and the Chinese, each comprising about 10 percent of the population.

Despite the formidable challenges of the unfamiliar geography, many newcomers after the Gold Rush boom settled in enclaves centered around farming or filled specialized niches in agriculture. Some of California's earliest successful farmers were German-born, as were several of the first capitalists who made fortunes based on agriculture—Henry Miller the "cattle king," whose partner, Charles Lux, was from Alsace; Claus Spreckels the sugar magnate; Isaac Friedlander the great grain ship-

CHINESE FIELDHANDS IN CALIFORNIA IN THE LATE NINETEENTH CENTURY.

per. Other Europeans included some who found the state's climate like that of their Mediterranean origins: Portuguese from the Azores, Northern Italians, French, and Spanish. Many of these tried vegetable growing or Old Country winemaking.

Those who lacked individual means to conquer the raw landscape tended to settle in colonies, which were encouraged by promoters—some carefully structured, others merely loose associations of like-minded settlers. German colonists prospered with vineyards and orchards as early as 1856 at Anaheim. In the 1870s the Fresno area developed around seven colonies, three of them Scandinavian. Later a banker started the Italian Swiss Colony at Asti in the Sonoma Valley. The Dutch tried settlements in the San Joaquin Valley, while English and Canadians settled around Arlington Heights near Riverside or in Placer County. These early agrarian colonies preceded many others formed after the turn of the century.

In a Yankee-dominated California, Europeans were readily accepted. Not so the Chinese. Arriving by the thousands, seeking the "Gold Mountain" of their dreams and establishing a lasting East-West connection, the Chinese labored everywhere: laying track for the railroads, building dikes in reclamation districts, planting and harvesting fruit orchards

8 and vineyards, cooking and cleaning on ranches or in city homes. They were so numerous and so active that they became a major irritant for whites irked by their competition and strange ways, particularly after the depression of 1873. Incidents of vandalism and terrorism against the Chinese were frequent, and anti-Chinese feeling finally culminated in passage of the Exclusion Act in 1882, which severely limited further immigration. Nevertheless, the Chinese presence in California remained: in rural areas like Riverside or the Sacramento Delta they contributed their labor and horticultural skills for decades, a thin trickle of "paper sons" renewing the supply until well into the twentieth century.[4]

## VENTURES IN A VIRGIN LAND

In the gradual shift of California's economy from mining to agriculture, the mentality of the gold seekers often lingered on. Speculation remained the temper of the times. When mining became more difficult, some fortune hunters hoped to cash in on the fertility of virgin soils;

many of California's bonanza wheat growers were speculators on a grand scale. Beginning in the mid-1860s ranchers planted millions of acres of wheat, in fields sometimes miles long. For more than a generation wheat growers mined the soil's fertility without replacing the nutrients given up to the grain crop.[5] On July 6, 1872, the *Pacific Rural Press* reported, in a story copied from the *Stockton Independent*, that "From Lathrop to Merced, a distance of over fifty miles, the railroad runs through an almost unbroken grain field, extending as far as the eye can see on either side." This area on the east side of the San Joaquin River, the story said, was "the largest wheat field in the world . . . 672 square miles, or 430,080 acres."

Livestock and grain did not demand the painstaking kind of husbandry necessary for establishing orchards or row crops. In this place where land was cheap but labor was scarce, agriculture remained largely pastoral for decades. Nevertheless, in scattered areas where nature was especially kind, there began to develop signs of what California might become agriculturally. A few talented European expatriates and American pioneers had even before statehood started modest mixed farming operations. George Yount received a Mexican land grant in 1836 and settled in the Napa Valley, where he planted grapes

NINETEENTH-CENTURY MULE-DRAWN HARVESTING MACHINE. CALIFORNIA'S ENORMOUS WHEAT FIELDS WERE COVERED BY HUGE TEAMS OF ANIMALS, WHOSE MAINTENANCE WAS A SIGNIFICANT YEAR-ROUND EXPENSE.

and tree crops. In the 1840s Johann Sutter and others established diversified ranchos in the Sacramento Valley. Near the pueblo of Los Angeles Jean Louis Vignes and William Wolfskill set out fruit trees, vines, and citrus. John Bidwell began building his magnificent estate at Chico in the 1850s, experimenting with many different crops and enterprises. South of San Francisco in the Santa Clara Valley, early farmers tried fruit culture and silkworm growing.[6]

After 1850 California's emerging institutions tried various ways to encourage the growth of a diverse and permanent agriculture. In May 1854 the California legislature chartered the State Agricultural Society, prodded by James Warren, a businessman and "one-man agricultural pressure group."[7] In its early years the society championed experiments with many kinds of crops and products, including sugar cane, flax, cotton, tobacco, hops, tea, coffee, indigo, and rice. Each year it sponsored a State Agricultural Fair, offering prizes for the best specimens in various agricultural categories. For a time there was even talk of the society overseeing an experimental farm, but this never materialized. Local agricultural societies also flourished between 1850 and 1870, members meeting at intervals to discuss problems and learn of new opportunities and methods.[8]

State government for a time offered bounties in certain industries such as silk or sugar manufacturing. The Legislature also commissioned Agoston Harazsthy's 1861 journey to Europe to collect cuttings for California vineyards; the thousands of cuttings he brought back became the basis for a greatly expanded state wine industry.

Agricultural journals arose in the state to bring their readers information on farming and related topics. James Warren launched his *California Farmer* and *Journal of Useful Sciences* in 1854 to promote horticulture as well as, incidentally, his nursery business. The state's best-known farm periodical, the *Pacific Rural Press*, began weekly publication in San Francisco in January 1871.

# A UNIVERSITY OF CALIFORNIA AND A COLLEGE OF AGRICULTURE

Although Californians were hard at work trying to build their fortunes and create a stable economy, a sense of community did not come easily, and public institution-building took place by fits and starts. In a state whose inhabitants were still primarily single men, the education of children long remained a hit-or-miss affair. State public school laws were passed in 1851, but not until 1874 was education compulsory, and even in that year 22 percent of California's children were not attending any school, public or private. During this period elementary schools were poorly funded and inconsistent in their standards of education, and as late as 1879 only sixteen public high schools existed in the state. In many areas throughout the 1880s, the only high schools were academies organized by religious denominations.[9] Creation of institutions of higher learning lagged as well.

Although the California Constitution of 1849 gave lip service to some kind of state university, early efforts at organizing and endowing one were largely ineffectual. Without money or much student interest, establishment of a public college took a back seat to more pressing matters. Before 1862, only a handful of private, mainly church-sponsored colleges offered higher education to California students—one of them the College of California in Oakland, founded by educational visionary Henry Durant. With congressional approval of the Agricultural College Land Grant Act that year, however, the possibility for a state university for California emerged more clearly.[10]

The national movement to establish state-supported colleges to prepare young people for careers in agriculture and commerce had been simmering for a number of years before Representative Justin S. Morrill, the son of a Vermont blacksmith, turned it into legislation. Morrill's first bill to

10 promote public higher education, introduced in the 1857 congressional session, narrowly passed both houses in 1859 but was vetoed by President Buchanan on grounds of expense and possible unconstitutionality. In 1861 Morrill reintroduced the bill, which again passed the House and Senate and was signed by President Lincoln on July 2, 1862. The act provided that each state might apply for 30,000 acres of public land for each of its federal representatives, which could then be sold for

> the endowment, support, and maintenance of at least one college where the leading object shall be, without excluding other scientific and classical studies, and including military tactics, to teach such branches of learning as are related to agriculture and the mechanic arts, in such manner as the legislatures of the States may respectively prescribe, in order to promote the liberal and practical education of the industrial classes in the several pursuits and professions in life.[11]

For several years after the Morrill Act was passed, the states grappled in various ways with the problems of organizing land-grant institutions. Several states in the East or Midwest used the newly available federal support to strengthen or reorganize already established colleges. It took a little longer in the West. In 1864 the California legislature formally accepted the land grants, but for two years took no further steps. On March 31, 1866, to meet the deadline for capturing federal incentives, the legislature officially created an "Agricultural, Mining and Mechanical Arts College." In June the board of directors of the new college met in San Francisco to authorize solicitation of offers for the sale or donation of lands for an Agricultural College and Farm. Seven proposals were received by September (from individuals and groups in Sacramento, Sutterville, and San Jose, as well as El Dorado, Santa Clara, Napa, and Alameda counties), but the directors took no action.[12]

The following June, Governor Frederick Low, chairman of the state college board, attended the commencement and sixth-anniversary celebration of the College of California in Oakland. Here he became convinced that the creation of an "Agricultural, Mining and Mechanical Arts College" had been too hasty. In a speech to the assembled alumni he suggested the possibility of combining the existing College of California with the mandate and resources of the Morrill Act. Reasoning that the state needed a complete university including literary and scholarly studies rather than a narrowly defined polytechnic school, Low continued to urge friends and trustees of the College of California to consider a combination of efforts. Trustees of the financially troubled college found the suggestion appealing, and in October they made a formal offer to the State Board of Directors of the Agricultural, Mining and Mechanical Arts College: they would donate the college's land and dissolve the institution if a university were organized on an academic level "equal to those of Eastern Colleges."

In November 1867 the State College directors accepted the College of California offer. A committee of trustees drafted a bill to create the University of California, stipulating its terms of organization. To meet the mandate of the land grant act, the new university would have to include a College of Mines and a College of Agriculture. John Dwinelle, principal author of the founding document, carefully outlined the structure and duties of a nonpolitical Board of Regents and Academic Senate and skillfully wove in reference to practical as well as classical studies. Carried by Dwinelle, who was newly elected to the Assembly by Alameda County, the bill quickly moved through the legislature, was passed on March 21, 1868, and was signed by the governor two days later. This "Organic Act" established the present University of California.[13]

The Organic Act provided that when the original Agricultural, Mining and Mechnical Arts College was annulled in favor of a University of California, the new institution would give special consideration to agriculture as a field of study. To quiet any fears of farmers and their representatives, the College of Agriculture was to be established first, before any other in the University.[14]

The place intended for the new state university was not the College of California's Oakland site but a tract about 4 miles north that had been acquired some years earlier and dedicated for future college use in May 1866. At that time the tract had been named Berkeley after the Irish bishop and philosopher who had penned a well-known poem containing the line "Westward the course of empire takes its way. . . ."[15] It was a beautiful setting for a college. Sloping upward toward the hills overlooking San Francisco Bay, the grounds were divided by two branches of a pretty stream named Strawberry Creek and punctuated with picturesque oaks. Tempered by proximity to the ocean, the climate was mild year-round, and the vista across the undeveloped land below, over the bay to the Golden Gate, with the Pacific beyond, was glorious.

EARLY VIEW TOWARD SAN FRANCISCO BAY FROM THE GROUNDS OF UC BERKELEY. THE FIRST BUILDING COMPLETED, SOUTH HALL (AT LEFT), HOUSED THE COLLEGE OF AGRICULTURE IN ITS BASEMENT.

In the flurry of activity that ensued, the University's Board of Regents had first of all to put together a faculty. A few instructors came directly from the old College of California. Others were rather hastily hired to fill immediate needs. The first Professor of Agriculture, Ezra Slocum Carr, was one of these.

## THE CASE OF PROFESSOR CARR    11

### CARR'S BACKGROUND

Professor Carr arrived in California with impressive credentials. Educated in Troy, New York, at the Rensselaer Institute, the pioneering school of technical education, he had subsequently earned a degree in medicine at Castleton College in Vermont. He taught chemistry there and at several other Eastern medical colleges before moving to the University of Wisconsin in 1856. There he remained for more than ten years as chair of chemistry and natural history, delivering lectures on, among other subjects, agricultural chemistry and the "application of science to the useful arts." He also worked on Wisconsin's state geological survey and served for a year on the University's Board of Regents.

Although Carr's letters of recommendation from Wisconsin were laudatory, the circumstances under which he had left Wisconsin were somewhat vague, and the Regents in California did not find out until later Carr's true reputation there. In a difficult period at the University of Wisconsin after a financial panic in 1857, Carr had been "active around the legislature" helping to stir up

12 enough dissatisfaction for a formal investigation to be mounted in 1858 to examine the university's budget and management. The university was subsequently reorganized into different departments, but disharmony between administration and faculty continued. Carr, who had gained a seat on the Wisconsin Board of Regents, was forced to resign to save his position on the faculty. He made some enemies by being "tactless" and "contemptuous" of his colleagues. In 1865 a faculty subcommittee accused him of "dereliction of duty," but nothing came of the charge. In 1867, however, the Regents, in a clean sweep of the faculty anticipating the arrival of a new president, voted not to re-elect Carr to his chair.[16] Though the new president, Paul Chadbourne, retained Carr on trial for a few months, he later informed Daniel Gilman's brother that he had ultimately judged Carr unfit for his office and ordered him to "leave quietly" or risk exposure before the scientific community.[17]

Carr, "the fractious one," headed west via steamship to San Francisco, arriving at just about the time the new University of California emerged as an institution. When the university advertised for applicants for its first faculty positions, Carr produced his extensive credentials and a letter of recommendation from a former fellow regent at Wisconsin. A second letter of recommendation commented that Carr's talented wife Jeanne would be an additional asset for the university. Carr was duly appointed Professor of Agriculture, Agricultural Chemistry, and Horticulture on July 7, 1869.[18]

### BUILDING A CONSTITUENCY

The new professor had no program, no students, no equipment, and no laboratory; everything was yet to be shaped. At the behest of the Regents in January 1870, Carr set about traveling to familiarize himself with California conditions, speaking to agricultural groups about the goals of the University and planning for development of the Department of Agriculture. In a report dated November 10, 1870, he

claimed to have traveled at least 2,000 miles, speaking to "not less than 30,000 people" in locations between Chico and Jackson, "endeavoring to interest them in a rational development of our industrial interests, and to show the relations of these to education, and especially to make the objects and scope of the University, and its practical value to the state, more thoroughly understood." In an address at the 1870 State Fair, Carr specifically alluded to the possibilities of research: "The University proposes to furnish the facilities for all needful experiments: to be the station where tests can be made of whatever claims attention."[19]

Carr also began appearing regularly in the pages of the *Pacific Rural Press*. To the inaugural issue of January 6, 1871, he contributed the first of four articles on agriculture and education. In "The Needs of Agricultural Communities" Carr argued the need for education to overcome the distaste of young people for farming, to build a more scientific agriculture, and to help develop more satisfying rural communities in California, like those created by European immigrant farmers in the Midwest.

Elsewhere in this first issue Carr was referred to as "one of California's most eloquent lecturers." His popular lectures on "Chemistry and Its Applications" for the Mechanics Art College in San Francisco were reported in the *Pacific Rural Press* in succeeding issues between March and June. Carr always accompanied his rather basic explanations of natural phenomena with entertaining demonstrations and "experiments," which his audiences greatly appreciated.

> The Professor has a peculiarly happy manner of handling scientific subjects, which gives them an unusual interest in the minds of the ordinarily educated, while they lose nothing of their value to the better informed listener. His illustrations are always of the most simple description, while the apparatus usually employed is in keeping with the simplicity of his language.[20]

To extend his influence Carr joined farm organizations. For a time he served as president of the Oakland Farming,

Horticultural and Industrial Club. He was a member of the committee that drafted the constitution of the California Farmers' Union in 1872, and he gave a major address to that organization's first convention in April 1873, at which the highly respected John Bidwell presided. When the union dissolved after establishment of the Order of the Patrons of Husbandry (the Grange), Carr was active in the new movement, which swept rapidly across California. By July 1873, 35 local granges had been organized in the state, and a regular "Patrons of Husbandry" section began appearing in the *Pacific Rural Press*. At the first annual meeting of the State Grange in San Jose in October 1873, when more than 100 local granges convened, Carr gave a "powerful and entirely interesting" address. Riding the wave of enthusiasm that lifted the Grange in California, as in other states, to a remarkable bloom of membership by 1874, Carr served as Worthy Lecturer (program chairman and officer in charge of member education) for his local Temescal Grange (Alameda County) and later as Master of that group.[21]

## DELAYS AND DISCONTENTS

Carr had been Professor of Agriculture not quite a year when construction began in May 1870 on the first permanent building for the Berkeley campus (later called South Hall), designed to meet the mandate of the Organic Act by providing space for the College of Agriculture. In January 1871, however, work on the building stopped for lack of funds and was not resumed until the following year. In letters to the Regents between 1871 and 1874, meanwhile, Carr continued to report extensive traveling to give lectures. He also discussed ambitious plans for horticultural plantings on the campus and proposed experimental gardens for the testing of plant varieties from other countries that might be adaptable to California conditions, urging appropriations for planting at the proper times and suggesting that students be paid for labor on the agricultural grounds. He outlined a course of instruction for agricultural students and asked for additional faculty to assist in giving specialized instruction. On several occasions he urged that a "model farmhouse" be built on campus, where the Professor of Agriculture might live and discharge his responsibilities as director of the agricultural program.[22]

Carr's reports to the Regents were always submitted in his wife's handwriting. Mrs. Carr may have contributed more than simple transcription. Jeanne Smith Carr was a strong character in her own right, with a more than amateur's interest in botany and horticulture; she wrote her own letters suggesting plantings for the University grounds and later developed the Carrs' beautifully landscaped estate "Carmelita" in Pasadena, which some years afterward became the site of the Norton Simon Museum. An early activist for women's rights, Jeanne Carr was an articulate advocate for useful education in domestic science and "outdoor industries" for women. She was also a lifelong friend of John Muir and supporter of his literary, scientific, and environmental work. Like her husband, she was very active in the Grange movement, and the Carrs' home in Oakland was known as a gathering place for distinguished visitors to California.[23]

Despite the Carrs' reports and proposals, the Regents moved slowly in responding to their requests. Much else needed to be done in establishing the University, and funds were short. Few students were interested in agricultural courses, and the grounds at Berkeley were not occupied until the autumn of 1873. When South Hall was completed and dedicated in October of that year, the College of Agriculture was assigned only limited quarters in the north half of the basement floor, for other departments also needed space while new buildings were going up.[24] Though the unobstructed view from the basement half-windows was very fine, the College of Agriculture was apparently being only nominally accommodated. Carr grew increasingly frustrated.

## CHALLENGE TO A YOUNG UNIVERSITY

The University's infant years in the early 1870s were difficult ones for both California and the nation. While capitalists were amassing fortunes, workers suffered from low wages and unemployment. Labor unrest was endemic. Some of California's labor turmoil surfaced in the virulent anti-Chinese demonstrations of the decade, when workers vented their anger against the growing number of Asian immigrants who would work for very low pay. Small business owners and farmers focused their anger against the power of the railroads and other shippers to control traffic and commerce. In 1873 a national financial panic was followed by a major depression; in 1875 the Bank of California collapsed after speculation in the Comstock mines ballooned into a debacle. The times were ripe for a populist movement against grievances, and widespread frustration underlay the organization and growth of groups like the Workingmen's Party, the Knights of Labor, and the Patrons of Husbandry. Few institutions escaped the backwash from these waves of discontent, and the young University was rocked by the resentment smoldering among farmers who felt victimized by the wealthy and powerful.

### RISE OF THE PATRONS OF HUSBANDRY

A national fraternal order of farmers begun by O. H. Kelley in 1867 in Washington, D.C., the Patrons of Husbandry became generally known as the Grange, probably after their local lodges or grange halls erected in rural areas as a base for their activities. There was a great surge in Grange membership between 1873 and 1875, the nadir of the national depression. At its peak in 1875, the National Grange claimed 21,697 local granges across the country and more than 750,000 individual members.

California Grange membership also peaked that year at about 15,200 in 264 local chapters; the number suggests that a high percentage of California's farmers had joined, for in 1870 there were 23,724 California farms. Many members came from other local farm organizations, and a certain class consciousness pervaded at least some of their thinking. Remarks by a Mr. Garrigus of the San Jose Farmers Club and Protective Association were recorded in the *Pacific Rural Press*: "He don't like to associate with such men as form the State Agricultural Society. They are a horse-racing, gambling, drinking and wine growing set of men."[25] Public statements by some Grangers were occasionally highly emotional, not to say rhetorically inflated—as in the opening address at the organization of the Elmira Grange, by Judge T. Hart Hyatt, Master of the Vacaville Grange:

> What Do the Patrons of Husbandry Propose to Do?—We propose to become revolutionists. Yes, we propose to try our hand at revolution, until we can overthrow the perverted, rotten system by which the industrial farmer, the producer of the very elements of man's existence and subsistence has been made to toil and sweat and suffer privation, and too often penury and ruin, in order that the bloated monopolist, the grasping middleman, and the ring sharks, who rob the farmer of all his profits, may roll in luxury and wealth, and by which the farmer has been made to support the political demagogues, who ride into place and power on the backs of the honest but duped tillers of the soil, who are taxed, and taxed, and taxed, and squeezed and robbed, to support these insatiable monopolists and political bummers, until it has come to be a serious question with many farmers whether they had not better abandon their farms and their homes to those who already absorb all the profits [that] their farms and labor can produce. . . . We propose to break up these monopolies, to combine our strength into one mighty power that shall be able to hurl from place and power all these dishonest harpies who steal into office, betray the farmers' interests, and make themselves millionaires and lordly aristocrats at the expense of the honest and confiding farmer.[26]

This kind of crusading spirit led to much vigorous action. Nationally the Grange of the 1870s has been most remembered for its efforts to fight the pricing policies of the railroads; enactment of various "Granger laws" in some of the midwestern states brought some relief against high commodity transportation rates. In California the Patrons not only organized protests against the railroads, they fought the sack manufacturers and the shipping interests handling sea freight of California wheat to European markets. Grangers tried to compete with "wheat king" Isaac Friedlander's stranglehold on the Liverpool grain trade by chartering their own vessels through Morgan and Sons in 1874. When Friedlander and his colleagues undercut the Morgan shipping prices, however, the Grange venture ended within a year in near-disaster. Members attracted by the promise of cheaper shipping rates deserted in droves, enrollment falling from more than 15,000 in 1875 to fewer than 2,000 by 1880.[27]

While the Grange gained high visibility for its economic activities, its role in supporting and shaping public education is not so well remembered. In many states, however, the Grange was deeply involved with the land-grant colleges as they developed. The Morrill Act had specified that states would have flexibility in organizing land-grant institutions according to the "various needs" of their constituencies. Thus states took different directions, some combining education in agriculture and the mechanic arts with traditional classical and literary studies within universities, while others created separate and distinct agricultural colleges. In states such as California, where organizers sought to combine the two kinds of education, the Grange frequently mounted efforts to disassociate the schools of agriculture from the university and establish them as independent institutions. In 1876 the National Grange directed state chapters to investigate their land-grant colleges for their effectiveness in offering agricultural education. At the same time, "Patrons resolved 'that these colleges ought to be . . . separate and distinct schools, where science as applied to agriculture, may be taught to farmers' children, fitting them for the high calling of farm-

ers.'"[28] Many Grangers distrusted the elitist proclivities of universities to value literary and classical studies above "practical" education, some farmers fearing (not without reason) that their sons would be looked down upon by "literary" students as being "inferior," or that they might acquire tastes that would induce them to leave farming. As early as 1871 Ezra Carr had revealed his sympathy with this position, when he wrote, in praise of the technical school approach in German agricultural education, that American colleges should not have "an Agricultural Professorship . . . tacked upon some classical institution, and left to flutter in the unkindly winds of competition with departments which have prestige and a class or aristocratic sentiment in their favor."[29]

## THE GRANGE AND DANIEL GILMAN

In California the Patrons became active on the issue of the land-grant university's mission and methods just at the time the infant University of California was feeling its way toward the future. Daniel Coit Gilman, the dynamic new young president of the University, arrived in California in 1872 from the Sheffield Scientific School at Yale. At his November inauguration he enunciated a vision for the University of California:

> First, it is a "University," and not a high-school, nor a college, nor an academy of sciences, nor an industrial-school, which we are charged to build. Some of these features may, indeed, be included in or developed with the University; but the University means more than any or all of them. The University is the most comprehensive term which can be employed to indicate a foundation for the promotion and diffusion of knowledge—a group of agencies organized to advance the arts and sciences of every sort, and to train young men as scholars for all the intellectual callings of life.

The work of the University, said Gilman, was "to fit young men for high and noble careers," to bring before society the failures and successes of societies in the past, "to discover and make known how the forces of nature may be

16 subservient to mankind," and to hand down to succeeding generations "the torch of experience by which we have been enlightened."[30] Noble words, though spoken at the edge of the continent: Gilman showed a vision far ahead of his time, and particularly so in California, a state still stumbling toward an identity.

On his way to becoming one of the great American educators of the nineteenth century, Gilman had firm opinions about goals for higher education, and they were based on a scientific view that emphasized the discovery of new knowledge through carefully focused research. For Gilman, as he demonstrated later at Johns Hopkins in his gathering of a brilliant faculty, a university was above all a body of scholars, "skilled in their specialties, eminent in their calling, loving to teach."[31] More important for the institution than buildings, laboratories, or libraries was the quality of the faculty, and that quality should be demonstrated through original investigations that could build up, brick by brick, the edifice of accumulated knowledge about the world.

Gilman's vision for the University of California was very unlike Carr's. Though Carr was a talented lecturer and had early in his California career stated that the University should serve as an experiment station, he himself did no research, and he continued to emphasize practical training for agricultural students. The clash in philosophy between president and professor soon erupted in political conflict.

In a December 1873 report to the California legislature, Gilman claimed, "The University domain is being developed . . . to be the station where new plants and processes will be tested and results made known to the public." As progress toward this goal was obviously not yet apparent, in January 1874 the California State Grange and Mechanics' Deliberative Assembly presented a memorial to the legislature charging that the University was not carrying out in good faith the intent of the Morrill Act. In his annual reports to the Regents for at least three years, Carr had petitioned for more resources with which to carry on his work. The Grange's memorial made recommendations "suspiciously similar in content and wording" to the requests made by Carr.[32]

> We earnestly recommend . . . the improvement of such portions of the University grounds as may be required to illustrate practically the subjects taught in the Department of Agriculture, and the adaptation of this state to various cultures. The erection of a plain, convenient, and commodious farm house, with suitable outhouses, to be occupied by the Professor of Agriculture, or some practical farmer to act under his direction. To this an orchard, vineyard, vegetable and flower garden, and a poultry yard should be attached; also, a propagating house, and . . . a conservatory. The culture of cereals, textiles, and other valuable vegetable productions; the rearing of stock, bees, and silkworms should be illustrated, on a small scale, epitomizing the entire range of agricultural industries.[33]

Stating that only one-twentieth of the funds for the University were being used for the Department of Agriculture and that only one professor was discharging all of the duties of instruction for agricultural students, the memorial claimed that putting the department in the basement of South Hall placed it "in a subordinate position" when it should be "the most prominent department of the State University." The memorial demanded that signs for the College of Agriculture be clearly displayed on the facade of the building, called for an investigation of the University's use of land-grant funds, and suggested reorganizing the Board of Regents to more adequately represent the interests of agriculturalists. This complaint on the behalf of a large and vocal constituency impelled the legislature to appoint a joint committee to investigate the charges. Committee members visited the Berkeley campus and interviewed various people including Professor Carr, whose responses to their probing questions were "masterfully noncommittal."[34]

In March the Regents responded to the questions of the joint committee in a formal report. This document contained a description of the general courses of instruction offered *all* students, including agricultural students, and a report by Carr on the status of agricultural instruction that recommended ways to improve the operations of the department (among other things, Carr recommended that the University sponsor annual Farmers' Institutes like those in other states such as Illinois—a suggestion not carried out in California until more than fifteen years later). Granting that development of the Berkeley grounds was slow, the Regents included a report from Wm. Hammond Hall, engineer, on principles to be considered in landscaping. Finally, in the appendix, "Special Information Respecting Agricultural Education," the Regents stated that, because agricultural students had been slow in appearing, they had directed the agricultural professor to travel and give lectures outside the University, that agricultural work on campus was not possible until the September 1873 move to Berkeley, that the professor had always been consulted for suggestions, that four surveys of the grounds had been made, and that appropriations had been solicited for experimental work.[35]

Ultimately the investigating committee vindicated the Regents' management of the University. Committee members concluded that "all had been done in the advancement of agricultural matters that could have been reasonably performed with the means at hand," considering the youth of the institution and the very recent surveying and laying out of the grounds. They attributed the controversy to "jealousy and bad feeling with some persons connected with the University," as well as to the "general spirit of rush, hurry, and impatience of our people" in expecting to see things done immediately.[36]

President Gilman and the Regents were greatly relieved, but Carr's career at the University had suffered irreparable damage. During the months preceding, Gilman had inquired among colleagues about Carr's former Wisconsin reputation, receiving the following unflattering comments:

"President Chadbourne . . . was dissatisfied with Dr. Carr . . . whom he had retained on trial. . . . He did his work in a slovenly and unsatisfactory manner . . .[and was] behind the times in his science, was a popular lecturer, rather than a scientific instructor. . . . He slighted his work."[37] In an April letter Gilman wrote, "The Grangers were determined to capture the [University],—up to the last moments were endeavoring to abolish the Board of Regents, and substitute a Board chosen by popular election—two from each Congressional district. Dr. Carr, who appears to have instigated the whole movement, at the last of it backed down."[38] In early summer Carr was invited to resign. When he would not, he was dismissed by the Board of Regents on August 11, 1874, by a vote of 11 to 6 (with 6 absent), on grounds of incompetence. Gilman himself prepared a handwritten list of Carr's deficiencies as a professor, including his failures to keep abreast of the sciences and to make experiments, his 50 percent absence rate from faculty meetings in 1873, and his having made the agricultural course notoriously easy for students.[39]

Though Gilman had carefully documented the case against Carr, the Regents' action did not sit well with the public. On August 15, the editor of the *Pacific Rural Press* protested the "unceremonious dismissal," calling it the culmination of a "personal squabble" and a great wrong done to an individual, though he did not defend Carr directly. Grangers were incensed at the action against their popular brother, calling in the *Press* for a complete explanation from the University. Resolutions came "pouring in from every quarter, denouncing the unwarranted and hasty actions of the Regents," expressing the views of perhaps nine-tenths of the farmers of the state.[40] The Santa Barbara Grange, endorsed by several others, angrily accused the Regents of dismissing Carr because of his association with the Grange. In late September the Regents issued a defense of their decision, stating that the University was offering appropriate instruction and

18 making progress in developing its agricultural facilities, and that the Regents had both the right and the responsibility to judge the fitness of faculty.

In the swirl of the controversy Carr sought to garner support from the press, going so far as to visit the offices of the *San Francisco Bulletin* to drop off a written justification of his cause (which the *Bulletin* refused to publish, but which subsequently appeared in the *Chronicle* and in the *Pacific Rural Press*).[41] The case attracted commentary in many newspapers, some of which called the Regents' action "treachery to the people," "a high-handed outrage," "double-dealing," and "a grievous wrong," although others defended the Regents.[42] Eventually the uproar died down.

### DENOUEMENT

Away from the University, Carr busied himself preparing pamphlets on education and a lengthy book about the Grange and agriculture in California. With the help of many supporters he won election in 1875 as state superintendent of public instruction. He held this post for four years, appointing his wife Jeanne as deputy superintendent. Ironically, one of his duties as superintendent was to serve as an ex officio member of the University's Board of Regents. He only sporadically attended meetings, however, and despite the apprehensions of his successor Eugene Hilgard, Carr "never opened his mouth," knowing that the other regents disliked him.[43] His term over, Carr retired to Pasadena and after some years of ill health died in 1894.

Though the University came through the turmoil with no real damage—even, in fact, with augmented appropriations for the next year—the fight with the Grange left Gilman discouraged and unhappy with the politics of a public university. To a friend Gilman wrote that, though he felt the structure of the institution was rising in a stately fashion, it seemed built above a "powder mill" that might endanger it at any moment.[44] In early 1875, only six months after Carr's dismissal, Gilman left California to become president of the newly established Johns Hopkins University in Maryland, where he would build an illustrious career.

## A LAST GLANCE

Probably Carr's most lasting legacy is his book *The Patrons of Husbandry on the Pacific Coast*, published in San Francisco in 1875. The book has been called "an unscholarly hodge-podge."[45] It consists variously of what seem to be lecture notes on the history of agriculture from the Babylonians to the Japanese, proceedings of meetings, a directory of local granges and charter members, and a long section on "Aids and Obstacles to Agriculture on the Pacific Coast," including chapters on land monopoly, the "irrigation problem," transportation, education, banking, and rural communities. As a collection of undigested material the book has no intellectual framework, but as a documentary source on the origins and early concerns of the Grange in California it remains an important historical reference work.

Carr's career illustrates the difficulties of staffing early agricultural colleges. California was not unique in its early problems with agricultural education. Though Carr and his wife sincerely tried to get the college going, he was apparently neither professionally competent nor politically astute enough to do the job; these deficiencies led to his downfall. Yet hindsight suggests at least a mixed evaluation of his efforts.

Carr was a great popularizer of scientific ideas; he was not really a scientist. He often signed himself M.D. because of his medical degree (although he never practiced medicine), but in this he was not untypical of his peers. With no clearly established body of agricultural sciences, early educators often simply foraged superficially among related branches of knowledge, and in the nineteenth century the study of medicine provided at least a passing acquaintance with the rudiments of chemistry, biology, and other scientific disciplines yet to be fully developed. Carr's visions for the land-grant college were certainly more limited in scope than Gilman's; he was nonetheless committed to the cause of education for the common man, and, influenced by his capable wife, he was an advocate of better opportunities for women as well. His arguments for practical education were valid, though perhaps ill-timed. Later establishment of a University Farm and of more vocationally oriented education at other institutional levels would eventually meet the needs he articulated. But for a young university trying to set its priorities clearly, Carr was an obstacle and an irritant. The charges of Carr's incompetence were documented, yet Frederick Slate, a later Berkeley faculty member, wrote in his biography of Eugene Hilgard that Carr had been dismissed "for political reasons."[46]

EZRA AND JEANNE CARR IN RETIREMENT AT THEIR PASADENA RANCH, CIRCA 1890.

The story of Carr's career illustrates two themes that have reverberated down through the history of the College of Agriculture—and the University as a whole—until now. The first is the difference in philosophy between proponents of the applied and the theoretical in agricultural education, those endorsing "practical" training emphasizing manual skills versus those urging the grounding of practice upon scientific understanding. Carr and the Grangers were defeated in their attempts to establish practical training, but the issue would resurface many times in the University of California's next eighty years as the state's agricultural and educational systems evolved.

The second theme is the sometimes uneasy relationship between the land-grant university and its legislature, still a living issue. Each university administration throughout the years has had to deal in some way with external political pressures, or, conversely, to find ways to leverage legislative response to internal needs. Carr may have misread the power of the Grange to give him what he thought he needed; almost certainly the pressure from the populist, class-conscious Grangers antagonized President Gilman and the Regents, who were committed to establishing California's land-grant university as a foundation for "intellectual callings" and "high and noble careers." Later college administrators would find ways quite different from Carr's to enlist political support in pursuit of their goals—by proving the value of science for economic development, and by nourishing a long-term cooperative relationship between the University and a stable constituency.

# NOTES

1. Earle D. Ross's authoritative *Democracy's College: The Land-Grant Movement in the Formative Stage* (Ames: Iowa State College Press, 1942) describes the evolution of the land-grant idea and the early history of the land-grant colleges. Another general account of the land-grant movement is found in Edward Danforth Eddy, Jr.'s *Colleges for Our Land and Time: The Land-Grant Idea in American Education* (New York: Harper, 1956).

2. For a concise history of U.S. farming, see Everett E. Edwards, "American Agriculture—The First 300 Years," in U.S. Department of Agriculture, *Yearbook of Agriculture* (Washington, D.C.: USDA, 1940), pp. 171–276.

3. The atmosphere of the period is described in several general histories of the state, including Walton Bean's *California: An Interpretive History* (New York: McGraw-Hill, 5th ed., 1988); Robert Glass Cleland's *From Wilderness to Empire: A History of California* (New York: Knopf, 1969); Kevin Starr's *Americans and the California Dream, 1850–1915* (New York: Oxford University Press, 1973); and T. H. Watkins's *California: An Illustrated History* (New York: American Legacy Press, 1983). Bean comments, "The gold rush was the product of a kind of mass hysteria, and it set a tone and created a state of mind in which greed predominated and disorder and violence were all too frequent" (p. 123). But see J. S. Holliday, *The World Rushed In: The California Gold Rush Experience* (New York: Simon and Schuster, 1981), for a view of well-educated, stable farming folk who also became gold seekers.

4. For an overview of ethnic groups in California agriculture, see the three-part series of articles by Ann Foley Scheuring, "From Many Lands," "Social Climbing," and "Off Limits," in *California Farmer* 267:8 and 9 (Nov. 21 and Dec. 12, 1987): 16–18 and 34–36; and 268:1 (Jan. 2, 1988): 26–28. "Paper sons" (next-generation Chinese applying for immigration on the basis of documented kinship to earlier immigrants) are described in Thomas W. Chinn, ed., *A History of the Chinese in California: A Syllabus* (San Francisco: Chinese Historical Society of America, 1969), p. 15. Other sources on the Chinese include the oral history compiled by Peter C. Y. Leung with editor L. Even Armentrout Ma, *One Day, One Dollar: Locke, California, and the Chinese Farming Experience in the Sacramento Delta* (El Cerrito, Calif.: Chinese American History Project, 1984) and Sucheng Chan's *This Bittersweet Soil: The Chinese in California Agriculture* (Berkeley: University of California Press, 1986). Source materials on other ethnic groups in California agriculture over time include Joseph A. McGowan, *History of the Sacramento Valley* (New York: Lewis Historical Publishing, 1961); Wallace Smith, *Garden of the Sun: A History of the San Joaquin Valley, 1772–1939* (Los Angeles: Lyman House, 1939); Carey McWilliams, *Factories in the Fields: The Story of Migratory Farm Labor in California* (Boston: Little, Brown, 1939); George E. Frakes and Curtis B. Solberg, eds., *Minorities in California History* (New York: Random House, 1971); Theodore Saloutos, "The Immigrant in Pacific Coast Agriculture, 1880–1940," *Agricultural History* 49 (Jan. 1975): 182–219; Andrew Rolle, *The Immigrant Upraised* (Norman: University of Oklahoma Press, 1968); Jerry R. Williams, *And Yet They Come* (New York: Center for Migration Studies, 1982).

5. See Rodman Paul, "The Great California Grain War: The Grangers Challenge the Wheat King," *Pacific Historical Review* 27 (Nov. 1958): 331–49.

6. See Frank Adams, "The Historical Background of California Agriculture," in Claude Hutchison, ed., *California Agriculture* (Berkeley: UC Press, 1946), pp. 1–50.

7. Walton Bean, "James Warren and the Beginnings of Agricultural Institutions in California," *Pacific Historical Review* 13 (Dec. 1944): 361–75.

8. Adams, "Historical Background," pp. 40–41.

9. William Warren Ferrier, *Ninety Years of Education in California, 1846–1936* (Berkeley: Sather Gate Book Shop, 1937), pp. 118, 88–91.

10. See William Warren Ferrier, *Origin and Development of the University of California* (Berkeley: Sather Gate Book Shop, 1930), and Verne Stadtman, *The University of California, 1868–1968* (New York: McGraw-Hill, 1970), for the story of California's early efforts to establish a state college.

11. Morrill's bill was "a generalized synthesis . . . the epitome of two decades of regional agitation and experimentation" (Ross, *Democracy's College*, p. 46). See also Wayne Rasmussen, ed., *Readings in the History of American Agriculture* (Urbana: University of Illinois Press, 1960), pp. 109–11.

12. Stadtman, *University of California, 1868–1968*, pp. 24–29.

13. Ibid., pp. 29–34.

14. Ibid., pp. 141–42.

15. Ibid., p. 14.

16. Carr's career prior to California has been pieced together through entries on Carr in Verne Stadtman, *The Centennial Record of the University of California*, p. 411, and entries on Carr in Merle Curti and Vernon Carstensen, *The University of Wisconsin: A History, 1848–1925* (Madison: University of Wisconsin Press, 1949), vol. 1, pp. 83–114 and 160–94 passim.

17. UC Archives, *Gilman Papers*, vol. 2, letter of February 1874.

18. UC Archives, *Regents' Records*, Box 2, "Faculty 1868–69." After his appointment Carr recommended Colonel John McMynn, his own recommender, for the position of Professor of Mathematics. Stadtman, *University of California 1868–1968*, pp. 51 and 518, fn. 3.

19. E. W. Hilgard, *Report on the Agricultural Experiment Stations of the University of California . . . Being a Part of the Combined Reports for 1888–89* (Sacramento: State Printing Office, 1890), p. 19.

20. *Pacific Rural Press*, Dec. 16, 1871, p. 369.

21. Carr's activities in the California Farmers' Union and the Grange are mentioned in numerous articles in the *Pacific Rural Press*, which served as the Patrons of Husbandry news organ.

22. UC Archives, *Regents' Records*, Box 1, "College of Agriculture 1870–79."

23. See Jane Apostol, "Jeanne Carr: One Woman and Sunshine," *American West* 15 (July–Aug. 1978): 28–33, 62–63. Jeanne Carr's personal papers are at the Huntington Library, San Marino, Calif. Eugene Hilgard's memoir mentions Mrs. Carr as "the better man of the two."

24. This building, the oldest on campus, still bears panels representing grain crops on its north and south sides, but today houses the School of Library and Information Studies.

25. *Pacific Rural Press*, October 19, 1872, p. 244.

26. Ibid., July 5, 1873, p. 4.

27. See Paul, "Great California Grain War."

28. See D. Sven Nordin, "The Grange and Higher Education," in *Rich Harvest, A History of the Grange, 1867–1900* (Jackson: University Press of Mississippi, 1974), chap. 4, pp. 62–83; also Solon Justus Buck, *The Granger Movement . . . 1870–1880*, Harvard Historical Studies (Cambridge, Mass.: Harvard University Press, 1913), vol. 19, pp. 290–93.

29. *Pacific Rural Press*, January 21, 1871, p. 36.

30. Daniel C. Gilman, "The Building of the University: An Inaugural Address Delivered at Oakland, Nov. 7th, 1872," in UC Archives, *Inaugurals, 1872–1899*.

31. Ibid. G. Stanley Hall, former Johns Hopkins faculty member, describes Gilman's emphasis on faculty research in Richard Hofstadter and Wilson Smith, eds., *American Higher Education: A Documentary History* (Chicago: University of Chicago Press, 1961), vol. 2, pp. 649–52.

32. Stadtman, *University of California, 1868–1968*, pp. 71–78, discusses the episode, taking a very negative view of Carr. Another reference appears in Francesco Cordasco, *Daniel Coit Gilman and the Protean Ph.D.: The Shaping of American Graduate Education* (Leiden, The Netherlands: E. J. Brill, 1960), pp. 40–49.

22

33. "Memorial of the California State Grange and Mechanics' Deliberative Assembly on the State University," in UC Archives, *Pamphlets Historical, relating to the University of California*, vol. 2. Italics are original.

34. Stadtman, *University of California 1868–1968*, p. 74.

35. "Statements of the Regents of the University of California to the Joint Committee of the Legislature, March 3, 1874," in *Pamphlets Historical*, vol. 2.

36. "Report of the Joint Committee," ibid.

37. UC Archives, *Gilman Papers*, vol. 2, "Letter from William T. Allen," Dec. 15, 1873.

38. Ibid., "Letter to Andrew D. White," April 5, 1874.

39. *Gilman Papers*, vol. 2.

40. *Pacific Rural Press*, Aug. 29, 1874, p. 132.

41. Ibid., Oct. 3, 1874, pp. 217, 220.

42. A small envelope of newspaper clippings on the Carr case is in UC Archives, *College of Agriculture Files*, Folder 1.

43. This statement and other brief references to Ezra Carr appear in Hilgard's unpublished autobiographical memoir in the Bancroft Library. Hilgard speculated that Carr wished to be president of a separate agricultural college.

44. *Gilman Papers*, vol. 2.

45. Buck, *Granger Movement*, p. 341.

46. UC Archives, *Frederick Slate Papers*, Box I, draft manuscript of a biography of E. W. Hilgard.

# 2

# The Hilgard Era

## 1875–1904

*View of the Berkeley campus about 1897, looking east. The College of Agriculture was still headquartered in South Hall, at right.*

L ATE-NINETEENTH-CENTURY CALIFORNIA WAS A DEVELOPING COUNTRY, ITS ENTREPRENEURIAL IMMIGRANTS SEARCHING FOR WAYS TO EXPLOIT ITS RESOURCES. ITS AGRICULTURE CONSISTED PRIMARILY OF ANIMAL AND GRAIN RANCHING ON VERY LARGE HOLDINGS. WITH THE ARRIVAL OF EUGENE HILGARD, A GERMAN-BORN AND -EDUCATED PHYSICAL SCIENTIST, FARMERS AND RANCHERS GAINED A STATE EXPERIMENT STATION WHERE NEW TECHNICAL AND SCIENTIFIC DISCOVERIES COULD AID THEIR EFFORTS TO IMPROVE AND DIVERSIFY PRODUCTION. HILGARD'S ABILITIES HELPED ESTAB-LISH THE UNIVERSITY OF CALIFORNIA AS A RESPECTED CENTER OF AGRICUL-TURAL RESEARCH, ESPECIALLY IN SOIL SCIENCE AND WINE MAKING. HIS INSISTENCE ON HIGH STANDARDS HELPED SET THE TONE FOR THE COLLEGE OF AGRICULTURE AS A PROFESSIONAL SCHOOL. HILGARD'S THIRTY-YEAR CAREER ALSO SAW THE COLLEGE MOVE INTO LOCAL COMMUNITIES THROUGH EXPERI-MENT SUBSTATIONS AND FARMERS' INSTITUTES.

# 2

# The Hilgard Era 1875–1904

During the 1870s and 1880s California's leading crops in acreage and value were wheat and barley, trailed by potatoes, corn, and oats. Favored by climate, early mechanization, and world trade patterns, winter wheat production grew steadily to a peak at about 1895 of 41 million bushels produced on 2.4 million acres. After the disastrous weather of the early 1860s livestock numbers declined for a time, particularly in southern counties, but the cattle population returned to about 670,000 in 1870, and by 1876 more than 6 million sheep grazed the ranges of California.[1] In areas where water was available, farmers began to experiment in a small way with fruit and vegetable crops, and viticulture attracted growing interest. Enthusiasm for other crops waxed and waned as experiments did or did not pan out: there were serious efforts in silk, ramie, tobacco, and opium poppy production, growing of eucalyptus for lumber and woodworking, and other exotic enterprises, but these remain footnotes in California history.[2]

Despite the breakup of the great *ranchos* of Mexican California, huge landholdings still predominated even a quarter century after statehood, partly because of the difficulties of developing an intensive agriculture and partly because of the opportunism of early speculators. In *The Patrons of Husbandry on the Pacific Coast*, Ezra Carr contrasted California's farm ownership patterns with that of other states:

> Wisconsin, in 1870, had 102,904 farms, only thirty-two of which contain more than 1,000 acres. In California five hundred and sixteen men owned 8,685,439 acres, nearly double the area of Massachusetts, and about one fifth of the arable land of the State. . . . In Fresno County there are forty-eight land-holders, that own from five to seventy-nine thousand acres each. In Santa Barbara forty-four men own over a million acres. Sixteen men in California own over eighty-four square miles.[3]

One of the state's most influential early journalists, Henry George, identified land monopoly as the greatest problem in California's economic and social development, proposing as a tool for reform the single (land) tax in his very popular book *Progress and Poverty* (1879). George's criticisms were to little avail, however, for the early pattern of land speculation continued to be a feature of California life. Men like William Chapman and Henry Miller amassed hundreds of thousands of acres; the Miller and Lux ranching empire alone was said to be larger than Belgium. Railroad land grants also took up enormous chunks of land, and though the rail companies eventually waged active promotional campaigns to attract California settlers, they were sometimes heavy-handed landlords. In the San Joaquin Valley in 1880, several settlers were killed in a gunfight when threatened with eviction by Southern Pacific railroad agents at Mussel Slough, an event immortalized by Frank Norris in his 1901 novel *The Octopus*.

In the semiarid conditions of California, water monopolies were more threatening than land monopolies. Private irrigation companies building large canals sometimes infuriated their neighbors by appropriating the streams running through valleys; Miller and Lux's Kern Water Company was involved in decades of legal battles over water rights. In other areas such as the Cache Creek district of Yolo County the "water wars" were smaller in scope, but feelings ran just as high. Years of struggle and adjudication took place before the Wright Act in 1887 enabled more orderly formation of public irrigation districts.[4]

Transportation monopolies also caused resentment. Until internal combustion engines and automobiles replaced steam power, Californians had to rely on the railroads or riverboats for any nonlocal transportation and trade. Between 1870 and 1880 the state's railroad track more than doubled from 925 to 2,195 miles; doubled again to 4,356 miles in 1890; and by 1900 covered 5,751 miles. Although the rail and shipping companies helped develop California economically, some rail users thought their pricing policies exorbitant. Neverthe-

EUGENE WOLDEMAR HILGARD, PROFESSOR OF AGRICULTURE AND DIRECTOR OF THE UNIVERSITY AGRICULTURAL EXPERIMENT STATION FROM 1875 TO 1905.

less, with its hammerlock on public transport, the Southern Pacific "octopus" retained a strong influence on the California legislature until the Progressives took over state government in 1910.

As ambitious new settlers converged on recently opened lands, they craved information—about soils and water, weather patterns, crops both traditional and experimental, farming techniques, labor-saving machines, processing, and transportation possibilities. The *Pacific Rural Press* kept them in touch with new developments, and local agricultural organizations brought them together to discuss mutual problems, but their appetite for rapidly evolving technology far exceeded satisfaction by these few resources. When Eugene Hilgard appeared on the scene to begin serious agricultural research at the University of California, it was only a matter of time before he was deluged with requests for advice and information.

## THE ARRIVAL OF EUGENE HILGARD

University President Daniel Gilman lost no time in finding a replacement for Professor of Agriculture Ezra Carr, dismissed from his position in August 1874. Gilman had, in fact, met a potential candidate three years earlier at the first meeting of the American Agricultural Colleges Association in Chicago. Gilman was then representing Yale, while Hilgard attended as the delegate of the University of Mississippi. In Hilgard, Gilman recognized an already accomplished

28 scientist with a broad understanding of agriculture and its needs, and Hilgard agreed with Gilman on the purposes of higher education. Both of them objected to the "Michigan plan" then under discussion, under which agricultural students did farm work in the mornings followed by lectures in the afternoon. When Gilman again met Hilgard at the August 1874 meetings of the American Association for the Advancement of Science in Connecticut, just after the dismissal of Professor Carr, he immediately invited him to give a series of special lectures in California during the fall. Gilman's philosophy of faculty building was to attract the best minds he could find and give them room to work. He must have eloquently presented to Hilgard the opportunities waiting in the West.

Although some friends warned him against going to such a "hornet's nest" as the University of California, Hilgard was attracted by both the opportunities and the climate.[5] He had just taken a new position in Michigan, but, troubled with life-long health problems, Hilgard thought that California might be more conducive to his own and his family's well-being than the cold winters of the upper Midwest. He returned with Gilman by train to Berkeley to deliver a six-week short course on soil science; his lectures "On the Origins, Properties and Functions of Soils" were printed subsequently in a University bulletin. He also gave a course on "household chemistry for women." By mid-October he had so impressed other members of the faculty that a six-person committee including President Gilman recommended to the Board of Regents that he be appointed the new Professor of Agriculture. Hilgard accepted the appointment beginning in January 1875, although he could not move his family and officially begin his duties until March.[6]

Like Carr before him, Hilgard began his career at the University by looking about him at the state's agriculture to determine the needs that the University might serve. Unlike Carr, however, Hilgard had a wide-ranging and rigorous scientific education, a great gift for research, and an extraordinary capacity for work. He would employ his talents in the service of California agriculture for the next twenty-nine years.

## HILGARD'S BACKGROUND

The man who came to the struggling young University of California to give lectures on soil science in the autumn of 1874 had a remarkable background. Born in Rhenish Bavaria in 1833, Eugene Woldemar Hilgard came to America as a small child when his father, a respected jurist with liberal political views, emigrated in the tumultuous years preceding the abortive German revolution of 1848. In southern Illinois young Hilgard grew up enjoying an unusual combination of experiences on an American frontier farm and a classical European education, drilled into him by his father. An apt scholar, Hilgard read extensively in his father's library, developing an interest in botany and natural history. Although a severe bout of malaria left him with permanently weak eyes, he left home at sixteen years of age to join his older brother Julius in Washington, D.C. There he worked briefly for the U.S. Coast Survey and went on to the Franklin Institute and the Homeopathic College in Philadelphia to hear lectures. Given his family background and interest in science, however, it was inevitable that he would return to Germany for more rigorous academic training.

German universities then led the world in the study of science. In 1849 the young Hilgard departed for Heidelberg to study analytic chemistry and botany, embarking eastward from New York at just the time that California-bound ships were frantically loading passengers on their way to the Gold Rush. Since German students typically studied at several universities, Hilgard also took coursework at the University of Zurich in Switzerland (natural history and geology) and at the University of Freiburg (mining and metallurgy). In Heidelberg again as a student of the famed Robert Bunsen he earned his doctorate in 1853, at the age of twenty, with a dissertation analyzing the process of combustion in a candle flame—a subject that honed his skill in the meticulous observation and analysis of ordinary chemical processes. Then, to recuperate from illness brought on by overwork, Hilgard spent two years in southern Spain taking temporary jobs, learning the language, and observing for the first time the life and culture of a semiarid land. He also met his future wife, the daughter of a prominent Spanish family.

In 1855 Hilgard returned to the United States and took a position as assistant to the State Geologist of Mississippi. Despite an incompetent supervisor and political quarreling in the legislature, he successfully performed the fieldwork for the Geological Survey of the State of Mississippi and was eventually named its director in 1858. He produced a respected report on Mississippi's soil resources, particularly as adaptable to agriculture. Through the Civil War Hilgard remained in Oxford, Mississippi. After the war he took the chair of chemistry at the University of Mississippi. Continuing his investigations into soils, he developed a solid professional reputation with publications in the *American Journal of Science*. In 1872 he was elected a member of the National Academy of Sciences.

As did its counterpart in California, the University of Mississippi in the early 1870s became embroiled in controversies over the nature of its agricultural program, and agitation began for a separate agricultural college. Hilgard opposed separation, arguing for scientific grounding rather than manual labor as the basis for effective agricultural education. Wearying of the struggle and unhappy with postwar conditions in the South, he decided in 1873 to move on to greater opportunities as professor of geology and natural history at the University of Michigan in Ann Arbor. At that time Michigan stressed teaching rather than research, however, and Hilgard missed his scientific studies. Barely a year later, he came to California.

Hilgard's background could scarcely have been better designed to fit him for successful work in California. He was a respected scientist with a solid record of accomplishment; he understood agriculture and was vitally interested in the soil resources on which it was based, a particularly important qualification; he possessed a firm sense of educational mission; and he was a fighter for what he believed in, with no mean ability at political jousting. Perhaps not least, he was a cosmopolitan of European birth and training, speaking five languages and certainly the intellectual equal of his university colleagues. No one in the growing University could think of Hilgard as provincial in outlook or lacking in scientific sophistication.

## HILGARD'S EARLY WORK IN CALIFORNIA

Although the Grangers' complaints had impelled the University to take steps in forwarding the College of Agriculture, on his arrival Hilgard had no students, little equipment to work with, and few reliable sources to acquaint him with the state's agricultural potential. He also had resentment to overcome among those who had sided with Professor Carr. Nevertheless, as a one-man College of Agriculture Hilgard set about preparing to be of service. At the end of two years, in his first formal report to the President and Regents in 1877, Hilgard presented a carefully reasoned plan for his department as well as results of some beginning empirical research and a discussion of research needs. Though he could report only two seniors in the agriculture course and no juniors, Hilgard outlined a series of classes for future students, consisting of the study of economic botany in the second year, agricultural chemistry in the third, and reviews of "special cultures, agricultural implements and operations, horticulture, stock breeding, dairying, and the principles of husbandry," all to be taught by special lecturers in the senior year. Unperturbed by the paucity of students, Hilgard reasoned that until the

fertile virgin soils of California began to show signs of deple-
tion, farmers would hardly be inclined to recognize a need for
education or scientific management. Meanwhile there was
plenty of research a professor of agriculture might do.

With only $250 appropriated for investigations, Hilgard
began his research work at Berkeley with a test of the results
of deep and shallow plowing on the production of wheat
(then something of a controversy) and a study of the effects of
different fertilizer regimes on wheat and oats. Although
unsuitable weather and heavy squirrel depredations prevented successful conclusions to these experiments, it was with
these 1875 projects that Hilgard later claimed to have begun
the first true agricultural experiment station work in the United States. In his first two years Hilgard also did analyses of
commercial manures, of sugar beets for their sugar content
and purity-coefficient, of Liberian coffee and California buck-
thorn as a possible coffee substitute (not advised), and of the
California sumac as a substitute for the Spanish, Virginian,
or Sicilian sumacs then used in the tanning industry.

In his first years at Berkeley Hilgard taught courses in general science, botany, and mineralogy. For a time he signed
himself Professor of Agriculture and Botany, but by 1882 he
urged appointment of a bona fide botanist to give instruction
so that he could concentrate on the course in agricultural
chemistry. It was difficult to find lecturers with both breadth
of knowledge and teaching ability for the "practical" course,
but in 1878 Hilgard engaged C. H. Dwinelle, who also assisted with experiments and correspondence. That year Hilgard
also arranged for young Edward J. Wickson to offer twelve
lectures on dairying, with two class excursions to nearby
dairies. Though this course was poorly attended at first, it
attracted students as the College grew.

Like Carr before him, Hilgard recognized the need for a
garden of general and economic botany—an outdoor museum of plants—for instructional and demonstration purposes on the University grounds. After the Grangers had

prompted the legislative investigation, the University had
begun some plantings in 1874 on about 40 acres of the
northwest part of the Berkeley grounds. The secretary of the
Board of Regents reported plantings of 584 varieties of tree
fruits, 73 of grapevines, and 95 of various small fruits,
whose dual purpose was to furnish a means of correcting
the nomenclature of the fruits already in cultivation and to
supply scions and plants for distribution. Unfortunately, it
was the secretary and not the Professor of Agriculture who
had charge of these early agricultural plantings, and they
were never very successful.

> In fact, the trees were mostly grubbed out in 1895, long in
> advance of need for building space, because of unthrift and
> because, being planted by a "very competent English garden-
> er" chosen by the secretary, they were grown with trunks four
> or five feet high and were laughed at by visiting California
> growers as a "frightful example of how not to do it in this
> country," this being about the only instructional purpose
> they served.[7]

Eventually Hilgard protested against "the overlordship" of
the Secretary, and in 1879 the Regents gave him responsibility for the agricultural grounds. A two-acre plot fronting on
Oxford Street was established as a Garden of Economic
Plants and for twenty years it was the "great showplace of the
Agricultural Department . . . maintained with great neatness
and cultural excellence, with all the small plots of plants accu-
rately labeled."[8]

To establish a better relationship between the College and
the farming community, Hilgard publicly invited correspondence from individuals and societies, and, despite the
"impossibility of making myself ubiquitous," he visited farm
groups whenever he could. Years later Wickson recalled his
first view of the new professor:

> I was present at a farmers' meeting in San Francisco in 1876,
> apparently called to see just how far the College of Agricul-
> ture had fallen. The room . . . was crowded with men of some

prominence in farming and hostile to the University because they really believed that the College of Agriculture ought to be snatched from ruinous association with a so-called "classical institution." It was a stormy assembly but when there came a lull the chairman asked Hilgard to speak. He rose alertly, showing then a slim, graceful figure, and when he had folded and pocketed the blue glasses which a long continued eye trouble forced him to wear, they saw a scholarly face illumined with an eagerness, cordiality and brightness of expression. . . . He had them transfixed with surprise and curiosity, and when he began to speak in a low, conversational voice, with an accent which compelled them to listen closely, every man was at attention.[9]

Hilgard modestly introduced himself, saying that he was glad to meet them, for no one could do much for farming unless he had personal knowledge and the support of farmers; he had listened with interest to their talk and much of it would be helpful to him; he had come to California to try to know it from the rocks to the sky, and would use all that he had learned elsewhere as a help to knowing California, which he had already perceived was different from any other land in which he had worked. He had always been interested in differences and wanted to see how they applied to farming. On his father's farm in Illinois he had learned that the soil was not all alike and had been told that soil came from different rocks, was moved about and mixed with other things in different ways, and since boyhood he had been studying soils and plants in the hope of matching them to get the best crops and the most money in farming. Then Hilgard briefly discussed soil formation and movement, tillage, fertilization, and other farming matters without a single scientific term or reference to chemistry. His captivated audience fired questions at him from all over the room, which he answered readily. When he asked whether California farmers had anything as hard to handle as the gumbo soil of the Mississippi Valley, half a dozen farmers swore they had soil many times worse; would he come to their farms and see it? Said Wickson, "As the meeting closed . . . a tall giant from the San Joaquin who was a leader in the opposition and who was known to be able to damn the classics all around a thousand acre grain-farm, leaned down and whispered in my ear: 'My God, that man knows something!'"

From the beginning, Hilgard was fascinated with the state's distinctive climate, which reminded him of his sojourn in Spain's Andalusia—"six months of clouds and flowers, six months of dust and sky." Trees stayed green despite rainless hot summers, and irrigation offered almost unlimited promise for annual crops—yet some irrigated lands soon turned alkaline and unproductive. There were great opportunities for agriculture here, but formidable problems to be overcome as well. Hilgard thought an objective survey of California's agricultural potential was very much needed. Promotional pamphlets were attracting settlers woefully ignorant of the difficulties they might face. Hilgard suggested that the College publish a handbook on agriculture in plain language for the public, the geological survey work of the previous decade having been "unsatisfactory" in its "practical deductions."[10] It was the kind of job he had done in Mississippi, and the prospect of doing it for California presented him with a fascinating lifelong challenge.

## HILGARD THE SCIENTIST

### INVENTORYING THE SOILS

Hilgard's soils work in California began immediately. His first report to the Regents discussed the value of soil and water analysis, giving details on samples from the campus grounds and university reservoir. In University of California *Bulletin 26*, issued in April 1877, Hilgard invited interested persons to send soil specimens to the University and specified exactly how samples should be collected and transported. Lacking the money for fieldwork, Hilgard hoped in this

32 way to accumulate knowledge about the soils of different regions and to construct a generalized soils map of California. By 1879 the University had more than 200 soil specimens from across the state, and the collection continued to grow.

What was really needed in this pioneer period, Hilgard knew, was the systematic field exploration of California's resources that might be suitable for farming, along with a compilation of available information on crops and methods of culture. He leaped at the chance offered him by U.S. Census Superintendent F. A. Walker to prepare a report on national cotton production for the Tenth Census. Though the report was proposed to cover primarily the southern states, Hilgard urged the inclusion of California, which then had only a few hundred acres of experimental plantings. In the fall of 1879 Hilgard went to Merced County and neighboring areas to collect soil samples; later he explored Fresno, Kern, and Tulare counties in the San Joaquin Valley, and the seaward counties of the central Coast Range—Santa Cruz, Monterey, and San Benito. He hired a young railroad engineer, N. J. Willson, to travel for three months on a handcar along the railroad tracks collecting soil samples and taking notes on features of the landscape from Redding in the north to Yuma in the south. Later, with the support of Henry Villard, president of the Northern Pacific Railroad, who asked him to study the asphalt deposits of southern California, Hilgard explored the region south of the Tehachapi Mountains.

In 1880 Hilgard published a major report on the alkali soils of the San Joaquin Valley. In it he discussed the effects of irrigation in bringing up alkali by capillary action, the possible remedies, suitable crops, and adaptive cultural methods. By 1882 he asserted that California's great agricultural resources demanded scientific management: "There is in California a more remunerative field for the exercise of discriminating judgment, and the application of science, than is the case in any other State of the Union." Part of his Tenth Census work was printed in 1883 as *A Report on the Physical and Agricultural Features of the State of California, with a Discussion of the Present and Future of Cotton Production in the States; Also, Remarks on Cotton Culture in New Mexico, Utah, Arizona, and Mexico.* A version of this publication was distributed through the *Pacific Rural Press.* Besides tabulating statistical information and describing farm production in California's counties, it discussed the climate, topography, and soil and water resources of the various regions, incorporating much of Hilgard's previous work in soil analysis. He commented years later that the report was but little noticed, but it was the first real attempt to produce a comprehensive scientific survey of California's agricultural resources.

From a historical standpoint the report's discussion of cotton culture in California is illuminating. Hilgard recognized the debilitating effects of the "bonanza" wheat-growing practices of these years well before they became widely understood:

> Apart from the general rule that the greater the variety of crops and industries of a country the more independent and the less liable it is to crop failures of a general character, there are two points that speak strongly in favor of at least the partial substitution of cotton for wheat. One is the well-known fact that wheat culture is very exhaustive of the soil, notably of the phosphates, especially when the grain is chiefly used for export, little or nothing being given back to the soil, and the same crop being repeated year after year. . . . This kind of farming, or rather planting, is doomed to speedy termination . . . while for the time being it enriches individuals it is of very doubtful permanent benefit to the country. The exhausted wheat-fields must wait for the coming generation of more careful farmers—true husbandmen, not skinners of the soil—to be rehabilitated into something like their original productive value.

He thought cotton growing might be good for other reasons as well:

> On lands affected with alkali the evil is steadily on the increase . . . as a consequence of continued surface irrigation. . . . More and more every year the "dead spots" in the wheat-

fields increase.... Something else must be substituted ... a deep and tap-rooted crop, requiring the least amount of irrigation.... Cotton fulfills pre-eminently both conditions. It [also] needs and responds generously to clean and frequent tillage, and in this it would tend to fill the period of comparative idleness experienced by the California grain-grower between harvest and seeding time that for the time ... throws a large number of laboring men out of employment. By the ... spreading out of the work over the entire twelve months cotton serves to secure steady employment, and therefore a steady laboring class.[11]

Throughout his career Hilgard continued to build a detailed database on the soils of California and to explore techniques and theories for analyzing soil quality. In the summers between 1879 and 1883 Hilgard worked for the Northern Pacific Railroad transcontinental survey in Montana, Washington, and Oregon, accumulating information about the soils and vegetation of the arid West beyond California.[12] His laboratory analyses of soils and waters appeared regularly in station publications, scientific journals, and transactions of learned societies for more than twenty years. His collection of soil samples and a representative soil map were exhibited at various national and international fairs, such as the Columbian World's Fair in Chicago, the Midwinter Fair in San Francisco, and the Paris Exposition.[13] During the exceptionally dry years of 1897 and 1898, Hilgard and his assistant R. H. Loughridge investigated how crop plants endure drought, seeking to learn the minimum of water needed for satisfactory growth in different soils. They measured the root penetration of cereal grasses, herbaceous plants, and orchard trees in the effort to understand how plants seek moisture.[14]

Hilgard's soils work culminated after his retirement with his book *Soils: Their Formation, Properties, Composition, and Relations to Climate and Plant Growth* (New York and London: Macmillan, 1906). In this volume Hilgard gave climate an essential role in the formation of soils and subsoils. The differences between the soils of arid and humid regions, he wrote, were due partly to the presence and influence of organic matter and microorganisms, and partly to physicochemical causes such as moisture, access of air (oxygen), temperature, and their interactions.

No scientific work could have been better suited to California agriculture's needs at the time. Hilgard helped demonstrate that alkali soils were unusually fertile, given proper management, and his experiments with tillage and irrigation added to practical understanding of

HARVESTING CREW DURING THE NINETEENTH-CENTURY BONANZA WHEAT YEARS. LARGE CREWS HAD TO BE ASSEMBLED FOR THIS HEAVY SEASONAL LABOR.

34 ways to farm on these soils. His descriptions of the physical effects of water percolation in the typical arid soil profile were to be of great importance to irrigation science. Shortly after his death in 1916 his colleague and successor R. H. Loughridge summed up his work: "[In] his studies on humid and arid soils . . . he was the first to point out their differences in depth and in physical and chemical characteristics; he was the first to explain endurance of drouth by culture crops in sand soils and why sandy soils are among the most productive in the arid region and least so in the humid. . . . He was also the first to maintain that the physical properties of the soil are equal in importance to the chemical in determining the cultural values."[15] Decades later Hans Jenny, another prominent UC soil scientist, commented, "Unmistakably, Hilgard [became] the scientific conquistador of the soils of the arid region, a region that comprises over half of the earth's surface."[16]

## VINES AND WINES

Although Hilgard was pre-eminent as a soil scientist, he devoted his next-greatest research efforts to grape growing and winemaking. Given his European background, Hilgard undoubtedly had some knowledge of grapes and wines before coming to California, but it was here that he developed a significant body of knowledge concerning both viticulture and enology.[17] Hilgard recognized ear-

EARLY IRRIGATION PUMPING SYSTEM. THE DEVELOPMENT OF WATER SUPPLIES FOR IRRIGATION MADE MORE INTENSIVE AGRICULTURE POSSIBLE IN CALIFORNIA.

ly the extraordinary promise of California for developing this industry, writing in 1879 that "in the natural course of things California can hardly fail to become one of the foremost grape-growing countries of the world, since it possesses all the natural advantages."[18] His investigations were shaped by strong demand, for many aspiring regional winemakers harbored hopes for a brilliant future. Doubtless Hilgard was also attracted by the opportunities for helping an infant industry achieve quality and permanence through the systematic collection of scientific data; like his soils work, viticultural research represented a massive challenge. Equally important, money for experiments materialized in the form of a legislative bill.

Hilgard's first foray into the field was a lecture in 1875 on the grapevine root louse phylloxera, delivered at the request of the State Vinicultural Association. Phylloxera, then beginning to decimate vineyards in Europe, had been introduced into California with European stock; it was first reported in Sonoma County in 1873. Hilgard's lecture, reviewing current knowledge about the pest and methods for its control, was published as University of California *Bulletin 23* in January 1876 and reprinted twice. While the pest spread relatively slowly in California, Hilgard pushed ahead with research on soil treatments and resistant vine varieties as funding allowed him to do so. When the University vineyard in Berkeley was found to be infested, nearby grape growers petitioned the Regents to remove it, but Hilgard had the planting preserved for research purposes. Hilgard and his assistant F. W. Morse observed the insect's life history and tried various remedies including soil fumigation with mercury vapor. Yet they found no truly effective mitigations for the plague other than planting resistant rootstocks. By 1900 Hilgard's own vineyard at Mission San Jose succumbed. Despite lack of success in controlling phylloxera—which threatens wine regions to this day—Hilgard's work was an important contribution toward understanding the problem.

After serving on the wine-tasting panel for the thirteenth exhibition of the Mechanics' Institute of San Francisco in 1878, Hilgard noted in his 1879 biennial report that many California wines were of inferior quality, suffering from excessive sugar in the grapes, and that winemakers definitely needed more information on wine grape varieties and winemaking techniques. (His memoir, years later, observed that winemaking of the time was "oftentimes simply horrible.") His offers to help did not fall on deaf ears. In April 1880 the legislature passed a bill creating a Board of State Viticultural Commissioners representing seven growing districts, with headquarters in San Francisco. Charles Wetmore, a University of California graduate, was appointed chief executive officer. Responsibility for viticultural research was assigned to both the Board and the University, and an annual appropriation of $3,000 was provided. An interested grower offered several acres of his Cupertino vineyard (Santa Clara County) for grapevine variety studies. At Berkeley an analytical winemaking laboratory was built. With regular appropriations for the next fifteen years Hilgard supervised fermentation studies on the University grounds, amassing mountains of data on wines made from grapes from the University's affiliated vineyards and from sample lots sent in by vintners.

Unfortunately, between Hilgard and the "practical" men among the Viticultural Commissioners (specifically, Wetmore and Arpad Haraszthy, son of Agoston) there existed a certain rivalry, and for a time their disagreements on goals and methods of research threatened to become disruptive. When in 1885 the legislature expanded its viticultural research appropriation to $10,000, the Commission proposed placing a new research laboratory in San Francisco, away from Hilgard's direct supervision. Hilgard, incensed, fought to keep the facility in Berkeley and finally succeeded, acquiring larger and better-equipped quarters for another decade of fermentation studies.

In 1892 the Experiment Station published a report of more than 400 pages summarizing its studies on red wine grapes. When the mid-1890s depression hit the wine industry after a decade of rapid expansion by enthusiastic but inexperienced vintners, the legislature disbanded the Board of Viticultural Commissioners and transferred its research functions solely to the University, with reduced appropriations. In his final comprehensive report on winemaking in 1896, Hilgard claimed,

> Our work in this line represents the largest and most complete systematic investigation of the kind on record thus far in any country," asserting that "with the proper understanding and utilization of the data . . . much of the uncertainty and haphazard heretofore prevailing will disappear, and . . . both in the selection of the grape-varieties to be planted, and of the proper blends to be made for particular purposes and types, the . . . analyses and the records of vinification will be found of the greatest practical use."[19]

After this report, University-directed fermentation studies declined until new research appropriations were granted in 1903. Although viticultural work continued, with emphasis on grafting, cultural practices, and testing of phylloxera-resistant rootstocks, winemaking activity was only a relatively minor portion of Experiment Station research until after the Prohibition era (1919–1933).[20]

36 ## "SUCH A PRESSURE TOWARD DIVERSIFIED KNOWLEDGE"

From the beginning of their experimental work in California Hilgard and his small staff found it hard to keep up with the demand for their services.

> There was such a pressure toward diversified knowledge that the experiment station was actually not allowed to classify, correlate and discriminate, but was forced to take up a bargain-counter business, by research into foreign records, by local observation, and by current experimentation, which would supply each of a throng of patrons with the particular goods which he conceived to be desirable.[21]

Hilgard had appealed to agriculturalists to get in touch with him, and they did. Their requests were so varied that it was difficult to lay out a single clear research program; on the other hand, as Wickson observed, "in California, scientific wing-shooting can drop many plump birds."[22] College staff and facilities gradually evolved in tandem with development of the state's agriculture on a broad variety of fronts.

### LOOKING FOR OPPORTUNITIES

Part of Hilgard's work on the University grounds was to oversee various plantations of trees introduced for trial under California conditions. By 1890 he could report that English oaks, acacias, eucalyptus, camphor, and mulberry were adaptable and fast growing in various parts of the campus. The College of Agriculture's primary variety-testing facility was the Garden of Economic Plants along Oxford Street, which also played a role in public relations.

> During this period the department had a great thirst for visitors as a means of securing desirable publicity. When a visitor of agricultural aspect entered the garden the workman in charge . . . sent a boy . . . to notify the Director . . . and it was his custom to send out all the rest of the teaching staff to explain the plants to the welcome guest, take him to lunch and afterwards keep him well entertained with plant lore until the western sun cast long shadows over the garden and then escort him to an outgoing train. In this way many good friends of the college were developed and many critics disarmed. And indeed there was much to see in that old garden. In 1890 there were . . . fifty-five plots of grasses, twenty-five of leguminous forage plants, eight of textile plants, twenty-four of aromatic herbs, fifty-nine of medicinal herbs, and forty-one of miscellaneous plants . . . foreign trees and shrubs yielding commercial products, such as tea, camphor, cinnamon, bamboos, carobs, cork oaks, etc., which were hardy and lived as permanent exhibits, and . . . others even more interesting in the ways they died, such as cinchona, coffee and many strictly tropical fruits.[23]

Although the early experimental orchard languished, its fruit unable to mature properly without summer heat, stock of a wide variety of species could be propagated in the moderate temperatures of Berkeley. Thus the Garden of Economic Plants became a source for seed and plant distribution for nearly thirty years. Like the U.S. Department of Agriculture, which also distributed stock gathered from other parts of the world through gift and collection, the College offered only experimental varieties to avoid competing with nurseries. Bulletins listing available seeds and scions were distributed at intervals, and applicants were asked only to pay a small handling fee and submit a brief report on adaptability of the plants for their areas. According to Wickson, in charge of the distribution for many years, 85,488 ounces of seed and 93,448 plants were distributed from the Berkeley Garden between 1886 and 1896, and a high of 1,477 applicants was reached in 1895. For years the station's reports duly included a section of "results" sent in by experimenting correspondents. The following are typical:

> L. C. Kinkaid, San Diego County: "I sowed the Shrader's brome grass seed March 28, and it came up in ten days. It grew until it nearly covered the ground, when the quail ate it up. I am satisfied it will be a good grass in this part of the state."

R. Hastie, Contra Costa County: "The Gopher Plant (Euphorbia lathyris) is a humbug. I have grown it along my garden fence . . . and the gopher runs under and around it all the time."

W. C. Bradford, Colusa County: "Australian Saltbush planted in the spring on moist, gravelly, clay soil (fair grain land), which had no rain and only about ten days of cool, cloudy weather, grew and fully one half lived through the hot, dry summer. It has no equal as feed for chickens, but stock will not eat it until everything else is gone."

E. A. Irish, Mendocino County: "The Defiance [variety] yields a little more than twice as much as our common wheats and showed no sign of rust. It is the best that I ever saw."

B. D. Vanderburgh, Fresno County: "Three out of five English Oak trees died, but the other two are alive and doing well . . . eleven inches in diameter, thirty feet high, with a spread of twenty-four feet, and have borne a heavy crop of acorns every year for several years."

Leslie E. Conklin, Santa Barbara County: "The Roselle made a very satisfactory growth. The unirrigated plants grew to about 15 inches high and produced from three to five pods. The irrigated plants would all measure three feet, and on one plant I counted 83 pods. From two quarts of the pods we made one quart of the most delicious jelly."

Jacob Veiteinger, San Diego County: "I have harvested four pounds of Fenugreek seed. The pods grew six and eight inches long. They were quite hard to open, and after working at it for a certain time I had to jump up—it made me vomit. . . . When I cleaned the seed in the wind, my chickens picked up some and it physicked them."

Eventually the garden drew unwelcome visitors from the growing town of Berkeley (including "small boys with a keen appetite for green fruit"), and Wickson complained that plants were being stolen right out of the ground. Distribution of seeds and stock by annual announcement was discontinued in 1908, and in 1918 the garden area was built over with wartime military structures.

With Californians always looking for new opportunities, olive culture began to attract great public interest beginning in the early 1880s. The olive tree of Spanish and Italian tradition seemed to be a natural for the state's Mediterranean climate, and its ease of cultivation suggested it might do well even in hard-to-farm areas. Early enthusiasts glowed with the possibilities. Promoters were quick to tout a new industry for both fruit and oil. The State Board of Horticultural Commissioners and several prominent nursery owners published popular pamphlets on olive growing.[24]

The College of Agriculture responded encouragingly to the clamor for information. In his 1885 report W. G. Klee, the gardener in charge of the agricultural grounds, stated, "It has often been said that the olive is the poor man's tree. . . . It is the richest and most nutritious of all fruits, for upon it and bread alone a man may be sustained so as to perform the hardest labor." He further commented that "the tree will thrive throughout California. . . . Hills and mountain slopes, not fit for the pasture of even a goat, can . . . produce olives."[25] Experiment Station bulletins gave detailed instruction on propagation from small wood cuttings. By the 1890s the College had planted dozens of olive varieties to investigate their adaptability and product quality. Research staff examined fruit size, pit content, and oil percentage, and concluded that the Mission olive, a California variety derived from seeds planted at the Spanish missions, remained the best all-around variety. By 1894 the College offered courses in olive culture along with viticulture. Experiment Station *Bulletin 123*, issued in January 1897, reviewed what was known about cultivation methods, oil making, pickling, and disease problems.

The number of olive trees in California increased from a few thousand in 1880 to 2.5 million in 1897. Not surprisingly, the craze brought problems. By 1900, state newspapers reported that the olive industry was a failure and market values of orchards were plummeting. The Experiment Station issued a "Report on the Condition of Olive Culture in California" (*Bulletin 129*) in which author A. P. Hayne warned that olives had been speculatively overplanted in many areas not appropriate for them; that neglect of orchards was common; and that California olive oil was often of poor quality and adulterated with cottonseed oil. Nevertheless, despite a "poorly organized market," American demand for olives was actually "good and growing," and California growers might yet prosper if they dropped their "false ideas" that olive trees needed no attention and paid more attention to quality in pickling and oil making.[26]

As it became obvious that olives were no easy road to riches, the boom in planting declined and other crops became more popular. The olive industry settled into certain areas, but the familiar gray-green tree rows along many California backroads serve as a reminder of the enthusiasm of the 1890s.

DROUGHT-TOLERANT OLIVE TREES. SOME OF THE UNIVERSITY AGRICULTURAL EXPERIMENT STATION'S EARLIEST PUBLICATIONS FOCUSED ON OLIVE CULTURE.

## PESTS IN THE GARDEN OF EDEN

Californians searching for failure-free crops soon discovered that they had competition from many voracious pests. Some of them, like phylloxera, were introduced through plants brought in from other places and easily proliferated in California's long growing season. Other native pests throve as expanding agriculture provided them with richer diets. Small vertebrates were particularly encouraged by the new largesse.

Hilgard's early cereal experiments at Berkeley had been ruined by the hungry hordes: "So soon as the grain began to form, all the squirrels inhabiting the vacant lots surrounding the University grounds, resorted to these grain plots as the most promising pasture within their reach." Hilgard estimated that squirrel depredations could cause losses of up to 50 percent of a grain harvest. One of his first publications, University of California *Bulletin 32* (April 1878), described fumigation of ground squirrel tunnels with carbon bisulfide, a practice Hilgard thought better than using poisoned grain, as it avoided endangering game birds and farm animals.

Hilgard met early requests for information on pest problems by lecturing at meetings or preparing bulletins, but he soon began more systematic instruction and research on potentially damaging insects. The College first offered a course in elementary entomology in 1882, given by the lecturer in agricultural practice. That year Hilgard stated that an "increase of noxious insects" in the state called for a specialist in "economic entomology." In 1884, *Bulletin 16* of the Agricultural Experiment Station proposed development of a $50,000 endowment for a chair in entomology, meanwhile summarizing current remedies for insect invasion, including sprays with tobacco extract, caustic soda and potash solution, lye, and kerosene emulsions. The endowment did not materialize, however, and instruction in entomology was continued by the lecturers in agricultural practice until a trained entomologist joined the staff in 1891. Research publications reported on alkaline washes, whale-oil soap washes, vine sulfuring, commercial insecticide mixtures, natural enemies of aphids, fumigation treatments, and tree banding to trap or cut off access by crawling insects. In 1887 an elaborate experiment in spraying with Paris green, used in the Eastern states, demonstrated its feasibility under California conditions. That year the legislature passed a law requiring instruction in economic entomology in the public schools, and though the requirement was later repealed, it "notably quickened public interest in crop protection."

In 1892 the new station entomologist C. W. Woodworth published a key to families of insects "to enable the unscientific public to determine the characters of insects suspected of injury to plants." He followed up with bulletins on pest control, including a major publication on orchard fumigation. By 1900 popular concern about insect and rodent predations rose to such levels that county governments began to grant special funds to the Experiment Station for local problem solving. Station agents were assigned to investigate outbreaks of grasshoppers in foothill counties, the codling moth in the Pajaro Valley, and the peach worm in Placer County. Between 1901 and 1903 ten major bulletins on

WINTER SPRAYING, CIRCA 1900. ORCHARDISTS VERY EARLY HAD TO LEARN TO COMBAT PESTS AND DISEASES THREATENING THEIR CROPS.

insects and insecticides appeared. In 1903 the College placed a special agent in the newly developed district around Turlock, where grasshoppers were causing heavy losses. He helped control the plague by supervising the burning of breeding grounds and use of a "hopper-doser." In 1904 Woodworth issued a bulletin on orchard fumigation by hoop tents. Campaigns against the mosquito, nemesis of marshland and irrigation districts, culminated in a 55-page bulletin on mosquito control in 1906.[27]

Until a specialist in plant diseases was appointed in 1903, Woodworth also supervised work in this area. During the 1890s Experiment Station research on root galls on fruit trees and vines was of particular interest. The Russian thistle (popularly known as tumbleweed), a pest that had already severely infested other states, caused some alarm among California ranchers, but in 1895 Experiment Station *Bulletin 107*, "The Russian Thistle in California," predicted that the weed would not be a major problem here.

In 1903 a disaster facing California asparagus growers brought Ralph E. Smith to the University as the first plant pathologist to be employed by the Experiment Station. Rust disease at that time was jeopardizing the future of the million-dollar industry in California, and leading growers

40 and canners had promised Hilgard $2,500 for a special investigation of the problem, plus a voluntary assessment of 75 cents an acre for a two-year "thorough study." At the Massachusetts Agricultural Experiment Station, Smith read about and volunteered for the project; his expenses in coming to California were paid by the California Fruit Canners Association. Fieldwork in the extensive asparagus fields south of San Francisco Bay and in the Sacramento Delta convinced him that "the day of bonanza asparagus farming has passed," and he began demonstrating the effectiveness of dusting the crop with sulfur. Within a year the rust problem was under control, and Smith went on to study other serious plant diseases in California. In 1905, at the request of fruit growers, Smith wrote the legislative bill appropriating funds for control of a pear blight epidemic, which the legislature augmented with another appropriation for research on walnut blight.[28]

## THE HATCH ACT EXPANDS FACILITIES

Because of his experiments at Berkeley in 1875, Hilgard claimed that the University of California was the "first to officially establish an agricultural experiment station within the United States."[29] Without regular and reliable appropriations, however, research was always a matter of balancing demands, and much remained undone. With minimal office and laboratory space—the College was still housed in the basement of South Hall in the 1880s—Hilgard produced an amazing amount of work, but he continually pressed for better support as requests for help increased. Agricultural research did not come cheaply. Every one of Hilgard's early reports asks the Regents for more money—for staff salary increases, for equipment, for operating expenses.

In 1887, 25 years after passage of the Morrill Act, Congress provided a more secure and permanent basis for agricultural research through the Hatch Act. This legislation provided formally for operation of agricultural experiment stations in conjunction with the land-grant colleges, appropriating $15,000 annually to each station:

> It shall be the object and duty of . . . experiment stations to conduct original researches . . . on the physiology of plants and animals; the diseases to which they are . . . subject, with the remedies for the same; the chemical composition of useful plants . . . the comparative advantages of rotative cropping . . . the capacity of new plants or trees for acclimation; the analysis of soils and water; the chemical composition of manures, natural or artificial . . . the adaptation and value of grasses and forage plants; the composition and digestibility of . . . food for domestic animals; the scientific and economic questions involved in the production of butter and cheese; and . . . other researches . . . bearing directly on the agricultural industry.[30]

Because of California's diversity in soils and climate, Hilgard had long recognized a need for local research stations. With Hatch Act funds becoming available in 1888, Hilgard negotiated the development of three substations across the state (Berkeley being the "Central Station") for experimental work. The criteria were three: stations should represent so far as possible the conditions in each geographic area, should be able to provide answers to questions on appropriate crops and agricultural methods, and should have the support of local citizens. The land for each substation was not to be purchased but lent for University use, with reversion to the owners in case of abandonment.

At Berkeley the first Hatch Act funds were used to erect a wood-frame Experiment Station building in 1889. Called Budd Hall, the new quarters included well-equipped laboratories for the study of entomology and plant diseases, fields in which Hilgard hoped to encourage more students to pursue careers. This building was destroyed by fire in 1897. Though it was subsequently rebuilt, Hilgard lost all his botanical, geological, and agricultural collections; stockpiles of bulletins, records of experiments, and research equipment were likewise destroyed, interrupting normal work for months.

In April 1890 Hilgard reported on the progress of the three "General Culture Stations," furnishing detailed descriptions. The Foothill Station, situated on 36 acres 5 miles north-north-east of Jackson in Amador County, began an experimental orchard planted with sixteen kinds of fruits and nuts, other miscellaneous trees, a vineyard, and plots for forage plants. The South Coast Range Station, 2 miles north-northeast of Paso Robles, consisted of 20 acres planted to orchard, vineyard, and small grains. The San Joaquin Valley (Tulare) Station, one mile southeast of Tulare City, contained 20 acres to be used for variety tests and work on reclamation of alkali soils, including underdrainage and gypsum treatments.

Hilgard's hope for a fourth substation in southern California was realized a few months later. Offered land in both Riverside and Pomona, he chose the more central Pomona site, lying between the San Gabriel and Santa Ana rivers, because of its wider applicability for the general area. The entire region, Hilgard predicted, would soon be "a continuous garden and orchard" and a notable center for horticultural industries. A special citrus station, he wrote, would be appropriate for the Riverside district to the east if financial backing could be obtained.[31]

The College of Agriculture came to acquire three more local research stations during Hilgard's tenure. The 1893 state legislature transferred two forestry stations from the control of the State Board of Forestry to the University agricultural department, with an appropriation of $4,000 to maintain them. Both had been intended for experimental tree nurseries but because of neglect were in poor condition. The 29-acre forestry station at Chico had formerly been part of the famous 26,000-acre Rancho Chico belonging to John Bidwell. The 20-acre Santa Monica station, spanning several elevations, consisted mainly of a collection of eucalyptus species. The third new station was established in 1904 at Petaluma in Sonoma County, which by 1900 had become the greatest poultry-producing area in the nation, shipping more than 3 million dozen eggs and nearly half a million fowl annually. The 5-acre poultry experiment station was organized to combat infectious diseases—fowl cholera, tuberculosis, croup—threatening the concentration of small poultry farms nearby.[32]

None of these stations lasted more than a decade or so. They were relatively expensive to maintain, and finding scientifically competent people to oversee them was difficult. "Their chief crime was poverty, which restricted their undertakings, reduced their custodians to care-takers, and made it impossible to even aim at results of wide significance."[33] By 1903 the stations at Jackson and Paso Robles were closed, about two years later those at Tulare and Pomona, and the others faded away as the College of Agriculture grew.

## 42 A PHILOSOPHY OF EDUCATION FOR AGRICULTURE

Hilgard was a practicing and problem-oriented scientist light-years beyond Ezra Carr in terms of his useful research contributions. He also championed a totally different concept of agricultural education. Whereas Carr, like his Grange supporters, endorsed "practical" education—the acquiring of physical skills through student labor in a model farm setting—Hilgard believed that higher education in agriculture should be intellectual in nature, based on the physical sciences and aimed at progress for the industry rather than training in specific farm skills.

### WHAT IS A COLLEGE OF AGRICULTURE FOR?

In the first of his many reports to the Regents, Hilgard wrote of his belief that education could best counteract the "growing tendency of our youth to abandon the country for the city" by acquainting students with the pleasures and challenges to be found in the study of the natural sciences:

> So long as they see in a farmer's life only the daily drudgery, without the cheerful background afforded to educated minds by the contact with nature, and the intellectual food so abundantly presented in the correct application of the principles governing the very complex profession of the truly rational farmers: so long will they continue in the vain attempt to find in our overcrowded cities a more satisfactory existence.... It is clear that the remedy lies in the elevation of the farmer's pursuit to its true dignity of a learned profession, second to none in the complexity and difficulty of the problems with which it deals, and superior to many in its fundamental importance, as well as in the rational enjoyment of life which it affords to those who understand the principles that underlie its practice.

Hilgard argued that university education in agriculture, as in other professions, should be for the leaders of the future—teachers, original researchers, and industry representatives.

> Twenty years of personal experience ... involving constant and intimate relations with both the leaders and the rank and file of the farming population, has left me strongly impressed ... that apart from a comparatively small number ... the general desire is not for more drill in handicraft, but for more use of brains trained in the branches of knowledge or science related to agriculture.... I have found no reason to believe that the unusually intelligent farming population of California is differently minded.... The complaint ... that the farmers' influence is not sufficiently felt in the legislative halls, strongly corroborates and tallies with my conviction, that the remedy lies more in the direction of the training of the mind than of that of the hand; and that the sound sense of the industrial population appreciates the fact that the safeguarding of their interests requires a more thorough education within their own ranks.[34]

A few years later, in a two-part article in the prestigious *Atlantic Monthly*, Hilgard decried the devastation of the nation's soil resources wrought by the ignorance of pioneer farmers and called for a "rational agriculture" based on scientific principles.[35] He noted that while "manual labor" agricultural schools had at first been popular, they had eventually proved to be of questionable educational value because they conveyed "little or nothing new after a few weeks' practice." Scientific studies, on the other hand, demanded at least four years of full-time work, and student labor requirements would only interfere with learning things of higher value. The agricultural colleges of Europe were not "peasant schools" but places to find new solutions to problems through experiment; these were the institutions needed in America. The Grange movement itself, noted Hilgard perceptively, recognized the need to counteract the "barrenness" of rural life through the social and intellectual development of country people; manual labor schools were thus actually inconsistent with Grange goals.

Throughout the 1880s in California as elsewhere, relatively few students came to study agriculture at the University.

Hilgard was undisturbed. In 1884 he noted that the College of Agriculture "has ceased to be a safe harbor for the indifferent student and an easy road to graduation," and he was pleased that among those who attended there was more "earnestness." As a body of solid information about farming in California developed through surveys and experiments, agricultural students gradually began to appear. Emerging problems increasingly brought forward-thinking farmers to the University for information and advice, and as they realized the value of scientific education they sent their sons and daughters to Berkeley.

Until 1896 fewer than 20 full-time "agricultural students" enrolled at Berkeley, but thereafter both students and courses of instruction increased rapidly, especially with the admission of "special students," those interested in a two-year course without degree.

> The status of "special students" became quite popular with those who had done so much farming that they had no opportunity to prepare for admission as regular students, and . . . also to others who had become of age without distinguishing themselves in the high-school work. . . . It was with students of this status, and of greater average age than that of students generally, that the college finally acquired a student body of respectable size. . . . In 1904 the enrollment in agriculture included fifty-one regular and fifty special students. Subsequently the ratio of special students to regular rapidly decreased, as more rational specializing in studies and purposes and fuller qualifications for the pursuit of it were insisted upon.[36]

In 1900 the agricultural course at Berkeley was still a single program of study, but it now included courses in agricultural chemistry, soil physics, animal industry, chemistry of dairy products, dietetics, apiculture, olive and grape culture and vinification, beet sugar industry, advanced horticulture, economic botany, current agricultural literature, several courses in entomology and plant diseases, and extension work in agriculture. By 1904 Hilgard reported rapidly increasing interest in agricultural studies as students recognized expanding career opportunities in public service, teaching, and private enterprise. He noted in particular a larger number of young women in the agricultural science classes.

## REACHING OUT TO FARMERS

From the beginning of his California career Hilgard turned his attention toward solving questions of practical importance to farmers, partly to further the University's role in assisting industrial development and partly because he needed popular support to pursue his goals for the College of Agriculture. He began writing up short research reports almost immediately, which were published as supplements to his annual reports or as University of California bulletins sent to the *Pacific Rural Press* and other newspapers for immediate distribution. In early articles for the *Press* Hilgard also invited farmers to correspond with him directly on questions of interest; eventually this correspondence became so voluminous that much of it was turned over to assistants, but Hilgard retained an interest in it until the end of his life. By 1903 the station staff was responding to nearly 15,000 letters a year.

In January 1884 the College of Agriculture began producing short bulletins in a regular series. The first four numbered bulletins, each one page long, were titled "Examination of the Water of the San Fernando Tunnel," "Plant Distribution," "Remedies for the Phylloxera; Failure of Cuttings," and "Analysis of Tanning Materials." When the Hatch Act in 1887 mandated quarterly distribution of bulletins and provided funds for this purpose, the Agricultural Experiment Station began issuing longer-format pamphlets available for the asking. By the late 1890s some of these bulletins amounted to 30 pages or more. At first Hilgard published most, particularly on soils, but soon other authors made important contributions: C. W. Woodworth on plant diseases and pests, F. T. Bioletti on grapes and olives, and M. E. Jaffa on animal feedstuffs and nutrition. By Hilgard's retirement in June 1905 the

44 Agricultural Experiment Station publications series included 171 bulletins, printed at that time in editions of 10,000 to meet the demand both at home and in the eastern states and Europe, and 14 circulars (shorter, less technical reports begun in 1903). Taken all together, these publications constitute not only a record of Experiment Station research but a history of the concerns of California farmers.

On December 31, 1890, the State Grange—still the most active agricultural organization in California—presented a resolution to the Board of Regents requesting Farmers' Institutes.

## .. PROGRAMME ..

### MORNING SESSION, JAN. 3, 10 O'CLOCK.

Piano Solo—"Song Without Words," . . . . . . . . . . . . . . . . *Mendelssohn*
  MISS CLARA BOSBYSHELL.
Invocation . . . . . . . . . . . . . . . . . . . . . . . . . . . . . . . . . . . . . . . . . . . . . .
  REV. WARREN F. DAY.
Address of Welcome . . . . . . . . . . . . . . . . . . . . . . . . . . . . . . . . . . . . .
  GEN. FORMAN, Pres. Chamber of Commerce.
Response . . . . . . . . . . . . . . . . . . . . . . . . . . . . . . . . . . . . . . . . . . . . . .
  DR. E. W. HILGARD, Berkeley.
Farmer's Clubs Institute . . . . . . . . . . . . . . . . . . . . . . . . . . . . . . . . .
  PROF. A. J. COOK, Claremont Club.
Home Improvement . . . . . . . . . . . . . . . . . . . . . . . . . . . . . . . . . . . . . .
  C. F. McDOUGALL, Escondido Club.
Solo—"Armorer's Song"—From Robin Hood . . . . . . . . . . . . *De Koven*
  MR. C. F. EDSON.
Diversified Farming . . . . . . . . . . . . . . . . . . . . . . . . . . . . . . . . . . . . . .
  ROBT. DUNN, Fillmore Club.
Almond Culture . . . . . . . . . . . . . . . . . . . . . . . . . . . . . . . . . . . . . . . . .
  PROF. A. R. SPRAGUE, Antelope Valley Association, Fairmont.

### AFTERNOON SESSION, 2 O'CLOCK.

Flute Solo . . . . . . . . . . . . . . . . . . . . . . . . . . . . . . . . . . . . . . . . . . . . .
  MR. W. H. MEAD.
Question Box.
Fruit Exchanges . . . . . . . . . . . . . . . . . . . . . . . . . . . . . . . . . . . . . . . . .
  J. H. HOAG, Redlands Club.
Fruit Exchanges . . . . . . . . . . . . . . . . . . . . . . . . . . . . . . . . . . . . . . . . .
  L. A. TAYLOR, Pomona Club.
Deciduous Fruit Exchanges . . . . . . . . . . . . . . . . . . . . . . . . . . . . . . .
  A. R. SPRAGUE, Organizer Southern California Deciduous
  Fruit Grower's Association.
Piano Solo . . . . . . . . . . . . . . . . . . . . . . . . . . . . . . . . . . . . . . . . . . . . .
  MR. WILL STROBRIDGE.
Deciduous Fruit Exchanges . . . . . . . . . . . . . . . . . . . . . . . . . . . . . . .
  HON. T. N. STOCKSLEDGER, San Jacinto Club.
Beekeeper's Exchange . . . . . . . . . . . . . . . . . . . . . . . . . . . . . . . . . . . .
  C. A. HATCH, Southern California Beekeepers
  Association, Pasadena.

### EVENING SESSION, 8 O'CLOCK.

Violin Solo—"Legende," . . . . . . . . . . . . . . . . . . . . . . . . . . *Wieniawski*
  MISS DAISY POLK.
Question Box.
Roads . . . . . . . . . . . . . . . . . . . . . . . . . . . . . . . . . . . . . . . . . . . . . . . . .
  A. P. GRIFFITH, Azusa Club.
Roads and Roadside Tree Planting . . . . . . . . . . . . . . . . . . . . . . . . . .
  ALBERT K. SMILEY, Redlands Club.
Solo—"Angel's Serenade," . . . . . . . . . . . . . . . . . . . . . . . . . . . *Braga*
  KATHERINE PHILYSS EDSON.
  With Violin Obligato, MISS DAISY POLK.
Promising New Varieties of Fruit . . . . . . . . . . . . . . . . . . . . . . . . . . .
  J. W. MILLS, Agricultural Experiment Station, Pomona.
Food Adulteration . . . . . . . . . . . . . . . . . . . . . . . . . . . . . . . . . . . . . . .
  HON. ELWOOD COOPER, Pres. State Board of Horticulture.

### PROGRAMME—Continued.

### MORNING SESSION, JAN. 4, 10 O'CLOCK.

Invocation . . . . . . . . . . . . . . . . . . . . . . . . . . . . . . . . . . . . . . . . . . . . .
  REV. DR. WALKER.
Reading . . . . . . . . . . . . . . . . . . . . . . . . . . . . . . . . . . . . . . . . . *Selected*
  MR. LEE BASSETT, Cummock School of Oratory and Arts.
Question Box.
Scale Insects: . . . . . . . . . . . . . . . . . . . . . . . . . . . . . . . . . . . . . . . . . .
  MISS JEAN LOOMIS, Claremont Club.
Fighting Scale Insects . . . . . . . . . . . . . . . . . . . . . . . . . . . . . . . . . . . .
  F. AUSTIN, Fallbrook; S. A. PEASE, San Bernardino;
  JUDSON WILLIAMS, Fallbrook.
The Purple Scale . . . . . . . . . . . . . . . . . . . . . . . . . . . . . . . . . . . . . . . .
  HERMAN COPELAND, Chula Vista Club.
Solo—"Oh, Rest in the Lord," . . . . . . . . . . . . . . . . . . . . *Mendelssohn*
  KATHERINE PHILYSS EDSON.
Thoroughbred Poultry . . . . . . . . . . . . . . . . . . . . . . . . . . . . . . . . . . . .
  V. TRESSLER, Sec. Riverside Poultry Association.
Bees and Horticulture . . . . . . . . . . . . . . . . . . . . . . . . . . . . . . . . . . . .
  T. W. COWAN, London, England.

### AFTERNOON SESSION, 2 O'CLOCK.

Solo—"Guide Me, Oh, Thou Great Jehovah," . . . . . . . . . . . . . *Flotow*
  MISS JESSIE MILLS.
Question Box.
The Fertilizer Question . . . . . . . . . . . . . . . . . . . . . . . . . . . . . . . . . . .
  S. M. WOODBRIDGE, PH. D., Southern California Pomological
  Society, South Pasadena.
Fertilization of Our Orchards . . . . . . . . . . . . . . . . . . . . . . . . . . . . . .
  GEO. F. FERRIS, Claremont Club.
Solo—"One Spring Morning," . . . . . . . . . . . . . . . . . . . . . . . . . *Nevin*
  MISS JESSIE MILLS.
Maintaining Fertility of Our Soils . . . . . . . . . . . . . . . . . . . . . . . . . . .
  DR. E. W. HILGARD, Berkeley.

### EVENING SESSION, 8 O'CLOCK.

Duet—"Oh That We Two Were Maying," . . . . . . . . . . . . . . *Herschel*
  KATHERINE PHILYSS EDSON AND MR. C. F. EDSON.
Question Box.
Disposing of Our Fruit Crops . . . . . . . . . . . . . . . . . . . . . . . . . . . . . .
  JAMES MORGAN, Santa Barbara Horticultural Association.
The Future of the Citrus Fruit Industry . . . . . . . . . . . . . . . . . . . . . .
  E. W. HOLMES, Riverside Club.
Beet Sugar and the Farmers . . . . . . . . . . . . . . . . . . . . . . . . . . . . . . .
  W. T. HAYHURST, Chino.
Solo—"Love's Old Sweet Song," . . . . . . . . . . . . . . . . . . . . . . *Molloy*
  KATHERINE PHILYSS EDSON.
Ornamentation of Home Grounds . . . . . . . . . . . . . . . . . . . . . . . . . . .
  ALFRED H. SMILEY, Redlands Club.
Influence of Stock on Scion and of Pollen on Carpels . . . . . . . .
  PROF. L. H. BAILEY, Cornell, Ithaca, N. Y.

PROGRAM FROM AN 1898 FARMERS' INSTITUTE MEETING IN LOS ANGELES. LECTURES ON HORTICULTURE, FERTILIZER, AND DAIRYING WERE INTERSPERSED WITH MUSICAL ENTERTAINMENT.

Already long established in Wisconsin and several other states, Farmers' Institutes were educational conference events for rural people, sponsored by the land-grant colleges in conjunction with local communities. When money from the second Morrill Act (1890) became available, the Regents deemed it fitting to use some of the funds to meet the request of the Grange and extend the work of the College out into rural areas. In April 1891 the first Farmers' Institute in California was held in Fresno under the direction of Edward J. Wickson; its main subject was "Alkali: Its Causes and Remedies,"

---

**PROGRAMME—Continued.**

**MORNING SESSION, JAN. 5, 10 O'CLOCK.**

Invocation...............................................
    REV. A. C. SMITHERS.
Piano Solo...............................................
    MR. WILL STROBRIDGE.
Question Box.
Handling Milk..........................................
    PROF. A. J. McCLATCHIE, Southern California Dairymen's
        Association, Los Angeles.
A Better Dairy Cow
    GEO. E. PLATT, Southern California Dairymen's Association,
        Los Angeles.
'Cello Solo.............................................
    MR. C. W. STEVENS.
The Silo................................................
    JAS. R. BOAL, Southern California Dairymen's Association,
        Los Angeles.
The Cereals in Southern California.....................
    OLIN L. LIVESEY, Antelope Valley Association, Fairmont.

**AFTERNOON SESSION, 2 O'CLOCK.**

Quartette—"Nocturne,".............................. *Doppler*
    MISS DAISY POLK, Violin; MR. C. W. STEVENS. 'Cello;
    MR. W. H. MEAD, Flute; MR. M. F, MASON, Piano.
Question Box.
Pruning the Lemon......................................
    WM. IRVING, Riverside Club.
Lemon Culture..........................................
    G. P. HALL, San Diego Horticultural Association.
Reading................................................
    MRS. PARSONS, Cumnock School of Oratory and Arts,
Lemons on the Coast....................................
    N. W. BLANCHARD, Santa Paula Club.
    Discussion led by H. C. DILLON, Long Beach Club.
Raisin Culture.........................................
    R. C. ALLEN, National City.

**EVENING SESSION, 8 O'CLOCK.**

Solo...................................................
    MRS. ABBOT KINNEY.
Question Box.
Preserving Our Forests.................................
    HON. ABBOT KINNEY, Pres. Southern California
        Pomological Society.
Preserving Our Forests.................................
    C. B. WILSIE, Nordhoff Club.
Solo...................................................
    MRS. ABBOT KINNEY.
Address................................................
    REV. BURT ESTES HOWARD.
The Rhizobius.
    H. C. DILLON, Long Beach Horticultural Club.
Concluding Exercises.

**ADJOURNMENT.**

The Piano used is from the Southern California Music Co., 216-218 West Third
Street, Los Angeles, Cal.

---

The Farmers' Institutes are held under the auspices of the University of
California. It is a University extension movement, carried to the farmers.
All farmers should come and bring their wives and families.

UNIVERSITY FARMERS' CLUB
INSTITUTE, TO BE HELD AT
CHAMBER OF COMMERCE, LOS
ANGELES, CAL., JAN. 3-4-5-1898

CONDUCTED BY

PROF. A. J. COOK OF POMONA COLLEGE
UNIVERSITY REPRESENTATIVE IN
SOUTHERN CALIFORNIA

**COMMITTEES:**

| | | |
|---|---|---|
| *Decoration*—FRANK WIGGINS. | | *Exhibit*—A. R. SPRAGUE. |
| | *Railroads*—ABBOT KINNEY, | |
| | C. H. SESSIONS, | |
| | A. P. GRIFFITH. | |
| *Programme*—G. H. A. GOODWIN. | | *Music*—C. F. EDSON. |
| | *Publicity*—C. H. SESSIONS. | |
| | *Finance*—PROF. A. J. COOK. | |

More money always follows intelligence and skill in orchard, field and
garden; in dairy, stockyard and apiary. This intelligence the Farmers'
Institute aims to disseminate.

A special rate has been secured on all railroads of one and one-
third fare. Ask your ticket agent for certificate and pay full fare
to Los Angeles. Return ticket will be issued at Los Angeles for
ONE-THIRD rate. Be sure to have your certificate signed at the
meeting by the Secretary.

CALIFORNIA CULTIVATOR PRESS,
LOS ANGELES, CAL.

46 and it drew a crowd. Because Californians were eager for information, institutes proved popular, sharing in the contemporaneous general interest in adult education events like those of the Chautauqua movement. Within three years 45 meetings were held in ten counties.[37]

Wickson used a circular letter to explain stipulations for organizing the institutes. If a community arranged and advertised the event, provided a hall, and took care of details, the University would send lecturers to speak on general subjects related to agriculture. Local speakers, both men and women, were to make presentations on area-specific farming or "home affairs," and part of the program should include music—which, Wickson wrote, "helps wonderfully to enliven the meetings." All "vexed questions" on political subjects were to be strictly out of order. Eventually, to use college staff efficiently, the institutes took a standard format: a week of three institutes would take place within a given county, each institute consisting of a day and a half of sessions starting in the afternoon and lasting until the next evening.

At first the greatest interest in Farmers' Institutes was shown in southern California below the Tehachapis, with a "measure of apathy" apparent in northern and central California, although this did not last long. Institutes became so popular that in 1897 the Regents created a Department of University Extension in Agriculture, headed by Wickson, who supervised two assistants in organizing the northern and southern portions of the state. From 1898 through 1901 more than 80 institutes each year attracted an average of 250 persons each, and Wickson estimated that about 20,000 people attended annually, scattered in rural communities from border to border. Demands on the staff eventually became so great, detracting from research and instruction at Berkeley, that in 1903 the legislature appropriated $6,000 per year to reorganize the work. That year the number of Institutes rose to 113, covering 41 out of 57 counties. Some were more ambitious than others; for example, the "Seaside Farmers'

Institute" in Long Beach lasted an entire week with "interest keenly maintained throughout."[38] By their high point about 1912, more than 150 Farmers' Institutes each year attracted more than 40,000 participants.

In addition to Institute work, University Extension in Agriculture inaugurated a series of reading courses to meet the demand for information among persons unable to attend courses or local programs. In 1902 about 100 students enrolled by mail for a reading course in animal industry covering stockbreeding, diseases of farm animals, and kindred subjects. Other courses were announced in economic entomology and irrigation.[39] These early correspondence courses were later supplanted by a more formal series prepared after 1913.

The outreach work of Farmers' Institutes served several purposes. Not only did they convey results of College work to farmers ("The farmers' institute is but a larger classroom of the university"), they brought back questions of pressing local importance, providing a conduit for communication between the College and the public. Farmers' Institutes also directly encouraged community development in rural areas, and many local clubs and cooperatives were formed as a result of institute meetings. Not least, as the most visible representatives of the University of California in communities across the state, College of Agriculture staff helped build good will for the entire institution.

## HILGARD'S LEGACY

Hilgard was truly a man for all seasons. Meticulous in detail but broad of vision, he moved with grace from laboratory and fieldwork to the international podium. In 1892-93 Hilgard took a sabbatical year in Europe, returning to California with a detailed report on agricultural schools and experiment stations in Germany and Switzerland.[40] In Berlin and Paris,

Hilgard delivered several lectures on California and its agriculture, enlightening listeners whose impressions of the state stemmed from the writings of Mark Twain and Bret Harte and establishing many useful contacts in the European scientific community. Later he was recognized with international awards for his contributions to soil science. In 1903 Hilgard received a "Golden Degree" from the University at Heidelberg on the fiftieth anniversary of his doctorate there, and he was also awarded the Liebig medal from the Academy of Sciences at Munich for distinguished achievement.

More than any other person, Hilgard set the course and established the solid scientific reputation of the College of Agriculture. He recognized that California experimental work had entirely different parameters than that in other states: "The unfamiliar agricultural practices of Southern Spain, Egypt, North Africa, Asia Minor, and the northernmost provinces of India, rather than that of the eastern United States, form the basis upon which the greater part of California must build its own, profoundly modifying many of the current practices of the old States. . . . Our line of investigations is necessarily laid in different and new directions."[41] Not only did he produce a pathbreaking body of work in his chosen field of soil science, he contributed important knowledge about viticulture and winemaking and supervised a broad variety of research projects in many other areas. Arguing again and again for the importance of Experiment Station work in developing rational management of the state's resources, he proved both a competent and an eloquent administrator. He firmly advocated the view of agriculture as a profession based on science and earned a real, if sometimes grudging, respect within the University for the College by making the agricultural sciences academically respectable.

Hilgard also recognized the entrepreneurial character of California agriculture and turned it to his institution's advantage. As limited state and federal support could not let him meet all requests for Experiment Station research, Hilgard convinced interest groups to sponsor research projects through legislative or private grants, augmenting general station resources. He withstood interference, however, with probity and skill, insisting on truly scientific investigations—for example, in wine research—even when some supporters would have preferred less "theoretical" work. As he grew older, some chafed at his "imperial" ways, but they never doubted his competence or his integrity.

By 1905, the end of Hilgard's tenure as Dean, the College of Agriculture had grown from a one-man operation to a staff of nearly 30. Since agricultural research had begun at Berkeley many changes had swept over the state: waves of immigration had brought in a richly diverse population; colonies and cooperatives were bringing group action to bear on farm and community problems; water law had begun to regulate stream diversions and rationalize distribution; enormous growth of rail and road networks was making remote regions more accessible. While all these factors were important in bringing about the transformation of California's agriculture from a pastoral to an irrigated economy, at least of equal import was the work of the Experiment Station, which by applying science to farm practice brought large gains in productivity, with far-reaching ramifications. Farmers were learning how to handle stubborn soils, overcome the vicissitudes of aridity, adapt crops to local circumstance, and fight the threats of disease and pests. With the help of the natural and biological sciences, agriculture in California seemed on the verge of vast opportunities, and the state's entire economy was benefiting. The growing diversity of enterprises after 1900 was reflected in the hiring of new college staff in animal industries, dairying, veterinary science and bacteriology, fermentative industries, horticulture, and irrigation engineering. The College had great popular and legislative support. With Hilgard's retirement would come a major reorganization of college administration and a great flowering of facilities.

# NOTES

1. See George Hart et al., "Wealth Pyramiding in the Production of Livestock," in Claude B. Hutchison, ed., *California Agriculture* (Berkeley: UC Press, 1946), pp. 52–53.

2. John E. Baur, "California Crops That Failed," *California Historical Quarterly* 45 (Mar. 1966): 41–68.

3. Ezra Slocum Carr, *The Patrons of Husbandry on the Pacific Coast* (San Francisco: A. L. Bancroft, 1875), p. 295.

4. See Elwood Mead, *Irrigation Institutions: A Discussion of the Economic and Legal Questions Created by the Growth of Irrigated Agriculture in the West* (New York: Macmillan, 1903), and Donald Pisani, *From the Family Farm to Agribusiness: The Irrigation Crusade in California and the West, 1850–1931* (Berkeley: UC Press, 1984).

5. Details of Hilgard's life are based on Hilgard's own unpublished biographic memoir written after his retirement and collected with his papers at the Bancroft Library (UC Archives, *Hilgard Papers*).

6. UC Archives, *Regents' Records*, "Faculty 1875–1879." Ironically, when Hilgard finally arrived in California, he found Daniel Gilman about to depart for his new position in Maryland; Hilgard was so disheartened that he nearly turned around.

7. Edward J. Wickson, "Beginnings of Education and Research in Agriculture," in *Annual Report of the Director, University of California Agricultural Experiment Station, 1918*, pp. 41–42.

8. Ibid., pp. 68–69.

9. From *In Memoriam: Eugene Woldemar Hilgard* (Berkeley: University of California Press, 1916). Reprinted from the University of California *Chronicle* 18:2, and distributed by the University of California Agricultural Experiment Station, pp. 10–12.

10. UC Archives, *College of Agriculture Files*, "Report of the Professor of Agriculture to the President of the University" (1877), pp. 11–13.

11. Hilgard, *Report on the Physical and Agricultural Features of the State of California . . .* (Washington, D.C.: Dept. of the Interior Census Office, 1884), pp. 77–78. Cotton did not, however, become a major commercial crop in California until well after the turn of the century.

12. Hilgard's consulting activities drew criticism a few years later, and Hilgard asked the Regents to examine the issue. Convinced by his arguments that his independent fieldwork had compiled much useful knowledge without expense to the University or the state, the Regents commended Hilgard's work.

13. See "The Experiment Station Exhibit," Appendix I in *Report of the Work of the Agricultural Experiment Station of the University of California, for the Year 1892–93 and Part of 1894: Being a Part of the Report of the Regents of the University.*

14. "Endurance of Drought in Soils of the Arid Region" and "Moisture in California Soils during the Dry Season of 1898," in *Report of the Work of the Agricultural Experiment Station of the University of California, for the Year 1897–98: Being a Part of the Report of the Regents of the University*, pp. 40–96.

15. James C. Malin evaluated Hilgard's soils work in *The Grassland of North America: Prolegomena to Its History* (Lawrence, Kans.: privately printed, 1947), pp. 212–21. Loughridge's quote is from pp. 50–51.

16. The only biography of Hilgard to date is by Hans Jenny, who described Hilgard's contributions in *E. W. Hilgard and the Birth of Modern Soil Science* (Pisa, Italy: Collana della Rivista Agrochimica, 1961). The quote is from p. 80.

17. The description of Hilgard's vicultural work in this section is based on Maynard Amerine, "Hilgard and California Viticulture," *Hilgardia* 33:1 (July 1962): 1–23. Although Hilgard's reputation as a wine researcher was largely forgotten during Prohibition, his work during the earliest years of the industry was both solid and useful.

18. UC College of Agriculture, *Supplement No. 1 to the Report of the Board of Regents, 1890*, p. 19.

19. "Work of the College of Agriculture and Experiment Stations," *Partial Report of the Work of the Agricultural Experiment Stations of the University of California for the Years 1895–96; 1896–97*, p. 15.

20. But see F. T. Bioletti, "Principles of Wine-Making," Agricultural Experiment Station *Bulletin 213* (1911); and Bioletti and W. V. Cruess, "Enological Investigations," *Bulletin 230* (1912).

21. Wickson, "Beginnings," p. 64.

22. Ibid., p. 63.

23. Ibid., pp. 68–69.

24. Pamphlets on olive culture from about 1883 to 1900 are in the collection of the Huntington Library, San Marino, Calif.

25. UC College of Agriculture, *Supplement to the Biennial Report of the Board of Regents, 1885–86*, Appendix 3, p. 109.

26. Over time the Experiment Station worked extensively on olive oil manufacturing technology, and a viable olive oil industry existed in California well into the 1930s. California olive oil is today a relatively minor industry, eclipsed by Italian and Spanish oils in both U.S. and world markets.

27. See Wickson, "Beginnings," pp. 83–85; also, C. W. Wickson's report on "Entomology" in *Report of the Work of the Agricultural Experiment Station, 1901–1903*, pp. 104–110. Some of Woodworth's students employed as field agents in the early 1900s eventually founded the California Spray Chemical Company, later known as Ortho and acquired by the Standard Oil Company in 1931.

28. William B. Hewitt, "R. E. Smith: Pioneer in Phytopathology," *Annual Review of Phytopathology* 25 (1987): 41–50. The quote is from Agricultural Experiment Station *Circular 9*, p. 19; Smith's report on asparagus work is "Asparagus and Asparagus Rust in California," *Bulletin 165* (Jan. 1905).

29. Letter of transmittal, Hilgard to President Horace Davis, April 7, 1890, *Report on the Agricultural Experiment Stations of the University of California, Being a Part of the Combined Reports for 1888 and 1889*, p. 15. Hans Jenny, in his book on Hilgard, and Wayne Rasmussen, in *Readings in the History of American Agriculture* (Urbana: University of Illinois Press, 1960), note that the University of Connecticut at Storrs claims to be the first (1875) Agricultural Experiment Station in the United States on the basis of funding by the state legislature. Hilgard insisted that California was the first state actually to do experimental work.

30. Act of 1887 Establishing Agricultural Experiment Stations, 24 U.S. Statutes at Large 440, Sec. 2. The Adams Experiment Station Act (1906) provided additional federal funds.

31. *Report . . . 1890*.

32. *Report . . . 1892–93* describes the newly acquired forestry stations, pp. 425–32. *Twenty-Second Report of the Work of the Agricultural Experiment Station of the University of California, from June 30, 1903, to June 30, 1904; Being a Part of the Report of the Regents of the University*, pp. 89–105, describes the establishment and work of the Petaluma poultry experiment station. At this time a family of five could support itself on a 5-acre poultry farm with a flock of 1,000 to 1,500 laying hens and a "thrifty family orchard."

33. Wickson, "Beginnings," p. 61.

34. *Report . . . 1877*, pp. 4 and 9.

35. Eugene Hilgard, "Progress in Agriculture by Education and Government Aid," *Atlantic Monthly*, April 1882: 531–41, and May 1882: 651–61.

36. Wickson, "Beginnings," p. 50.

37. Emmett Fiske's 1979 dissertation, "The College and Its Constituency: Research and Community Development at the University of California, 1875–1978" (University of California, Davis), pp. 41–85, describes California's Farmers' Institutes in detail. See also UC Archives, *Regents' Records*, "Farmers' Institutes 1890–99."

38. *Report . . . 1903–04*, pp. 24–26.

39. Ibid., pp. 26–27.

40. "Report of Observations Made on European Agricultural Schools and Experiment Stations, 1892–93," in *Report . . . 1892–93*, pp. 27–41.

41. *Report . . . 1890*, p. 18.

# 3

# Land of Promise

## 1905–1918

A young farm advisor in his Model T, which covered many miles of country road. Beginning in 1913, the Agricultural Extension Service helped farmers and their families achieve better livelihoods through outreach of land-grant university research.

THE EARLY TWENTIETH CENTURY WAS AN EXCITING PERIOD OF PROGRES-
SIVE REFORM AND OPTIMISM. POPULATION GROWTH IN CALIFORNIA
BROUGHT IN A WIDE VARIETY OF NEW RESIDENTS, AND NEW OPPORTU-
NITIES IN IRRIGATED FARMING CONTRIBUTED TO THE BREAKUP OF MANY LARGE
RANCHES INTO SMALLER UNITS. THE UNIVERSITY OF CALIFORNIA FLOURISHED.
THE COLLEGE OF AGRICULTURE ACQUIRED TWO IMPORTANT NEW OUTLYING
FACILITIES, THE UNIVERSITY FARM AT DAVIS AND THE CITRUS EXPERIMENT STA-
TION AT RIVERSIDE. IN 1913 THE COLLEGE GAINED A NEW DEAN WHO UNDER-
TOOK MANY NEW INITIATIVES. THE PREWAR YEARS SAW THE ESTABLISHMENT OF
THE AGRICULTURAL EXTENSION SERVICE AND A DIVISION OF RURAL INSTITU-
TIONS, WHICH TOGETHER WITH THE STATE OF CALIFORNIA ATTEMPTED A MODEL
STATE LAND SETTLEMENT PROGRAM. WORLD WAR I MADE NEW DEMANDS ON
FARMERS AND BROUGHT AN END TO THE PROGRESSIVE PERIOD.

# 3

# Land of Promise 1905–1918

## WINDS OF CHANGE

The turn of the century and the waning years of Hilgard's career saw the passing of an era. After the economic and political struggles of the 1890s a different spirit seemed to take hold around the world. Liberation movements gathered strength in such strongholds of despotism as China, Russia, and the Ottoman Empire, and in England the long Victorian era ended with the death of the queen in 1901. That same year catapulted 42-year-old Theodore Roosevelt into the U.S. presidency.

Roosevelt's entry into office began an innovative period of federal reforms and new programs, and his vigorous personal style influenced daily life across the nation. Roosevelt threw his powers behind the effort to regulate industrial monopolies, and called rhetorically for establishing a "square deal" for all. Perhaps his greatest impact came through his active support for the protection and rational development of the nation's natural resources. His administration strengthened the irrigation movement in the arid West, established the U.S. Forest Service, began federal regulation of coal and mineral deposits, doubled the number of national parks, and established dozens of national wildlife refuges.

In California the early years of the twentieth century saw sweeping changes along with attempts to forge a new social vision. Based on growing opposition to corrupt machine politics dominated by the Southern Pacific Railroad, the Good Government movement spread through the state, led by a coalition of prominent newspaper editors and other citizen politicians. In 1910 these progressives elected Hiram Johnson as governor with a reform agenda. (In 1912, Johnson became the vice presidential candidate on Roosevelt's Progressive Party ticket.) The colorful governor was supported by those bent on developing state institutions responsive to the needs of the people rather than the desires of special interests. The most thoughtful and sensitive of the progressives also cherished an idealistic ambition to build a better society on the foundations of the new wealth developing in California. With optimism based on technical advancement buoying their hopes, they turned their energies toward many good causes, and some of California's most prestigious institutions flowered during this period. Benjamin Ide Wheeler, inaugurated as President of the University of California in 1899, brought a large sense of mission to his twenty-year task of leading the University. Scientists and nature enthusiasts followed the charismatic John Muir to promote a growing conservation movement through the Sierra Club, organized in 1892. The Commonwealth Club of San Francisco, formed in 1903, became an influential forum for debate on state policy issues.[1]

## NEW FRONTIERS, NEW FARMS

In 1911 Ishi, the last "wild Indian," walked out of the Lassen wilderness to confront a white man's culture that had irrevocably changed the natural world he knew. Protected by University anthropologist Alfred Kroeber, Ishi spent his remaining five years as a living resource in the University's museum, leaving behind him a record of his people's customs and a better understanding of the modest grace of their vanished way of life.[2] But by 1911 more than Ishi's way of life had vanished: twenty years earlier the Superintendent of the U.S. Census had observed that "there can hardly be said to be a frontier line." The era of open land in the West, available for homesteading and sodbreaking, had come more or less to an end. Historian Frederick Jackson Turner, for whom the frontier possessed great significance as an essential factor in the development of American institutions, held that the brief official statement marked the closing of a great historic movement.[3]

PRESIDENT THEODORE ROOSEVELT POSES WITH JOHN MUIR ABOVE YOSEMITE VALLEY, 1903.

Access to open land had long served the nation as a safety valve for population pressures and discontents, and the shrinking of that opportunity encouraged the reclamation movement. Throughout the 1890s leaders like William Ellsworth Smythe and George Maxwell headed a broad-based effort to transform the arid and semiarid regions of the West into productive farms. For Smythe, an influential journalist, irrigation was not only a vehicle for economic development but a "program of practical statesmanship" that offered the opportunity to enact agrarian reforms. In southern California talented engineers had already proved that well-planned private irrigation projects could provide comfortable livelihoods for settlers on small acreages in formerly dry regions. In 1902 the National Reclamation (Newlands) Act, wholeheartedly endorsed by President Roosevelt, became another means of extending the frontier through federally sponsored irrigation projects. Specifically written into the legislation were acreage limitations (160 acres) on water subsidies, intended to preserve opportunities for family farmers.[4]

By 1900 California's wheat boom was fading. Declining soil fertility, increased competition for world markets, and opportunities for more intensive cropping made wheat growing less profitable, and production fell from more than 40 million bushels in 1895 to less than 18 million ten years later. Many of the huge grain ranches of the nineteenth century began to break up. In 1904, for example, the *Pacific Rural Press* ran advertisements for the subdivision of former wheat baron Hugh Glenn's estate in the Sacramento Valley. Announcements of 20- and 40-acre farms carved out of larger landholdings proliferated in newspapers and magazines.

Although land promotion was not new in California, the euphoria of the "irrigation crusade" gave promotional efforts more scope and intensity. After 1900 the railroads grew even more active in trying to attract settlers. As early as the 1880s the Southern Pacific Rail Company had published a guide for California immigrants extolling the healthful climate ("Nowhere in the United States are the children so rosy and fat as in California"); throughout the 1890s the railroad distributed alluring pamphlets in several languages including German, Italian, and Portuguese. Then, in 1898, Southern Pacific began *Sunset Magazine* as a regular vehicle for publicizing "the attractions and advantages of the Western Empire." The distribution and size of this monthly grew quickly—from a printing of 15,000 in its first issue to 60,000 by 1905, and from 15 pages to more than 200. At first geared toward tourists and health seekers and serving largely as an advertising medium, the magazine soon became a major popular information source on agricultural development and resource management along the Pacific coast. By 1914, when employees purchased it from the railroad company, *Sunset* was running a variety of feature articles on California, including profiles of "interesting Westerners" like agricultural researchers Eugene Hilgard and Luther Burbank.[5]

At the 1904 World's Fair in St. Louis, state government and commercial interests backed an elaborate promotional display extolling California's agricultural possibilities—it included "an obelisk made of 2,000 bottles of olive oil," a bear made of prunes, a horse of hops, portieres of peanuts, a miniature palace of oranges, and the replica of a mission covered with dried fruits. Land agents put out increasingly large and attractive booklets aimed at attracting an "industrious agricultural population." "California is not a lazy man's country," proclaimed one pocket-sized handbook distributed by the California Promotion Committee in San Francisco about 1906, but "there is a wonderful future for intensive farming." In 1914 the Southern Pacific Passenger Department published a beautifully illustrated 96-page booklet on the attractions of California for the "plain American farmer" who is "something of a scientist as well," stating emphatically that "more farmers are needed" for the expansion of "another stage in the evolution of California agriculture."[6]

Rapid improvements in transportation during this period encouraged immigration. Railroad miles continually expanded, and the opening of the Panama Canal in 1914 greatly decreased ocean transport time and costs from the East coast and Europe. The magnificent Panama-Pacific International Exposition held in San Francisco in 1915 celebrated not only the opening of the canal but the rebuilding of the city after the 1906 earthquake and fire. A five-car automobile caravan from New York to the exposition advertised the official opening (not completion) of the transcontinental Lincoln Highway.

The great opportunities touted by promoters and hucksters drew a wide variety of newcomers. Between 1890 and 1910 California's population doubled, from about 1.2 million to 2.4 million, and another million flooded in by 1920. Many eastern and midwestern Americans had already settled in the state, particularly in the citrus colonies of southern California, and promoters continued attempts to convince more Americans to relocate. Twentieth-century ethnic settlement included new waves from southern and central Europe—Italy, Portugal, the Balkan states, and Armenia—many of whom successfully went into specialty crops, dairying, or poultry production. New immigrants from Asia also began to change the face of California agriculture, but while other "foreign farmers" were often admired for their thrifty, hardworking habits, the Asians were commonly resented.

"John Chinaman as a crop-coaxer" may have been unexcelled.[8] Yet Chinese laborers were prohibited from bringing wives to this country, and many of them eventually returned to Asia or migrated to California's growing cities, leaving a gap in rural areas just as the demand for labor increased with rapid conversion to intensive crops. Other Asians filled the niche. Japanese immigration started as early as 1888 with the importation of harvest workers for fruit growers in the Vacaville district. Their numbers swelled after 1900, particularly after the Russo-Japanese war of 1904. Alarm about the "yellow peril" surfaced again, fanned by the Hearst newspapers. The arrival of 30,000 Japanese in 1907 caused so much public concern that the Roosevelt administration negotiated a "Gentlemen's Agreement" between the United States and Japan: if the United States would not pass an exclusion act like that against the Chinese, Japan would voluntarily restrict the number of laboring men allowed to emigrate. Despite the agreement the Japanese influx continued, and since their women had not been barred, many Japanese already here sent for "picture brides" from the old country, who soon began producing babies—further alarming anti-Asian critics.

Seizing on the new opportunities offered by the subdivision of large ranches, industrious Japanese quickly moved from working for others to leasing or owning land for themselves. From 1900 to 1910, the number of Japanese farmers in California grew from 37 to 1,816; between 1904 and 1909 Japanese land ownership increased from 2,442 to 16,449 acres and their land leases from 54,830 to 139,233 acres. Their endurance of hardship and backbreaking work did not endear them to other California farmers, who viewed them as clannish, grasping, and "unassimilable." While the Japanese forged a growing success, resentment simmered: admiration mingles with exasperation in the contemporary comment, "What a clever Jap will do with a one-acre farm is almost past belief."[9] Under mounting public pressure the legislature passed the California Alien Land Law (1913) prohibiting ownership of California land by persons not eligible for citizenship—that is, all immigrants from Asia. Because this law had some loopholes, two stronger laws prohibiting such ownership were passed by initiative in 1921 and 1923.[9]

A smaller group of Asians, from the Punjab province of northern India, also settled in California during the early 1900s. They came originally as farm laborers into the Imperial Valley and parts of the San Joaquin and Sacramento valleys, where their experience with cotton and rice growing proved useful. Eventually, like the Japanese, they seized on opportunities to lease or buy land, and with their business sense strengthened by ethnic solidarity they also achieved agricultural success.[10]

The farms so carefully tended by immigrants, either as tenants or owners, demonstrated the rapid conversion of land to more intensive uses. Between 1900 and 1914 the number of farms in California ballooned from 72,542 to 110,000. Many factors contributed to the expansion. Developments in irrigation and agricultural science made more feasible the establishment of profitable orchards, vineyards, sugar beet plantings, and vegetable farms, and developments in transportation made it easier to ship products. By trial and error farmers learned to organize into cooperatives to meet the challenge of marketing across the great distances separating them from major U.S. urban areas.[11] And California's own internal markets grew, bringing greater demand for dairy and poultry products and fresh fruits and vegetables.

Between 1900 and World War I California agriculture entered an exciting new era. It was a good time for all American agriculture, but in California optimism ran especially high. Promoters made a great effort to attract settlers, for science and technology seemed to offer effective means for overcoming natural obstacles to land development. The legislature was generous in its support, and during this period the College of Agriculture significantly extended its activities and influence.

58

# THE FLOWERING OF THE UNIVERSITY OF CALIFORNIA

## BENJAMIN IDE WHEELER, PATRIARCH AND BUILDER

Benjamin Ide Wheeler, President of the University from 1899 to 1919, was a renowned scholar and linguist, benevolent patriarch, and consummate politician. He shared with his friend Theodore Roosevelt an enthusiasm for vigorous action and an abiding concern for the common weal. Like Roosevelt, Wheeler used his office as "a bully pulpit" to urge students and citizens alike toward the good life. His famous talks to undergraduates combined fatherly advice with reflections on the course of western civilization; his habit of riding horseback around campus endeared him to a generation of students.[12] Inspired by Wheeler's hopes and concerns so persuasively expressed, those students would become teachers, engineers, business owners, lawyers, scientists, managers, and journalists, influencing much of California's twentieth-century development.

For the University the Wheeler years brought beautiful buildings, ambitious new academic programs, increased emphasis on faculty quality, and a quadrupling of student enrollments from about 2,000 in 1900 to 8,600 in 1919. Wheeler was instrumental in persuading Californians, in a

AGRICULTURE HALL (LATER NAMED WELLMAN HALL), CONSTRUCTED IN 1912 ON THE BERKELEY CAMPUS.

remarkable common flowering of private philanthropy and public support, to underwrite a great construction program for the Berkeley campus based on Frenchman Henri Benard's comprehensive design, which won Phoebe Apperson Hearst's international architectural competition in 1897.[13]

Under the Benard plan the northwest corner of the campus was reserved for agriculture. A complex of four buildings was planned for the west knoll overlooking the north fork of Strawberry Creek. Long before Hilgard's retirement in 1905 the College of Agriculture had outgrown its limited quarters, the faculty pressing into service any horse- or toolshed it could commandeer for experimental needs. Always the persistent lobbyist, Hilgard argued powerfully in his last report for more classroom, laboratory, and office space ("painfully inadequate . . . the possibilities even of the garret now being exhausted").[14] But the new agricultural complex came into being only after both Hilgard and his successor had ended their active careers.

In 1912 the first building in the group, Agriculture Hall (renamed Wellman Hall in 1968), was completed for $250,000 and dedicated for the use of the departments of entomology, horticulture, viticulture, plant pathology, apiculture, and irrigation. In 1917 Hilgard Hall was dedicated to serve the agronomy, citriculture, forestry, genetics, pomology, soil technology, and other departments. This building, one of the most beautiful on campus, cost $350,000, raised through a special university bond issue passed by California voters in 1914. University Architect John Galen Howard designed the structure to face west toward the Golden Gate; its east front bordered an inner courtyard inspired by the idea of an old Tuscan farmstead. Of reinforced concrete and roofed in tile, Hilgard Hall contained 111 rooms on three floors, plus a basement. Sgraffito work (sculptured pink layers of plaster) decorated its exterior; worked into the plaster were symbols of agriculture including fruit and flowers, sheaves of grain, animal heads, and farm implements. Along the west attic wall ran an inscription penned by Wheeler himself: "To Rescue for Human Society the Native Values of Rural Life."[15]

## THE WOOING OF LIBERTY HYDE BAILEY

As one of the conditions of his presidency, Wheeler insisted on the power to appoint faculty. On Hilgard's retirement Wheeler felt compelled to seek a man of equal stature to head the College of Agriculture. Though Wickson, Hilgard's lieutenant for more than 25 years, desired the appointment and had many supporters, Wheeler hoped to find a more scholarly man with a national reputation.

The person Wheeler wanted was the renowned Liberty Hyde Bailey, dean of the college of agriculture at Cornell University. Wheeler had known Bailey during his own years at Cornell and shared his conviction that education could—and should—bring a "new rural civilization" to the American countryside. Bailey, a horticulturalist, was the leading spirit

HILGARD HALL, BUILT IN 1915. THE QUOTATION ACROSS THE PEDIMENT REFLECTS THE PHILOSOPHY OF THE COUNTRY LIFE MOVEMENT.

in the emerging "Country Life" movement and an articulate writer on the values of husbandry and the needs of farm communities. He was also an eloquent conservationist, calling for a deeper understanding of man's relationship with "the holy earth" ("We are parts in a living, sensitive creation").[16]

Wheeler had already brought Bailey to Berkeley to lecture on nature study during the summer session of 1901 before "very large audiences of very interesting people." And Bailey had clearly enjoyed it, visiting among other places the Santa Rosa gardens of Luther Burbank as part of the "most interesting and profitable summer I have ever had." But he declined Wheeler's invitations to return in 1902 and 1904. In early 1905, with Hilgard's retirement imminent, Wheeler pressed Bailey in a series of letters to consider the California deanship. On April 6 Bailey replied: "I am of course much complimented. . . . If I were desiring the directorship of an agricultural college I should, I think, prefer yours to any other. . . . The field is white for the harvest in California." But he pointed out his happiness with his home and work in Ithaca and the advantage of his location in pursuing his literary interests with publishers in New York. In late April Wheeler urged him again, citing the challenges and opportunities emerging in California—appropriations forthcoming for a University farm, a citrus experiment station, a pathology laboratory, broadened Farmers' Institutes, and special investigations:

The situation has entirely outgrown us. We need a man of large view, with high courage, and broad wisdom to come in. . . . If you should come here, there would not be a question from

60

one end of the State to the other concerning anything you would choose to do. People would have entire confidence in you. . . . There is a strong feeling that we must break with our past. I am earnestly resolved to have, if possible, the best agricultural school in the United States. California deserves it. Californians do not like second-rate things. Now is the time to make the change. . . . If we delay a year longer, I fear that the [university] farm problem will be settled and perhaps settled wrong.

Bailey replied: "I should like the larger opportunity and the freer atmosphere of the Pacific Coast. You certainly have a great opportunity to make an institution that will stand in a very bold and large way for the very best interests of agriculture and country life." But he firmly declined Wheeler's importuning, although he agreed to teach once more in the Berkeley summer session and to consult with the State Farm Commission regarding criteria for selecting a University Farm site.[17]

In May 1905 the disappointed Wheeler named Wickson as Acting Dean and Director of the Experiment Station, while he continued his search for a permanent dean. He asked many colleagues, including Hilgard, for recommendations. Hilgard's suggestions did not include Wickson, nor did those of Dean W. A. Henry of Wisconsin, who thought that Wickson, though of great value in a secondary

PICNIC DAY AT THE UNIVERSITY STATE FARM. ON LEFT, BENJAMIN IDE WHEELER, PRESIDENT OF THE UNIVERSITY OF CALIFORNIA; SECOND FROM RIGHT, EDWARD J. WICKSON, DEAN OF THE COLLEGE OF AGRICULTURE; ON RIGHT, NORMAN VAN LEAR, DIRECTOR OF THE UNIVERSITY FARM.

position, had "confined himself too closely to routine duties" to be the best leader for the College.[18] Nevertheless, Acting Dean Wickson, believing that it was time for the College to have a "democratic rather than an imperial government" with "new efforts along practical lines," plunged immediately into reorganizing the College into departments by subject. Clearly no one man could assume all the responsibilities that Hilgard had carried. Research requests and college enrollments were on the rise, and the 1905 legislature, taking a very active interest in the future of the College, had debated twelve college-related bills, passing half of them.[19] Wickson had much to do just to keep up.

Perhaps not least among Bailey's reasons for declining the deanship was the knowledge that, as Hilgard commented in a letter to a friend, the "extremely captious public" in California would likely make life difficult for an eastern man. Wickson had written to Wheeler that farmers would insist on a man who "understood California conditions." In July, Bailey's remarks at Berkeley on the role of a University farm brought forth a spasm of criticism, partly stirred up by Peter Shields, author of and lobbyist for the State Farm bill.[20] Bailey, who was increasingly revered at Cornell, could hardly have been attracted by the problems he would have to endure as Dean in California.

# A TALE OF TWO DEANS

## EDWARD J. WICKSON

Edward J. Wickson arrived in California in 1875 as a young journalist from upstate New York. In 1869 he had graduated from Hamilton College in classics and chemistry, expecting to go into business with his father. When the business was destroyed by fire, he took a job writing for a dairy journal and subsequently became secretary of the New York Dairyman's Association. Invited by the publisher of the *Pacific Rural Press* to become its editor, he came to San Francisco to hold that position for nearly fifty years.

In 1878 at Eugene Hilgard's request, Wickson organized a university lecture course on dairying. Whatever Wickson's practical expertise in the dairy industry may have been, he was a master at organizing information, and his lecture outline, published in an early bulletin, is comprehensive if occasionally quaint ("The Philosophy of Butter-Making"). Over time Wickson became the college fill-in man; as "lecturer in practical agriculture" he organized courses in animal husbandry and livestock breeding, elementary entomology, and horticulture, supervised the operations of the agricultural grounds at Berkeley, took charge of the distribution of seeds and plants, and wrote early bulletins. In 1891 he became superintendent of the Farmers' Institutes and directed their growth.

A prolific writer and popular speaker, Wickson was "keen of observation . . . and gifted with a phenomenal memory . . . not only the chronicler, but the prophet of California's amazing rural progress."[21] His connection with the *Pacific Rural Press* was useful both in giving the University much favorable publicity and in disseminating information on scientific and technical developments. The weekly's circulation grew from about 2,000 subscribers in 1875 to more than 35,000 by 1923, the year Wickson died. Throughout his deanship Wickson continued to write weekly editorials and special articles, and though he retired from the University he never retired from the *Press*.

Wickson's connection with the University also helped him become a recognized horticultural expert. From 1888 to 1897 he reported on distributions of seeds and plants from the University trial gardens, incorporating observations from statewide collaborators. In 1889 the *Pacific Rural Press* published Wickson's classic *California Fruits and How To Grow Them*, which went through nine editions in thirty years. In 1898 came *California Vegetables in Garden and Field* (five editions, one translated into Japanese). Wickson wrote articles on Luther Burbank for *Sunset* and other popular periodicals and frequently spoke before horticultural associations.[22] After his retirement he prepared *One Thousand Questions in Agriculture Answered* (1914), *California Garden Flowers, Shrubs, Trees and Vines* (1915), and *A Second One Thousand Answered Questions in California Agriculture* (1916), the latter two volumes compiled from the popular newspaper column in which he answered readers' questions. Wickson's last book, *Rural California* (1922), was prepared for Bailey's series, published by Macmillan, on country and farm life in selected states.

As Acting Dean Wickson performed yeoman service, helping establish new institutions at Davis and Riverside while overseeing rapid expansion of the College at Berkeley. Nonetheless, President Wheeler let Wickson dangle for more than two years while he continued to search for a prominent successor to Hilgard. By November 1906 Wickson fretted to a friend about his "very depressing and discouraging" situation at the University. He was convinced that California farmers were bound to distrust any eastern men who "might be inclined to policies in the development of the agricultural work of the University" that they did not believe to be best for California.[23] Although Wickson's many friends lobbied on his behalf, it was September 1907 before Wheeler

62 made formal Wickson's appointment, citing his "proved wisdom . . . and wide acquaintanceship with men and affairs" as determinants for his selection after a "careful and persistent canvass."[24] Though Wheeler would have preferred a man with better scientific credentials, he settled for a popular figure and capable administrator.

Wickson's years as dean were busy ones—so busy, in fact, that he submitted no formal reports as Dean of the College of Agriculture from 1905 to 1912, breaking the series that otherwise documents the history of the College from 1877 through 1940. (A record of the College's activities during this period is found in the official *University Chronicles*.)

In 1905, after assuming the deanship, Wickson took on not only the job of selecting a site for the University Farm, but the controversial case of the Tulare Experiment Station. This 20-acre tract had been established in 1888 to study drainage and soil salinity problems in the Tulare area. From 1890 to 1893 experimental plantings of wheat and barley on

the station's poorest soils attracted considerable attention from visiting farmers, and throughout the 1890s the station tested crops that might be adaptable to saline conditions, including Australian saltbush (*Atriplex semibaccatum*), which for a time aroused enthusiasm. By 1898 the Tulare station drew about 500 visitors a year. Nevertheless, the USDA's Office of Experiment Stations, under director A. C. True, became critical of such locally oriented research, insisting that the state experiment stations conduct more "original" research or have their Hatch Act funding withdrawn. Hilgard defended research work geared toward the needs of regional farmers, but Wickson recommended closing the station in July 1905. In August the county board of supervisors and

CHICO STATE NORMAL SCHOOL STUDENTS VISITING AN AGRICULTURAL DEMONSTRATION TRAIN, NOVEMBER 1908.

the Tulare Grange sent a delegation of six to argue the case before the Regents, who were persuaded to continue the station. True again threatened to withdraw federal funds, however, and the Tulare Station remained open only because of state appropriations for cereal experiments. In 1909 the facility finally closed, its research work going to the Kearney Estate near Fresno.[25]

Among the other activities of Wickson's tenure were the popular Farmers' Institutes and correspondence courses, the offering of farmers' short courses in many aspects of agricultural production, and, in 1911, creation of a division of agricultural education to train public school teachers in nature study and elementary agriculture. From 1908 to 1912, the College also organized the agricultural demonstration trains running the length of the state in cooperation with the Southern Pacific Rail Company.[26]

In 1912 Wickson, the "all-round generalist" and "apostle of optimism," was close to 65 and eligible for retirement. Wheeler again began a major search for a successor, this time under somewhat different circumstances. Floods of newcomers after 1900 had swelled the population, the Progressives were in office, and the University was becoming very well known. The College of Agriculture had a major new building under construction at Berkeley, an operating University Farm, and a Citrus Experiment Station. This time Wheeler was determined, with the support of the Regents, to make the College "positively the best agricultural school in the country."[27]

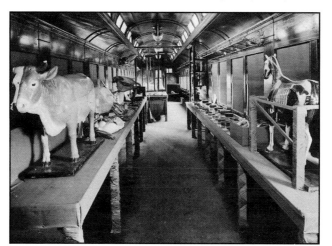

ANIMAL HUSBANDRY DISPLAYS IN AN AGRICULTURAL DEMONSTRATION TRAIN, 1909.

## THOMAS FORSYTH HUNT

In May 1912 Wheeler telegraphed Thomas Forsyth Hunt at Pennsylvania State University to discuss the California deanship. When Hunt demurred, Wheeler went east and within a few days convinced him to accept the position. At Wheeler's request Hunt also made a list of the "best men in American agricultural research"—many of whom Hunt and Wheeler subsequently brought to California.[28]

Hunt was an agronomist with degrees from the University of Illinois and Michigan Agricultural College. During the 1890s he taught at Pennsylvania State College and at Ohio State University, where he also became dean. From 1903 to 1907 Hunt was professor of agronomy at Cornell and right-hand man to Liberty Bailey, who considered him one of the greatest teachers he knew. In 1907 Hunt became dean and director of the experiment station at Pennsylvania State, where he started several new departments. A strong writer and speaker, Hunt was also an eloquent advocate for family farming and the necessity for improving life in rural America.[29]

In California Hunt became an innovative dean; like Wheeler, he was interested in using the resources of the University to build a better society, and he had the courage to make bold statements of his beliefs:

A successful system of agriculture in a country which has universal free public school education can only exist permanently where there is a successful and attractive family life in

64

the open country. . . . A farm is not a place for a permanent bachelor. . . . The fertile land of the United States must be reserved for those who wish to rear and educate children. . . . If we are compelled to admit that food and clothing can be produced only under conditions requiring submerged foreign laboring classes, then we must make the further admission that democracy will fail and that Americanization is a will-o'-the-wisp. Only under autocracy can a large group of people be kept permanently submerged. . . . The primary purpose of better farming is not necessarily cheap food, however important that may be; the primary purpose is a virile, educated citizenship.[30]

Hunt's arrival began a new epoch in the College. His inauguration on October 1, 1912, coincided with the dedication of Agriculture Hall. Before the assembled dignitaries Hunt announced his goals for the College: to help promote the state's agriculture by contributing not only to its economic prosperity but to its "social, moral, and spiritual ideals." Like others of his time concerned about immigration issues, Hunt expressed the hope that immigration would bring to California not the "offscourings" of other nations, but the "intelligent, thrifty, moral countryman whose generations of experience will help to develop this country." He stressed the work of the College of Agriculture as statewide rather than confined to campuses, its goal the public good rather than local interest.[31]

Hunt moved quickly, for the College was booming. In 1912 its budget was $358,957, including $76,900 earned from sales of the University Farm Creamery and products of the Experiment Stations. More than 400 students were majoring in agriculture at Berkeley or Davis, including 155 at the University Farm School, and altogether about 1,000 students were enrolled in the various agricultural courses, many from other majors taking them as electives. Farmers' Institutes reported nearly 40,000 participants; the agricultural demonstration train of 1912, covering 6,847 miles in 237 stops, attracted 102,600 visitors. A new event was the "mov-

able school," a week-long course of intensive instruction for practical farmers on a single subject. The College had been given responsibility for a state-sponsored Pure Food Laboratory, which issued 1,850 citations for food or drug adulteration or mislabeling out of 8,500 samples taken during 1911–12. By state decree employees of the College also inspected commercial fertilizers and insecticides and manufactured hog cholera serum for immunizations.

Given full support by Wheeler and a generous legislature, Dean Hunt recruited a star-studded staff by offering attractive salaries and handsome new facilities. Within a year of Hunt's arrival the College had seven new full professors, including the distinguished Herbert John Webber from Cornell to head the Riverside Station, Charles F. Shaw from Pennsylvania State to direct the important soils work, and Hubert E. Van Norman, an authority in dairying and livestock, to oversee the University Farm. At the same time Hunt organized several new divisions. A division of pomology began in 1912. Walter Mulford came from Cornell to head forestry work in 1913. John William Gregg arrived from Pennsylvania State to lead a new division of landscape gardening and floriculture. Irrigation expert Elwood Mead returned from Australia to organize a division of rural institutions. Anticipating passage of the Smith-Lever Act, Hunt brought B. H. Crocheron from Maryland in 1913 to organize California's Agricultural Extension Service.[32]

The agricultural teaching curriculum was reorganized into four general courses for underclassmen (agricultural chemistry, soils, plant propagation, and principles of breeding plants and animals), with specialization beginning in the junior year in one of fifteen fields. As students recognized emerging opportunities in both farming and the agricultural sciences, agriculture became a more popular major. The number of graduates rose from 2 in 1900 to 79 in 1915, with 36 completions at the Farm School in Davis. For a brief period the administration considered dividing the Kearney Estate near Fresno into units that would house and employ 15 to 30 students at a "Kearney Ranch School," but the dream never came to fruition. A new series of correspondence courses inaugurated in fall 1913 enrolled more than 1,000 students by mail, rising to 8,000 the following year and 19,000 in 1916. Reflecting the day's "back-to-the-land" sentiment, in 1916 an audience of more than 500 attended fifteen college-organized lectures on "The City Man in Agriculture" at the San Francisco YMCA.[33]

More than 600 agricultural research projects were undertaken between 1912 and 1920, and they were very diverse. The College published bulletins and circulars on topics from mushrooms and meadowlarks to potato and cabbage growing; avocados, belladonna, dates, loquats, and pomegranates; silkworm culture; honeybees; goats; control of gophers; rotation experiments; bulk handling of grain; jelly and marmalade making, and many other topics. Hunt authored several publications, including the 64-page "Some Things the Prospective Settler Should Know" (Experiment Station *Bulletin 121*, 1914)—an informative but cautionary guide on opportunities and pitfalls for aspiring farmers trying various enterprises on small parcels of land.

Very prominent in College priorities was the work on pests and plant diseases. When Hunt arrived in 1912, the plant pathologist who had begun work in 1903 had a laboratory and headquarters at Berkeley, two laboratories in southern California, and twelve field and laboratory assistants, whose bulletins made up a large portion of total station publications. Between 1913 and 1916 additional staff took up the work in plant protection, and the divisions of agronomy, pomology, and viticulture began to broaden their work to include the tests of varieties and rootstocks for disease resistance. Researchers experimented with spraying, surgery, cultural practices, and other methods including the introduction of natural parasites.

One particularly important achievement of the prewar period was the formation of local mosquito control districts, made possible by the 1915 Mosquito Abatement Districts Act and aided by College staff who conducted surveys and gave presentations. Shortly after the war parasitologist W. B. Herms supervised a statewide survey that pinpointed the distribution of anopheline mosquitoes, the carriers of malaria, then a serious problem in parts of California. In June 1919 entomologist S. B. Freeborn took charge of a cooperative antimalaria campaign financed by the State Board of Health to combat the illness in southern Shasta County. There nearly a quarter of the population carried the infection, and the death rate, at 64 per 100,000, was higher than in Mississippi. A dramatic decline in malarial outbreaks was reported soon after the project opened a free dispensary, furnished screening material at cost, and constructed 76,000 feet of drainage ditches to prevent mosquito breeding.[34]

## THE UNIVERSITY GETS A FARM

### RENEWED ARGUMENTS FOR PRACTICAL EDUCATION

Although the College of Agriculture had gained a loyal constituency during Hilgard's tenure, grumblings still surfaced now and then about the nature and direction of its work. Some Grangers and others believed that Hilgard's "theoretical" work was of scant use on individual farms.[35] While entomological work sometimes had quick results, variety testing could take years before results were clear, and laboratory studies of the chemical composition of soils or plant tissue had little immediate application in the field. Investigating long-range solutions to large problems like decreasing soil fertility required years of concentrated effort far removed from short-term profits. Farmers interested in "how-to" education for

66 their sons and daughters wanted research work useful for next year's production cycle.

Latent dissatisfaction with Berkeley-based agricultural studies assumed greater importance as the dairy industry of California expanded during the late 1890s. The California Dairy Association, established in 1894, began to advocate a dairy education school. By this time Wisconsin and other states were making great strides in milk testing, cheese making, and other matters. Although instruction in livestock subjects had begun at Berkeley in 1878, it was largely by the "picture book and farm-visiting method" until 1900, when focused instruction in dairying began with the appointment of Leroy Anderson. In May 1901 the College established a dairy division and began a small "dairy school" in the basement of the agricultural building, offering a nine-week "practical" course for 38 students, using purchased milk and borrowed appliances. In 1902 a small herd of dairy cattle was installed in Strawberry Canyon behind the Berkeley campus. Though these arrangements were not really adequate, the growing city of Berkeley and expansion of the campus itself left little room for improvement. As requests for dairy research and education became more insistent, dairy and rancher associations urged that the University acquire a real farm in a location more representative of California conditions than Berkeley.[36]

Peter Shields, then secretary of the State Agricultural Society, became interested in the issue when he heard of dairying progress in other states. A young enthusiast with a facile pen and many connections, he queried land-grant institutions in several states about their dairy facilities and with the support of California dairy farmers drafted a bill proposing a State Dairy School. The bill passed through the 1903 legislature, but was vetoed by Governor Pardee for being "too narrow." Shields then drafted a more comprehensive bill describing a University State Farm that would serve all the needs of the College for a demonstration farm, research center, practical agricultural school, and dairy school. Intense lobbying by Shields and others publicized the proposal widely, and Marshall Diggs of Yolo County carried the bill into the Senate for the second time.[37]

Despite the enthusiasm of supporters, President Wheeler was apprehensive, and Hilgard was disgusted. Both saw the dangers of splitting the College of Agriculture into two parts—the drive for "practical" work seemed reminiscent of earlier controversies about the functions of agricultural education—and both were concerned about keeping land-grant university work on a relatively high level. To one correspondent Hilgard wrote, "There is an awful mixup of agricultural and University bills at Sacramento. . . . It is a case of 'Save me from my friends.'" Not convinced of the need for a first-class farm as described in the bill, he thought that a "boom farm" where "any fool can be a farmer" was ill considered. His opinion was that a university farm should be for experimental purposes, contain variable soils, and be situated for convenience close to Berkeley. He warned that proponents were really envisioning an "*agricultural high school*," which, though it might be beneficial, was a "wholly distinct proposition" from the intent of the Morrill Act to support "the branches of *learning* related to agriculture."[38] Nevertheless, Hilgard was about to retire, and Shields and his colleagues were determined to have their way.

Passed by the legislature and signed by Governor Pardee on March 18, 1905, the State Farm bill provided $150,000 for purchase of a farm with at least 320 acres of "first-class tillable soils" typifying the best farming conditions in the state and provided with an irrigation system. A five-member State Farm Commission, comprising the governor, the lieutenant governor, the President of the University, the president of the State Board of Agriculture, and the state commissioner of horticulture, was to select an appropriate site.

## SELECTING A SITE

In April the commission solicited land offers through newspaper announcements, while consulting with various experts regarding the best criteria for a university farm. In May the commission inspected three properties offered in Contra Costa County and several in Yolo County, but made no decision. Wheeler's concern mounted. In July he wrote to Governor Pardee, "The State and the University are on the verge of a possible mistake of colossal proportions."[39] He requested that the commission meet for discussion with Liberty Hyde Bailey. In Berkeley Bailey stated publicly that he thought a college farm should be a laboratory rather than a "model farm," and that 10 acres close to the University would be better than 400 far away. His comments, unpalatable to Central Valley promoters, caused something of a furor.[40]

Meanwhile, offers of land poured in from individuals and community groups across the state. The commission considered sites on the lower San Francisco Peninsula, including the Flood estate in San Mateo County, which had already been deeded to the University, and part of the Stanford estate, suggested by Stanford's president David Starr Jordan, but these did not fit the stipulations of the legislation. By November, with more than 70 offers in hand, including a proposed gift of 320 acres by prosperous raisin grower and land developer Theodore M. Kearney of Fresno County, the commission delegated the task of site visits to Acting Dean Wickson. Wickson decided to limit his investigations to Central Valley sites served by a railroad, with easily irrigated deep loam soils not subject to waterway overflow.

On February 9, 1906, Wickson presented the commission with a 14-page report detailing 77 sites offered up and down the state from Butte County in the north to San Luis

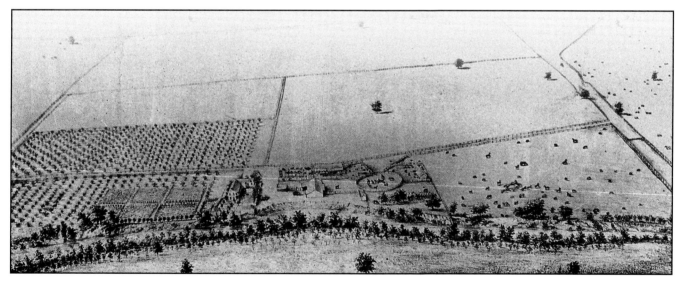

THE JEROME DAVIS RANCH IN 1857, LATER TO BECOME THE UNIVERSITY FARM. PUTAH CREEK CROSSES AT THE BOTTOM.

68 Obispo in the south. Sonoma, Yolo, and Contra Costa counties were the leading contenders, with eight sites each. During the next six weeks the commission made inspection visits within these three counties. On March 31 the commission voted unanimously to select a tract containing a former award-winning stock and grain farm, offered for $103,290 near Davisville in Yolo County. The 776-acre tract combined three fertile properties abutting Putah Creek, and the offer contained water rights worth $1,500, raised by donation from the citizens of Davisville. Perhaps not least in importance, the tract lay along the railroad line between Berkeley and Sacramento, the state capital.

On April 5, 1906, the commission announced the Davisville choice, setting off a great local celebration. From Woodland, the Yolo County seat 12 miles to the north, the disgruntled Chamber of Commerce immediately wrote to the commission that their town offered many more amenities than dusty little Davisville, but the choice was final. The opinionated Hilgard, meanwhile, grumped to a friend that the 800-acre farm was a "big elephant" with "just one kind of exuberantly fertile soil . . . just the thing to teach boys how to farm under difficulties. . . . Faugh!"[41]

EARLY (ABOUT 1910) VIEW OF THE UNIVERSITY FARM, DAVIS CENTRAL QUADRANGLE. THE THREE BUILDINGS ON THE EAST SIDE OF THE QUAD (NORTH HALL, SOUTH HALL, AND THE COTTAGE) ARE STILL IN USE.

Twelve days later the great San Francisco earthquake and fire distracted Californians from the mundane details of setting up the University Farm, but this was not the only startling event. In early May Theodore Kearney died suddenly at sea en route to England, and it was learned that he had bequeathed his entire 5,400-acre "Fruitvale" estate to the University of California. It was a "princely bequest" with a value of "something like a million dollars." A striking ten-mile drive lined with palm trees and oleanders led from the ranch headquarters to the city of Fresno. It seemed an embarrassment of riches. For a time there was talk of abandoning the Davisville farm—until the Regents learned that a $250,000 mortgage came with the Kearney property and it would be at least two years before Kearney's will was cleared. They decided to run the Fresno ranch as a money-making enterprise, and Davisville (almost immediately renamed Davis, thought to sound less rustic) remained the site for the University Farm.

In July the Davis purchase papers were signed, and on September 1, 1906, at the stroke of midnight, the new University Farm superintendent, John Rogers, symbolically "opened the gate" for the people of California.[42]

## THE FARM SCHOOL BEGINS

Despite construction delays caused by the rebuilding of San Francisco, four structures at the Farm were completed in 1907: an octagonal livestock judging pavilion, which doubled as a meeting hall; a two-story building containing a "capacious creamery" plus administrative offices, a library, and classrooms; and two cottage residences for the farm manager and the creamery manager. The first public event at the Farm was a three-day State Farmers' Institute held in late October 1907. Dedication ceremonies included addresses by President Wheeler, Peter Shields (now a judge), and a representative of the governor.

Three types of instruction were offered at the University Farm: short courses for farmers, a three-year farm school curriculum, and agricultural practice courses for university students. Beginning in fall 1908, the short courses for nonresident men and women from age seventeen upward ranged from two to eight weeks and covered dairy manufac-

ture, poultry husbandry, animal husbandry, irrigation, soils, forage and cereal crops, veterinary science, horticulture, viticulture, and entomology. The Farm School opening, first scheduled for September 1908, was delayed until January 1909. The School offered a three-year course open to any boy over the age of fifteen with a grammar school education, consisting of secondary-level courses in English, mathematics, and all phases of farm practice. (With the growth of agricultural education in the state's high schools a few years later, Dean Hunt raised the minimum entering age to eighteen and restructured the curriculum to two years.) University students working toward a degree in agriculture at Berkeley were encouraged to come to Davis in the spring of their junior year for a few months' practicum to supplement their more scientific work. Beginning in 1913 they could attend classes at the Farm in the spring of both their junior and senior years.

In the first semester of instruction the student body at Davis comprised just fifteen Farm School students and six University students. Enrollment soon increased. By 1912

SHORT COURSE IN ANIMAL HUSBANDRY CONDUCTED AT THE UNIVERSITY FARM ABOUT 1910. CLARENCE M. HARING, BERKELEY PROFESSOR OF VETERINARY SCIENCE (FAR LEFT), PARTICIPATED IN THIS DEMONSTRATION OF THROWING A BULL.

more than 100 were attending the Farm School. Students came from across the state, some from abroad. Their small community was friendly and close-knit, for they lived and studied in a truly rural atmosphere. Two hours and twenty minutes by rail from Berkeley and twenty-five minutes from Sacramento, the semi-isolated campus consisted of farm buildings, grain and alfalfa fields, and assorted experimental plots, orchards, and vineyards. Though up to thirteen trains stopped each day, Davis was hardly more than a cluster of modest houses and a few stores, and, until completion of the Yolo Causeway in 1915 across the Sacramento River floodplain, no all-weather road to Sacramento existed.

Growth at the University Farm was slow but steady. Chief among the Farm resources was the model creamery, where young men and women learned the principles of dairying. As herds of prize-winning dairy and beef animals were established, the Farm began to win many championships in state and national competitions between 1910 and 1918. Students learned the fine points of judging livestock, and student judging teams did well in Western show rings. Eventually the fields, vineyards, and orchards became demonstration sites for new crop varieties and better techniques in planting and cultiva-

NURSERY OF THE UNIVERSITY FARM IN DAVIS, 1915.

tion; joint funding with the U.S. Department of Agriculture supported the development of irrigation research; and early instruction in farm mechanics and farm accounting paved the way for later work in agricultural engineering and economics. In 1917, needing more space, the University leased the adjoining 300-acre Armstrong Ranch on the south with an option to buy (finally exercised in 1931).[43]

An excerpt from a series of letters from "two Paradise boys at the University Farm" describes something of student life in those days:

Tell [grandfather] that I am judging hogs this time. . . . I find they are deceitful critters, as a hog can look pretty good and yet have bad points. You must consider the form, as straightness of back and width across shoulders must balance that across the hips. All points between must be even . . . sides deep, neck short, head trim, jowl neat and snout small. Condition means the state of development of the animal's flesh. Quality is fineness of hair, quality of skin, as coarse, medium or fine; and lastly the way the animal stands. . . . I mention all these tedious details just to give an idea of all the different points which must be considered . . . and some idea of the difficulty in sizing up . . . four animals in a small portable pen, with a class of thirty or forty all gathered around . . . and when the pigs themselves insist on lying down and going to sleep.[44]

## SOUTHERN CALIFORNIA GROWING

### ORANGE HEAVEN

By 1900 great changes had come to the dry "cattle counties" of southern California. The region began to boom after large water distribution systems were developed in the 1880s by ingenious engineers like the Chaffee brothers and the visionary Canadian promoter Matthew Gage. Their pioneering arrangements for linking water rights with land parcels made possible the formation of early colonies like Riverside, Etiwanda, Ontario, and Covina. By 1890 the state's citrus belt was well established, and the dusty valleys below the Tehachapis were transformed into an empire of mixed farming under irrigation: orange groves, fruit and walnut orchards, vineyards, poultry farms, and dairies. Rail network expansions and aggressive land promotion schemes continued to bring people to the sunny Los Angeles basin; real estate developers broke large tracts into 10- or 20-acre lots, constructed irrigation works, planted citrus trees, and sold the lots to settlers. Often these were not farmers at all, but professionals seeking a healthier climate or city folk from the East or Midwest lured by promises of lotusland. On 20 acres of oranges they hoped to live a comfortable life in a land of sunshine, unperturbed by the weather vagaries and illnesses of harsher climates.[45]

By the early 1890s, however, economic problems began to emerge. Speculative overplanting inevitably resulted in much worthless nursery stock placed on lands not particularly suited for citrus culture, and unfavorable weather and marketing problems deflated optimistic expectations. Competition from Florida for eastern buyers, abuses by commission men and fruit brokers, production expanding more rapidly than markets—all combined to bring uncertain pricing, sporadic gluts, and general instability to the California citrus industry. In addition, diseases, pests, and fruit quality problems underscored the need for growers to organize. Because the background of many of the new southern Californians was in business or the professions, they early showed "a progressive attitude, a belief in technology, and urban organizational skills."[46] Citrus growers formed the state's first permanently successful commodity cooperative, the Southern California Fruit Growers Exchange, in 1895. Later reorganized as the California Fruit Growers Exchange (1904)—and still later renamed Sunkist Growers—the cooperative developed rational marketing strategies and protective mechanisms and began to provide assistance in production-related tasks like cultivation and harvesting.

The Riverside Horticultural Club was also formed in 1895. Led by John Henry Reed, the club emphasized cooperative research from the start. Many of the members' experiments in soil preparation, planting, budding, irrigation, cultivation, and frost protection were included in the first bulletin on citrus culture published by the Agricultural Experiment Station in 1902. Not content with individual experiments, the Riverside Club wanted to have professional scientific research conducted on citrus problems. Because the University's Pomona station was being closed down, and the USDA pomologist assigned to study fruit decay at Riverside in 1903 was only temporary, the club began to work for a permanent citrus experiment station with resident scientists.

### THE FOUNDING OF THE CITRUS EXPERIMENT STATION

Late in 1904 a group of orange growers came together to draft a state bill for a research station. Assemblyman Miguel Estudillo of Riverside carried the bill, which combined the citrus growers' request with that of another group proposing a plant pathology laboratory to study disease problems in other crops. On March 18, 1905, the legislature passed the

72 citrus experiment station bill along with the University Farm bill. Carrying an appropriation of $30,000, the bill provided for a commission of three—Governor Pardee, President Wheeler, and Acting Dean Wickson—to select sites for both laboratory and station.

After examining a number of sites, the commission on May 21, 1906, announced plans for a new institution with two branches: a citrus experiment station to be situated on 23 acres in the heart of the citrus belt on the eastern slope of Mount Rubidoux overlooking the town of Riverside (the Huntington Park Association owning the property leased it to the University nearly rent-free), and a pathology laboratory to be housed in a two-story frame building with a greenhouse on a 1-acre site donated by the Whittier Board of Trade—a more central location close to walnut, lemon, vegetable, and berry production.

After a research plan was drawn up for the two sites, the Regents appointed plant pathologist Ralph E. Smith as superintendent of the combined Southern California Pathological Laboratory and Experiment Station. Smith arrived in Riverside on August 27, 1906, and announced that work on a reservoir would begin the next day.[47] In January 1907 the largest Farmers' Institute ever held in California heralded the opening of the station. The Regents formally approved the Riverside leases on February 14, 1907, the University's official founding date for the station.

ORIGINAL STAFF OF THE CITRUS EXPERIMENT STATION AT THE RUBIDOUX LABORATORY. DIRECTOR HERBERT J. WEBBER IS IN LEFT FOREGROUND.

From its inception the Rubidoux unit focused on soil studies, including fertilization and irrigation experiments, and on the improvement of citrus varieties by grafting and bud selection. An experimental orchard of citrus species and varieties was begun, later to be world famous. Whittier served as headquarters for plant pathology and entomology investigations. Meager funding, minimal research direction, and staffing changes prevented much progress in the early years, however, and though the 1911 legislature approved $25,000 for site purchase and a main office and laboratory building at Riverside, citrus growers were not wholly satisfied.

## REORGANIZATION AT THE RIVERSIDE STATION

Thomas Hunt became Dean in 1912 with the goal of reorganizing the College of Agriculture. Among his immediate steps was the formation of a Graduate School of Tropical Agriculture along with a division of citriculture. Among the group of faculty "stars" attracted by Hunt was Herbert John Webber, a nationally renowned expert in plant breeding, who came from Cornell to take charge of the Citrus Experiment Station and the new Graduate School in January 1913.

That same month a massive killing freeze struck southern California, causing great damage to orchards and near-panic among growers. The citrus industry, by then worth more than $175 million, petitioned the legislature for increased citrus research to assist in its recovery, and lawmakers immediately passed three bills providing $185,000 for land, water rights, and buildings for an enlarged experiment station to be located in one of the eight southern counties. Governor Hiram Johnson approved the bill in June 1913.

Although Riverside hoped to retain the Rubidoux station, there was strong competition for a new site. The San Fernando Valley, anticipating completion of the Owens Valley aqueduct in 1914, became a leading contender. A bidding war brought in 167 site offers, but of these only about a third were seriously considered. The site selection committee narrowed the choices to four, including Riverside and the San Fernando Valley. Convinced that Riverside was the best site, Webber selected a new 475-acre tract about 2 miles from downtown Riverside, close to the Box Springs Mountains. A series of votes by University advisory committees, however, selected the San Fernando Valley proposal.

DEDICATION CEREMONY AT THE NEW CITRUS EXPERIMENT STATION AND GRADUATE SCHOOL OF TROPICAL AGRICULTURE, MARCH 1918. (FROM A BROKEN GLASS-PLATE NEGATIVE.)

Controversy and outrage swept southern California. Protests came to the Regents from growers, packinghouses, chambers of commerce, boards of trade, civic groups in more than 30 cities, and boards of supervisors of 7 counties. The San Fernando site seemed to offer a number of advantages, including a more moderate climate and proximity to a metropolitan center, but opponents argued that it was not in the real citrus belt, and many accused the "gentlemen in Los Angeles" of promoting the valley location for their own private gain. In fall 1914 a joint meeting of three Regents' committees examined the accumulated testimony, and on December 23, in executive session, the Regents voted to retain the station at Riverside.[48]

Construction of the farm, laboratory, and residence buildings on the Box Springs site began in 1916. With completion of these new quarters came the official demise of the Southern California Pathological Laboratory at Whittier, and the Division of Agricultural Chemistry moved to the Rubidoux site. Dean Hunt presided at the dedication ceremonies held on March 27, 1918, and President Wheeler gave a "stirring patriotic speech" appropriate for a nation at war.[49]

Although the Graduate School of Tropical Agriculture began formal operation at Riverside in 1917, only those students who had completed course requirements at Berkeley were permitted to enroll for dissertation work. The school subsequently languished, and years later (1932) its responsibilities were transferred to the Division of Subtropical Horticulture at UCLA.

One other southern California research station was established during this prewar period. In 1910, at Meloland 6 miles east of El Centro in the rapidly developing Imperial Valley, county supervisors donated 40 acres for research in general agronomy. At first difficult to staff because of its isolation and hot desert climate, the Meloland station eventually grew to 250 acres; it is now the University's oldest local research station.

## 74 NEW VISIONS FOR RURAL CALIFORNIA

### THE COUNTRY LIFE MOVEMENT

Between 1900 and World War I the national "Country Life Movement" manifested mounting concern over the quality of American rural life. The need to increase farm productivity had been the basis for founding the land-grant college and agricultural experiment station system; this system, though effective in developing technical improvements in farming, did not seem to relieve some economic and social problems. Many rural communities remained rough, backward places from which their best and brightest youth fled as soon as they were able. The bleak late-nineteenth-century backwaters of Hamlin Garland's stories in *Main Travelled Roads* and his autobiographical *Son of the Middle Border* had by the turn of the century improved in some regions, but in others farm life was still physically grueling, economically precarious, and socially retarded.

American agriculture was still struggling with the conflict between traditional ideals and the demands of an industrializing society. On the one hand lingered Thomas Jefferson's view of the freeholder farmer as the backbone of democracy, his independence and his property interests ensuring his political rectitude and stability. The Jeffersonian vision saw farming as a family-centered, physically healthy, and morally virtuous way of life. On the other hand, a new view gradually developing since the Civil War saw farming primarily as a business, integrated into a wider economy and dependent for its success on its efficiency. After the turn of the century this conflict became keener. With the help of the agricultural experiment stations, agriculture was becoming at least potentially more productive and profitable; it was also becoming more competitive.

Farmers themselves were not always enthusiastic about the new developments.[50]

Young people from farming areas continued their flight to the cities, drawn not only by greater economic opportunities but by the social and cultural attractions there. A group of concerned educators, journalists, and others began to form a consensus that something more had to be done to help country people achieve satisfying lives. These social reformers, largely from the East or Midwest, hoped to stem the rural exodus, which they saw as weakening the fiber of the nation. They extolled the virtues of country life while proposing various reforms to make country living more appealing. The most prominent figures in the movement were Liberty Hyde Bailey of Cornell and rural sociologist Kenyon Butterfield of the Massachusetts State College of Agriculture, but they were joined by many other educators, newspaper editors, clergy, and community groups. Writing widely on the rural question, these "country lifers" suggested ways to meet rural needs including direct technical assistance, better cooperatives, improved country schools, stronger community churches, a rural postal delivery service, better banking and credit facilities, improved roads, healthier sanitation practices, and more labor-saving devices for farm women.

The movement reached a high point in 1908, when President Theodore Roosevelt in the closing months of his administration persuaded Bailey to head a Country Life Commission to investigate the "problems of the open countryside" and make recommendations for action. Roosevelt's belief that sturdy farmers were still the backbone of the nation coexisted with his view of industrialists as the brains and moving power. In taking up the country life cause, he was strongly committed to improving conditions for rural areas, but the commission's report came at the very end of his term, and actions on its recommendations were implemented only gradually.[51]

Possibly because agriculture in California had developed quite differently than in other states, an organized Country Life Movement here was never very strong. Even within the College of Agriculture there were no special advocates of the "family farm" philosophy at the time. Though intellectually interested in broad questions like the development of society in arid cultures, Hilgard, the quintessential scientist, had remained relatively remote from social reform issues. Wickson's métier was journalism, yet as editor of the *Pacific Rural Press* he chose to emphasize scientific and economic information rather than discussion of social problems. In the Grange section of the journal, to be sure, readers corresponded on family farm issues, but Wickson himself–though he routinely encouraged improvements–was actually quite complacent in his views of California agriculture.

When the Country Life Commission toured the country to collect information in the fall of 1908, four late-November hearings were scheduled in California at Los Angeles, San Francisco, Fresno, and Sacramento. The local press covered them well, and the commission itself considered them successful, but the hearings did not turn up much illuminating information. Indeed, the tone of the November 25 hearing at the Los Angeles Chamber of Commerce was patently self-congratulatory. "Country life has no problems here," proclaimed the *Los Angeles Times*, citing descriptions of happy southern California farming communities where "ranchmen" did not have to work half so hard as farmers elsewhere and could get on a streetcar at the end of the day to attend a theater performance in the city just a few miles away. Wickson himself read a statement describing why California farming was superior, citing (1) the high quality of settlers, with their "nerve and ability," "high plane of intelligence," and "mastery of funds and business . . . enterprise"–altogether a "select

population"; (2) the excellence of agricultural education in California; (3) the social standing of agriculturalists based on the value of their property holdings; (4) the comfort of California country homes, with their running water and modern plumbing; and (5) the "benign influence" of cooperatives as a powerful agency for advancement. After this hearing Bailey remarked that although "it is not within the power or scope of the commission to advise wholesale immigration to Los Angeles County," southern California could stand as an ideal for other rural areas.[52]

At the other California hearings the outlook was not quite so sanguine. In San Francisco, before a "notable gathering" in the hall of the California State Board of Trade at the Ferry Building, the commission heard statements about very poor sanitary conditions for Asian farm laborers. In Sacramento, "the most instructive of the California meetings" according to Bailey, speakers testified on problems in marketing, flood control, drainage, and irrigation. Two large-scale Yuba City growers spoke on farm labor, saying that white farmworkers were useless "scum" and "no account drunks" and that California needed from 10,000 to 50,000 "intelligent Chinamen" annually for farm work. Another witness suggested alleviating the farm labor problem by cutting up big farms so that young men could become owners instead of having to compete with Asiatic labor.[53]

Despite the lingering legacy of land monopoly and uneasy dependence on seasonal immigrant farm labor, the national Country Life Commission, by Californians' own testimony, found few rural problems in this part of the nation. In Sacramento Judge Peter Shields stated that California farm life had not the "gloom and drudgery" of the East, and in the December 12 *Pacific Rural Press* Wickson reprinted his declaration that the agriculturalist in this state was a cut above his counterparts elsewhere.

Perhaps a part of California's self-satisfaction was rooted in the promise of the brilliant future apparently offered by irrigation. The "irrigation crusade" preached the possibilities not only of extending the farming frontier into semiarid regions but of redesigning Western communities through careful planning. The principles of engineering, suggested contemporary thinkers, could be applied not only to physical but to social problems, and irrigation could serve as a catalyst for social change, as it already seemed to have done in southern California.[54]

One of the most effective of the irrigationists was Elwood Mead, whose long and varied career included two stints at the University of California. Known internationally as an engineer and administrator of irrigation agencies, Mead was also a social visionary. Though not all his projects were successful, Mead was greatly respected throughout his long career. After his death in 1936, the reservoir behind Hoover Dam was named Lake Mead in his honor.[55]

Elwood Mead took a degree in civil engineering in 1883 at Iowa State College and became the nation's first professor of irrigation engineering at Colorado State Agricultural College. In 1888 he became engineer for the Territory of Wyoming, where he drafted the laws governing water rights. Wyoming water law, in which all water rights were vested in the state, ended some legal snarls over "ownership" and became a model for other Western states (though not for California). In 1899 Mead became chief of the Office of Irrigation Investigations in the U.S. Department of Agriculture, producing among other publications USDA *Bulletin 100*, "Irrigation Investigations in California" (1901), a comprehensive report on the state's irrigation practices and legal framework at that time.

In 1901 Mead accepted Wheeler's invitation to head a new division of irrigation in the College of Agriculture. The conditions of his appointment were that he would spend one-third of his time teaching and doing research as Professor of the Institutions and Practices of Irrigation at the University, the other two-thirds continuing his work for the federal government. Mead presented a very popular lecture series each spring in Berkeley, some of which later appeared as a book, *Irrigation Institutions: A Discussion of the Economic and Legal Questions Created by the Growth of Irrigated Agriculture in the West*. In 1902 Mead supervised a federal drainage study of the Fresno area, then beginning to experience severe problems with rising underground water tables and accumulation of alkali on thousands of acres of irrigated farmland.

In 1907 the Australian government invited Mead to take charge of the State Rivers and Water Supply Commission of Victoria, overseeing 32 irrigation projects and the district's colonization plans. For the next seven years Mead supervised a successful government-sponsored land settlement program there. In Australia Mead won many admirers through his "stout-hearted . . . optimism," his ability to "calmly face the most hostile audience" with "cool, persuasive and convincing" arguments, and his good humor and "genuine kindliness of heart."[56]

In 1913 Mead accepted a new appointment as Professor of Rural Institutions at the University of California, though he did not return to Berkeley until 1914. In an exchange of letters with Wheeler, who described the "great influx of population seeking farm homes . . . at the mercy of land sharks," Mead wrote, "The more I learn of conditions here, the more confident I am that the time has arrived for the University to become a law-giver to the State of California, in the development and use of both land and water." Mead felt a "measure of paternalism" was sorely needed in California, and thought his University position would provide a great opportunity to plan model settlements, using state resources to protect and help new family farmers.[57]

## THE DIVISION OF RURAL INSTITUTIONS

In a report he had prepared for the Association of American Agricultural Colleges and Experiment Stations in 1911, Hunt had made an assessment of unmet needs in land-grant agricultural education:

> [We are] deeply impressed with the importance of developing strong courses in rural economics and sociology. . . . These all involve the human element in agriculture and country life. They tend to raise the college courses in agriculture above the materialistic plane, to emphasize broadly the human interest that properly inheres in agricultural studies, and thus to inspire both faculties and students . . . with a higher sense of the wide responsibilities attaching to leadership in agricultural affairs. Pedagogically they serve to show that agriculture, when broadly treated, is to be enrolled among the humanities, as well as the sciences; ethically, they point out the vital connection between agricultural science and the welfare of rural people . . . even of all mankind.[58]

Convinced of the need for broadening the outlook of the College of Agriculture in 1913, Dean Hunt established a new department to pursue work in these subjects. Rural economics and sociology were already recognized as worthy of consideration at several land-grant colleges, including Cornell, but not at the University of California. Hunt recognized that, despite the promotional enthusiasm of land developers and the complacency of entrenched interests, there were real problems in California's hinterlands. To assist the state in grappling with some of these, Hunt planned a "division of rural institutions," to engage in research on rural communities and apply the knowledge gained toward solution of standing concerns.

Hunt chose Elwood Mead to head the division, citing his "statesman-like vision coupled with a scientific habit of mind . . . wide experience and ripe judgment," and he was fully prepared to support Mead in a "revolutionary" and "constructive programme of the highest importance to society." In a formal description of the division's goals, Mead wrote:

> When the Regents of the University created the Division of Rural Institutions they broke new grounds in the field of American education and political thought. They believed that there was need for a better social and economic organization of rural life and that it was the duty of this University to help bring this about. . . . It should create an agency fitted to study existing conditions, to speak with candor, and advise without bias. . . . Its purpose should be to help create institutions, established either by law or the efforts of individuals, which would rescue rural life from some of the dangers which now menace it, make it socially more attractive, and enable farmers to cope more successfully with conditions created by the growth of cities, the combinations in business and industrial life, and the increasing competition of other countries.[59]

Mead may have been speaking more for himself than for the Regents, but from hindsight it is clear that personalities, progressive idealism, and opportunity had converged to begin a most interesting venture: an initiation of state-sponsored land settlements that might serve as model rural communities. California was already home to a number of utopian colonies.[60] The University's involvement with the California Land Settlement projects would, however, be both unprecedented and unparalleled, and Mead would wear several hats: educator and advocate, planner and administrator.

Like many of his contemporaries, Mead idealized the small farm freeholder, and California's old problem of land monopoly troubled him. Despite the promise of irrigation, many large tracts remained in few hands, and small-acreage settlers often failed. Mead thought that their greatest barrier to success was the high cost of land and development.[61] He was disturbed by the state's increase in farm tenancy, for he thought that farmers without a vested interest in their land would be less interested in supporting their local communities. As an engineer Mead was convinced that good planning and rational management could be the key to social and economic reform, and his experience in Australia had convinced him that state-sponsored colonies could succeed in California.

Progressives were ready to back such visions; but the darker side of the issue was an undercurrent of racism. Like others of the time, Mead was apprehensive about the upward rise of the Japanese in California agriculture after 1900. He touched on the subject in his book about land settlement published in 1920:

> The owners of great landed properties derived their income mainly from rentals. As the demand for land grew, the rent rose through the competition of tenants. The one who would pay the most . . . got the land. In these competitions, Oriental farmers or other aliens who could pay high prices because they have a low standard of living, secured control of a larger and larger percentage of the best farming land. As citizens and as builders of rural society, these aliens were in sorry contrast to the State's first settlers, who were the finest type of American citizen this nation had produced. The California pioneer had been a citizen first, a money maker second. He was generous and public spirited to a fault. In contrast, the alien renter had no interest in rural welfare. He had a racial aloofness and he farmed the land to get all he could out of it in the period of his lease. Wherever he displaced the American, he put rural life on the downgrade.[62]

Japanese immigrant farmers in California during this period were making remarkable progress, but their isolation from the mainstream represented a threat to traditional American communities. Mead's and others' answer to the problem was not to include the Japanese in planning for a better future, but to supplant them if possible by state aid to American citizens. As head of the new Division of Rural Institutions, Mead methodically built support for a California land settlement program that would assist new small-scale farmers. In May 1914 he convinced the Commonwealth Club to consider the subject of state colonization and was elected chairman of the study committee. His chief aide was Frank Adams, under joint appointment with USDA and the University, an energetic young man whose father had organized the club. The committee recommended that some type of state credit system should be available to support organized settlement, and after considerable debate the club endorsed this view.

In 1915 Governor Johnson requested legislative authority to form an investigatory State Commission on Colonization and Rural Credits. Mead was appointed its chairman. Other members were professor of political science David Barrows (later University President), progressive businessmen Harris Weinstock and Mortimer Fleishhacker, and prominent editor and University Regent Chester H. Rowell. The commission toured California farming areas, studied reports on colonization in other countries, and reviewed data collected by University graduate students paid by the Commonwealth Club to conduct a summer survey of 991 California settlers in 1916. In November 1916 the commission held public hearings and then issued a report to the legislature. The report stated that a large proportion of the new settlers in California were failures; of those who prospered, many did so by selling their land under speculative price changes, the profits of which were used in further speculation. These problems could be corrected, said the report, by state aid and direction. The state should provide bona fide settlers with liberal credit and technical services; the report specifically recommended that a long-term credit program be established to enable desirable settlers to acquire land and start small farms.[63]

## THE CALIFORNIA STATE LAND SETTLEMENT AT DURHAM

Impressed with all the data and arguments, the 1917 legislature enacted a bill (prepared by the Commonwealth Club; that is, probably by Mead himself) creating a Board of Land Settlement and appropriating $260,000 to underwrite a model colonization project. Once more Mead was appointed chairman. Other board members were Fleishhacker, Judge William Langdon, State Senator Frank Flint, and businessman-farmer Prescott Cogswell. Mead's dual appointment as director of a University department and head of a state agency drew some protest from other faculty members, but the arrangement continued until 1923.[64]

Of the money allocated for land settlement, $250,000 was a loan to be repaid in 50 years at 4 percent interest. The board used this money in early 1918 to acquire a tract of 6,240 acres in the upper Sacramento Valley, 7 miles south of Chico, a city of about 18,000, and a half mile from Durham, a railroad station. The tract was purchased from two separate owners—Stanford University and Richard White—for a total cost of $534,000. Running through the attractive oak-studded property was Butte Creek, which would provide irrigation water. The College of Agriculture's Division of Soil Technology prepared a soils map showing considerable variation in the tract, from silty loams close to the creek to adobe clays on the east.

Careful planning preceded the opening of the colony for settlement. After design of an irrigation system, farm sites and sizes were laid out according to the soils map. Adobe

ELWOOD MEAD, ARCHITECT OF THE CALIFORNIA LAND SETTLEMENT PLANS, FLANKED BY HIS TWO SETTLEMENT SUPERVISORS, WALTER PACKARD AND GEORGE KREUTZER.

soils were to be used for livestock and grain farms; the loams were planned for alfalfa and orchards. While farm units ranged from 9 to 300 acres, most were in a middle range of between 20 and 80 acres. About two dozen 2-acre plots were set aside for farm laborers' allotments. With spring already under way, the board arranged for land leveling and seeding some of the land to grain and alfalfa. Prices for individual units, fixed according to size, soils, preparation, and cropping potential, ranged from $48.50 to $235 an acre. To protect the health of settlers, a mosquito abatement district was organized. The state architect drew up plans for farmhouses, farm buildings, and a community park and center. Because all of these improvements cost more than anticipated, the board took an additional loan of $125,000 from the Federal Land Bank.

In May 1918 the first allotments were offered for sale. Almost all the units were considered desirable by someone, and some attracted several applicants. Since the board wanted settlers with the best chance to succeed, it stipulated that they should have some previous farm experience as well as $1,500 to $2,500 or more of capital to carry through the first years of development. When there were several

80 applicants for a farm, the board interviewed them to judge their fitness for the challenge.

Development at Durham proceeded very rapidly. Within the first year settlers took up 120 farms and 26 laborer's allotments. Houses and farm buildings went up, alfalfa and grain crops made good progress, and small orchards were laid out. The Durham cooperative livestock association purchased high-quality dairy cows, a pedigreed herd sire, and prizewinning hogs, and it undertook purchasing and marketing efforts to cut supply costs and pool milk sales from the colony's small dairy herds. Settlers built a cold storage warehouse and a community dance pavilion. Farm advisors and faculty from the College provided technical advice, and a resident supervisor kept in touch with all colonists to lend assistance as needed.[65]

With the advantages of advance planning and cooperative activity during the first years at Durham, settlers' spirits were high. The colony attracted national attention. Mead was a tireless publicizer, recounting Durham's plans and activities in many articles and speeches. Even the Southern Pacific Rail Company cited the colony as an example of success in its new promotional publication after the war, *California for the Settler* (San Francisco, circa 1921).

The first exuberant year at Durham, however, coincided with heavy U.S. involvement in the Great War. American farm prices had shot up dramatically with war-related demands for food. The coincidence might have suggested a more cautionary approach, but the smashing early success of the Durham colony encouraged both Mead and his supporters to pursue further state-sponsored settlements. They reasoned that returning war veterans would make ideal candidates as settlers. Carried forward on a wave of popular enthusiasm, Mead's benevolent paternalism seemed to provide at least some of the solutions for California's rural problems. (Chapter 4 continues the land settlement story into the 1920s.)

## THE BEGINNINGS OF THE AGRICULTURAL EXTENSION SERVICE

In the long run, another organization established during this period proved more effective than state land settlement in shaping change in the countryside. A major recommendation of the Country Life Commission's 1909 report had been to establish a nationwide "extension service" to bring the research knowledge of the land-grant colleges directly into rural areas. Such extension work by Seaman Knapp's "county agents" had already helped poor farmers in sections of the South. The signing of the Smith-Lever Act in May 1914 by President Woodrow Wilson enabled all the states to employ such agents. Their salaries paid by joint agreement between the federal and state governments, their local expenses would be covered by the counties they worked in. They would be available to assist individual farmers or farm groups in improving their production techniques and living conditions.[66]

Months before the legislation was actually passed, Dean Hunt called thirty-one-year-old B. H. Crocheron from Maryland to take charge of organizing extension work in California. Like Hunt, Crocheron had a Cornell connection. He had entered the College of Agriculture there in 1904, eventually taking a master's degree in 1909, and had been profoundly influenced by Liberty Hyde Bailey. At Ithaca Crocheron honed his writing skills by editing *The Cornell Countryman*, the college newspaper, and worked for Bailey on the nation's first scientific survey of rural conditions. Subsequently he became head of a rural high school in Sparks, Maryland, where his innovative teaching methods drew favorable attention. Crocheron began his 35-year career at the University of California on July 1, 1913.[67]

Crocheron laid the groundwork for deploying farm advisers.[68] He contacted counties, spoke to local farmers, and prepared the information necessary for formation of support groups called "farm bureaus." Stipulations for placement of an adviser were that the county board of supervisors appropriate at least $2,000 for local office and travel expenses, and that at least 20 percent of the county's farmers belong to a local farm bureau, with whom he would work. Each farm bureau member was to pay $1 in dues and help support a local farm center to house meetings with the farm adviser. Usually the local school-house doubled as the farm center.

Why did the Extension Service seek to establish a new farm organization for support of its activities? Why not use the Grange, the already established Patrons of Husbandry? For one thing, the Grange was a fraternal organization with secret ceremonies and rituals; for another, its populist political baggage might not attract some farmers who would otherwise be ideal candidates for extension work. In encouraging the formation of farm bureaus, the Extension Service could make a clean start in attracting members to support its work, particularly those middle-class, conservative farmers with whom it would be easy to interact because of their generally high educations and solid standing in their communities. Pragmatically, the land-grant colleges needed stable, noncontroversial groups with whom to collaborate. Farm bureaus drew the progressive local opinion leaders who could influence other farmers to adopt new practices.

Even before the official signing of the Smith-Lever Act, four California counties (Humboldt, Yolo, San Joaquin, and

THE YOUNG B. H. CROCHERON. THE MAN IN THE AUTOMOBILE IS PROBABLY DEAN HUNT.

San Diego) agreed to sponsor farm advisers. A bucolic description of the formation of the Yolo County Farm Bureau, written by a University Farm student in 1914, reveals the optimism of the time:

> Across the warm green plains, past the blossoming almond orchards and the gray olive trees, fifteen hundred country people came to the little town of Yolo to organize the Yolo Farm Bureau and to picnic through the pleasant March day. The bent, gray couple meeting one more spring together, the sun-tanned farmer and his wife, the bright-eyed children bubbling over with outdoor life and spirits, all were glad to leave the farms a little while and spend the holiday together. . . .
>
> The little hall, set close to the white orchards was soon crowded to the doors. The State Leader . . . spoke of the Farm Adviser's work and of his opportunity. He told how hundreds of such trained "Farm Doctors" had come at the request of the farmers to as many counties in the nation, connecting every ranch with the University experiment stations and the federal department of agriculture. He suggested that the Farm Advisers' work was not alone to promote better crops, but also to help country people to work together, and to live more interesting and broader lives. . . .
>
> After this hour in the warm noon sun, various farmers spoke, county issues, such as state highway bonds, were discussed, the band played, the Woodland Quartet sang. . . .
>
> Yet beneath it all rang the motto of the meeting "Knowledge + Economy = Efficiency," and the outcome of the day was the organization of the Yolo Farm Bureau . . . and one more step taken in Yolo County towards a fuller and richer country life.[69]

82 During his first year in California Crocheron also helped organize a very successful Ministers' Week at the University Farm. In December 1913, with the assistance of special rates from the railroads, more than 700 clergy from all over the state converged on Davis for three days of lectures, discussions, and cultural events. The conference was designed to aid the rural clergy in their ministry to farm people by promoting the educational discussion of farm problems and those in the "borderland between agriculture and social service." Hunt called the event the largest gathering of its kind held anywhere.

Crocheron's energy and organizing skills were exceptional, and by the end of 1916 thirteen California counties had farm advisers. (The spelling was changed about this time to farm advisor.) The farm advisor's role was to investigate and help solve local farm problems—by setting up demonstrations in cooperation with interested farmers, visiting farms when called, making regular visits to farm centers, and generally offering assistance as needed. The early technical work of the Extension Service consisted largely of practical demonstrations applying information already gathered through research at the University: better pruning techniques for fruit trees, results of grain variety trials, treatment for insect and other pests, methods for dealing with alkali soils, organization of cow-testing associations, and other improved production practices.

Hunt and Crocheron were interested in more than just farm production, however. Crocheron's first bulletin, "The

FARM BUREAU CENTER FIRE STATION IN A TRAILER.

County Farm Adviser" (*Circular 112*, January 1914), stated that farm advisors would cooperate with the "civilizing forces of the community"—youth clubs, farmers' associations, schools, and churches. "The County Farm Bureau" (*Circular 118*, June 1914) described the organization not only as a sponsor for local agricultural education but as a "guardian of rural affairs" helping to "promote the social institutions of country life." Farm advisors soon began to report on rodent control campaigns, better-roads movements, the establishment of restroom facilities for farm families visiting town, community beautification through landscaping, hot lunch programs in rural schools, first aid demonstrations, and many other local improvement activities. To combat range and grain field fires in California's hot dry summers, farm advisors and farm bureaus also began to organize, for the first time, portable fire fighting units for public use.

To encourage youthful interest in agriculture and provide yet another means of extending information on better farming methods, farm advisors began to oversee the boys' and girls' agricultural clubs begun in 1912 in California schools—forerunners of the 4-H clubs. They encouraged club members to enter crop-growing contests: contestants had to keep track of costs and sales as well as production, and the competitor with the highest profits won. Contest winners were awarded trips to visit the College of Agriculture at Berkeley or the University Farm. In the years 1914 through 1916, Crocheron arranged special transcontinental railroad tours for the top 20 or so statewide boys' club winners. These month-long trips covered several farming regions and were capped by a visit to Washington, D.C. In some cases the experience of seeing the world beyond California influenced the boys' entire lives.[70]

## AGRICULTURE GOES TO WAR

Between Hunt's arrival in California in 1912 and the entry of the United States into the European war were nearly five years of intense and innovative efforts in the College of Agriculture. A vigorous and farsighted leader, with broad interests in all aspects of farming, Hunt encouraged his staff to pursue a variety of pathbreaking activities. Hunt's program was interrupted, however, with the formal announcement of war on April 6, 1917.

CALIFORNIA AGRICULTURAL CLUB CONTEST WINNERS VISITING WASHINGTON, D.C. ON THEIR 1915 TRANSCONTINENTAL TOUR.

Impelled to turn the energies of the College toward increasing the food supply, Hunt now organized a campaign to mobilize California's farmers for wartime needs.

## NATIONAL PLANS FOR FOOD PRODUCTION

By 1917, the great conflict that began in 1914 had reduced much of the European continent to rubble and chaos. Despite President Wilson's reluctance to commit American forces to the fray, many volunteers from the United States had already gone abroad to serve in the military units of other nations. When, after a series of incidents, the United States came into the war on the side of the Allies, the nation was ready for mobilization. Along with rapid military buildup, U.S. policy concentrated heavily on supplying foodstuffs to the Allies, whose armies and peoples were suffering from food deficiencies after three years of war. A short American wheat crop in 1916 and rising prices in 1917 contributed to an emphasis on increasing production and eliminating as much waste as possible.[71]

Congress gave the president broad powers over agricultural production, purchasing, and transport, and provided funds for greatly expanding the Agricultural Extension Service. President Wilson named Herbert Hoover head of the U.S. Food Administration. In an all-out campaign urging citizens to conserve food, the administration promoted strategies stressing "wheatless Mondays," "meatless Tuesdays and Thursdays," and the use of wheat-saving "Victory bread." The Bureau of Reclamation undertook a drive to increase production on reclaimed land, and the Department of the Interior encouraged new homesteading. The Commissioner of Education urged schools to cooperate in a food-growing campaign. The Department of Labor waived restrictions on immigration of Mexican farm laborers and helped organized a domestic force for farm work.

84 Farm prices shot up phenomenally, from less than a dollar per bushel of wheat in 1915 to $2.26 in 1918; it would not fall below that price until June 1, 1920. A barrage of posters and pamphlets encouraged farmers to plant fencerow to fencerow. Farmers responded to the challenge—and the prices. For nearly three years American farmers poured grain, meat, and other products in increasing quantities into the marketplace. Farm income rose greatly. Just slightly behind came an inflationary upswing in consumer prices and farmland values.[72]

### CALIFORNIA AND THE FOOD EFFORT

Immediately after the declaration of war, the California State Council of Defense convened in Sacramento to map out strategies for complying with the food production campaign. By the end of April a statewide survey of the potential for increasing food production was completed. Hunt wrote the report, incorporating a number of suggestions based on practices in other states that until then had not been common in California: grain sorghums were to be more widely planted and storage silos constructed; on-farm poultry production was to be encouraged to better utilize farm by-products; high school boys and women were to be used for farm labor; irrigation was to be extended; tractor garages were to be organized for equipment rental or custom work; home economics teachers were to conduct food conservation campaigns, aided by women's clubs; and information on backyard poultry raising and vegetable gardens was to be made available for city residents.

Funded by the Emergency Food Production Act, the number of farm advisors in California more than doubled by the end of 1917. By early 1919, 39 of California's 58 counties had Extension offices, compared with 19 before the declaration of war. Home demonstration work also received a big boost. Although only three itinerant home agents were employed

before the war, federal money allowed the California Extension Service to hire six more. In 1918-19 these home agents became county based. Holding monthly demonstration meetings with farm bureau home departments, they taught food preservation techniques—canning, jelly making, and fruit drying—and food substitution strategies, encouraged farm home gardens, and helped start small-scale poultry flocks.

Anticipating a possible farm labor crisis, the College assigned R. L. Adams to work with government agencies in organizing a plan for mobilizing high school boys, a "Women's Land Army," and city residents for harvest help. To encourage the use of labor-saving machinery, the College sponsored special courses on tractor operation and maintenance.

Within a year the College issued 14 special bulletins, 39 circulars, and 50 emergency leaflets on almost every aspect of wartime food production or conservation. These efforts were very rewarding. Hunt claimed that California shipped more food per capita than any other state in the nation, and reported that production of grain sorghum, wheat, Sudan grass, rye, barley, potatoes, and beans increased by some 150,000 acres in two years while livestock production ("liberty pigs" and "liberty flocks") also grew.[73]

American participation in the war lasted only a year and a half, but it had a marked influence on the nation's agriculture; before long, some of the results would be very unhappy (see chapter 4). For a brief period, however, buoyed by wartime demand, farmers enjoyed a nearly unprecedented prosperity.

### END OF AN EPOCH

Though no one knew the extent to which the world had been changed by the Great War, the signing of the Armistice in November 1918 marked the closing of not just a conflict but a unique two decades of history. Nowhere was this more true than in California, which on the western edge of the continent seemed paradoxically to lag behind some national trends while at the same time it presaged movements of the future. In the years between 1900 and 1918, while it still struggled with the legacies of land monopoly, racism, and immature social and cultural institutions, California leaped forward economically and politically, experimenting with a number of more or less successful progressive reforms. The University's interactive relationship with the legislature during the period itself epitomized the creative uses of political power—from the constituent-led establishment of new facilities and problem-solving projects to University-led proposals for entirely new programs.

Carried forward by the rapid advancement of agriculture under irrigation, the University of California's College of Agriculture grew enormously. Applied scientific work produced remarkable achievements. The soil scientist Hilgard was followed as Dean by the genial generalist Wickson, whose administrative abilities and journalistic skills helped the College diversify its activities and cement a loyal following. Wickson's tenure saw the establishment of the University Farm at Davis and the Citrus Experiment Station at Riverside. Organization of these permanent outlying facilities broadened the work of the Berkeley campus, making the College a truly statewide entity and strengthening its connections with rural California.

For a time, despite Hilgard's objections, the University Farm served as an agricultural high school, until development of agricultural education at the secondary level provided local opportunities for learning good farm practices. Thus proponents of "practical" education had their way, and for several decades to come the University of California offered both production-oriented training at Davis and more theoretical academic work at Berkeley. The difference in outlook between the two institutions had long-range ramifications, in terms of both campus "culture" and alumni loyalty years later.

Wickson's successor, Thomas Hunt, was a man of breadth and vision. He reorganized the College, built a strong scientific staff, and boldly introduced a social policy program. He encouraged students and staff alike to consider the human values in agriculture, and he brought a comparative perspective and a sense of history to the study of agriculture. He helped lay the foundations for development of a strong department of agricultural economics.[74] Under his deanship his energetic colleague Elwood Mead skillfully maneuvered the legislature into funding an innovative University-designed land settlement project, and B. H. Crocheron began a long career building one of the most effective extension services in the nation.

Had the war not intervened, Hunt's leadership might have shaped yet more changes within the College. But the Progressive movement faded in the wake of wartime upheavals, and by the time the war was over many of that era's stalwarts were approaching the end of their careers. After a score of extraordinarily uplifting years, University President Wheeler resigned in 1919. Hunt was tapped that year by the federal government to serve on the postwar Commission on Agricultural Conditions in Allied Countries, and in 1920 he spent a year in Rome as U.S. delegate to the International Institute of Agriculture. Thus the war brought to a close a uniquely exciting period in California agriculture. The pendulum of history began to swing toward a new generation.

# NOTES

1. See Walton Bean, *California: An Interpretive History* (New York: McGraw-Hill, 1988), pp. 312–53, on the progressive period; Michael L. Smith, *Pacific Visions: California Scientists and the Environment, 1850–1915* (New Haven: Yale University Press, 1987), pp. 143–85, on the conservation movement; Frank Adams, *Edward F. Adams, 1839–1929* (Berkeley: privately printed, 1987), on the founding of the Commonwealth Club.

2. See Theodora Kroeber, *Ishi in Two Worlds: A Biography of the Last Wild Indian in North America* (Berkeley: UC Press, 1962).

3. Frederick Jackson Turner, *The Frontier in American History* (New York: Holt, 1920), p. 1.

4. See Stanley R. Davison, *The Leadership of the Reclamation Movement, 1875–1902* (New York: Arno Press, 1979); Frederick D. Kershner, Jr., "George Chaffey and the Irrigation Frontier," *Agricultural History* 27 (Oct. 1953): 115–22; Michael C. Robinson, *Water for the West: The Bureau of Reclamation, 1902–1977* (Chicago: Public Works Historical Society, 1979); Donald J. Pisani, "Reclamation and Social Engineering in the Progressive Era," *Agricultural History* 57 (Jan. 1983): 46–63.

5. Charles Nordhoff, "California for Immigrants" (San Francisco: Southern Pacific Railroad Company, 1883); Richard J. Orsi, "The Octopus Reconsidered: The Southern Pacific and Agricultural Modernization in California, 1865–1915," *California Historical Quarterly* 54 (Fall 1975): 197–220. Historical files of *Sunset* provide a wealth of information on California's development until about 1929, when the magazine became primarily a consumer publication.

6. *Pacific Rural Press*, July 9, 1904, p. 22; Hand Book Series (San Francisco: California Promotion Committee, 1906), preserved in the California State Library; A. J. Wells, *California for the Settler* (San Francisco: Southern Pacific Railroad, circa 1914).

7. See Forest Crissey, *Where Opportunity Knocks Twice* (Chicago: Reilly & Britton, 1914; first copyright 1910), pp. 37–58. The book was prepared from a series of *Saturday Evening Post* articles describing the success of small farmers, especially ethnic farmers, in California.

8. Ibid., p. 131.

9. On the Japanese in California agriculture, see Roger Daniels, *The Politics of Prejudice: The Anti-Japanese Movement in California and the Struggle for Japanese Exclusion* (Berkeley: University of California Press, 1962); Robert F. Heizer and Alan F. Almquist, *The Other Californians: Prejudice and Discrimination under Spain, Mexico, and the United States to 1920* (Berkeley: University of California Press, 1971); Masakazu Iwata, "The Japanese Immigrants in California Agriculture," *Agricultural History* 36 (Jan. 1962): 25–37; *The Japanese Farmers in California* (San Francisco: The Japanese Agricultural Association, circa 1919); Kuchi Kanzaki, *California and the Japanese* (San Francisco: Japanese Association of America, 1921).

10. See Rajani Kanta Das, *Hindustani Workers on the Pacific Coast* (Berlin: Walter de Gruyter, 1923); Carey McWilliams, *Factories in the Fields: The Story of Migratory Farm Labor in California* (Boston: Little, Brown, 1939), pp. 116–19; Lawrence A. Wenzel, "The Rural Punjabis of California: A Religio-Ethnic Group," *Phylon* 29 (Fall 1968): 245–56; Karen Leonard, "Punjabi Farmers and California's Alien Land Law," *Agricultural History* 59 (Oct. 1985): 549–62.

11. H. E. Erdman, "The Development and Significance of California Cooperatives, 1900–1915," *Agricultural History* 32 (July 1958):

179–84. See also Mansel Blackford, *The Politics of Business in California, 1890–1920* (Columbus: Ohio State University Press, 1977), pp. 15–17. By 1920 cooperatives marketed "well over half of California's agricultural output," according to Blackford (p. 21).

12. See Verne A. Stadtman, *The Centennial Record of the University of California* (Berkeley: UC Printing, 1967), p. 15, for a brief biography of Wheeler, and *In Memoriam: Benjamin Ide Wheeler* (Berkeley: UC Press, 1928), a 40-page booklet containing addresses given Oct. 3, 1927, at Wheeler's memorial service. Monroe Deutsch, ed., *The Abundant Life* (Berkeley: UC Press, 1926) offers a collection of Wheeler's addresses.

13. See Verne A. Stadtman, *The University of California, 1868–1968* (New York: McGraw-Hill, 1970), Chapter 13, "Benjamin Ide Wheeler," pp. 179–201.

14. *Twenty-second Report of the Work of the Agricultural Experiment Station of the University of California, from June 30, 1903, to June 30, 1904, Being a Part of the Report of the Regents of the University*, p. 8.

15. Robert W. Hodgson, "Hilgard Hall: A Gift of the Citizens of California" (Berkeley: University of California, 1917), pamphlet issued for Oct. 11, 1917, dedication of Hilgard Hall; Wheeler's words are attributed by Paul S. Taylor in "Foundations of California Rural Society," *California Historical Quarterly* 24 (Sept. 1945): 193–228.

16. Bailey's numerous books demonstrate the breadth of his thought. Best known for editing the *Cyclopedia of American Horticulture* (1900–02), the *Cyclopedia of American Agriculture* (1907–09), and *Hortus* (1930), he also wrote *The Country-Life Movement in the United States* (New York: Macmillan, 1911).

17. UC Archives, *Presidents' Records*, 1905.

18. Ibid. Quote from W. A. Henry to Wheeler, Oct. 10, 1905.

19. Ibid. Quote from Wickson to Wheeler, Feb. 28, 1905. In Peter J. Shields, *The Birth of an Institution: The Agricultural College at Davis* (Sacramento: privately printed, 1954), Shields describes his part in the farm school legislation and claims that he "roused such opposition" to Bailey's views that Bailey was dissuaded from becoming Dean of the College (p. 20).

20. See *University of California Chronicle* 7 (1905): 231–32.

21. Frank Swett, "Wickson as Editor," in *In Memoriam: Edward James Wickson, Addresses Delivered at a Memorial Service October 14, 1923* (Berkeley: University of California, 1924). The synopsis of Wickson's lecture course on dairy industry was published as a University of California *Bulletin* in 1879.

22. Wickson did what he could to strengthen the University's offerings in horticulture. As early as 1901, writing to Wheeler, he urged formation of a division of horticulture, referring to a "feeling of rivalry . . . almost antagonism" between the State Board of Horticulture and the Agriculture Department of the University. In 1902 Wickson, a great admirer of Luther Burbank, suggested to President Wheeler that Burbank be appointed Professor of Plant Breeding in a new department of horticulture with a faculty of six. Although overtures were made, Burbank declined, and Wickson conceded that the University probably could not afford to support Burbank's mass-production hybridization experiments. Wickson also proposed an endowed Carnegie Institute for Horticultural Research, but this did not materialize.

23. UC Archives, *Wickson Papers*, "Wickson to Judge Chipman," Nov. 1, 1906.

24. *University of California Chronicle* 9 (1907): 361.

25. Ronald L. Nye, "Federal versus State Agricultural Research Policy: The Case of California's Tulare Experiment Station, 1888–1909," *Agricultural History* 57 (Oct. 1983): 436–49.

26. See Orsi, "Octopus Reconsidered."

27. *University of California Chronicle* 14 (1912): 481.

28. UC Archives, *Presidents' Records*, 1912: Faculty, Hunt file.

29. Hunt's career is described by Henry C. Taylor and Anne Dewees Taylor in *The Story of Agricultural Economics in the United States, 1840–1932* (Ames: Iowa State College Press, 1952), pp. 60–71, 90–96.

30. T. F. Hunt, "The Motive for Better Farming," *University of California Chronicle* 22 (1920): 408–20.

31. *University of California Chronicle* 15 (1913): 111–51, contains the addresses at the 1912 ceremony.

32. All facts are from *University of California Chronicle* 14 (1912), 15 (1913), and 16 (1914).

88   33. All facts are from *University of California Chronicle* 17 (1915) and 18 (1916).

34. For research work, see the annual *Reports* of the Agricultural Experiment Station; also, Axel Borg's bibliography of agricultural publications. A narrative of plant protection work appears in Ralph E. Smith et al., "Protecting Plants from Their Enemies," in Claude B. Hutchison, ed., *California Agriculture* (Berkeley: UC Press, 1946), pp. 239–315. The mosquito campaign is mentioned in *Report of the College of Agriculture and the Work of the Agricultural Experiment Station of the University of California from July 1, 1919, to June 30, 1920*, pp. 60–61.

35. See S. M. Woodbridge, "Criticism on the Agricultural College at Berkeley" (Los Angeles: Herald Bulletin No. 1, circa late 1890s), leaflet available at the California State Library, Sacramento. This harsh indictment of Hilgard's work may be partly explained by the fact that Hilgard would not endorse Woodbridge's fertilizer products.

36. Claude B. Hutchison, *California Agriculture* (Berkeley, UC Press), p. 88. Also E. J. Wickson, "Beginnings of Agricultural Education and Research in California," in *Report of the College of Agriculture and the Agricultural Experiment Station of the University of California from July 1, 1917, to June 30, 1918*," pp. 54, 91.

37. Shields, *Birth of an Institution*, p. 15.

38. UC Archives, *Hilgard Papers*, Hilgard to M. H. Durst, January 20, 1905; Hilgard to Wheeler, January 28, 1905; *Report . . . 1903–04*, pp. 8–11. Italics are in the original.

39. UC Archives, *Presidents' Records*, Wheeler to Pardee, July 7, 1905.

40. Bailey's remarks, "What a University Farm Is For," were published as Agricultural Experiment Station *Circular 15* in August 1905 and in *University of California Chronicle* 8 (1905–06): 49–54.

41. UC Archives, *Hilgard Papers*, Hilgard to N. A. Cobb, May 31, 1906.

42. UC Archives at the Bancroft Library, Berkeley, and at the Department of Special Collections, Shields Library, Davis, are the sources of details on the siting of the University Farm. Another source, somewhat garbled, is Alyce Williams Jewett's *Saga of UCD* (Davis: privately printed, 1982). The quote about the opening of Kearney's estate is from Wickson, "The Advancement of Agricul-tural Education," Agricultural Experiment Station *Circular 21* (July 1906).

43. All facts are from *University of California Chronicle* 9–19 (1907–1917) or from materials in the Department of Special Collections, Shields Library, UC Davis.

44. UC College of Agriculture miscellaneous publications, "Harry and I at the University Farm" (Berkeley: UC Press, 1917), p. 26.

45. See Harry W. Lawton and Lewis G. Weathers, "The Origins of Citrus Research in California and the Founding of the Citrus Research Center and Agricultural Experiment Station," in Walter Reuther, E. Clair Calavan, and Glenn E. Carman, eds., *The Citrus Industry* (Oakland: UC Division of Agriculture and Natural Resources, 1989), vol. 5, pp. 281–335. I am indebted throughout this section to Lawton and Weathers for details on the founding of the Riverside Station.

46. Ibid., p. 291.

47. Ibid., p. 310.

48. Ibid., pp. 312–17.

49. Ibid., pp. 320–22. The Whittier building was later (1920) placed at the disposal of the State Department of Agriculture for the study of parasites to combat scale insects. This work was transferred back to the University in 1923.

50. See Paul H. Johnstone's classic essay "Old Ideals Versus New Ideas in Farm Life," in U.S. Department of Agriculture, *Yearbook of Agriculture* (Washington, D.C., 1940), pp. 111–69. Also, David B. Danbom, *The Resisted Revolution: Urban America and the Industrialization of Agriculture, 1900–1930* (Ames: Iowa State University Press, 1979), especially pp. 3–22.

51. William L. Bowers, in *The Country Life Movement in America, 1900–1920* (New York: Kennikat Press, 1974) pointed out that Roosevelt, like others in the country life movement, "tried to face in two directions at once, looking backward to a largely mythical Arcadia of simple rusticism and forward to a twentieth-century society in which farmers would need to rely on scientific efficiency and business practices to succeed" (p. 43). See also Danbom, *Resisted Revolution*, pp. 23–74; Samuel P. Hays, *Conservation and the Gospel of Efficiency: The Progressive Conservation Movement, 1890–1920* (Cambridge, Mass.: Harvard University Press, 1959), pp. 269–71;

Clayton Ellsworth, "Theodore Roosevelt's Country Life Commission," *Agricultural History* 34 (Fall 1960): 155–72.

52. *Los Angeles Times*, November 26, 1908, editorial section, p. 1.

53. *San Francisco Chronicle*, November 29, 1908, p. 36; and *Sacramento Union*, December 1, 1906, p. 1. By this time antagonism toward the Chinese had evidently waned, judging by the testimony of one woman at the Sacramento hearing who ungrammatically gushed, "The dear old Chinamen! I feel like hugging one every time I see him."

54. For a description of the influence of new industrial management techniques on social thinking during the progressive era, see Samuel Haber, *Efficiency and Uplift: Scientific Management in the Progressive Era, 1890–1920* (Chicago: University of Chicago Press, 1964).

55. Paul Conkin, "The Vision of Elwood Mead," *Agricultural History* 34 (Apr. 1960): 88–97.

56. Mead's book, which even today is a lucid examination of basic questions, was published by Macmillan in 1903 in its Citizens Library of Economics, Politics, and Sociology. Characterizations of Mead are from the *Bendigo Advertiser*, an Australian periodical quoted in *Irrigation Age*, June 1915, in UC Archives, *Land Settlement Papers*.

57. UC Archives, *Presidents Records*, Box 72, File 143.

58. Quoted in Taylor and Taylor, *Story of Agricultural Economics*, p. 95. The inception and progress of the Division of Rural Institutions is described in Emmett Fiske's 1979 UC Davis dissertation, "The College and Its Constituency: Research and Community Development at the University of California, 1875–1978," pp. 144–95.

59. "Rural Institutions," *University of California Chronicle* 19 (1917): 464–65.

60. See Robert V. Hine, *California's Utopian Colonies* (New York: Norton, 1953).

61. Ellen Liebman, in *California Farmland: A History of Large Agricultural Landholdings* (Montclair, N.J.: Rowman & Allanheld, 1983), suggests that subdivision of large estates into small farms did not happen as often as might have been expected during this period because of high costs of development, a readily available cheap labor force agreeable to tenantry, and the value of holding even underutilized land as an investment (pp. 79–81).

62. Elwood Mead, *Helping Men Own Farms: A Practical Discussion of Government Aid in Land Settlement* (New York: Macmillan, 1920), p. 5.

63. See "Land Settlement in California," *Transactions of the Commonwealth Club of California*, 11:8 (Dec. 1916): 369–465; UC Archives, *Land Settlement Papers*; Roy J. Smith, "The California Land Settlements at Durham and Delhi," *Hilgardia* 15 (Oct. 1943), pp. 399–492.

64. Fiske, *The College and Its Constituency*, pp. 180–81.

65. Details are from Mead, *Helping Men Own Farms*, pp. 106–60; and Smith, "Settlements at Durham and Delhi."

66. Histories of the extension movement include A. C. True, *A History of Agricultural Extension Work in the United States, 1785–1923* (Washington, D.C.: GPO, 1928); Gladys Baker, *The County Agent* (Chicago: University of Chicago Press, 1939); Roy V. Scott, *The Reluctant Farmer: The Rise of Agricultural Extension to 1914* (Urbana: University of Illinois Press, 1970); and Wayne Rasmussen, *Taking the University to the People: Seventy-Five Years of Cooperative Extension* (Ames: Iowa University Press, 1989).

67. Biographical material relating to Crocheron is scanty; details here are from his file in the University Archives. See also *Bertram Hanford Crocheron, Architect and Builder of the California Agricultural Extension Service* (UC Agricultural Extension Service, 1967). For a short history of the California Agricultural Extension Service, see Ann Foley Scheuring, *A Sustaining Comradeship: A Brief History of University of California Cooperative Extension, 1913–1988* (Berkeley: UC Division of Agriculture and Natural Resources, 1988).

68. Hunt preferred the title "farm adviser" to "county agent" because he thought the latter "smacks of police powers"; *University of California Chronicle* 18 (1916): 28.

69. Report of the College of Agriculture and the Agricultural Experiment Station of the University of California, 1913–1914, "The County Farm Bureau," *Circular 118* (June 1914), pp. 13–14. This circular contains the constitution and by-laws for farm bureaus written by Crocheron.

70. See "Boys' and Girls' Clubs," *Circular 80* (Oct. 1912), describing early contests; also J. Earl Coke, *Reminiscences on People and Change in California Agriculture, 1900–1975* (Davis: UC Oral History Center, 1975), pp. 6–8.

71. Murray Benedict, *Farm Policies of the United States, 1790–1950* (New York: The Twentieth Century Fund, 1953), pp. 160–68.

72. Ibid.

73. College war activities are described in the *Report of the College of Agriculture . . . 1916–17,* pp. 39–95, and *University of California Chronicle* 20 (1918): 334–76.

74. Henry C. Taylor gave Hunt credit for doing "more than any of his contemporary agriculturalists to blaze the trail and open the administrative minds in the colleges of agriculture for work in agricultural economics." Taylor and Taylor, *Story of Agricultural Economics,* p. 63.

# 4

# Transition and Change

## 1919 – 1929

*Family farm at Durham, site of the first California Land Settlement project, about 1920.*

AFTER WORLD WAR I RAPID POPULATION GROWTH BEGAN TO CHANGE CALIFORNIA DRAMATICALLY, WHILE THE POSTWAR AGRICULTURAL DEPRESSION HIT THE STATE'S FARMERS. THE COLLEGE OF AGRICULTURE REORGANIZED UNDER NEW LEADERSHIP. THE UNIVERSITY FARM WAS STRENGTHENED ACADEMICALLY AND AGRICULTURAL RESEARCH FLOURISHED, BUT THE STATE LAND SETTLEMENTS AT DURHAM AND DELHI FAILED. AGRICULTURAL ECONOMICS BECAME AN IMPORTANT FIELD OF STUDY, SUPPORTED BY A BANK OF AMERICA ENDOWMENT. THE AGRICULTURAL EXTENSION SERVICE AND LOCAL FARM BUREAUS COLLABORATED IN FARM AND COMMUNITY DEVELOPMENT. BY THE DECADE'S END ECONOMIC PRESSURES WERE INTENSIFYING AND THE OUTLOOK FOR MANY FARMERS WAS GRIM.

# 4

# Transition and Change  1919–1929

## THE POSTWAR WORLD

World War I ineluctably changed American views, mores, and expectations. In some ways the Great War brought an end to innocence—individually, in the case of the "lost generation" of expatriates who prowled the boulevards and bistros of France and Spain, and more generally as national values began to erode in the social revolution after the war. New attitudes stemming from wartime experiences were deftly captured in a popular song of 1919:

> How 'ya gonna keep 'em down on the farm,
> After they've seen Paree?
> How 'ya gonna keep 'em away from Broadway,
> Jazzin' aroun' an' paintin' the town? . . .
> They'll never want to see a rake or plow,
> And who the deuce can parley-vouz a cow?
> How 'ya gonna keep 'em down on the farm,
> After they've seen Paree?[1]

The song was an updated comic recitation of what had been a serious national concern since the Civil War. Keeping rural people content "down on the farm" while encouraging greater agricultural productivity had been a goal of the

Morrill and Hatch acts, the Country Life Movement, the Agricultural Extension Service, and California's Land Settlement Act. Despite regional variations, results of these legislative interventions had generally been successful: the years before World War I have been recalled as a kind of golden age for American agriculture, when production and markets seemed fairly synchronized, and prices received by farmers became the standard for later "parity" arguments. Nevertheless, this apparent prosperity was accompanied by, perhaps achieved through, a steadily declining farm-city ratio: the nation's population on farms decreased from about 37 percent in 1900 to 30 percent by 1920.

Very soon after the war American farm conditions suddenly soured. Agricultural commodity prices, which had soared as wartime-spurred farm production rose to new heights, collapsed. Export markets dried up as European agriculture began to recover from the trauma of war. The support price for wheat, pegged at $2.26 a bushel in July 1918, remained under government guarantee until May 31, 1920, but when futures trading resumed on the Chicago Board of Trade on July 15 of that year, prices for wheat and other staples broke sharply. By May 1921 average prices for ten leading crops were only a third of what they had been the preceding June.[2]

The three years of high profits, however, had encouraged farmers to invest in more land, and across the country farmland values had risen greatly as a result of demand. In 1920 improved land was valued at an average of 70 percent above prewar levels. Though land prices eventually dropped as farmers pulled back from the market, mortgage debt already assumed remained burdensome. So did prices for necessary farm purchases such as machinery and fencing, running approximately double their prewar costs. Purebred livestock prices soared to record highs. Postwar wages for farm labor reflected new labor scarcity, and other expenses added to the farmers' load. The combination of slashed income and heavy financial commitments proved to be a tightening economic vise that eventually squeezed many out of business.[3]

Meanwhile, other segments of the economy boomed. Urban jobs were plentiful as emerging industries of the prewar years—automobiles, oil, aircraft, and movies—moved rapidly into larger commercial production. Consumers were eager for the mobility offered by the automobile, and Detroit poured out vehicles on the assembly lines. Highway building, fuel production, and associated businesses all prospered. While airplanes were not yet commonplace, the fascinated public followed the exploits of barnstorming stunt pilots with enthusiasm, and beginnings were made in air postal service and commercial passenger transportation. The new mobility also brought more opportunities for entertainment. With advances in filmmaking the movie industry flourished, bringing new views of the world and new attitudes even into conservative small towns. Challenged by a constitutional amendment outlawing alcoholic beverages, some citizens found illicit ways to acquire liquor, and bootlegging encouraged a lighter view of lawbreaking.

The contrast between the doldrums in agriculture and the boom in transportation and entertainment reflected a mounting disjunction in the economy. The formation of many new companies made stock transactions an attractive financial game for the rich and the near-rich. Speculators began taking gradually greater risks. Toward the end of the decade many were making paper fortunes in a matter of months, even weeks. The mania for buying and selling on margin pyramided noncollateralized stock issues into increasingly tenuous arrangements based on holding companies, but few economic observers were prescient—or brave—enough to warn of potential disaster: those who urged caution were discounted as doomsayers. Income disparities widened between rich and poor: by 1929 the upper 5 percent of the population received 30 percent of all personal income, the lower 40 percent only 12.5 percent.[4]

Although President Calvin Coolidge complacently reported to Congress in December 1928 that the nation could "regard the present with satisfaction and anticipate the future with optimism," the country stood on the eve of the stock market disaster. Beneath the surface of apparent prosperity, ominous trends had been building for some time. Farmers had been tightening their belts for most of the decade; working-class families were finding their spending power eroded by inflation; capitalists and brokers were playing dangerously with illusional stocks. The "roaring twenties" came to a dramatic end when the stock market collapsed in the fall of 1929.[5]

## CALIFORNIA CONVERTING

While California shared the nation's general postwar readjustments, its geographical and historical position helped shape its own unique adaptations to the 1920s. Increased mobility and new jobs brought rapid in-migration and increasing urbanization, especially below the Tehachapis. In 1920 Californians were 3.2 percent of the U.S. population;

by 1930 the figure was 4.6 percent. Even though the number of California farms grew during the twenties from 117,670 to 135,676, the proportion of its farm population shrank. In 1920 only 15 percent of Californians lived on farms, compared with the nation's 30 percent; by 1930 the figures were 11 percent compared with 25 percent.[6]

Attracting the newcomers were many of the booming industries that characterized the decade—aviation, oil production, and filmmaking. Douglas and Lockheed set up airplane production in the Los Angeles basin in the early 1920s, and the first daily air passenger service in the country began between Los Angeles and San Diego in 1922. The discovery of major oil deposits in southern California made petroleum refining the state's largest manufacturing industry. Hollywood moviemaking evolved into the studio system, and with the advent of "talkies" in 1927 the film industry entered a period of prosperity that continued even through the Great Depression.

After World War I southern California leaped ahead of the north in population, gross income, and general affluence. Los Angeles surpassed San Francisco in population for the first time in the 1920 census (576,000 to 506,000), and by 1930 had doubled it (1,238,000 to 634,000). As job seekers attracted by new industries settled in, their search for homes triggered a new land rush in the Los Angeles basin. Farm properties were subdivided, towns flourished around the oil refineries, and from its modest beginnings Hollywood developed into the glamor capital of the West.[7]

Reflecting the shift in population and prosperity, the University of California in 1919 established a Southern Branch on the Vermont Avenue site of the Los Angeles State Normal School. The two-year program was expanded to four, and by 1924 the school outgrew its facilities. In October 1926 the University formally dedicated its Westwood campus, changing its name to the University of California at Los Angeles—UCLA—the following year. In May 1929 four large Romanesque buildings were completed around the main quadrangle.[8]

## AGRICULTURAL SHIFTS

In some parts of California the 1920s were still a pioneer period. Much new land came under the plow, and many older areas saw cropping shifts. In the Sacramento Delta and the Sutter Basin north of Sacramento, large reclamation projects brought thousands of new acres into agricultural production.[9] In San Luis Obispo, Colusa, and other counties, orchard developers peddled 20-acre parcels to midwesterners and other buyers lured by the sunshine mystique and promises of easy profits.

Experienced California farmers continued experimenting with new crops, and several major industries emerged during this decade. Shipping improvements, including the development of iced freight cars, encouraged the production of fresh vegetables for distant markets. Better canning technologies aided the growth of processing companies. In some areas growers began to produce two, even three crops of vegetables. Monterey County's production of lettuce rose from 4 acres in 1921 to 1,500 acres in 1923, and in 1925 California shipped seven times the carloads of lettuce shipped in 1917.[10] In the Imperial Valley and parts of the San Joaquin, an equally dramatic expansion took place in melon and vegetable production. Cotton and rice became major enterprises; legislative restriction (in 1925) of San Joaquin Valley cotton planting to the Acala variety helped increase yield and quality and standardize the industry, while rice pioneered by Japanese farmers proved a profitable use for the heavy basin soils of the Sacramento Valley.[11]

Low postwar prices for wheat and other cereal crops convinced many California farmers to convert their fields to vineyards or orchards. Growth of the banking system, particularly the spectacular rise of A. P. Giannini's Bank of Italy (later the Bank of America) with its many rural branches, made more credit available for conversion costs.[12] With climate and irrigation offering a flexibility of opportunity not available in many other states, farmers continued to turn former grain acreage into the more profitable specialty crops, and for a few years California seemed to escape the nationwide agricultural depression.

Perennial crops, however, had their problems. Prohibition decimated the winemaking industry after 1919; the continued planting of raisin and table grapes resulted in an eventual market glut as bearing vineyards came to maturity. Many grape growers were financially ruined, and a "drastic reorganization" of the entire industry took place in the twenties.[13] Overplanting of various fruits encouraged by high prices between 1919 and 1921 also brought price reversals by the time new orchards came into produc-

UC AGRICULTURAL FACULTY AND STAFF ASSOCIATED WITH THE 1928 REVIVAL OF THE TRAVELING EDUCATIONAL TRAINS OF THE EARLY 1900S. BY THIS TIME THE COLLEGE OF AGRICULTURE STRESSED MORE EFFICIENT FARM MANAGEMENT AS WELL AS BETTER FARMING TECHNIQUES.

tion a few years later. Thus by the end of the decade the postwar farm crisis humbled California in its own way.

In March 1928 the College of Agriculture revived its "demonstration train" to provide information for troubled farmers in 24 rural communities throughout the Central Valley. From the platform of the "California Agriculture Spe-

cial" college staff explained basic economic outlook data for more than a dozen crops, stressing the need for realism and efficiency in farm management.[14] The next year, at the request of the state legislature, the College began compiling a special report describing the problems facing the state's farmers and ranchers (see chapter 5).

## FARM SIZE AND FARM LABOR

What of the promise of irrigation for bringing "family farming" to California? In areas like Stanislaus and San Joaquin counties, where soils, water supply, and climate were particularly favorable, the prewar conversion of nineteenth-century grain ranches to 40- or even 20-acre farms indeed proved successful. In the first two decades of the Turlock Irrigation District (its main canal completed in 1901) the number of farms increased from 140 dryland ranches averaging 1,250 acres each to more than 4,000 irrigated farms averaging 40 acres, while district population soared from 950 to more than 15,000. A study of two California counties published in 1922 by the National Council of Churches—titled *Irrigation and Religion*—reported that prosperous small farms and rural communities (and churches) followed in the wake of good irrigation projects.[15]

98 Small family farms were not necessarily to be the wave of California's future, however. Given fertile soil, abundant water, and intelligent management, it was true that in some areas a small specialized farm could be productive enough to provide a comfortable family living; yet probably not more than 15 percent of the state's total farmland was actually suited for this kind of agriculture. This fact did not stop land speculators, who continued to subdivide and promote farmland in many areas, leading to disappointments and bankruptcies down the line. Apart from the importance of basic resources, the small farm was also highly dependent on a stable economic climate—reliable markets and favorable prices—that would allow the farmer to recoup the relatively high costs of development and production. Nor was specialized irrigated agriculture for everyone. By the mid-1920s it was clear that such enterprises demanded a complex combination of horticultural, engineering, and business skills. Enmeshed in a complex of factors and forces beyond the limits of individual farms or local water districts, irrigated agriculture was actually quite vulnerable to shocks. With operating costs greater than those of the mixed grain-and-animal farms of the Midwest, California farms also depended on a complicated support system—water and drainage districts, marketing associations, credit agencies, transportation and supply networks—that needed adequate financing and intelligent management at all levels. Farm profitability hinged on equilibrium between supply and demand, which might easily be tipped with too many plantings. Thus small enterprises, while feasible, were also fragile; like venturesome small boats, they could be threatened by ocean swells, and the competence of their captains was crucial.

Large farms, on the other hand, often had more cropping options, could spread their risk, and could benefit from lower costs of production per unit. The continued availability of low-paid immigrant farm labor in California also tended to support the dominance of large-scale farming and undercut small owner-operated units. While many big nineteenth-century ranches went on the auction block in the early years of the new century, others were converted to more intensive uses not by new family owners but by ethnic tenants operating blocks within the larger landholdings. The Chinese, conveniently available at a crucial stage in the state's development, had been supplanted in turn by the Japanese or Punjabis. After the 1924 immigration act stopped the Asian influx, Mexicans and Filipinos, who were exempt from immigration quotas, increasingly supplied California's needs for seasonal farm labor.[16] Thus California farmers nearly always had enough cheap labor to harvest developing specialty crops, and labor scarcity in itself was not a reason to break up large holdings. According to an analysis by agricultural economist Varden Fuller, landholders came, perhaps unconsciously, to include the availability of labor as a component in pricing their land—to the disadvantage of smaller buyers. Some of the difficulties California's small farms experienced in the 1920s could be traced to the historical pattern established some 50 years earlier:

> The failure to subdivide the land and the consequent establishment of large units must be attributed principally to the fact that purchasers to buy and establish small farms at the land prices asked by the large holders were absent and that in their stead cheap and convenient labor, principally Chinese, was available for intensive cultivation. . . .

> What the significance to the future of employing the Chinese would be may not have been appreciated by farm employers. More realistically, we must look upon it as one of the aspects of social accounting of which individual interest cannot be expected to take cognizance. . . . With sufficient labor available . . . it was feasible to convert large acreages into intensively cultivated fruit farms. This was the most profitable

alternative and the one which self-interest dictated. . . . The prospective purchaser of a small acreage, to be operated as a "family farm," principally with the labor of himself and his family, found that the capitalized value of the land was too high to permit a labor return equal to his other wage alternatives. An established farmer of the eastern states stood a good chance to lose if he attempted to migrate to California. He must sell less highly capitalized land to purchase the more highly capitalized land of California and must pay the cost of migration in addition.17

In the early 1900s immigrant labor had been generally considered only a stopgap supply while the state was becoming fully populated. In part, the widespread promotion of small-acreage parcels at that time was an attempt to attract reliable American labor; promoters thought that a permanent rural population would not only develop the country but provide seasonal workers for large ranches. By 1910, however, established growers began to give up notions of a settled American work force and focus increasingly on the imperatives of an industrializing agriculture, simply employing the least expensive and most convenient labor available. Because circumstance continued to provide a foreign, migrant labor force for California, it became the accepted norm, and little effort was put into trying to restructure the system.[18]

The 1920s brought a gradual jelling of what would later become known as "agribusiness"—the complex of related marketing and supply businesses serving relatively large-scale agriculture. The economic stresses of the time made cost-efficiency a major goal. In some regions the quality of soils and the cost of supplying water precluded the survival of small units. In others, small farms were caught between high costs and small if any profits, with little cushion for bad years and a miserable return on investment. As price-to-income ratios tightened further, the College of Agriculture itself began to suggest that it might make economic sense for some small operators to simply sell out to their neighbors.[19]

## CHANGES IN THE UNIVERSITY AND IN THE COLLEGE OF AGRICULTURE

Within a few months after the Armistice students came flocking back to the University. In September 1919 Berkeley registered a record-breaking 8,600 students. At the University Farm at Davis, the enrollment doubled from the prewar 314 to more than 700 in the Farm School and short courses. For a few months the University Farm also provided training for several dozen Australian veterans sent by their government to study alfalfa growing, hog raising, and irrigation in California.[20]

Along with the surge in students came pressure for several major changes within the University and the College of Agriculture. A constitutional amendment approved by voters in November 1918 had materially increased the autonomy of the University and freed administration and faculty to restructure its organization and governance. Upon President Wheeler's retirement in July 1919, the Academic Senate took steps toward greater authority in the University's internal administration. For years Wheeler had dominated faculty hiring and personnel matters; the Senate now negotiated a lessening of presidential powers and a broadening of its own under departmental structures. In October the faculty presented a memorial to the Regents demanding, in effect, greater authority for the Academic Senate. By June 1920 the "faculty revolt" resulted in several organizational shifts.[21]

One big change affecting the College of Agriculture was a new restriction on Senate membership. Until 1920 all agricultural faculty, research staff, and farm advisors held academic titles with the right to vote in the Academic Senate. The rapid growth of the agricultural staff, from 47 in 1914 to more than 200 in 1919, obviously had an effect on the balance of power within the University. When farm advisors on campus for an Extension conference in 1919 exercised their voting privileges in the Academic Senate over the objection of other members, the Berkeley faculty moved to restrict membership to those in academic teaching positions. This ruling barred farm advisors, some researchers, and many of the Davis teaching staff, because instruction at the University Farm was not then at university level. Thus the decision dealt a blow to the status of at least half of the agricultural staff. It also led to reorganization of internal structure for the agricultural group.[22]

In 1919 Dean Hunt had announced a major delegation of functions, appointing associate directors Walter Mulford to supervise resident instruction, H. J. Webber to oversee the Agricultural Experiment Station, and B. H. Crocheron to lead the Extension Service. In October 1920, with Hunt away on leave, Acting Dean Mulford recommended a new plan of organization for the agricultural group as a whole. The College of Agriculture was now officially to comprise four parts: the Department of Agriculture for academic instruction leading to university degrees, the Agricultural Experiment Station for original research, the Agricultural Extension Service for statewide public outreach, and the University Farm School. The Dean of Agriculture would continue to be the general administrative officer for the College, but each part would have its own head as well. Only faculty in the Department of Agriculture would be entitled to membership in the Academic Senate, but all members of the College were to have a voice in matters of internal concern.[23]

Another postwar change for the College came with the creation of a new state agency to protect and regulate Califor-

THOMAS FORSYTH HUNT, DEAN OF UC'S COLLEGE OF AGRICULTURE FROM 1912 TO 1923.

nia agriculture. In 1919 the legislature created the State Department of Agriculture to combine the regulatory functions of nine lesser boards and commissions established over the previous twenty years. The new agency immediately took on several of the tasks formerly delegated to the College, such as fertilizer and insecticide testing and hog cholera serum production. Freed of these "police duties," the College was able to concentrate more completely on research and education.[24]

These transitions in the College accompanied a serious and far-reaching re-examination of the functions of the University Farm. In the ferment of the postwar period, an old issue resurfaced: What was the role of the College of Agriculture, to train California farmers in "practical" matters or provide them with theoretical background? Was it doing its job adequately? Returning veterans apparently voiced considerable criticism of work at the University Farm, and some claimed that students seeking high-quality agricultural courses were choosing Oregon State Agricultural College at Corvallis over Davis. Meanwhile a contingent of agriculturalists resenting Berkeley domination called for complete separation of the University Farm from the University of California, charging that division of instruction and research between Berkeley and Davis was inefficient and costly.

Once again, as in 1874 and in 1905, the University found itself on the defensive about its agricultural program. At a meeting in Sacramento, University President David Barrows and others spoke against the separation proposal, and in Berkeley in October 1920, the Regents' Committee on Agriculture, along with University officers, met with representatives of more than 40 important agricultural organizations to discuss "matters of mutual interest."[25]

In January 1921 the legislature appointed a Special Legislative Commission on Agricultural Education to review agricultural education across California—including the University, the high schools, the junior colleges, and the California Polytechnic Institute at San Luis Obispo. The seven-member commission included Elwood Mead and the newly appointed young university comptroller, Robert G. Sproul.[26] The commission's charge was to examine agricultural education in other states and recommend possible improvements for California.

With a $10,000 budget, the group spent almost a year investigating the agricultural education system in fifteen states, including Illinois, Michigan, Minnesota, New York, Oregon, and Wisconsin, traveling to ten institutions to view their physical facilities and learn about their governance, curricula, and standards. One chief objective was to compare the advantages and disadvantages of incorporating a college of agriculture within a university, in contrast with maintaining such a college as a separate institution. After talking with administrators at the state institutions and the U.S. Department of Agriculture, members came to a consensus that colleges within the state university (as in Illinois, Wisconsin, and, in New York, Cornell University) were superior in offering "much broader possibilities of research and . . . finer training . . . for agricultural leadership."

> [Interviewees] were unanimous in opposition to separation, either physical or administrative, of a college of agriculture from the State University; doubtful of divided instruction except as an alternative to separation, and generally favorable to the location of the whole college at the site of the State University even if highly expensive land must be condemned to make this possible.[27]

The commission's final report came down firmly in favor of keeping the College of Agriculture permanently within the larger University of California and defined its goals for instruction:

> Agriculture, from being a simple art, has become one of the most complex of modern occupations . . . and agricultural education must . . . comprehend the practice, the science, and the business of farming, in order that men may be trained not only as tillers of the soils but as rural leaders, scientific investigators, managers of cooperative enterprises, agricultural teachers and for the many other branches of human endeavor that closely affect farm life and rural progress. . . .
>
> For teaching the economics and science of agriculture, the college of agriculture in contact with the broad life of a university and directed by the same board of trustees is the best agency. It can not be expected to train the great army of farmers any more than the engineering colleges are expected to train the mechanics of the country, but it is the only source from which agricultural leadership can be looked for with confidence.[28]

Several other of the commission's recommendations were to have a pronounced effect on the state's agricultural education in general and the University Farm in particular. Specifically, the commission recommended extending vocational education under the Smith Hughes Act of 1917 into California's junior colleges; transferring the "farm school" for students under twenty-one from Davis to the California Polytechnic Institute at San Luis Obispo; acquiring more land, greenhouses, and laboratories for agricultural research at Berkeley; developing better facilities at Davis to compare with those in other state institutions and restructuring the Davis undergraduate curriculum; adding home economics for women students and more professional short courses for adult farmers; applying the same admission standards for agricultural students as for other university students; and allowing autonomy for the College of Agriculture to the largest degree compatible with the unity of the University. Other recommendations were directed toward solution of apparent political problems: authority over Experiment Station work should be exercised by the Board of Regents rather than by the legislature; the Board of Regents should include representatives of rural interests; and the College of Agriculture should more widely distribute information through bulletins and circulars to the public.[29]

Nearly every one of the commission's recommendations eventually became fact. Reorganization of the University Farm took place immediately. The Farm School was discontinued, and the University Farm became the College of Agriculture, Northern Branch. In 1922 the Regents approved the initiation of university work for freshmen and sophomores at Davis. Dean Hunt brought in a young professor of plant breeding from Cornell, Claude B. Hutchison, as the new director of the campus, and under his supervision class offerings at Davis were broadened and physical facilities improved. In the first year of reorganized coursework, 253 of the 388 students enrolled chose the new "degree program," which offered two years of production and business education at Davis followed by two years of science and economics at Berkeley. A two-year vocational "nondegree program" continued the equivalent of junior college work until well after World War II.[30]

In Berkeley, private fund-raising supplemented a $100,000 legislative appropriation to acquire the Schmidt tract, a block of 18 acres northwest of the campus, for an additional agricultural research area, and the Regents assigned the strip of land along Hearst Avenue from Hilgard Hall to Oxford Street for construction of new greenhouses, which remained there until campus expansion in the 1960s.[31]

At the Citrus Experiment Station in Riverside, the Graduate School of Tropical Agriculture drew only a handful of graduate students during the 1920s. Between 1924 and 1932, when undergraduate instruction in agriculture began at UCLA, eight-week summer sessions at Riverside offered classes in subtropical horticulture, but the primary focus at Riverside until much later was experimental research.[32]

A marked transition in leadership took place in both the University and the College of Agriculture. University President David P. Barrows, successor to Wheeler, submitted his resignation effective June 30, 1923. His successor was William W. Campbell, longtime director of the Lick Observatory. In 1923 Hunt also resigned as Dean of the College of Agriculture. Aware that the Dean of Agriculture was considered the second-most-important executive officer in the University, President Campbell selected Elmer P. Merrill as Hunt's successor, largely because of his excellent reputation as a scholar and an administrator. As a botanist recently returned from 22 years in the Philippines, however, Merrill possessed little direct knowledge of either agriculture or California, and in his six years as Dean he made little effort to acquire it. For the rest of the decade, Campbell and Merrill shepherded the University and the College through various internal changes and a period of quiet growth, essentially caretakers and stabilizers in a period marked by no further controversy.[33]

## RESEARCH PRIORITIES IN THE 1920S

In his first report as director of the Agricultural Experiment Station H. J. Webber submitted a lengthy discussion of the station's work, its place in the College and in the University, its methods of operation, and the demands for its services.[34] While recognizing California's diversity of problems and the responsibility of the station to respond to them, he argued for a strong program of basic research:

> A considerable portion of the energy of the Station staff should be given to the study of fundamental problems.... One function of an experiment station is to conduct purely scientific research for the single purpose of discovering new truth which may or may not have immediate practical value.

Like Hilgard before him, Webber emphasized the role of science in discovering causes and relationships. Fundamental research, he wrote, necessarily precedes much applied work; it provides the understanding of principles that lies behind practice. Basic knowledge of the physical and morphological principles of tree growth better determines good pruning techniques, for example, than any number of simple empirical trials; and knowledge of soil structure and composition underlies the most effective use of fertilizers. To help cope with the constant distraction of requests for special research projects, Webber recommended establishing clearer priorities for a fundamental research program. He also strongly supported the concept of interdisciplinary work, even urging the inclusion of non-College scientists in projects. And he called for the segregation of teaching, research, and extension functions:

> I am firmly convinced that the Agricultural Experiment Station should have its own corps. . . . The investigator may give occasional lectures to students and may direct the work of a few graduate students . . . but he should not be required to teach regular undergraduate classes. . . . The extension workers . . . already . . . have enough to do.

At the Citrus Experiment Station where Webber was in residence, such a segregation of functions was already practiced and worked well. Later research administrators would have different views on the subject.

The research activities of the Agricultural Experiment Station during the 1920s were many and varied, covering soil studies, the animal and plant sciences, investigations into pest and plant disease control, the new field of agricultural engineering, nutrition and food science, and forestry.

## SOIL STUDIES

As the state's agriculture expanded and intensified, the soil investigations begun in California by Hilgard continued to be of paramount importance. Under the leadership of C. F. Shaw, soil mapping and classification work was enlarged.

Between 1913 and 1918 the soils division, in cooperation with state and federal agencies, produced seven detailed reconnaissance maps covering 22 million acres. By 1920 the division had identified and mapped dozens of California soil series, developing a much better understanding of the state's resources. As this work went on, soils were classified according to texture, subsoil, lime content, acidity or alkalinity, water-holding capacity, drainage, and relief—all factors important in crop production and soil management.[35]

Soil reclamation research became increasingly important. In 1920 Webber cited the spread of alkali as "probably now the dominant agricultural problem of the state. . . . The permanent welfare of the state is threatened."[36] W. P. Kelley told a gathering of farm advisors that hundreds of thousands of acres in the Central Valley were deteriorating as irrigation raised the water table, allowing alkali to rise through capillary action. Many acres of vineyards at the University's Kearney Ranch near Fresno had been ruined. Though Kelley held out little hope for reclamation of "black" alkali soils, he described treatments for "white" alkali through better drainage, leaching, and application of gypsum or other flocculating agents.[37]

In succeeding years University scientists focused intensively on the alkali problem in cooperation with federal and state agencies. In drainage districts organized throughout the affected parts of the Central Valley, deep pumping wells began to lower the water table. Fundamental laboratory studies on base exchange began to yield important results on the chemical processes in soils, and pot experiments helped determine plant response to various soil treatments. With the help of farm advisors, researchers conducted field trials treating soil deficiencies with various additives including sulfur and lime. By the end of the decade these measures had materially improved the outlook for affected lands, and experiments at the Kearney Ranch began to offer hope for reclamation of black-alkali areas.

104    Other soils work included experiments with subsoiling and blasting to make heavy soils more permeable, measurements of the "duty of water" (requirements to satisfy the needs of plant growth) in irrigation on sandy soils, measurements of subsidence in the peat soils of the Delta due to cultivation (farmland on the Lower Jones Tract, for instance, was measured to sink 6 feet between 1902 and 1929), experiments with mulches to aid early seed germination, and study of the importance of various trace elements or micronutrients to plant growth.[38]

### ANIMAL SCIENCE

During the 1920s the east half of the Berkeley campus (about 260 acres) was still used for a foothill pasture and a certified dairy (which sold products in the community), but most of the University's animal science research took place at Davis. The breeding studies begun earlier at the University Farm continued to dominate. College purebred herds of beef cattle and dairy cows won awards in state and national exhibitions all through the decade, adding to the prestige of the University. Stockmen's Week at Davis became an annual event. In 1921 the U.S. War Department established an army remount stallion-breeding station at Davis to provide high-quality cavalry stock and saddle horses, and the famous stallion "Gunrock" in the next ten years provided stud service for nearly 500 mares. In 1923 Hunt and Hutchison arranged

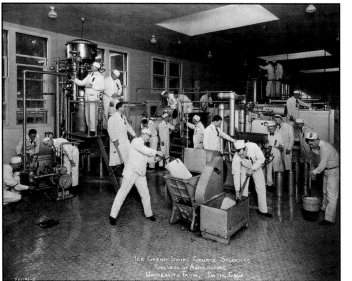

SHORT COURSE IN ICE CREAM PRODUCTION AT THE UNIVERSITY FARM IN DAVIS, ABOUT 1925.

for William M. Regan to come from the New Jersey Experiment Station with his entire dairy herd, and for many years at Davis Regan continued his long-term project in crossbreeding and inbreeding, in cooperation with the USDA.

In 1921 animal scientists began a project in range cattle feeding on a leased 3,500-acre ranch in El Dorado County, and the University purchased a herd of 475 head. This venture ended two years later because of its expense, but at Davis cattle-feeding trials continued, using various farm by-products including raisin pulp, dried orange pulp, and even pineapple pulp from Hawaii. By the end of the 1920s animal scientists were pursuing long-range nutritional trials to study the effects of diet on animal weight gain, metabolism, and reproductive health. These experiments were particularly significant at a time when large cattle feedlots were being established in the Imperial and southern San Joaquin valleys and near the major urban centers of Los Angeles and San Francisco. These studies also proved useful for better understanding of human nutrition, particularly the importance of vitamins in maintaining optimal health.

California dairy production received enormous boosts from University research and extension work during the decade. In 1920 the University announced a two-year State Dairy Cow Competition with large prizes offered by the dairy industry; more than 1,200 cows belonging to more than 70 owners from Del Norte to Imperial counties enrolled, and many production records were broken. In 1922 the Extension Service undertook a statewide dairy campaign aimed at doubling milk butterfat production in participating herds from the 1920 average of 182 pounds to 265 pounds by 1930. That goal was achieved through an educational campaign emphasizing the importance of cow-testing associations, purebred bulls, herd health, and better management.

Animal science facilities at Davis improved and expanded. In 1921 sheep specialist James Wilson helped establish a laboratory for research on wool technology, including biological aspects of wool production, and sheep crossbreeding experiments began to significantly improve wool output and fiber characteristics.[39] In 1922 a new dairy building opened. Research projects included cheese making (jack, Neufchâtel, cheddar, and a goat's-milk Roquefort), investigation of off-flavors in milk, studies of ice-cream quality and "sticky butter" problems, and the keeping quality of various types of milk container. In 1927 the legislature appropriated $300,000 for a large, new, modern animal science building, dedicated a year later (now known as Hart Hall in honor of George H. Hart, chairman of the animal science division from 1926 to 1948 and later Dean of the School of Veterinary Medicine).

CEREAL HYBRIDIZATION WORK, A COOPERATIVE PROJECT BETWEEN THE USDA AND FACULTY AT THE UNIVERSITY FARM.

Animal disease control work was varied and important. Cooperative work between the College, the State Department of Agriculture, and the USDA stopped a serious epidemic of foot-and-mouth disease in 1924. Researchers continued to work on ways to combat other serious common diseases, such as infectious abortion and anaplasmosis in cattle and typhoid, "blackhead," and coccidiosis in poultry.

With poultry production flourishing in the 1920s, the Experiment Station assisted producers with general brooding and feeding improvements and better storage methods. County farm bureaus sponsored statewide egg-laying contests that markedly increased farmer interest. Two Extension poultry specialists visited large and small laying operations. In 1928 a two-story poultry laboratory with several poultry houses went up in Strawberry Canyon behind the Berkeley campus, supplanting the discontinued Petaluma research station and retaining a bit of rural flavor in that area of the campus until the 1960s.[40]

## PLANT SCIENCE

Plant scientists of the 1920s continued variety testing and improvement of cultural practices for a wide range of crops. Postharvest handling studies, particularly packing and shipping techniques, also became important as the interstate fresh fruit and vegetable trade grew.

"Better seed" campaigns brought big improvements in the cereal crops. New varieties increased yields in wheat, barley, oats, and several economic range grasses; the agronomy division distributed free seed to farmers who would cooperate in expanding the supply. In 1928 an Extension agronomist began to supervise replication trials, eventually helping to develop the Cal Approved Seed certification program.[41] Plant breeders selected strains of dwarf milo to avoid lodging (flattening of the crop by wind or bad weather), making machine harvesting feasible and improving recovery of product. They also worked toward developing disease and insect resistance in alfalfa, which for a time in the 1920s suffered

106 from a severe bacterial wilt that threatened many stands. The College continued to introduce new forage crops, such as Ladino clover, Egyptian berseem, vetches, and cowpeas.

Although the College had conducted cotton trials at the Kearney vineyard in 1910 and in the Imperial Valley in 1912, California cotton really began to flourish in the 1920s because of high postwar prices. In 1922 the U.S. Bureau of Plant Industry established a Cotton Field Station at Shafter. To help standardize the industry and prevent hybridization problems, the state legislature passed a one-variety law in 1925, restricting cotton planting to the Acala variety in the nine southern San Joaquin Valley counties. With this regulation and the aid of farm advisors, the valley's cotton yield per acre nearly doubled in the next twenty years.

The College began collaborating in USDA rice experiments at the Biggs station in the Sacramento Valley in 1927, and that year the Meloland station began variety trials with flax from India.

Horticultural work expanded. Exploratory studies of potential new crops focused on "exotics" including dates, carob, pomegranates, and persimmons, and the Experiment Station issued major bulletins on almonds, figs, and avocadoes. Researchers produced a bulletin on Turkish tobacco growing after a cigarette manufacturing company began business in California in the early 1920s, but this industry did not become permanently established. Horticultural experiment facilities included the Mountain View Deciduous Fruit Station in Santa Clara County and twelve permanent demonstration vineyards in six counties. At Davis a new Horticulture Hall opened in 1922, a truck crops division was organized, and several new staff members began work in olericulture (vegetable production). By 1927 there were 1,350 named varieties of fruits and nuts in the Davis experimental orchards, and a major peach- and nectarine-breeding program began in 1928. At Riverside citrus research included new studies on fertilization, pruning, windbreaks, and protective orchard heating devices. Riverside also began permanent plantings of figs, olives, and persimmons in 1928.

Rapid growth of the Extension Service and the farm bureaus brought the results of research more quickly to the field. By the mid-1920s farm advisors were running hundreds of test plots and extension demonstrations annually. The important vegetable-growing counties—Imperial, Los Angeles, Monterey, San Joaquin, and Sacramento—began to prosper as a result of Extension trials with asparagus, cabbage, melons, potatoes, sweet corn, squash, spinach, tomatoes, and root crops.

Though much of the work of plant scientists was geared toward fairly rapid application, many breeding studies in annual and perennial crops were a long-range commitment requiring years for accurate assessment, as was the basic genetics work on the genus *Crepis* (the chicory tribe of the sunflower family), supported by Adams Act funds of 1906.[42]

## PEST AND PLANT DISEASE CONTROL

After some twenty years of constantly increasing research in pest control, the University of California became nationally known for its work in entomology and plant pathology. In 1918 a division of entomology was established at Riverside, and the research of H. J. Quayle and others eventually brought international recognition. (Quayle was one of the first to recognize that insects could develop resistance to treatments, noting in 1918 that both the black scale and the California red scale had become resistant to fumigation with hydrocyanic acid.)[43] In 1919 the legislature appropriated $100,000 for horticultural research on the management of plant diseases. In 1923 the State Department of Agriculture officially transferred its work in biological control to the University.

Research in pest control during this period was immensely varied. At the Mountain View Deciduous Fruit Station, work concentrated on fruit brown rot, oak root fungus, and other problems, until the station was abandoned in 1925. Three years later the station was re-established near San Jose in a fertile area of orchards and truck farms. At Davis, Riverside, Berkeley, and across the state, scientists studied the peach borer, alfalfa weevil, grape leafhopper, beet leafhopper, various aphids, and other pests too numerous to mention; fig rot, strawberry yellows, recurring serious problems with smut and rust of cereal crops, walnut blight, curly top of sugar beets, and other diseases. Their work helped overcome many serious problems in the fields of California. From Australia, for example, researchers adapted the use of copper carbonate dust as a fungicidal treatment for cereal seed, preventing bunt or "stinking smut" and several other diseases of wheat and barley. They demonstrated that other dusts, such as pulverized organic mercury compounds and red copper oxide, were effective in controlling seed- and soilborne fungi, and that in orchards nicotine dust treatment could control pear thrips and the

grape leafhopper. They pursued biological controls for some pests, following up on practices established in California in the 1890s when USDA agents imported the predacious ladybird or Vedalia beetle from Australia to control the cottony cushion scale then threatening the citrus industry. Until political upheavals ended some travel, College affiliates made collecting trips to China, North Africa, and other areas to find the natural enemies of pests causing problems in California.

The introduction of new crops and expansion of others brought continual appearance of new pest problems. During the 1920s staff members developed much useful information about pest life cycles, remedies, and preventive cultural practices. Gradually, as the study of plant nutrition developed, researchers began to recognize that some diseases resulted from previously unknown imbalances in soil elements, and that others were caused by viruses just beginning to be understood.[44]

## AGRICULTURAL ENGINEERING

The University Farm's farm mechanics courses developed into an organized division of agricultural engineering in 1915. As farmers began to invest in tractors after the war,

TRACTOR REPAIR LABORATORY SECTION IN THE FARM MECHANICS COURSE IN DAVIS, 1920S.

interest in engineering expanded. The division trained increasing numbers of students and held dozens of traveling "tractor schools" in outlying areas. In 1921 alone twelve one-week schools attracted more than 500 enrollees to learn about the overhaul and repair of tractor engines and moving parts. Using a set of portable displays, engineering staff explained the principles of internal combustion to thousands of curious farmers and encouraged the widespread adoption of labor-saving machinery. A few years later, faculty member A. H. Hoffman's work on dust separation in tractor engines drew interest from the automobile industry for its applicability to general problems of engine wear.

Agricultural engineers also designed plans for better barns, silos, milk houses, poultry houses, lambing sheds, and other farm buildings. Eventually more than 60 types of plans were available on request for a modest charge, and farm operators bought thousands during the interwar years. During the 1920s agricultural engineers also tested farm fencing, solar heaters, and adobe and earth wall construction, studied the use of electricity on farms; improved methods for bulk grain handling, investigated the kinematics and dynamics of wheel-type tractors, tested rice combine harvesters, and designed new milk containers, dairy sterilizers, can washers, and orchard heaters.

In 1926 a professional agricultural engineering program began at Davis as a major in the College of Mechanical Engineering at Berkeley. By 1928 the importance of agricultural engineering on the Davis campus was celebrated with the opening of a modern engineering building (later named Walker Hall for Harry B. Walker, chairman of agricultural engineering from 1928 to 1947).[45]

## NUTRITION AND FOOD SCIENCE

Until M. E. Jaffa retired in 1926, the division of nutrition in the College of Agriculture continued food analysis and dietary studies. For a decade or so after the establishment of the division of household science within the College of Letters and Science at Berkeley (1918), research conducted there overlapped to some degree with that in the College of Agriculture. In 1927 some of the Purnell funds allotted to the Experiment Station were used to support joint projects in the study of vitamins in dried fruits, but it was not until the late 1930s that household science entered the College of Agriculture as part of a new department of home economics.[46]

The division of viticulture and enology, its work in wine-making terminated by passage of the Volstead Act in 1919, became the division of viticulture and fruit products. Staff research during Prohibition concentrated on food preservation and processing. W. V. Cruess and others continued to search for new ways to utilize California's excess agricultural products. Some of their projects included refinements in grape and other fruit juices, fruit concentrates and syrups, marmalade, candy, dried fruit products, pear "butter," and avocado oil. Cruess undertook a special study of olive canning and oil refining after several deaths from botulism were attributed to California canned olives in 1919. His trips to southern Europe, where olives were a staple crop, contributed to a better understanding of olive-processing methods, and two Experiment Station bulletins were issued on the subject in 1925. Eventually UC researchers, in cooperation with the Stanford Medical School, conquered the botulism problem by introducing pasteurization and other controls in canning, and the olive industry, in decline for almost a decade, began to revive. In the late 1920s Cruess and M. A. Joslyn began research on freezing technology, anticipating what would later become a major industry outlet for California fruits and vegetables.[47]

## FORESTRY

Until 1939, when it became a full-fledged department, the division of forestry remained in the College of Agriculture.

During the 1920s forestry research expanded at Whitaker's Forest, a 320-acre Sierra forest reserve in Tulare County bequeathed to the University in 1914. This was a decade in which California conservationists became greatly concerned about exploitation of California's great redwood forests, and popular groups including the Sierra Club and the Save-the-Redwoods League actively lobbied for a state park system, permanent state forest reserves, and greater control over the lumber industry. The University's division of forestry helped the lumber industry begin to make progress in silviculture and sound forest management practices, including plans for second-growth harvesting. Forest and rangeland specialists also inventoried Sierra pine regions, measured eucalyptus growth rates, experimented with wood technologies, and performed time studies to measure the cost-efficiency of tractor logging, then beginning to revolutionize logging operations in California. The first Extension forestry specialist, Woodbridge Metcalf, focused particularly on timber species evaluation, growth and yield studies, and lumber mill efficiency.

In 1927 the U.S. Forest Experiment Station and Educational Headquarters of the National Park Service took up residence in Hilgard Hall. That same year Walter Mulford, head of the division of forestry, took his sabbatical year in Europe to study forest policy in Germany and other timber-producing countries with the hope of helping California develop a sound policy. Subsequent policy studies by the University included attention to the problems of private use of government lands, especially grazing and recreation.[48]

FIELD TRIP TO DURHAM BY AUSTRALIAN SOLDIERS STUDYING AT THE UNIVERSITY FARM, ABOUT 1920. ELWOOD MEAD STANDS IN THE FOREGROUND, HAND IN POCKET.

## "RURAL INSTITUTIONS" AND AGRICULTURAL ECONOMICS

By 1919, under Elwood Mead's supervision, the Division of Rural Institutions was fully occupied with the land settlement colony at Durham. The apparent rousing success of that project had attracted national attention, and U.S. Secretary of the Interior Franklin K. Lane promoted the idea of similar ventures in other states for soldiers returning from the war.[49] The postwar agricultural crisis, however, changed conditions and plans, and state-sponsored land settlements turned out to be short-lived. The Division of Rural Institutions was to share their fate.

## THE DEMISE OF THE STATE LAND SETTLEMENT EXPERIMENT

The enthusiasm for state land settlement projects that began in the prewar period reached its height at just about the time America entered the Great War. The California Land Settlement Board created by the legislature in 1917 began its work, in fact, under the cloud of that conflict. Five months after the declaration of war, in September 1917, the board issued its first announcement of terms for offers of land. The purchase of the Durham tract in Butte County was made in early 1918; the first allotments were offered for sale on May 15. With excellent planning and organization, the first year's activities appeared to go extremely well, and the success and excitement of the first year carried past the November Armistice into 1919. The legislature that year appropriated $1 million for further land settlement work, even approving a $10 million revolving fund for development, although this "was rendered void by the California Supreme Court for technical reasons."[50]

With Durham thriving, the board pressed forward with a plan for a second settlement in the San Joaquin Valley, this one for returning war veterans. In November 1919 the board purchased a tract of 7,654 acres at Delhi, a few miles southeast of Turlock, center of one of the state's most successful early public irrigation districts. Six miles south of the Delhi site was the community of Livingston, which had been settled by Japanese immigrants about 1906. The Japanese colony had struggled through some grim years in a dusty, windy area invaded periodically by plagues of grasshoppers, but their skills as farmers—and their powers of endurance—had eventually brought them a modest prosperity. Organizers of the Delhi colony must have reasoned that a state-sponsored settlement could do as well.[51]

The Delhi tract was divided into four units to be developed in annual phases. Engineers planned an elaborate irrigation system, necessary because of the porous soils and rolling topography, and construction began on ditches and laterals for the first unit. Because small laborers' allotments had sold so well at Durham, the board authorized twice the relative number at Delhi. Two townsites, at Delhi and at Ballico, were plotted according to plans drawn up in the College division of landscape design, and construction on several community buildings began along with road grading and tree planting. About 150 acres of the first unit were planted to alfalfa and 170 set out in vineyard.

Publicity for Delhi was widespread. Mead himself contributed a number of articles to periodicals, including the popular *Sunset* (June 1923), and kept up an extensive correspondence with editors and advertising agencies. The board reported receiving 8,000 inquiry letters from across the country. Yet when the first unit opened in May 1920, sales were sluggish. By September 30 about a third of the farms and 11 of the 58 workers' allotments were still for sale. While the settlers at Durham, chosen from a pool of applicants, were generally "of a type that any community would consider desirable," the dearth of applications at Delhi contributed to "a curiously diverse group" of colonists. Many were inexperienced in California farming, some were apparently convinced that state aid would ensure success regardless of effort, and many who purchased the small allotments were evidently attracted primarily by the inexpensive homes. Depending on their allotments, settlers were encouraged to try alfalfa and dairying, orchards and vineyards, and, on the poorest soils, poultry farms. By 1922 about half the settlers were veterans receiving vocational training and a monthly stipend from the federal government. Many other settlers, discouraged with the sand-dune soils and general difficulties, left to seek other opportunities. By the time the third and fourth units opened in 1922 and 1923, few applicants appeared. In 1924 nearly half of the entire settlement—3,528 acres—remained unsold.[52]

With costs in both Delhi and Durham running much higher than anticipated and little income coming in, settler resentment began to develop, particularly at Delhi. Although the board made great efforts to assist settlers in both colonies, soliciting technical advice from the College of Agriculture and employing resident managers, production problems arose and got worse. In Durham the adobe clay areas became waterlogged after a few years of irrigation, and due to an inadequate drainage system alfalfa did poorly. Disease—especially prune dieback—hit the orchards, and even on the good soils the high water table menaced tree survival. In Delhi the problems were wind, rabbits, undulating topography, and a heavy, sandy soil that swallowed water as fast as it could be applied. The expensive irrigation system proved insufficient; lateral pipes were too small, and long irrigation runs were impossible in the porous ground. Crops suffered from soil nutrient deficiencies, diseases such as bacterial wilt and little-leaf, and nematodes—all problems that were as yet poorly understood.

IRRIGATION IN A YOUNG VINEYARD AT THE DELHI LAND SETTLEMENT PROJECT, EARLY 1920S.

These physical and biological difficulties combined with the unfavorable economic climate to discourage even the most committed settlers. By 1922 many in both colonies were in deep financial trouble, unable to meet their loan repayment schedules and in need of more investment capital to deal with needs that had been underestimated. In November a potential infusion of state funds through a $3 million bond issue for land settlement work was rejected by the voters. In Delhi settlers became embittered and hostile, forming a Settlers Welfare League in 1923 to demand a reorganization of financing. When the Veterans Bureau investigated conditions at Delhi, it heard much critical testimony against the administration.

The crucial leader, Elwood Mead, left for several months in 1923 to conduct some international consulting work. On his return he decided that the board should foreclose on delinquent loan repayments. Governor Friend Richardson, though no advocate for the projects, called this action "inhuman" and immediately appointed C. M. Wooster, a critic of land settlement, to replace Mead as head of the board. At that point Mead decided to leave California permanently to work for the U.S. Bureau of Reclamation (where he served as director until his death in 1936).

Although the legislature passed some relief measures and settler debts were adjusted in 1925, the improved attitudes that followed did not last. At both Durham and Delhi the orchards and vineyards planted as long-term investments turned out to be disappointments. Problems mounted with each season, economic conditions in agriculture remained depressed, and for several years both communities languished, their settlers going deeper and deeper into debt. In 1927 the new Governor, C. C. Young, appointed an investigating committee, which ultimately reported that "land settlement under the State . . . from

112 its inception was a mistaken theory. . . . We earnestly recommend that no other or further attempt be made in that direction." In 1929 the legislature took action to buy out all delinquent settlers and assume all losses. In 1931 the State Land Settlement Board was finally dissolved.[53]

Perhaps it was partly the land settlement crisis that prompted the departure of both Hunt and Mead in 1923. Certainly the change of leadership within the College brought about a shift of emphasis within the Division of Rural Institutions. Nevertheless, the experiment continued to have some educational impact. Until his death in 1927, retired Dean Hunt pursued an Experiment Station project related to the broad topic of colonization; he began but did not complete a study of factors in the success of the private colony at Patterson in Stanislaus County. He also organized a popular two-semester course in "Comparative Agriculture," which reviewed agricultural conditions and practices from ancient to present times and then surveyed progress and problems in several California counties. Meanwhile, Mead in the mid-1920s participated in a national fact-finding commission study of similar project failures for the Bureau of Reclamation. For economists the failure of the settlements at Durham and Delhi provided an opportunity for some close analysis that in the long run gave a better understanding of pivotal factors in the success of irrigated agriculture. For years afterward University staff members debated the implications of the land settlement experience, and several of their research projects were at least obliquely related.

One publication of 1927, "The Problem of Securing Closer Relationship between Agricultural Development and Irrigation Construction," provides some interesting insights not only into the Durham and Delhi failures, but into the problems of all those attempting to farm in the 1920s:

> Farmers who bought and developed their farms in any year prior to 1919 made improvements under conditions of cost . . . better than those which have confronted the farmer making improvements in any year since. The farmer developing prior to 1918 had the added advantage of an increased ability to make repayment during the years 1918, 1919, and 1920, due to high prices for commodities sold. Farmers purchasing farms and improving them in 1919 and 1920 were unfortunate and will be compelled to write off some of their invested capital. . . .
>
> The cost of development in 1918 was 44 percent greater than it would have been had the farm been developed in 1914. At costs prevailing in 1920, it would have required an outlay 110 percent greater than in 1914. . . .
>
> Capital requirements [for irrigated agriculture] so frequently exceed the amount possessed by the settler, that even the generous terms of [the California Land Settlement Act] may not have provided funds sufficient for economic development.[54]

## THE RISE OF AGRICULTURAL ECONOMICS

California's state land colonies ran into difficulties at about the same time that interest in the study of agricultural economics was on the rise. Well before the war "country lifers" including Bailey and Hunt had emphasized the importance of understanding the business as well as the science of farming. In 1910 a group in the American Association of Agricultural Colleges and Experiment Stations (AAACES) organized the American Farm Management Association. Hunt clarified some disagreements over terminology and subject matter (the distinction between rural economics and farm management) in the report he prepared for the AAACES in 1911. In 1919 the American Farm Management Association became the American Farm Economic Association, and the Office of Farm Management in the U.S. Department of Agriculture was reorganized to reflect new thinking along broader lines. In 1920 Cornell established the first university department of agricultural economics in the nation. When the early 1920s demonstrated that American farmers were operating in a changing world of forces beyond their individual control, Congress approved the Purnell Act (1925), which allocated funds for the study of agricultural economics and rural sociology in the land-grant universities. At that time the USDA also launched a series of "outlook" studies to better understand trends in agricultural marketing.[55]

Developments at the University paralleled these trends. In 1922 economist Henry Erdman joined the division of rural institutions to begin compiling information on the operation of various kinds of cooperative organizations in California. (Some of Erdman's early work appeared in *Circular 298*, "The Possibilities and Limitations of Cooperative Marketing," and a couple of years later he produced a model constitution for organizing a cooperative.) After the departures of Hunt and Mead, Dean Merrill appointed Erdman head of the renamed division of rural economics in 1924. Two years later the division metamorphosed into the division of agricultural economics.[56] Just as drastic problems arising from the overplanting of several California crops were becoming apparent, the Purnell Act made federal funds available for "investigations . . . bearing directly on the production, manufacture, preparation, use, distribution, and marketing of agricultural products," with the express purpose of fostering a "permanent and efficient agricultural industry."[57] Although California at first had trouble attracting top-ranked economists because of salary differentials, several new young staff members began work on commodity studies, including Berkeley's first Ph.D. in agricultural economics, Harry R. Wellman, also the first economics specialist in the Extension Service.

In 1926 E. C. Voorhies produced the first crop and price outlook study, a detailed description of the California poultry industry reviewing historic production and consumption trends along with factors influencing current prices and projections, including the competition from other states and abroad. Wellman's analysis of the apricot industry, the first Extension Circular in the Series on Crops and Prices,

appeared about the same time. In it Wellman described the expansion in apricot acreage between 1918 and 1926 and gave warning of future low incomes as a result of higher production. Two more publications, on peaches and lettuce, followed. By the end of 1929 the series included studies thoroughly analyzing the apple, almond, asparagus, bean, cattle, cherry, dairy, grape, pear, plum, and prune industries. At more than 300 local Extension meetings, the economics staff distributed and explained this information to more than 16,000 California farmers. Much of the material was condensed into a comprehensive bulletin issued in 1928, "The Agricultural Situation in California."[58]

Other work in agricultural economics in the 1920s included a report on farm tenancy in California, an analysis of "work horse economics," reviews of operating costs for equipment and machinery, an investigation of factors influencing land values, and a state-requested study on Mexican farm labor.

## THE GIANNINI FOUNDATION

Inextricably linked with agricultural economics at the University of California is the name of Amadeo Peter Giannini, founder of the Bank of America. The son of immigrant Italian vegetable growers in the Santa Clara Valley, Giannini in 1904 established the Bank of Italy to serve the needs of Bay Area farmers for credit. Energetic and enterprising, Giannini was the first San Francisco banker to reopen for business after the 1906 earthquake and fire. His business prospered, and by World War I the Bank of Italy was handling many millions of dollars. Giannini understood the needs of farmers and recognized opportunities in rural California; his bank pioneered with branch banking at a time when few others wanted to venture into the small towns and cities of the interior valleys. By the mid-1920s the Bank of Italy was a force to be reckoned with. In subsuming smaller banking operations during the decade, its directors decided to give it

114 the name of a subsidiary purchased in New York in 1927, and in early 1928 the Bank of Italy became the Bank of America.[59]

About that time the bank's directors, wanting to honor Giannini on his sixtieth birthday, offered him a generous bonus. Giannini recommended that the money be given instead to the University for its work in agricultural economics. On February 14, 1928, the Regents accepted the bank's offer, announcing formation of the Giannini Foundation with an endowment of $1.5 million—a gift probably unique in the history of agricultural research at American universities.

One-third of the gift was earmarked for building the third and easternmost structure in the agriculture group at the Berkeley campus, to be called Giannini Hall. The rest went into a permanent endowment fund for research bearing on "the economic status of California agriculturalists," so that they might "profit from the existence of favorable facts and conditions, and . . . protect themselves as well as possible from adverse facts and conditions." The gift document laid out in detail the subject matter of the Foundation's work:

> The activities of the Foundation shall be embraced by the great field of Agricultural Economics, and relate to such subjects as: (a) the economic consequences of increased production which result from improved seed grains, improved nursery stock, improved live stock, improved machinery, and improved methods of farming; (b) the economic consequences of overproduction arising from unusually favorable seasons or unusually unfavorable seasons as to weather and other conditions in the producing nations; (c) the relations between conditions existing in the farming industry and the general economic conditions prevailing in the nation, and internationally; (d) the acquiring of such knowledge concerning soil qualities and climatic and other conditions in any or all parts of the State of California, and of such knowledge concerning existing or prospective supply and demand conditions for the various agricultural products of this State, as will enable the appropriate representatives of the foundation to advise the farmers of California as to wise plantings, sowings,

> breedings, etc., in relation to areas and kinds; (e) the methods and problems of disposing of farm products on terms or conditions giving maximum degree of satisfaction to the producers; (f) any economic questions which concern the individual farmer and the members of his family, and affect their living conditions.[60]

It specified that the University, in selecting members of the staff, should appoint "the most competent persons whose services are available, without restriction as to citizenship or race."

Claude B. Hutchison, former director of the Northern Branch of the College at Davis, returned from four years abroad with the Rockefeller Foundation to become the first director of the Giannini Foundation. Its seventeen charter members included all the faculty in agricultural economics and the economics specialists of the Agricultural Extension Service; B. H. Crocheron received a special appointment as an associate.

Among the first Giannini Foundation research activities were a study of the practices of foreign governments in promoting agricultural commodities competitive with those of California; a study of the factors responsible for yearly variations in prices of peaches and grapes, for use in stabilization programs; and partial support of an eight-month information-gathering tour by Crocheron and two assistants to seven Asian countries to investigate their market potential for California crops.[61]

In 1930 Giannini Hall was completed and dedicated. The new building provided space for administrative and faculty offices and for the Giannini Foundation library, which would become an outstanding research facility. Also housed in the building were the state offices of the California Farm Bureau Federation and several USDA agencies. In the marble lobby was placed a large portrait of Amadeo Giannini—which still dominates the space, along with another large portrait of Elwood Mead.

## THE EXTENSION SERVICE AND THE FARM BUREAU

By 1919 more than 3,500 of the nation's 4,000 counties had extension agents. When special appropriations ceased after the war, however, both nationally and in California the Extension Service suffered a temporary decline. Nearly half of California's farm and home advisors resigned in 1919. Nevertheless, local governments had seen the benefits of extension work, and state and county funds began to replace lost federal monies. By 1923, when Crocheron submitted his tenth-anniversary report, 41 of the state's 58 counties had farm advisors and 21 had home demonstration agents. There were also 33 assistant farm advisors and 12 state specialists in the fields of agricultural engineering, citriculture, dairying, farm management, home economics (3), illustrative materials, irrigation, poultry (2), and walnut growing.[62]

The decade of the twenties became the golden age for extension work. Farm and home advisors had enormous opportunities for helping farm families achieve more reliable livelihoods and better lives. Typically young, energetic, and idealistic, Extension agents were always on the go, their motorcycles or Model T's familiar sights along rural roads.

### B. H. CROCHERON

In 1919, at the age of 35, B. H. Crocheron was appointed director of the California Agricultural Extension Service. He held the position for nearly 30 years until his death in 1948, shaping its evolution and influencing two generations of farm advisors. Meticulous in his attention to detail, tall and elegant in appearance, Bertram Hanford Crocheron commanded great respect rather than affection among his staff. He was a careful administrator, strict but fair, requiring detailed weekly reports from the county offices, on which he based the impressive statistics contained in his

EARLY FARM BUREAU TRAVEL CONFERENCE ON THE BERKELEY CAMPUS.

116 own annual reports. A highly regarded public speaker and natural teacher, Crocheron had the power to motivate and inspire. Over the years his nickname became "the Chief"; while some idolized him, others described him as an autocrat running a quasi-military organization. Despite his visibility in his public role, in some ways he was a remote and mysterious figure. He had roots in the Country Life Movement and was a profound admirer of Liberty Hyde Bailey, yet when he arrived in Berkeley for the first time he was wearing spats and a top hat. His life's work revolved around farm people, but his personal interests included a small yacht and an elegant home with furnishings from Asia. He read widely and wrote eloquently, but he was a lifelong bachelor and rarely socialized. After the heady days of the Progressive period he became politically conservative, adamantly opposing Extension participation in "New Deal" farm programs during the Depression. Like Dean Hutchison, in the 1930s he was seriously concerned about the Communist threat to American institutions. A dominant leader and a master at organizing, he developed a separatist kind of governance for the Extension Service that left its legacy for many years.[63]

Throughout his years as director Crocheron mandated attendance at an annual conference for Extension staff on the Berkeley campus. He greeted each person by name and usually delivered a noteworthy address at the evening banquet. Another traditional Extension event during the 1920s was the weeklong "traveling conference," during which a caravan of cars containing county farm advisors and farm bureau representatives traveled for several hundred miles through a series of statewide stops viewing selected farms and other sites. Crocheron's orchestration of this event even included a bugle call to signal each day's caravan formation.[64]

DEMONSTRATION OF TREE PLANTING BY THE AGRICULTURAL EXTENSION SERVICE, 1920S.

## THE COLLEGE IN THE COUNTRYSIDE

Since its beginnings the primary role of the Agricultural Extension Service has been to disseminate, on the local level, information gathered through the research of the Agricultural Experiment Station. Extension work is basically adult education. The most effective farm and home advisors are those who can directly adapt research knowledge to local conditions, persuading progressive-minded farmers and others to collaborate. Thus advisors must be both technically competent and articulate teachers and leaders. Above all, they must be able to relate well to skeptical, independent adults who may range widely in schooling and experience.

The demonstration methods pioneered by Seaman Knapp and his county agents in the South were core to early extension teaching: demonstrations of *methods*, such as seed selection or pruning techniques, or of *results*, such as fertilizer trials in test plots. Another effective educational device was the production contest, mounted at levels from the local farm center to the statewide Farm Bureau.

During the 1920s Extension work included in its goals not just the transmission of information about ways to improve farm productivity, but the encouragement of social connections and leadership among rural people. Monthly meetings at the local farm centers drew together many families who otherwise might have remained in semi-isolation on their farms. As they became better acquainted and exposed to the possibilities of group action, they began to build effective coalitions for change. One early function of the local farm bureaus, for example, was to develop by consensus an annual community program of work, which called on members to organize projects in rural improvement. Community-based work during the 1920s included the organization of rural fire protection districts; large-scale rodent control campaigns; cooperative construction of farm septic systems; home demonstrations in first aid, family nutrition, and healthy child development; landscaping around schools and homes; local economic outlook meetings; and businessmen's tours of rural areas (initiated by Crocheron to discourage uninformed land speculation). These projects worked together with production-based activities to develop a more healthful and satisfying life in rural areas.

Some extension work had long-range impacts whose significance was probably not fully appreciated at the time. Home demonstration activities helped combat the isolation and expand the horizons of many overworked farm women, improving their self-confidence and leadership skills while teaching better homemaking methods. Youth work—the popular 4-H clubs in which boys and girls took on practical annual projects raising crops or animals, preserving food, or constructing clothing—brought to a growing generation many new interests, opportunities, and aspirations.

Unquestionably, extension work had a great impact on its clientele and on the development of rural communities. Crocheron, who kept careful records, reported in 1926 that farm and home advisors were making more than half a million contacts annually. He wrote (perhaps tongue in cheek), "The number of persons attending meetings conducted by members of the Agricultural Extension Service in a given year are more than double . . . those attending all football games

VENTURA COUNTY BOYS' CLUB EXHIBIT BEFORE A TRAVELING FARM BUREAU CONFERENCE SPONSORED BY THE AGRICULTURAL EXTENSION SERVICE, EARLY 1920S.

118 played by the University team."[65] The farm bureau centers were true grassroots units through which farm and home advisors could multiply their efforts in education and community improvement many times over. Part of the genius of the extension system was its involvement of the whole farm family in projects bringing both economic and social returns.

## THE FARM BUREAU BECOMES AN INDEPENDENT ENTITY

Although originally the local farm bureaus were organized as support groups for the educational work of the Agricultural Extension Service, within a few years farmers across the country realized their potential for acting on many general economic and political concerns. Even before the war some farm bureaus had begun to organize cooperatives for purchasing supplies and pooling marketable products; some had formed commodity interest groups; and others had seen swift results from political activity at the county level. Postwar concerns encouraged the affiliation of these local groups into a larger organization able to act in the state or national arena.

In October 1919 representatives of all the county farm bureaus in California met on the Berkeley campus to organize the California Farm Bureau Federation (CFBF). In Chicago the next month this fledgling organization participated in the formation of a national federation, the American Farm Bureau Federation (AFBF), officially ratified by state groups in March 1920. AFBF immediately opened an office in Washington, D.C., to participate in national farm policy discussions. As the postwar agricultural crisis spurred farmers to seek congressional help for their problems, AFBF membership soared to 466,421 by 1921.[66] So rapid was the transformation of the Farm Bureau into a political entity—and so critical became other farm organizations of the Farm Bureau's connections with Extension—that a congressional investigation was held, and the U.S. Department of Agriculture issued a "memorandum of understanding" to better define the relationship of the Farm Bureau to the Extension Service.[67]

CFBF family membership doubled from 10,794 in 1920 to 20,421 in 1930. Crocheron reported what seems to have been a peak of 568 local farm centers in 41 counties about 1925, with an average attendance of about 46 at monthly meetings. Besides cooperating with Extension educational work, these local bureaus purchased fuel, fertilizer, and feed for their members, held livestock auctions, set up cow-testing associations, organized labor bureaus for recruiting seasonal workers, and actively entered into county politics regarding budget and special district matters. Meanwhile, the statewide CFBF monitored legislative matters of both major and minor importance, although the organization generally kept aloof from partisan politics. Like most of the generally middle-class farmers it represented, the Farm Bureau maintained a careful conservatism in most of its activities. Other farm groups like the more populist Grange continued to complain occasionally about the linkage between the Farm Bureau and Extension, but for nearly twenty years CFBF headquarters stayed on the Berkeley campus, close to the offices of Crocheron.[68]

## REFLECTIONS ON A DECADE

The troubled twenties brought a recapitulation of old themes in the history of the College of Agriculture. The decade began with a new attempt to separate the College from the rest of the University, pushed by a farm constituency still distrustful of academic dominance at Berkeley, and for the third time in College history the state legislature intervened in its governance. In 1874 the legislative investigation of Grange complaints about the status of agriculture at Berkeley had brought about a reorganization of activities under Eugene Hilgard, who deftly handled political problems while firmly establishing the scientific reputation of the College. In 1905, as Hilgard retired, the "practical" men won their case by passing a State Farm bill establishing the University Farm School at Davis. In 1921 the Special Legislative Commission on Agricultural Education recommended a far-reaching reorganization of the University Farm by greatly expanding facilities at Davis and strengthening the academic standing of agricultural instruction there. Thus over a period of years the College of Agriculture, nudged by its clientele, adapted its work to fit the needs of the time.

These developments at the University of California generally paralleled what was also going on in other states at intervals of roughly a generation: first, the push to lay credible foundations for scientific research in agriculture; then, a drive to expand college facilities and physical plants; and, in the 1920s, a re-examination of structure and content in the agricultural curricula. The adaptations in each case were an effort to deal with the tensions engendered by mandated college commitment to "two masters"—the basic sciences and the agricultural industry. Land-grant colleges of agriculture had continually to keep in mind the twin goals of discovery and service, finding as they could a balance between the pursuit of knowledge for its own sake and the pursuit of solutions to client problems.

As the College of Agriculture completed a half century of work in California during the 1920s, its balance seemed fairly well achieved. The Agricultural Experiment Station had gained a national reputation, was attracting outstanding staff members, and continued to produce a solid record of research accomplishments both fundamental and applied. Research during this period was particularly significant in the fields of soil and plant science, animal physiology, entomology, and plant pathology. Because of their importance to California agriculture, the disciplines linked with pest control attracted a large number of research grants. Between 1920 and 1930 hundreds of bulletins and circulars appeared on an astonishing variety of subjects, and in 1925 the College began publication of *Hilgardia*, a highly respected journal of agricultural science, continuing a technical paper series begun two years before.[69]

Applied work by Extension emphasized more efficient farm management from both the technical and business points of view. The Purnell Act and later the Giannini endowment encouraged development of a strong division of agricultural economics in the College. Economists conducted pathbreaking outlook studies for most of the major commodities, took the information to farmers in public meetings, and strongly encouraged the formation of effective marketing cooperatives.

The collapse of the land settlement colonies at Durham and Delhi brought an end to the division of rural institutions. The colony experiment, though noble in intent, may have been doomed from its inception. Few utopian schemes have ever lasted long; this one met a rapid demise because of unforeseen economic and technical crises. The disaster probably influenced the future of sociological research in the College. Although several other state land-grant colleges, including Cornell and Wisconsin, supported active departments of rural sociology through the 1920s and 1930s, the whole focus of "social science" work in California shifted to agricultural economics.[70]

Meanwhile, the optimism and social activism of the Progressive era were supplanted in the 1920s by a much more conservative political climate both within the state as a whole and within the College. That conservatism would be shaken by events of the next decade.

# NOTES

1. "How 'Ya Gonna Keep 'Em Down on the Farm" by Sam M. Lewis and Joe Young, with music by Walter Donaldson, copyright 1919 by Mills Music, Inc., in Wanda Willson Whitman, ed., *Songs That Changed the World* (New York: Crown Publishers, 1969), pp. 190–91.

2. Murray Benedict, *Farm Policies of the United States, 1790–1950* (New York: The Twentieth Century Fund, 1953), p. 166; James Shideler, *Farm Crisis, 1919–1923* (Berkeley: University of California Press, 1957), p. 46.

3. Shideler, *Farm Crisis, 1919–1923* (Berkeley: UC Press), pp. 38–41.

4. Robert S. McElvaine, *The Great Depression: America 1929–1941* (New York: Random House, 1984), p. 331.

5. John Kenneth Galbraith, *The Great Crash, 1929* (Boston: Houghton Mifflin, 1954; reprinted with new introduction, 1988), pp. 168–94.

6. Rural Development Service, "Farm Population Estimates 1910–70," USDA *Statistical Bulletin 523* (July 1973).

7. Sources on the urbanization of southern California in the 1920s include Walton Bean, *California: An Interpretive History* (New York: McGraw-Hill, 1988), pp. 368–91; Carey McWilliams, *Southern California Country: An Island on the Land* (New York: Duell, Sloan and Pearce, 1946), pp. 135–37; and Robert Cleland and Osgood Hardy, *The March of Industry* (Los Angeles: Powell Publishing, 1929), passim.

8. Verne A. Stadtman, "Expansion in the Southland," in Stadtman, *The University of California, 1868–1968* (New York: McGraw-Hill, 1970), pp. 213–35.

9. See William J. Duffy, *The Sutter Basin and Its People* (Davis: privately printed, 1972).

10. H. R. Wellman, "Lettuce: Series on California Crops and Prices," Agricultural Extension Service *Circular 5* (Nov. 1926).

11. On cotton and rice, see Robert Glass Cleland, *From Wilderness to Empire: A History of California* (New York: Knopf, 1969), pp. 120–23.

12. Marquis James and Bessie R. James, *Biography of a Bank: The Story of Bank of America NT & SA* (New York: Harper & Row, 1954), pp. 72–92, 248–64.

13. Cleland, *Wilderness to Empire*, p. 115. Between 1900 and 1926 the annual production of California table grapes leaped from 12,000 to more than 366,000 tons, raisin production from 189,000 to 1,261,000 tons. See also S. W. Shear and H. F. Gould, "Economic Status of the Grape Industry," Agricultural Experiment Station *Bulletin 429* (June 1927), pp. 10, 95–109.

14. "The Agricultural Situation in California," California Agricultural Extension Service *Circular 18* (Apr. 1928), is the printed version of the California Agriculture Special Lecture series.

15. R. L. Adams, *The Marvel of Irrigation: A Record of a Quarter Century in the Turlock and Modesto Irrigation Districts, California* (San Francisco: Bond Department of The Anglo and London Paris National Bank, 1921); Edmund de S. Brunner and Mary V. Brunner, *Irrigation and Religion: A Study of Religion and Social Conditions in Two California Counties* (New York: G. H. Doran, 1922).

16. See Lorraine Jacobs Crouchett, *Filipinos in California* (El Cerrito, Calif.: Downey Place Publishing, 1982); Carey McWilliams, *Factories in the Fields: The Story of Migratory Farm Labor in California* (Boston: Little, Brown, 1939).

17. Varden Fuller, "The Supply of Agricultural Labor as a Factor in the Evolution of Farm Organization in California" (Ph.D. diss., University of California, Berkeley, 1939). Reprinted in *Violations of Free Speech and the Rights of Labor*, Senate Hearings, Subcommittee of the Committee on Education and Labor (aka La Follette Committee hearings), 76th Congress, 3rd Session (1940), Pt. 54, pp. 19777–19898, as Exhibit 8792–A. Quotes are from pp. 19811 and 19825.

18. Cletus E. Daniel, *Bitter Harvest: A History of California Farmworkers, 1870–1941* (Ithaca, N.Y.: Cornell University Press, 1981; reprinted by University of California Press, 1982), pp. 51–56, 61.

19. According to the *Oxford English Dictionary* (2nd ed., 1989), the word *agribusiness* was coined in a Harvard Business School Bulletin in 1955 to define the "many diverse enterprises which produce, process, and distribute farm products or which provide supporting services." Dictionaries do not attribute to the word any pejorative connotations, unlike some users of the term. For a discussion of the 1920s as a transition period in California agriculture, see Donald Pisani, *From the Family Farm to Agribusiness: The Irrigation Crusade in California and the West, 1850–1931* (Berkeley: University of California Press, 1984), pp. 440–52. "The Agricultural Situation in California" states, "California farms have tended to become rather small in acreage, too small in many cases to provide an income needed to care for a family and to meet business tests. . . . There may be a need these days for a readjustment in the size of acreage. Possibly some will move off, selling their holdings to their neighbors" (p. 23).

20. Facts are from *University of California Chronicle* 21 (1919).

21. Stadtman, *University of California, 1868–1968*, pp. 199–200, 242–44.

22. Ibid., pp. 252–53.

23. *Report of the College of Agriculture and the Agricultural Experiment Station of the University of California, From July 1, 1920 to June 30, 1921*, pp. 12–13.

24. On the creation of the State Department of Agriculture, see *Report of the California Department of Agriculture for the Year Ending June 30, 1920*, pp. 399–410. The agreement between the State Department of Agriculture and the College is cited in the *Report of the College of Agriculture and the Agricultural Experiment Station of the University of California, From July 1, 1922, to June 30, 1923*, p. 12.

25. Alyce Williams Jewett, *Saga of UCD* (Davis: privately printed, 1982), p. 40; *Report . . . 1920–1921*, p. 14.

26. Sproul's role in the agricultural education controversy is described in George A. Pettitt, *Twenty-Eight Years in the Life of a University President* (Berkeley: University of California, 1966), pp. 11–20.

27. *Report of the Special Legislative Commission on Agricultural Education, as authorized by A.B. 1335, 44th Session of the Legislature of California* (Sacramento: State GPO, 1923), pp. 64–65.

28. Ibid.

29. Ibid., pp. 32, 67–69.

30. *Report . . . 1922–1923*, pp. 32–37.

31. *Report of the Agricultural Experiment Station of the University of California, From July 1, 1923, to June 20, 1924*, p. 10.

32. Harry W. Lawton and Lewis G. Weathers, "The Origins of Citrus Research in California and the Founding of the Citrus Research Center and Agricultural Experiment Station," in Walter Reuther, E. Clair Calavan, and Glenn E. Carman, eds., *The Citrus Industry* (Oakland: UC Division of Agriculture and Natural Resources), vol. 5, p. 322.

33. See Stadtman, *University of California, 1868–1968*, pp. 255–57, on Campbell's accession to the presidency, and UC Archives, *Presidents' Papers*, 1923, on Campbell's deliberations regarding Merrill. In 1929 Merrill left California to become director of the New York Botanical Garden.

34. *Report of the College of Agriculture and the Agricultural Experiment Station of the University of California, From July 1, 1919 to June 30, 1920*, pp. 14–32.

35. Hans Jenny et al., "Exploring the Soils of California," in Claude B. Hutchison, ed., *California Agriculture* (Berkeley: University of California Press, 1946), p. 317–34.

36. *Report . . . 1919–1920*, p. 22.

37. See W. B. Kelley, "The Present Status of Alkali," University of California Agricultural Experiment Station *Circular 219* (May 1920). "Black" alkali soils have a high sodium content and severe

122    absorption problems; "white" alkali soils are less saline and more amenable to leaching.

38. Details on soils work were gleaned from the annual College of Agriculture and Experiment Station *Reports* of the 1920s, passim.

39. See *James F. Wilson, James F. Wilson, The Oral Reminiscences of an Old Sheepherder* (Davis: Oral History Program, 1976).

40. Animal and poultry science research projects are described in Experiment Station *Reports* of the 1920s, passim; also see Harold H. Cole, *Adventurer in Animal Science: Harold H. Cole* (Davis: Oral History Center, 1976).

41. J. Earl Coke, *Reminiscences on People and Change in California Agriculture, 1900–1975* (Davis: UC Oral History Center, 1975), pp. 23–27.

42. *Reports* of the 1920s, passim; also, Warren P. Tufts et al., "The Rich Pattern of California Crops," in Hutchison, *California Agriculture*, pp. 113–232, passim.

43. Lawton and Weathers, "Origins of Citrus Research in California," pp. 323–24.

44. Ralph E. Smith et al., "Protecting Plants from Their Enemies," in Hutchison, *California Agriculture*, pp. 239–315, passim; and College of Agriculture *Reports* of the 1920s, passim. The Vedalia story is also told in Wayne Rasmussen, *Agriculture in the United States: A Documentary History* (New York: Random House, 1975), vol. 3, pp. 2492–95.

45. Verne A. Stadtman, *Centennial Record of the University of California* (Berkeley: UC Printing Dept., 1967), pp. 169–70; College of Agriculture *Reports* of the 1920s, passim; see also *The Engineering of Abundance: An Oral History Memoir of Roy Bainer* (Davis: Oral History Center, 1975).

46. Agnes Fay Morgan, "The History of Nutrition and Home Economics in the University of California, Berkeley, 1914–1962" (unpublished manuscript in Bancroft Library, n.d.), pp. 32–35; also Stadtman, *Centennial Record*, pp. 94–95.

47. College of Agriculture *Reports* of the 1920s, passim; also William V. Cruess, *A Half Century in Food and Wine Technology* (Berkeley: Regional Oral History Office, 1967).

48. For information on the political activities of the conservation groups, see Michael P. Cohen, *The History of the Sierra Club,* *1892–1970* (San Francisco: Sierra Club Books, 1988), pp. 53–56. On forestry research, see College of Agriculture *Reports* of the 1920s, passim, especially 1928, pp. 77–80; *Woodbridge Metcalf, Extension Forester, 1926–1956* (Berkeley: Regional Oral History Office, 1969).

49. Bill G. Reid, "Franklin K. Lane's Idea for Veterans' Colonization, 1918–21," *Pacific Historical Review* 33 (Nov. 1964): 447–66.

50. Roy J. Smith, "The California State Land Settlements at Durham and Delhi," *Hilgardia* 15 (Oct. 1943), p. 410.

51. See Kesa Noda, *Yamato Colony, 1906–1960: Livingston, California* (Livingston: Livingston-Merced JACL chapter, 1981). In a letter in *California and the Oriental: Japanese, Chinese, and Hindus, Report of the State Board of Control to Governor Wm. D. Stephens,* pp. 123–25, Mead stated that one reason the board chose the Delhi land was to drive a wedge into increasing Japanese ownership in the area: in Livingston the Japanese owned 4,000 acres, and to the north of Delhi they owned 1,200. The board's haste to buy land in part caused the ultimate fiasco. Local farmers were said to describe the Delhi tract as land where even the jackrabbits had to carry their lunches; Frank Adams, *University of California, On Irrigation, Reclamation, and Water Administration* (Berkeley: Regional Cultural History Project, 1959), p. 288.

52. Smith, "Settlements at Durham and Delhi," pp. 418–21. See also Walter Packard, *Land and Power Development in California, Greece, and Latin America* (Berkeley: Regional Oral History Office, 1970), pp. 140–200.

53. Smith, "Settlements at Durham and Delhi," p. 468. In 1989, some 60 years after the land settlement experiment, the Durham rural area was prosperous, with traces of its early history still evident. The Delhi area was still not thriving.

54. David Weeks and Charles H. West, Experiment Station *Bulletin 435* (Sept. 1927), pp. 5, 75, 99.

55. Henry C. Taylor and Anne Dewees Taylor, *The Story of Agricultural Economics in the United States, 1840–1932* (Ames: Iowa State College Press, 1952), pp. 84–96.

56. For descriptions of the beginnings of agricultural economics at the University of California in the 1920s, see Henry E. Erdman, *Agricultural Economics: Teaching, Research and Writing, University of California, Berkeley, 1922–1969* (Berkeley: Regional Oral His-

tory Office, 1971), pp. 74–88, 107–23; also E. C. Voorhies, "The Beginnings of Agricultural Economics at the University of California" (unpublished manuscript dated 1939, in UC Davis Agricultural Economics Library); and Emmett Fiske, "The College and Its Constituency: Research and Community Development at the University of California, 1875–1978" (Ph.D. diss., University of California, Davis, 1979), pp. 200–207.

57. *An Act to Authorize the More Complete Endowment of Agricultural Experiment Stations, and for Other Purposes (43 Stat. 970), Approved February 24, 1925.* Sec. 1 also approves "such economic and sociological investigations as have for their purpose the development and improvement of the rural home and rural life."

58. Taylor and Taylor, *Agricultural Economics in the United States,* pp. 469–76, discusses and quotes several of these studies. See also Harry R. Wellman, *Teaching, Research and Administration, University of California 1925–1968* (Berkeley: Regional Oral History Office, 1976), pp. 33–37; and California Agricultural Extension Service *Circular 18,* "The Agricultural Situation in California."

59. James and James, *Biography of a Bank,* passim.

60. "Giannini Foundation Fund," from Regents' Minutes of February 14, 1928, copy in the Giannini Foundation Library.

61. H. R. Tolley, *How California Agriculture Profits by Economic Research: Accomplishments of the Giannini Foundation of Agricultural Economics* (Berkeley: University of California Printing Office, 1934).

62. *Report . . . 1922–1923,* pp. 316–21.

63. Details about Crocheron have been gleaned from a series of oral histories including George E. Wilson, *Farmer to Farmer Around the World* (Stockton, Calif.: University of the Pacific, 1987); Packard, *Land and Power Development;* and Wellman, *Teaching, Research and Administration;* as well as from personal interviews by the author between October and December 1987 with Extension

emeriti. For other information and several of Crocheron's public addresses, see *Bertram Hanford Crocheron, Architect and Builder of the California Agricultural Extension Service* (Berkeley: Agricultural Extension Service, 1967).

64. Ibid. Schedules of some of the traveling conferences are found in UC Archives, *College of Agriculture Files* for the 1920s.

65. *Report of the Agricultural Experiment Station of the University of California, From July 1, 1926, to June 30, 1927,* p. 104. The first ten years of extension work are reviewed in *Report . . . 1922–1923,* pp. 315–463.

66. David B. Danbom, *The Resisted Revolution: Urban America and the Industrialization of Agriculture, 1900–1930* (Ames: Iowa State University Press, 1979), p. 132.

67. See Benedict, *Farm Policies of the United States, 1790–1950,* pp. 176–78, on the history of the AFBF formation, and pp. 190–91 on criticism of the Farm Bureaus; see A. C. True, *A History of Agricultural Extension Work in the United States, 1785–1923* (Washington, D.C.: U.S. GPO, 1928), pp. 168–71, on the memorandum of understanding. Political scientist Grant McConnell gives a critical review of Farm Bureau activities and politics in *The Decline of Agrarian Democracy* (Berkeley: University of California Press, 1953).

68. See Clarke A. Chambers, *California Farm Organizations: A Historical Study of the Grange, the Farm Bureau and the Associated Farmers 1929–1941* (Berkeley: University of California Press, 1952), pp. 21–25.

69. See Axel Borg, *Bibliography of California Agricultural Experiment Station Publications, 1877 to 1975* (unpublished manuscript in UC Davis Shields Library, Bio-Ag section, 1987).

70. For a history of the development of rural sociology as a discipline, see Lowry Nelson, *Rural Sociology: Its Origin and Growth in the United States* (Minneapolis: University of Minnesota Press, 1969).

# 5

## Challenges in Peace and War

### *1930–1947*

*Postwar students on steps of North Hall, Davis, 1947. (Students unofficially dubbed it "Titus Hall," after longtime resident and favorite faculty member Charles Titus.)*

LIKE THE REST OF THE NATION, CALIFORNIA STAGGERED UNDER THE BLOWS OF THE GREAT DEPRESSION. FARM FORECLOSURES DIMINISHED THE NUMBER OF FARMS WHILE MIGRATION OF THE UNEMPLOYED FROM OUTSIDE THE STATE BROUGHT IN THOUSANDS SEEKING FARM WORK. LABOR STRIKES FLARED, AND CALIFORNIA'S AGRICULTURAL ESTABLISHMENT FOUGHT BACK. THE COLLEGE OF AGRICULTURE OPENED A BRANCH AT LOS ANGELES. RESEARCH AND EXTENSION WORK CONCENTRATED ON EFFICIENCY IN FARM MANAGEMENT BUT IGNORED THE KIND OF SOCIAL PROJECTS UNDERTAKEN BY THE U.S. BUREAU OF AGRICULTURAL ECONOMICS. WHEN WORLD WAR II BROUGHT A RENEWED EMPHASIS ON PRODUCTION, THE EXTENSION SERVICE SUPERVISED THE EMERGENCY FARM LABOR PROJECT. PLANNING FOR THE POSTWAR ERA INCLUDED A NATIONAL AGRICULTURAL POLICY STUDY AND A STATE-SPONSORED AGRICULTURAL RESEARCH STUDY.

# 5

# Challenges in Peace and War  1930–1947

## CALIFORNIA AGRICULTURE IN THE 1930S

In November 1930 University President Robert G. Sproul transmitted to Governor C. C. Young a report on the economic problems of California agriculture prepared by the staff of the College of Agriculture. The report described the serious difficulties besetting the state's farmers:

> Prices for most agricultural products are low relative to the prices farmers have to pay. . . . The unsatisfactory returns . . . have been reflected in reduced real-estate values and in many cases have prevented farmers from paying their debts. The farmers' equity in mortgaged property has been greatly reduced and tax delinquencies have increased. Banks and other lending agencies have acquired thousands of farms.[1]

To "safeguard the interests of established farmers and make possible a better standard of living," the report recommended a number of state actions including tax reform, surplus control, and regulation of marketing. Many of these recommendations would eventually be implemented through state or federal legislation during the following decade, but it would take years for California agriculture to climb out of the doldrums.

California farm prospects took a marked downturn a few years behind the nationwide agricultural depression of the early 1920s. Conditions after World War I encouraged the state's farmers to invest in more potentially profitable orchards and vineyards, particularly on the east side of the Central Valley. In the early 1920s the acreage of every one of the important field crops grown in California declined, by amounts ranging from 13 percent in the case of hay to over 40 percent in corn, wheat, sorghum, and beans. Meanwhile, the total fruit acreage increased by 573,000 acres, or about 43 percent, with even larger relative gains in fig, almond, apricot, pear, peach, and plum acreage. When these thousands of new acres came into bearing, the market could not absorb the additional production.[2] Lower prices often could not cover the high costs of production and fixed charges for mortgage and irrigation district debts. By 1930 many of California's farmers were in deep trouble.

As California, with the rest of the nation, slid into the deepening Great Depression, it was troubled with many of the same problems experienced elsewhere—and with some uniquely its own. Economic activity ground to a virtual standstill. In 1932 California farm income sank to little more than half of what it had been three years earlier. Across the state unemployment rose to unprecedented levels. In 1935 more than 1.2 million Californians—nearly 20 percent of the state's population—were dependent on public relief. New and bitter struggles between labor and employers broke out in violent confrontations in city streets and in farm fields. Political leaders seemed helpless. Social messiahs like Upton Sinclair and Francis Townsend offered utopian assistance schemes that were eagerly embraced by thousands of desperate and gullible people. And in an epic interstate migration of the destitute, hundreds of thousands of displaced American sharecroppers streamed forlornly out of the dustblown, dreary backcountry of Oklahoma, Texas, and Arkansas, seeking jobs that did not exist in the land of dreams along the Pacific coast.[3]

## WEATHER AND WATER

American farm problems were exacerbated by a series of drought years starting toward the end of the decade. By the mid-1930s the dry-farmed Great Plains were "blowing in the wind," crops withering in the unrelenting sun. Huge clouds of brown silt roiled across the arid land, sign of ill-considered agricultural expansion and harbinger of painful adjustments to come.

In California a seven-year drought reminiscent of the biblical story of Joseph began in most of the state during the mid-1920s. Long-term state precipitation records, though variable across sections, show a general sharp drop from the relatively moist years before 1925 to a low in the early 1930s. From about 1928 to 1934 weather stations in the Sacramento Valley reported far-below-average precipitation.[4] Although native Californians knew that periodic drought was part of their Mediterranean climate, arid conditions combined with the economic crisis to give farmers a double blow. Central Valley farmers turned to groundwater pumping to save themselves from ruin, but the hunt for water intensified.

Throughout the 1920s Californians had tried to put together a comprehensive state water plan to serve areas not included in the successful but scattered early irrigation districts. That need now made more urgent, the State Division of Water Resources laid the first State Water Plan on the desks of the legislature in 1931. The massive report cataloged California's water resources and needs, focusing on the Central Valley. The plan laid out an ambitious system for storing and transferring water from the northern and western mountains and the High Sierra to the plains of the great interior valley. The legislature authorized the Central Valley Project in 1933; voters endorsed a $170 million bond proposition to start construction. When there were no buyers for the bonds, promoters began to look toward Washington for assistance. Because the project fell within the parameters of the public works program supported by the Roosevelt administration, the U.S. Bureau of Reclamation undertook responsibility for it in 1935, beginning construction two years later.[5]

## SMALL FARM FALLOUT

Investors continued to buy into the California dream of owning a small piece of farm property during the 1920s despite the ominous postwar situation in agriculture. The division of farmland went on even in the early 1930s. Some farm owners probably tried to recoup losses by selling parts of their properties, and some of the unemployed may have tried their hand at subsistence farming; whatever the reasons, in 1935 the number of California farms peaked at about 150,000, an all-time high.[6]

As economic conditions worsened, however, defaults on farm mortgage debt became common. In 1929 the Bank of America, the state's biggest agricultural lender, formed a special holding company, California Lands, Inc., to manage the farms transferred to its ownership by foreclosures. Between 1932 and 1934 about 40 of every 1,000 farms were in default or forced sale, and this figure is probably conservative in estimating

130

distress transfers.[7] By the middle of the Depression many modest farm bungalows were empty, and much acreage stood idle as dairy herds were sold off, vineyards and orchards were abandoned, and open land reverted to weeds.

As more stable farmers began to absorb the foreclosures, a period of consolidations began. While the nation slowly climbed out of the Depression, average farm size in the nation and in California began to rise. Across the country sharecroppers and tenants literally lost their ground with increasing mechanization of farm operations by their landlords. Many other farmers were forced to leave farming altogether. Even the New Deal series of alphabetic rural assistance programs could not stem the flow.[8]

## LABOR STRIFE, INTERSTATE MIGRATION, AND INVESTIGATIONS

With unemployment at record highs and employers cutting wages across the board, the 1930s became the stage for labor turmoil. Violent confrontations between labor and management took place in many industries. Probably the single most dramatic conflict in California took place in San Francisco in 1934 between longshoremen and their employers. Led by Harry Bridges and supported by

"THAT SEASON THE WINTER PEA CROP FROZE. HE HAD WAITED FOR WEEKS," WROTE PHOTOGRAPHER DOROTHEA LANGE ABOUT AN IMPERIAL VALLEY MIGRANT WORKER IN 1937.

thousands of strikers, several hundred of the city's longshoremen battled with police on July 5. After two workers were killed and more than 70 injured, a general strike in sympathy with the longshoremen's demands shut down the entire city for nearly four days.[9]

Hostility also flared in California's fields. Apart from the 1913 Wheatland riot, in which the International Workers of the World attempted to mobilize disgruntled hop pickers, California farmworkers had borne their lot relatively stoically through the years, opting to find other jobs when they could. The ethnic groups doing much of the state's fieldwork had rarely been combative; yet even among them an incipient revolt was brewing. In 1928 Mexican workers in the Imperial Valley unsuccessfully attempted to strike for higher wages, and soon Mexicans were being sent back over the border as unemployed Americans began to replace them. In 1930 the communist-backed Trade Union Unity League supported several farm labor strikes. By then the leader of the Filipino Labor Union, organized in Hawaii a few years earlier, was also urging Filipinos in California to organize.[10]

In 1933 and 1934—the nadir of the Depression—a series of strikes rocked the Imperial and Salinas valleys and parts of the San Joaquin Valley. Workers protesting poor earnings and miserable living conditions were encouraged by the Cannery and Agricultural Workers Industrial Union, another communist organizing group. Some farmers met the strikes with violence. Attorneys and clergy who came to the Imperial Valley in early 1934 to check stories of oppression reported mistreatment by residents averse to their presence. Eventually a federal investigatory commission corroborated laborers' charges of infringement on their rights to organize and protest working conditions. Shortly thereafter, farm groups asked the governor to appoint a state investigatory commission, which was to take a view more sympathetic to the growers.[11] As unrest spread to other spots across the state, farmers, fearing loss of their perishable crops and determined to oppose any radical labor movement, responded by organizing the Associated Farmers. Supported in part by contributions from banking and industrial interests, the Associated Farmers used strong-arm tactics—billy clubs and police patrols—to defuse potential labor disturbances, much to the distaste and outrage of some observers.

Compounding California's agricultural labor problems, a mass migration from the southern states and the Dust Bowl in the mid-1930s brought in hundreds of thousands of displaced "Okies," "Arkies," and other American citizens seeking jobs. Destitute families camped along ditchbanks in agricultural areas, building shacks of cardboard and scrap wood and living in squalor while they searched for work. California was unprepared for these new migrants either physically or psychologically. While state agencies scrambled for resources to aid them, the federal government tried various housing and employment schemes. In 1935 the Resettlement Administration erected federal labor camps at Arvin in the San Joaquin Valley and at Marysville in the Sacramento Valley. In 1937 the agency, rechristened the Farm Security Administration, undertook a program of demonstration projects, which grew to include 69 installations throughout the state. By 1940 fifteen federal migratory labor camps were completed or under construction, three mobile camps were planned, and relief was available for hundreds of families. The FSA even attempted two full-time and several part-time cooperative farms in Arizona and California, offering subsistence farm plots and managed farming opportunities for selected applicants. These experiments died a quiet death during World War II.[12]

In late 1939 the Senate Committee on Education and Labor (the La Follette subcommittee) held a series of hearings to determine whether the rights of California's farm labor to organize had been violated. The hearings were decidedly unsympathetic to California's agricultural establishment. By the time they were concluded, however, the nation stood on the brink of war, and labor problems were about to be solved by mobilization for defense.[13]

## THE UNIVERSITY AND THE COLLEGE IN THE 1930S

In 1930 two very competent administrators took up the reins at the University of California. Within six months of each other Robert G. Sproul and Claude B. Hutchison respectively became President of the University and Dean of the College of Agriculture, the first- and second-most-influential positions within the institution. Sproul was a native son of California, an alumnus of the University, and former UC comptroller, land agent, and secretary to the Regents. His gift for oratory and his phenomenal memory, along with his good humor and common sense, helped him achieve great popularity with his colleagues, the public, and the legislature. Hutchison was a Missouri-born farm boy who had taken degrees at Cornell and Harvard, served for two years as director of the University Farm at Davis (1922-24), gone abroad for four years as administrator for Rockefeller Foundation

132

agricultural education programs in Europe, and returned to California to head the Giannini Foundation in 1928.

Both Sproul and Hutchison were professional administrators rather than academics in the strict sense; neither had a doctorate, though Hutchison had a master's degree in agronomy and some teaching experience. Both were absolutely dedicated to and tireless promoters of the University. They would serve in their respective positions for well over twenty years: Hutchison until 1952, Sproul until 1958. Both would leave their personal stamp on the institution. Hutchison, a "large, handsome, and highly self-confident man . . . excellently informed on all matters concerning the college," would lead the College of Agriculture into a whole new epoch.[14]

## FLAGSHIP BERKELEY: SPROUL AND HUTCHISON SETTLE IN

DEAN CLAUDE HUTCHISON SPEAKING AT THE DEDICATION OF GIANNINI HALL ON BERKELEY CAMPUS, OCTOBER 1930. BANK OF AMERICA PRESIDENT A. P. GIANNINI SITS IN FRONT ROW, HAND ON KNEE.

The two new administrators were immediately faced with Depression cutbacks in the University budget. State appropriations for the University dropped from $9.9 million in 1929-30 to $8.6 million in 1931-32, necessitating reduction in staff salaries and deferral of many expenditures. Anticipating further slashes in the University's proposed 1933-34 budget, Sproul urged departmental chairs to practice the "most exigent economy" while he campaigned vigorously against the threatened legislative reductions of $2 million. He carried his message to the public via the radio and his many speaking engagements, while Hutchison exerted his influence across rural California through the Agricultural Extension Service. Mobilized farmers sent hundreds of letters and telegrams to their legislators and joined B. H. Crocheron in a caravan of farm bureau members to Sacramento. After marathon discussions the legislature and governor restored most of the University's budget, but some University activities remained curtailed, and many needs for maintenance, construction, and new programs went unmet until better days.[15]

Hutchison found the assistance of several agricultural interest groups invaluable in these straitened times. The Agricultural Legislative Committee, consisting of representatives of the leading farm organizations, especially grower cooperatives, had been formed in the early 1920s to monitor legislation. Hutchison met with this group at intervals; it was a mutually advantageous association, keeping the College apprised of agricultural concerns while providing it with effective political support. A similar organization in southern California was the San Andreas Club, an informal group of prominent agriculturalists begun in 1930 by Dr. George Clements of the Los Angeles Chamber of Commerce. This group met periodically for recreational camping weekends on a rustic property in the San Andreas Canyon not far from Palm Springs. These semiannual "bull sessions" provided yet another opportunity for the movers and shakers in California agriculture to confer informally with political leaders and university administrators. (Another, later, informal "power group" was called the Executive Bulls.) Participants considered these associations extremely useful in setting mutual agendas.[16]

Despite the dreary financial outlook and social unrest of the 1930s, the University and the College of Agriculture remained relatively quiet, pursuing research and education in accustomed modes. Student numbers even increased. Between 1930 and 1940 general enrollments grew 50 percent, from 19,235 to 28,851, while those in the College of Agriculture more than doubled, from 1,020 to 2,871. At Berkeley alone agricultural enrollments nearly tripled, from 437 (graduates and undergraduates) to 1,297.[17]

## DAVIS SCENES

The Depression years saw steady growth at the University Farm—a name that lingered on among old-timers but gradually faded away in the 1930s. Davis became the "Cal Aggie" campus, focusing on the agricultural subjects for which Berkeley had insufficient space or inadequate facilities. Its chief programs were in animal science, agricultural engineering, and crop production; its atmosphere was relaxed and rural, its student body small and friendly. Until permanent grass was planted, the center "Quad" supported a stand of alfalfa, and butterflies and gurgling irrigation water were part of the memories of those living in South Hall.[18] Many of the faculty commuted from

HOME ECONOMICS PRACTICE LABORATORY
AT DAVIS, 1936.

Berkeley to Davis by train, the trip across the Carquinez Strait taking little more than an hour. Berkeley faculty viewed Davis as a "cow college" of less academic standing, and in fact there were usually about twice as many students in the two-year "practical" program as there were undergraduates studying for a degree. In 1930 there were 391 nondegree students compared with 184 undergraduates; by 1940 there were 937 and 483, respectively.

Growth at Davis began to change the nature of the place in the mid-1930s. After the repeal of Prohibition in 1933, the department of viticulture was officially moved from Berkeley and courses in wine-making were resumed at Davis in 1935. More important at the time, however, was Hutchison's decision to establish a department of home economics in the College of Agriculture, combining elements from Berkeley's two departments of household art and household sciences then in the College of Letters and Sciences. Hutchison's goal was to broaden the student body at Davis by offering what he called a "liberal education" in home economics for women; and, in fact, the Davis campus became truly coeducational because of the new program. A two-year nondegree curriculum in "home ec" was offered in 1936, and a four-year degree program was offered through Berkeley in 1938. The number of women enrolled at Davis increased from seventeen in 1934 to nearly ten times that figure by 1939. A small "practice cottage" afforded opportunity for meal preparation and other home-based project work, and courses were

134 offered in clothing design, child development, and family sociology. At Berkeley the renowned chemist Agnes Fay Morgan, head of the academic department there, emphasized scientific studies, especially research on the role of vitamins in human nutrition.[19]

In 1938 the University Farm was formally renamed the College of Agriculture at Davis, and its programs and facilities were reorganized. Horticulturalist Knowles Ryerson, an early University Farm student who had become chief of the U.S. Bureau of Plant Industry, was named assistant dean in charge of the Davis campus. Besides the continuing two-year nondegree program, Davis now offered four major degree programs in animal production, plant production, dairy industry, and home economics. Although the degrees in these fields were still granted through Berkeley, most of the course work was conducted at Davis. The look of the campus began to change. In 1938

a new gymnasium and swimming pool gave students and faculty badly needed recreational facilities; a new library and administration building went up along the south side of the main quadrangle; a new chemistry building (today's Young Hall) on the west side was completed just in time to be commandeered for national security work during World War II. In 1941 the California legislature authorized a School of Veterinary Medicine at Davis, which would not be developed until after the war was over.[20]

## UCLA AND RIVERSIDE: THE COLLEGE IN THE SOUTHLAND

In 1930 the Regents created the Branch of the College of Agriculture in Southern California, which included under its umbrella the research center at the Citrus Experiment Station in Riverside and instructional activities planned for the Los Angeles campus.

HERBERT WEBBER, DIRECTOR OF THE CITRUS EXPERIMENT STATION IN RIVERSIDE, PLANTS A TANGELO TREE (A TANGERINE /GRAPEFRUIT HYBRID) TO MARK THE TWENTIETH ANNIVERSARY OF THE STATION IN 1933.

From its beginnings UCLA was an urban campus concentrating on the letters, arts, and sciences; nevertheless, on the Westwood campus a 10-acre tract was reserved for an experimental orchard, and the Regents allotted more land and funds for agricultural facilities including substantial greenhouses. In 1932 Berkeley's Division of Subtropical Horticulture was transferred to UCLA, and the agricultural staff headed by Robert W. Hodgson moved into the recently completed north wing of the physics-biology building (Kinsey Hall). Formal undergraduate instruction in agriculture was first offered during the spring of 1933, and by the mid-1930s agricultural enrollments at UCLA hovered at around 100. The new college offered a small but well-balanced mix of degree programs in agricultural economics, botany, entomology, floriculture, irrigation and soils, plant pathology, and subtropical horticulture. It became especially well known for horticultural science, attracting many international students. The laboratory-orchard supported significant research in the production and handling of subtropical fruit crops. Though limited in size (about 14 acres), its collection included 71 different kinds of fruits and nuts, among which were 335 named cultivars. In 1938 William H. Chandler was appointed Assistant Dean of the Los Angeles Section of the College of Agriculture.[21]

At Riverside, after H. J. Webber's retirement in 1929, horticulturalist Leon C. Batchelor became the second director of the Citrus Experiment Station, where he stayed until his retirement in 1951. Under his supervision the facilities and operational budget expanded substantially, and the station moved into new areas of research on all the major crops of southern California. CES scientists pioneered in studies of the use of herbicides, new compounds to fight insect pests, and methods for disease control. With the transfer of instructional programs to Los Angeles in the 1930s, the Graduate School of Tropical Agriculture, which had never flourished, closed in 1939.[22]

## AGRICULTURAL RESEARCH HIGHLIGHTS, 1930-1946

Farmers trying to survive during the Depression needed all the help they could get. Scientists in the Agricultural Experiment Station continued to work on ways to improve farm productivity and conserve resources, and although the economic climate hindered the implementation of some innovations, a number of advancements were made.

Dean Hutchison's book-length biennial reports on research work in the 1930s were prepared with the help of assistant dean Stanley B. Freeborn and later of writer Henry Schacht. After four of these appeared, they were discontinued, but subsequently Hutchison oversaw the preparation of another book titled *California Agriculture*, published in 1946. This collection of chapters by College staff reviewed the state's agricultural development over the previous 75 years and described the role of UC agricultural research in improving productivity. The main thrusts of agricultural research from 1930 to 1946, as reported in those five volumes, are summarized in the remainder of this section.[23]

### SOIL AND WATER INVESTIGATIONS

Continuing their comprehensive field surveys of soils in California, soil scientists eventually completed a master soils map, classifying California's complex resources into six major profile groups and cataloging 250 different soil series. Detailed surveys were made available of the Mojave Desert, parts of the San Joaquin Valley, the Napa Valley, and the Modoc Plateau. In 1934 R. Earl Storie published his classic agricultural rating system based on soil texture and other modifying factors such as drainage and alkali content. His system of numerical expressions became known as the Storie Index, and it is still used to rank soils for their productive potential.[24]

136 Many research projects of the 1930s examined the relationship between soil water and plants in both field and laboratory. Experiments with seedbed preparation, cover crops, and furrowing led to better control of soil erosion, and researchers tried low-tillage soil management techniques in deciduous orchards. Other studies included measurements of soil permeability and field capacity, water requirements for various crops, salt accumulation under irrigation, and capillary movement of water under field conditions. Laboratory investigations focused on better understanding of the processes of soil formation and structure, water culture of plants, and the thermodynamics of soil moisture.

In 1933 Dean Hutchison convened a meeting at Berkeley for foresters, ranchers, and others to discuss the effects of brushland burning on the water supply and grazing capacity of range areas. At the time California had an estimated 12 to 18 million brushland acres with potential value for grazing, but range burning was controversial—many conservationists objected to brush removal because of its supposed effects on runoff and soil erosion. As a result of the Berkeley meeting, the College established a Range Committee composed of members from related departments including agronomy, forestry, and animal science. In the years following, coordinated UC research projects investigated the long-term effects of brush burning on controlled plots. These studies found no deleterious effects from systematic brush removal; there was in fact a net gain in water supply and grazing capacity, and improved soil conditions from an erosion viewpoint. The evidence eventually convinced the legislature to remove some prohibitions against brushland burning.

Development of plans for the Central Valley Project brought steadily increasing demands on the irrigation division. At the request of the State Engineer, University scientists analyzed water costs, reviewed state and federal flood control project reports, and commented on proposed soil conservation legislation. Irrigation engineers worked on many aspects of water application and system design: pumping plants, water-measuring devices, and the hydraulics of distribution through various flumes, siphons, sprinklers, and pipes.[25]

A 1931 SOILS LABORATORY AT THE BRANCH OF THE COLLEGE, DAVIS.

## PLANT BREEDING

Painstaking work by College plant breeders continued to develop "bred to order" varieties for California agriculture, bringing higher crop yields and greater resistance to adverse climatic conditions, pests, and diseases. Research in the 1930s succeeded in developing a wheat resistant to smut, better malting barley for brewing, improved-yield Sudan grass for forage, disease-resistant beans, leguminous cover crops for soil building, onions resistant to downy mildew and pinkroot, hardier citrus and grape rootstocks, heat-resistant maize, and better strawberries, melons, tomatoes, peaches, almonds, and grapes.

In 1934, in cooperation with the State Department of Agriculture and the California Farm Bureau Federation, the College began the California Approved Seed Plan to ensure a steady supply of pure seed of standard and improved field crop varieties. Under this plan, pure seed from certified sources was distributed to cooperating farmers, who produced more seed under strict supervision. After inspection, the final product was labeled "Calapproved," guaranteeing its freedom from contamination. This program was an immediate success and contributed greatly to higher crop yields in following years.[26]

The historic Wolfskill tract of more than 1,000 acres, near Winters, was bequeathed to the College in 1934. Although it was not fully to become university property until all heirs were deceased, the courts granted immediate possession of 108 acres, which became the Wolfskill Experimental Orchard under the direction of the experiment station at Davis. Here long-range fruit variety work began in cooperation with the U.S. Department of Agriculture.

## PLANT HEALTH AND PROTECTION

Attesting to the number of problems confronted in California's fields, research in crop protection continued to diversify. In 1931 scientists identified the cause of little-leaf disease—one reason for the colony failure at Delhi—as a soil deficiency of zinc available for plant nutrition.[27] Later the prune dieback experienced at Durham was found to be associated with a lack of available potassium in heavy soils. Scientists also identified deficiencies of copper, manganese, boron, and molybdenum as causes of other plant disorders. With these micronutrients identified, application of soil additives began to bring remarkable relief to crops suffering from previously little-understood nutritional problems.

The cumulative list of studies in plant protection is impressive and demonstrates the vulnerability to pests and disease of California farmers. The Experiment Station mounted projects on diseases such as shot-hole, citrus fruit rot and mold, date decline, bean rust, fig smut, spotted wilt, oakroot fungus, carrot blight, hop mildew, and tomato canker; and on pests like codling moth, red spider, orange tortrix, thrips, aphids, mites, purple and black scale, snowy tree cricket, and lygus. Researchers tried many methods of control for old enemies and new: fumigation, fungicides, oil sprays, water sprays, and beneficial parasitic insects. And they continued to seek ways to control the 150 different kinds of noxious weeds inhabiting the state's cultivated lands, ditchbanks, and roadsides.

## ANIMAL INDUSTRIES

Under the chairmanship of George Hart in the late 1920s, the animal science department at Davis divided into two groups, one focusing primarily on production and related problems, the other on basic research in the biological sciences—genetics, physiology, nutrition, and biochemistry.

In the following years production scientists increased their understanding of breeding, reproduction, diet, and disease control, helping ranchers, dairy farmers, and other animal producers achieve better production and quality in their herds and flocks. The systematic dairy cattle breeding begun in the 1920s produced Jersey cows with very high milk-production records, and commercial dairies were able to use University-bred bulls to upgrade their herds. Scientific

138 breeding work also resulted in earlier maturity and better carcass quality in beef cattle. University feeding studies monitored the effects of various diets on farm animals: combinations of irrigated pasture, field residue, and agricultural by-products for fattening cattle; better forage mixes for fattening lambs; least-cost rations for more efficient commercial poultry production; and the use of nutritional supplements for improving wool quality and egg production. Extension specialists collaborating with the U.S. Bureau of Animal Industry reduced the incidence of brucellosis in cattle and encephalomyelitis in horses by promoting vaccination campaigns.

Scientists in basic research studied the details of animal metabolism, the significance of vitamin levels in feeding, the process of cell division, and cell growth rates. Their research determined how to isolate and extract the gonadotrophic hormone secreted by pregnant mares, allowing its use in treating equine reproductive disorders.[28] Other long-range experiments enlarged understanding of animal physiology, genetics, and nutrition, which later was applied to improve production.

For a time during the 1930s it appeared that the University's animal science department had received a unique gift.

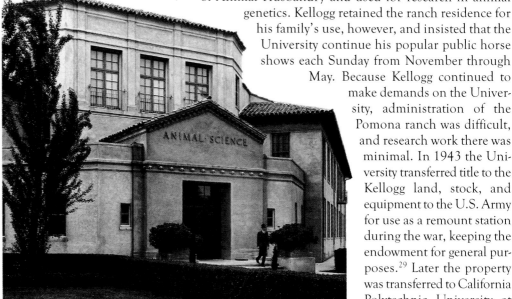

THE ANIMAL SCIENCE BUILDING ON THE DAVIS CAMPUS, LATER RENAMED HART HALL AFTER GEORGE HART, CHAIR OF THE DEPARTMENT IN THE 1920S.

In 1932 the Regents accepted an offer by W. K. Kellogg of Battle Creek, Michigan, to give the University his 800-acre ranch near Pomona, along with 60 purebred Arabian horses and an endowment of $600,000 to maintain the herd for 50 years as breeding stock. The formal agreement stipulated that the facility should be named the W. K. Kellogg Institute of Animal Husbandry and used for research in animal genetics. Kellogg retained the ranch residence for his family's use, however, and insisted that the University continue his popular public horse shows each Sunday from November through May. Because Kellogg continued to make demands on the University, administration of the Pomona ranch was difficult, and research work there was minimal. In 1943 the University transferred title to the Kellogg land, stock, and equipment to the U.S. Army for use as a remount station during the war, keeping the endowment for general purposes.[29] Later the property was transferred to California Polytechnic University at Pomona.

## AGRICULTURAL ENGINEERING

Engineering projects at Davis during the 1930s ran the gamut from simple gadgetry to analysis and resolution of highly complex problems in designing machinery for various crop operations. Early in the decade engineers designed mechanical rice-harvesting and -drying equipment, which was widely adopted by the outbreak of World War II; it allowed the tripling of rice acreage under wartime demands. Other engineering work developed a hay crusher-mower, a lima bean rubber-roller thresher that reduced seed bean injury, and an effective thresher for the Punjab flax earlier introduced to the Imperial Valley from India. Extension's engineering specialist worked to develop a spark arrester for motorized equipment used in grain harvesting, which helped avoid field fires. Other projects designed new orchard-heating devices for frost protection, air-cooled greenhouse and poultry buildings, pest control equipment, land graders, portable sprinkler irrigation systems, and precooling chambers for truck crops awaiting shipment. To discourage bears from raiding local apiaries, a problem in mountain areas, engineers designed electric fences for use around hives.

In 1932 the Extension Service began to offer farmers, at modest cost, professionally designed plans for construction of various farm buildings. This service proved extremely popular. In four years farmers purchased more than 5,000 sets of plans. University plans for market milk dairy barns were adopted as standard by the legislature in 1937.

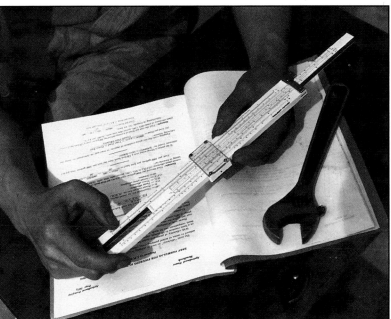

AGRICULTURAL ENGINEERING STUDENT AT WORK, 1930S.

One particularly ingenious device developed during the 1930s at Davis was an "internal combustion nut cracker" that "blew up" walnuts by introducing gas under the shell, thus avoiding crushing the kernel by breaking the nut from the outside. This invention, though greatly admired, did not become widely used because it was supplanted by an electronic nut cracker developed elsewhere; but the device so impressed the U.S. Sugar Beet Association that it gave $80,000—a huge sum in 1938—to the Davis engineering department to mechanize sugar beet operations. From then through the war years, Roy Bainer and other scientists and engineers in cooperation with USDA and Colorado State College worked on the development of segmented or decorticated seed balls, mechanical planters and thinners, and machine harvesters for the labor-intensive sugar beet industry. Eventually their team efforts revolutionized that industry by eliminating the backbreaking labor associated with hand thinning, topping, and harvesting.[30]

## FOOD AND DAIRY SCIENCE AND TECHNOLOGY

The Prohibition era suppressed enological research but contributed to the development of food science and technology. Scientists turned to projects in utilizing and improving unfermented fruit products, gaining along the way a much better understanding of food safety and quality. Although food technologists sometimes came in for ribbing by their colleagues as the "jams and jellies" people, their work helped the California food industry expand and provide better consumer products. Until the 1950s dairy scientists formed a unit of their own, working on ways to improve the flavor of milk, the consistency of skim milk powder, and the texture and quality of butter and ice cream. Other scientists investigated the keeping quality of dried fruits, the palatability of fruit and vegetable juices, the role of carbon dioxide and other gases during fruit storage, new uses for surplus commodities, sterilization in canning, processes for controlling enzyme changes in frozen products, and better storage techniques for deciduous fruits, potatoes, and citrus.[31]

STUDENT OF DAIRY SCIENCE, 1930S.

## ECONOMIC INFORMATION AND SOCIOLOGICAL QUESTS

The work of agricultural scientists and extension advisors had paid off handsomely in increased farm production before and after World War I. Those increases, however, were part of the problem of the 1920s. Agricultural economics became a legitimate discipline when it was recognized that successful farming depended not just on production but on efficient management. Starting in the 1920s, economists developed cost studies to determine what it took to make a profit and began to compile data on the marketing and distribution of farm products. During the Depression federal and state government policymakers also enlisted agricultural economists in the search for solutions to the complex issues troubling rural America.

Among farm journalists, educators, and other opinion leaders in the interwar period, there was a gradual but distinct transformation of attitudes toward agriculture, moving from the agrarian idealism of the Country Life Movement, with its emphasis on the moral values to be found in farm life, to a subtle but widespread kind of economic secularism, in which agriculture was considered a basic industry not just because it fed and clothed the nation but because farmers' purchasing power was essential to national prosperity. Contributing to this shift was the general recognition that the nation's urban and rural sectors were in fact interdependent—cities and towns needed food, and agriculture needed urban markets. Thus farmers became viewed more and more as businessmen and capitalists or, alternatively, as industrial workers seeking higher wages for their labor on the land. Farmers themselves, who continued to insist on the importance of their differences from other industries (real enough, though sometimes exaggerated), nevertheless increasingly accepted the benefits of industrialism and were eager to acquire such amenities as automobiles, washing machines, radios, and electricity. The Depression, with all its painful dislocations and economic hardships, helped bring to fruition a social and economic transition in agriculture that had been building for some half a century.[32]

## EARLY GIANNINI FOUNDATION WORK

The Giannini Foundation endowment of 1928 provided support for research in agricultural economics at the University of California during the Depression. The complexity of problems facing the state's agriculture demanded a broad-spectrum approach. In scores of publications and hundreds of meetings, staff provided meticulously collected statistical information on production costs and marketing trends in dozens of California commodities. At the urgent request of the State Department of Agriculture, economists made an extensive study of milk marketing in seven regions, to determine formulas for fair pricing under different cost and distribution arrangements. They also investigated the marketing and storage of eggs, the optimal organization of cooperatives, honey grades and standards, the effects of market control programs for various fruits and vegetables, raisin pooling

operations, California farm exports, farm enterprise efficiency, trade barriers between states including agricultural quarantines, advertising methods and policies, problems of irrigation districts, and still other subjects.[33]

New federal directives were the basis for several projects. In 1932, in conjunction with the U.S. Bureau of Agricultural Economics (BAE), Giannini economists began a type-of-farming study to determine the distribution of California's agricultural enterprises in an effort to analyze resource management strategies. Later, as the Resettlement Administration tried to relocate dispossessed farm people to cooperative farms and subsistence units, researchers reviewed the problems of the state land settlements of the previous decade.

Howard R. Tolley was appointed Acting Director of the Giannini Foundation in 1931 after Dean Hutchison's first choice, John D. Black of Harvard University, declined the position. A skilled mathematician highly recommended for his work as assistant chief of research in the BAE, Tolley had close ties with the New Deal. Between 1931 and 1936 he took two leaves of absence from Berkeley to assist in formulation of agricultural policy in Washington, D.C. In 1936 he left California permanently to oversee the restructuring of the Agricultural Adjustment Administration. Later he became head of the BAE, where he supervised programs in land use planning and resource management.[34]

Tolley was not the only Giannini Foundation contribution to national economic planning in the New Deal, or later. Several other UC agricultural economists including Harry Wellman, Murray Benedict, and Varden Fuller served temporarily in federal positions during the thirties and forties. A junior appointee from Canada named John Kenneth Galbraith, who authored three Experiment Station bulletins at Berkeley and taught two years at Davis during the Depression, went into federal price administration during the war and later distinguished himself at Harvard, in various presidential administrations, and as a writer.[35]

**FARM MANAGEMENT AND FARM LABOR**

Among the charter members of the Giannini Foundation was Richard L. Adams, specialist in farm management and a member of the Experiment Station since World War I. His studies in farm efficiency during the 1920s ranged from optimal dairy size to workhorse economics (in 1925 there were still nearly 400,000 horses and mules on California farms, providing animal power at an average cost of $1 for a nine-hour day). While other economists studied production trends, marketing mechanisms, and government policy, Adams concentrated on improving individual farm management by providing information on costs of production, farm leasing strategies, and farm organization. Until his retirement in 1954 Adams influenced two generations of students and farmers, convincing them of the necessity for good record keeping and rational use of resources.

Adams also became, more or less by default, California's first farm labor specialist. Labor was not his primary interest, however, and he expended relatively little effort on work in this area. Only during periods of crisis did he conduct studies relating to the use of human resources in agriculture. Some of these are worth noting in chronological order.

Until World War I the College of Agriculture simply did not address the issue of farm labor. To meet the wartime emergency, however, Adams was appointed State Farm Labor Agent in charge of gathering information; he conducted an extensive survey of seventeen counties and helped arrange for temporary workers to meet harvest needs, including high school boys, city residents, and women. In March 1918 his report appeared as the Experiment Station's first publication on farm labor, making a number of observations on working relationships, food and living conditions, and distinctions among California laborers:

> All men are not equally capable. A great variation exists among Mexicans and Hindus, some variation among Japanese, and the greatest among the floating white labor. . . . Among the latter are many who may correctly be classed as "unemployables"—mentally defective and wrecked physically. Many of these men are literally incapable of doing a reasonable day's work on any farm. It is these that largely make up the crowds hanging around poolrooms, saloons, and employment agencies.

Adams commented as well as on employer negligence:

> Difficulty in holding men not used to the ordinary living conditions on the average California ranch will be partly overcome by a recognition of the practical and pressing necessity of providing proper living conditions. Quarters provided for peon, coolie, or Oriental labor are generally not suitable for men demanding American standards of living.

Prophetically, he remarked on the long-range outlook for farm labor:

> It is the growing conviction of the authors that the American farms are conducted best when labor-saving machinery is applied to a variety of work. Hand labor does not appeal to a nation of strongly marked mechanical genius, and the monotony of often repeated routine operations does not commend itself to Americans. California has much of this kind of work, which is difficult of accomplishment without constant replenishment of the labor supply from sources which produce men able to do it. Obviously, therefore, one of the future methods of meeting the labor needs is a greater use of animal or gasoline power.[36]

With the war crisis over, Adams dropped his work on farm labor until growing Mexican immigration during the 1920s sparked public concern about its impact. As part of a state-commissioned report on Mexicans in California, Adams prepared a section on the use of Mexican labor in agriculture. His survey, encompassing hundreds of interviews, concluded that many farmers preferred Mexican workers to whites because they were dependable, hardy, patient, and cooperative.[37] Later, as thousands of the unemployed competed for farm jobs during the 1930s and the meager wages and living conditions of farm workers drew media attention, Adams served as an arbitration agent in some labor disputes. For the most part, however, Adams and other college staff stayed out of labor controversies. One notable exception was the participation of Dean Hutchison in the governor's select committee investigating the Imperial Valley disturbances.

Disturbed by the federal commission report on strikebreaking activities in the Imperial Valley in 1933 and 1934 (which concluded that the lawful rights of labor to organize had been abused), the California State Board of Agriculture, the California Farm Bureau Federation, and the agricultural section of the California State Chamber of Commerce asked Governor Young to appoint a special investigating committee to make an independent report. Hutchison was named to this committee along with W. C. Jacobsen of the State Department of Agriculture and John Phillips, Assemblyman from the 76th District (Banning). The committee's report, titled "The Imperial Valley Farm Labor Situation," was released on April 20, 1934; it concluded that labor agitation in the Imperial Valley was part of a "definite program" with "broad and sinister motives" by the Communist Party to stir up social discontent. Included in their evidence were copies of communist pamphlets and testimony by local citizens. While the report made many sensible recommendations for reform of poor local labor conditions, it stressed that much of the agitation on the part of workers had been fostered by communist agents. In general the committee seemed to side with residents who were "accustomed to meet their problems firmly" and to minimize worker complaints. Hutchison was, in fact, so convinced of the communist threat that he arranged for copies of the report to be sent to all state offices of the American Farm Bureau Federation. His participation in the Imperial Valley episode and his defense of growers attracted some criticism, including a letter to President Sproul from the director of the California Department of Commerce, Simon J. Lubin, who had served on the federal investigating commission. Asked by Lubin if Hutchison was officially representing the University, Sproul replied that he was not, but serving as an interested individual.[38]

Thereafter, both the Dean and the College kept a low profile on labor matters in agriculture. Experiment Station investigations were confined to the collection of statistical data. In 1938 Adams conducted a labor survey of Kern County that reported a "marked excess of manpower" in rural areas, with up to seven workers for every available job. He also prepared a statewide seasonal labor report at the request of the State Department of Agriculture, in which he reviewed labor needs by crop, area, tasks, worker-days, and number of workers needed. Giannini economist George Peterson's broader review of California's rural population changes in the 1930s, taken from census data, appeared in 1939, but his early death ended his plans to widen the scope of this study.[39]

## MISSING LINKS

While members of the College of Agriculture quietly went about their business, labor conditions and other social issues in agriculture attracted the keen interest of others outside the College. At Berkeley Paul S. Taylor of the Department of Economics, who had grown interested in Mexican migrant labor during the 1920s, pursued a pathbreaking series of studies in California and several other states. A reputable scholar, Taylor also began to publish articles on California's land policy and rural characteristics. His collaboration with photographer Dorothea Lange, who became his wife, provided outstanding documentation of the "Okie" migration.[40] Despite the fact that much of his work focused on California farm issues, Taylor's academic affiliation was in Letters and Science, and there was little apparent contact between Taylor and the agricultural staff. Taylor was an advocate of reform, critical of California's land tenure system and an outspoken supporter of the 160-acre "family-size" farm.

144    The popular books of Carey McWilliams and John Steinbeck, both published in 1939, also brought unflattering attention to the state's agricultural establishment. First came McWilliams's *Factories in the Fields*. McWilliams, an attorney and political activist, had been appointed by Democratic Governor Olson to head the State Division of Immigration and Housing, in which position he had made himself "Agricultural Pest Number One, outranking pear blight and the boll weevil," according to the Associated Farmers.[41] His book recounted the long history of agricultural labor relations in California, describing the ethnic waves that had long served the state's industrialized farms, documenting many grievances, and emphasizing the pathetic imbalance of power between employee and employer in a chapter on the Associated Farmers titled "The Rise of Farm Fascism." Then came Steinbeck's powerful novel *The Grapes of Wrath*. This simple, dramatic story, about an "Okie" family "tractored out" from its small plains farm and demeaned by suffering and mistreatment in its search for work in California, became an instant national best-seller and was made into a major Hollywood film.

Despite these evidences of increasing public interest in agricultural issues, the College of Agriculture did not engage in research on the socioeconomic problems being spotlighted and apparently ignored the possibilities for work in the field of rural sociology. The reasons were not financial. While the College certainly had to count pennies during the Depression, both Purnell funds and the Giannini charter offered some scope for sociological investigations. Some colleges of agriculture did in fact support such studies. In California, however, a combination of factors political and pragmatic seems to have inhibited initiative along this line.

With the departures of Thomas Hunt and Elwood Mead and the demise of the division of rural institutions in the 1920s, the College had turned away from a "social" agenda to concentrate on scientific and economic research. The state land settlement experiences at Durham and Delhi had apparently left a lingering discomfort with staff involvement in any potentially embarrassing positions of advocacy. Meanwhile the Giannini endowment had generously encouraged economic studies. Extension work in the counties had also developed a broad base of support from Farm Bureau cooperators, who tended to be the better-established and more politically conservative members of their farming communities. Few of these College allies would be inclined to approve of projects that might somehow unsettle the status quo.

Another reason for ignoring the field of rural sociology within the College was Hutchison's own expressed opinion that the discipline had little methodological credibility. In his oral history prepared three decades later, Hutchison stated that College staff were "somewhat interested in this rather ephemeral field of rural sociology" but that "we couldn't get our teeth into it."[42] In 1938 he wrote:

> A true man of science seeks neither to control nor influence the actions of any man save through the convincing weight of indisputable fact, developed by the most rigorous research discipline and tested by the precisions of science. . . . But it is easier to do this when dealing with physical and biological matters than when studying some important and complex social or economic problem. In the social sciences, yardsticks for measuring accomplishments and for estimating the truth have not been so clearly defined as in the physical and biological sciences. Too much depends upon opinion and emotion and no opportunity is at hand to check those . . . by subjecting them to rigorous experimental test. The social scientist must depend largely upon his logic. His thinking must, therefore be sound. . . . In the social field . . . so-called "experiments" are not experiments at all in the scientific sense. They are merely trial and error attempts, often supported by none too good logic, at finding a remedy for some pressing problems. Too often they are merely panaceas, with the inevitable result of more confusion and even harm to those they were designed to help.[43]

Neither Hutchison's background as a scientist nor his viewpoint as a political conservative were likely to lead him to justify social science research in the College of Agriculture. Others, however, argued for it. That same year Paul Taylor suggested to George Pettit, assistant to President Sproul, that a department of rural sociology ought to be established in the College of Agriculture, analogous to the department of agricultural economics. Pettit's memorandum to Sproul on the subject downplayed the suggestion but observed, "Dr. Taylor's emphatic statement that rural problems in sociology are not receiving adequate attention probably has some truth in it, at least from the research point of view."[44]

Despite California's reluctance to engage in social science research, some activists on the national level were attempting to use the social sciences to address some of the Depression's problems. The Roosevelt administration gave the U.S. Bureau of Agricultural Economics a role in such efforts. As the principal policy-formulating agency in USDA, the BAE drew together a core of social scientists to undertake ambitious studies of land use planning, types of farming, and the relationship between farm systems and community development in several parts of the United States.[45]

One BAE undertaking was a set of studies organized around the Central Valley Project to help formulate policy for its operation. In December 1942 the Bureau of Reclamation set up several interagency committees to investigate 24 questions ranging from appropriate charges for project water users to policies for distribution of project-generated power.

The University of California was invited to participate in two of these committees. Dean Hutchison, chairman of the University coordinating committee, asked two agricultural economists to serve. Adams was assigned to the committee for Problem 19—the question of whether land receiving irrigation water should be subject to acreage limitations; he declined to sign the final report, which recommended that it should. Murray Benedict, the College representative for Problem 24—the last, broadest, and most difficult question ("What effect will the project have on the agricultural economy and rural life in the Central Valley?")—took a wartime assignment in Washington and dropped off that committee, leaving E. T. Grether from the Department of Commerce as the University representative and Paul Taylor as an advisor. Thus the two committee reports submitted in 1945 did not reflect views from the College of Agriculture—whose staff in any event was preoccupied with meeting wartime demands and not eager to participate in controversial studies, knowing there was a local "very real and great fear" that the Central Valley Project would attempt to socialize agriculture in California.[46]

A spin-off from one of these studies caused a mild uproar. Walter Goldschmidt, a graduate in anthropology from UCLA, was employed briefly by BAE to gather data for Problem 19, the question of acreage limitations. In the spring of 1944 he conducted extensive surveys of two towns in the San Joaquin Valley, Arvin and Dinuba, communities of roughly the same size and in areas producing an equivalent dollar revenue from agriculture. Because economic and social conditions were superior in Dinuba, a community surrounded by small farms, Goldschmidt concluded that size of surrounding farm operations was linked inversely with healthy community development. Carl Taylor, director of the BAE studies, was uncomfortable with the Arvin-Dinuba comparison and refused to publish Goldschmidt's work, but the research appeared as a publication of the Small Business Administration (1946) and later was published as a book, *As You Sow*. For years afterward, the two-town study stimulated debate about both its methodology and its conclusions.[47]

The Arvin-Dinuba project produced some hostility in farm circles. Another BAE survey done about the same time in Coahoma County, Mississippi, drew even more hostile reaction because it was thought to raise racial issues. Congressional criticism of these community-based studies eventually brought about substantial cuts in the BAE budget, and the Bureau discontinued sociological research in 1946.[48]

146 **RURAL SOCIOLOGY AND DOROTHY SWAINE THOMAS**

Despite Hutchison's reservations about rural sociology as a discipline, Carl L. Alsberg, appointed director of the Giannini Foundation in 1937, believed there was indeed a need for a sociologist on the Giannini staff. He invited Dorothy Swaine Thomas, who had developed a reputation on the East coast for her work in population movements, to come to Berkeley in 1940 on a temporary appointment as a lecturer in sociology. Although the male members of the Giannini staff were markedly unenthusiastic about having a female colleague, Thomas quickly gained their respect—and a career appointment as professor of rural sociology and rural sociologist in the Experiment Station.[49]

In 1942 Thomas recognized the research opportunity provided by the wartime relocation of California's Japanese population to internment camps. With support from the Rockefeller Foundation, the Social Science Research Council, and the Giannini Foundation, she undertook an ambitious project to document the camp experience. The U.S. Department of Justice gave her access to confidential files on the evacuation, and she and her colleagues gathered information on camp life in three states with the aid of several bilingual Japanese-American graduate students. After the war the University of California Press published their three-volume documentary study. A doctoral thesis based on the project was turned into a controversial book, much to the displeasure of Thomas, who thought the author had used some of the data dishonestly.[50]

Despite the success of her research, Thomas left the University of California in 1948 to take a position at Pennsylvania's Wharton School of Commerce. There would not be another rural sociologist in the Experiment Station until 1964, fourteen years later.[51]

## EXTENSION IN THE DEPRESSION

### NEW ROLES FOR THE EXTENSION SERVICE

The Agricultural Extension Service was not quite twenty years old when Franklin Roosevelt was elected to lead the nation out of the worst depression in its history. Extension had been designed as the "bridge" between the land-grant colleges and farmers in the countryside. Its role was to bring the results of Experiment Station research directly to the people who could use it, through individual consultations, group meetings, and local demonstration plots where the skeptical could see with their own eyes the results of new practices. Much of the increased productivity of American farms during the twenties and thirties was a direct result of Extension work in rural counties. During the Depression the traditional educational role of Extension agents changed, however, when the federal government mandated Extension participation in programs aimed at relieving the economic doldrums.

During Roosevelt's first hundred days in office Congress passed the Agricultural Adjustment Act (AAA), its goal to raise farm commodity prices by regulating production. The responsibility for carrying out the program at the local level was assigned to the Agricultural Extension Service. Farm advisors were to explain the details and sign up interested farmers. States' response to this federal mandate were variable, ranging from enthusiastic acceptance in the South to serious reservations in the Northeast and West.[52] Among those disapproving was B. H. Crocheron of California. The California Extension Service took on the chores of AAA administration as required, but Crocheron strongly resisted its forced participation in an action program directed from Washington. Despite his disapproval, farm advisors spent about 20 percent of their time on AAA activities, until the program was dropped. One California farm advisor even wrote to Assistant Secretary of Agriculture M. L. Wilson of the positive advantages of participation: though the work load was large, he said, AAA work established new contacts with many farmers not otherwise familiar with Extension work, who then became new clients for more traditional educational services.[53]

Extension work received strengthened support through the Bankhead-Jones Act of 1935.[54] By the mid-1930s farm advisors were resident in 42 of California's 58 counties. Early in 1936, to replace the AAA program invalidated by the Supreme Court, Congress approved the Soil Conservation and Domestic Allotment Act, and again the Extension Service was given the responsibility of carrying out organizing work.

As the Depression dragged on, the idea of land use planning attracted considerable attention both nationally and in California. In San Francisco the Commonwealth Club took up a two-year study of the subject, to which several members of the College contributed their time and thoughts. Agricultural economist Henry Erdman wrote the club's final report, which concluded that the state needed better land use planning and recommended the development of regional planning commissions.[55] In 1938 federal-state agreements brought about a pilot program of land use planning in selected counties of each state. The California Agricultural Extension Service undertook such an effort in 1939, focusing on Riverside, Kern, Sonoma, and

PORTRAIT OF B. H. CROCHERON, DIRECTOR OF THE AGRICULTURAL EXTENSION SERVICE, COMMISSIONED BY THE CALIFORNIA FARM BUREAU FEDERATION TOWARD THE END OF HIS LENGTHY CAREER (1913 TO 1948).

Yuba counties because they represented different regions and types of farming. Under the general supervision of each county's farm advisor, county planning committees began to prepare maps and discuss optimal uses for local lands. Although participants considered the process valuable and plans were under way to expand the number of counties participating, this work was discontinued in the early 1940s.[56]

## FARM GROUPS AND EXTENSION

The number of local farm centers where families gathered for monthly meetings with their farm advisors gradually declined in the 1930s, but the close working relationship between the Extension Service and the county farm bureaus continued. Until 1931 the state office of the California Farm Bureau Federation was housed in two rooms of Hilgard Hall on the Berkeley campus. From 1931 to 1936 the CFBF occupied three rooms in Giannini Hall, then moved into six rooms in Hilgard until 1938. Then mounting pressures for space—and perhaps too for more distance—took the CFBF headquarters to an off-campus site nearby.

The symbiotic relationship of the CFBF with Extension continued to irritate other farm groups, such as the Grange, which criticized the Farm Bureau's unfair advantage in recruiting members and some of the activities it sponsored. Some of this resentment surfaced in 1935 in Santa Clara County. There the county farm bureau, organized in

1934, petitioned the board of supervisors to appropriate money for Extension work. According to a report on the public hearing, the California Extension Service became the butt of a number of "scurrilous remarks . . . by a few poorly informed and wild-eyed citizens." Critics from the Farmers' Union and a local taxpayers' league, thought to be angered by Giannini Foundation support of marketing orders for orchard crops, claimed that farm advisors practiced "regimentation" of farmers, that Crocheron was "some hombre" who "throttled" those who disagreed with him, and that home demonstration work was "frivolous" (homemaker clubs' hat-making activities drew particular scorn). Santa Clara County did not in fact open an Extension office until 1945.[57]

Such criticisms were relatively simple to shrug off, but the Farm Bureau's relationship with Associated Farmers was more problematical. After the Imperial Valley controversy of 1934, some Farm Bureau members helped organize the Associated Farmers for the specific purpose of dealing with labor issues. Many farmers had overlapping memberships, and the two groups often cooperated at the local level.[58] Nevertheless, not everyone within the Farm Bureau agreed with the stance of the Associated Farmers. In 1937 Alex Johnson, CFBF Secretary, wrote to S. P. Frisselle, AF representative, that he "felt that some of these local groups were inclined to get too militant"; later, when asked if CFBF would "carry a message of goodwill" from the Associated Farmers to the national FB convention in December 1938, Johnson polled his board of directors and got a mixed response: some were "much in favor of open and active support" while others expressed discomfort ("I think the Associated Farmers is our 'problem child' and we are going to have as much trouble as parents sometimes have with a headstrong adolescent boy.").[59]

The relationship caused trouble in at least one county agricultural economic conference sponsored by the Extension Service. These conferences were popular annual events, many of them two-day meetings including local bankers, merchants, and county officials besides Farm Bureau members. Ordinarily these meetings provided useful information and discussed agricultural policy and action programs that could help farmers plan for the next year, but occasionally they touched on more sensitive political issues. When one Sutter County conference endorsed the activities of the Associated Farmers and opposed federal labor camps, two incensed labor union councils wrote to President Sproul demanding that the University "immediately cease giving aid or comfort to the Associated Farmers or any similar anti-union group." Sproul disclaimed UC responsibility for conference statements, and thereafter Extension-sponsored conferences apparently made no more such recommendations.[60]

The Associated Farmers group received generally unfavorable publicity during the LaFollette hearings for its extralegal methods of strikebreaking. Nevertheless, Dean Hutchison—who in his oral history years later described himself as "one of the midwives" of the Associated Farmers and said he was "rather closely associated with that organization in a friendly and advisory capacity"—to the end of his career defended the organization for its role in fighting communism in California.[61]

## WORLD WAR II AND RURAL CALIFORNIA

By the time Pearl Harbor was bombed in December 1941, the military power of Japan had already overtaken countries in Asia like a juggernaut. After the Japanese air force demonstrated its effectiveness in Hawaii, many Americans began to be genuinely alarmed over the potential for invasion. There was talk in California of sightings of Japanese submarines along the coast and of possibly subversive activities on land. In early 1942 these fears combined with the prejudice or distrust of many white Californians to bring about the relocation of Japanese-American families to detention centers, under the rationale that such a move would increase national security. Given California's strategic location, its history of access to and from Asia, and its role in war industries and military staging, security was on nearly everybody's mind.

## EMERGENCY PREPAREDNESS: EXTENSION SWINGS INTO ACTION

For the second time in its history the Agricultural Extension Service swung into action as a public service agency in a nation at war, ready to mobilize citizens for wartime needs.

Galvanized by a sense of emergency, Crocheron presented a rural defense plan through President Sproul to Governor Olsen in March 1942. Modeled on the Home Guard of Great Britain, Crocheron's plan suggested organizing a rural militia—the "California Minute Men"—to be ready for action in the event of Japanese attack by parachute drop in concert with fifth-column sympathizers. Because many California farmers and ranchers were already expert marksmen, reasoned Crocheron, their skills would be useful for civil defense; he estimated that up to 100,000 men and boys could be enlisted through county farm advisors. Governor Olsen endorsed the plan, commending it to the commander of the state's armed forces, and in April Crocheron sent informational directives to all farm advisors. Although military authorities initially contemplated giving each farm advisor a military commission as a recruiting officer—an action that would have made Crocheron a lieutenant colonel—President Sproul declined that proposal. During the following months county Extension offices did recruit men for rural militia units, though not to the extent envisioned by Crocheron. In July, reporting that 20,000 men had signed up for reserve duty through the Extension Service, the University of California officially "signed off" the militia project, and civil defense authorities took over the tasks of organization and training.[62]

Extension also immediately undertook several public safety projects, including an inventory of rural emergency water supplies. Farm advisors and specialists identified and mapped water sources that could provide safe drinking supplies even if electricity for pumping were cut off, and helped farmers develop better on-farm water storage facilities. For the public at large, local Extension offices provided instruction leaflets and demonstrations on how to purify water from contaminated sources.

Farm advisors helped farmers expand production even with reduced resources. They organized tractor "cooperatives" to share machinery, and engineering specialists ran repair clinics for unreplaceable older equipment. Other Extension activities included strengthening rural fire protection in case of incendiary bomb drops (which could have been disastrous under California's summer range and forest conditions); distributing "blackout" instructions to keep rural enterprises like dairy barns from serving as beacons for enemy airplanes; directing "victory garden" programs, in which urban and rural citizens were encouraged to grow some of their own food; conducting home demonstrations of food preservation and other ways to conserve needed war materials; and disseminating general information in weekly "farm wargrams" distributed to all county offices.[63]

## THE EMERGENCY FARM LABOR PROJECT

As America's commitment to the war intensified, farmers lost much of their hired help to military duty or wartime industries. In California the farm labor problems of the 1930s were transformed into a new set of concerns. Job opportunities drew many of the "Okie" migrants into the cities, and the Depression's oversupply of seasonal farm workers vanished. Intensive farm labor users like the sugar beet industry in California and Colorado called for a return of Mexican workers, many of whom had been repatriated

150 during the Depression. In 1942 Congress negotiated a formal agreement with the government of Mexico to allow employment of Mexican *braceros* (day laborers, from the Spanish for "arm," *brazo*) in the United States under stipulated conditions for wages and housing. Under this program, important primarily to larger farm employers, nearly 90,000 workers were brought north between 1942 and 1945.[64]

Until 1943 general farm labor recruitment and placement came under the regulation of the U.S. Employment Service, but in April that year Congress assigned these responsibilities to the nation's Agricultural Extension Service. Neither Hutchison nor Crocheron was happy about the assignment, for the labor struggles of the 1930s had left bitterness in their wake. "Distinctly reluctant" to take on the new responsibility, Crocheron wrote to M. L. Wilson of the USDA: "The feeling in this State is strong among farm people against the Federal handling of the farm labor problem. . . . They believe that the objective of certain governmental bureaus and agencies has been the ultimate nationalization of the land and the unionization of farm labor." Hutchison and Crocheron submitted a joint memo to President Sproul on the issue of allowing the Extension Service to be "federalized" and controlled by Washington, but in this power struggle they had to capitulate.[65]

The Emergency Farm Labor Project developed rapidly under Extension administration in cooperation with the USDA, the War Food Administration, the California Farm Production Council, the State Department of Education, and the U.S. Army. Recruitment and placement took place in nine districts through a system of 125 local farm labor offices employing a staff of 443. These offices, directed by county farm advisors, were strategically placed along all major highways and in many towns. In each county a local labor advisory committee, composed of men familiar with local agriculture and labor needs, helped plan community mobilization and housing campaigns.

In its brief existence, from June 1943 through December 1945, the Farm Labor Project filled about 1,750,000 jobs on farms and in packing houses. Three-quarters of these were filled by domestic workers, 9 percent by Mexican nationals, 5 percent by prisoners of war, and the remaining 11 percent by miscellaneous workers, including Jamaicans, members of the armed forces, conscientious objectors, and prison inmates. The inexperienced were trained through demonstrations and instructional leaflets, which—complete with detailed line drawings—explained harvesting and other farm tasks in English, Spanish, German, or Japanese. Labor supervisors also received training. The project employed an architect to advise farmers on ways to improve labor housing. The California Farm Production Council constructed 359 demountable buildings and provided tents and tent platforms. The project also issued weather forecasts in critical labor periods, performed draft deferment investigations, and distributed gasoline coupons for worker transportation.

Because of the Emergency Farm Labor Project no material loss of crops occurred in California during the war years due to a shortage of labor.[66] Not the least significant legacy of the project may have been its demonstration that careful planning and attention to the details of recruitment, placement, training, and housing could go a long way toward solving the perennial farm labor problem in California.

## THE WAR'S IMPACT ON CAMPUSES

Wartime mobilization rapidly decimated the male student populations of UC campuses as well as the ranks of younger faculty and staff. The most dramatic single physical impact on the UC system was at the Davis campus. There, in the newly completed chemistry building, a small research group began in 1942 to work under conditions of high secrecy on certain aspects of the Manhattan Project, which would later develop the atomic bomb. The following year the entire campus was closed to collegiate instruction while the lands and buildings were used as a training school for the Army Signal Corps. Regular students did not return until 1945. Meanwhile, a reduced staff maintained the agricultural field experiments and animal herds, anticipating the resumption of research after the war.

Research activities of the University during World War II included the scientific contributions of physicists, engineers, and others toward national defense. Food and nutrition scientists made substantial progress in developing dehydrated meats, fruits, and vegetables at the request of the Office of Scientific Research and Development and the Quartermaster General of the Army and other military agencies. Home economists also served as consultants on housing and child care for local civilian groups.[67]

## AFTER THE WAR, WHAT THEN?

By the war's end, after fifteen years of unprecedented domestic and international upheavals, Americans were longing for a return to normalcy—whatever that might mean in a world that had been convulsed and forever changed. As the end of active conflict appeared within sight, two things were clear to those charged with preparing for the future: (1) unless careful planning took place, postwar adjustments might be as painful as those after World War I, and (2) the scientific and technological expertise that had been harnessed in the cause of war should eventually be used for the objectives of peace. Land-grant colleges of agriculture began to gear up for greatly expanded research and extension efforts after the war.

### PLANNING FOR POSTWAR AGRICULTURE

Land-grant college administrators hoped to use their influence to prevent postwar problems and encourage renewed focus on issues of concern during the Depression. In 1944 a special committee of the Association of Land-Grant Colleges and Universities (ALGCU) prepared a lengthy report to offer guidance. Entitled "Postwar Agricultural Policy," the report appeared under the signatures of nineteen land-grant officials from across the country, including Claude Hutchison, then serving as national president of the Association, and Harry Wellman, director of the Giannini Foundation. The document was a synthesis of opinions and policy recommendations gathered from a series of regional conferences and consultations with agencies, organizations, and scores of agricultural leaders and experts. Sections dealt with agriculture and the national welfare; adjustments in production; agricultural prices and price controls; land tenure, including ownership and tenancy and the use of credit; conservation of land, water, and forests; rural life and social facilities; and the role of farm people in policymaking. Generally, the report reaffirmed the desirability of the free market; the preservation of the family owner-operated farm as the typical basis for American agriculture; the urgent need for better land, water, and other resource management; and the importance of coordinated planning by government agencies, educational institutions, and farm organizations.[68]

The ALGCU document attracted widespread attention in academic and policymaking circles throughout the nation, and California was no exception. In 1945 the California legislature issued a joint resolution commending the report and recommending implementation of its policy goals in California. In 1946 the Commonwealth Club used the ALGCU report as the basis for undertaking a three-part study series on the future of agriculture in California, with section members including several faculty from the College and a number of prominent civic leaders. In 1947 the California State Reconstruction and Reemployment Commission published a 192-page document titled *Suggested Agricultural Policies for California*, which included discussions on sixteen "subjects of major

152 importance to the future of agriculture in California," ranging from the California State Water Plan to farm mortgage financing to sponsorship of a World Trade Center. Claude Hutchison was chairman of the editorial committee for this work.[69]

## THE AGRICULTURAL RESEARCH STUDY COMMITTEE

Hutchison's national connections and contacts in state legislative circles made him a powerful advocate for an expanded research and extension system in California. Recognizing the need to make up for time lost during the Depression and the war, Hutchison skillfully mobilized organized political support for renovation and expansion of county as well as campus agricultural facilities.

Although he would not live to see it fully implemented, Crocheron in 1945 prepared a postwar plan for the California Agricultural Extension Service. His county-by-county and program-by-program analysis stated:

> The size of the present staff . . . is manifestly inadequate to serve the rural interests of the state. . . . To meet the present problems of California agriculture in a manner comparable to that now operative in certain other states will require about an 85 percent increase in the staff of this Extension Service.

He went on to describe staff increases funded by new federal allocations to other states "of far less agricultural importance." Because the California farm population in comparison with these other states (for example, New York, Texas, North Carolina, and Iowa) was relatively small, wrote Crocheron, "Despite the fact that these states have lesser production and fewer problems, the total resources available to them will be far beyond those available to the California Extension Service unless and until the state and the counties materially increase their investment in the enterprise." The appraisal reviewed in detail the needs in each county and rec-

ommended increasing the current county staff from 156 to 292, the statewide specialist staff from 54 to 97. The total proposed increase in state funding for extension purposes: half a million dollars yearly.[70]

Hutchison adroitly maneuvered the push for better research and extension facilities. In a special session in January 1946, the legislature appropriated $1 million to augment the $6.2 million budget of the College of Agriculture for 1946-47. In March Governor Earl Warren signed Senate Bill 124, creating an Agricultural Research Study Committee consisting of nine appointed members, the state Director of Agriculture, and the Dean of the College of Agriculture. The committee was charged with studying the scope and general progress of agricultural research in California and the extent of "the practical application of the results thereof," with attention to the needs for new research on production, processing, and distribution of agricultural products and its "widest possible dissemination . . . to the end that the prosperity of this State shall remain unimpaired."[71]

After seventeen committee meetings, eight public hearings from Eureka to El Centro, and visits to UC facilities at Berkeley, Davis, Riverside, Meloland, and the USDA Western Regional Laboratory at Albany, the committee submitted its first report in 1946. According to the report, more than 800 people attended the hearings, nearly 300 presented oral statements, and 179 organizations and individuals filed written statements requesting research ranging from investigation of new insecticides such as DDT to a study of standards for consumer goods. In summary, the committee stated, "There exists with our farm people a universal desire to have an expanded, aggressive program of agricultural research, and the application of such research to production, processing, and marketing problems." The expanded research agenda included studies of irrigation efficiency, breeding of disease-resistant strains of plants and animals, basic work on soil improvement, effects of farm practices on the nutritional values of crops, rangeland improvement, mechanization of farm operations, utilization of waste products, improved forestry practices, economic analysis of marketing and distribution, methods for stabilizing farm labor, and expanded home economics information. The committee recommended an increase of $2 million in the College of Agriculture's next budget, more collaboration between federal and state research agencies, augmented county support for Extension facilities, and more rapid release and publication of research findings "in language readily understood by farmers."[72]

Within a year many of the recommendations became fact. With a legislative appropriation of $1.5 million for the biennium, the College hired new research staff, initiated many new projects, and began distributing a free monthly publication reporting research progress. Extension increased its technical staff from 242 to 302 in one year, anticipated hiring up to 42 more, and doubled its local field tests and demonstration plots, while county boards of supervisors substantially increased their support for local Extension work.[73] Rapid growth in campus and county facilities was made possible by taxes levied on California parimutuel racetrack betting. By 1948 a new forestry building was nearing completion on the Berkeley campus; buildings for soils and irrigation, plant science, and veterinary medicine were under construction at Davis; and there was a new insecticide laboratory at Riverside. In the planning stages were new buildings for viticulture, poultry, horticulture, and home economics. New county facilities included improved quarters for Extension and regulatory staff and better buildings and show rings at county fairgrounds.

In its final report the committee concluded, "of necessity much agricultural research work is laboriously slow and unspectacular in nature. Nevertheless, real progress is being made."[74] And so it was; a new era had begun.

### PRAGMATIC PARTNERSHIPS AND POLITICAL ALIGNMENTS

The College of Agriculture relied heavily on its traditional alliance with the agricultural community for political support during the Depression and immediate postwar years. With up to 25 percent of the entire University's budget assigned to the College during the Depression, the influence of groups like the Farm Bureau, the Agricultural Legislative Committee, and the San Andreas Canyon Club helped the College—and the rest of the University—fend off budget cuts and continue public service. After the war the support of these groups brought greatly increased appropriations for expansion and improvement in facilities and staff. The pragmatic partnership between the College and farm interests not only served an important sector of the state's economy, it strengthened the University as well.

Yet it was in the Depression decade that the College began to be perceived as a tool of big business. The hopes of many of California's small-scale farmers were dashed by the economic crises of the time; as farm foreclosures began to shrink the number of individual enterprises, California agriculture became increasingly associated with business and capital rather than family-farm or labor interests. For leftist critics in particular, the rise of the Associated Farmers during the 1930s represented an anti-union industrialist coalition. Even by its tenuous marginal association with such a group, the College became linked in some eyes with its views.

Leaders in the College of Agriculture were a fairly diverse and independent set of men, but clearly their opinions had to be palatable to their political supporters. Both Hutchison and Crocheron, widely respected for their administrative talents and grasp of affairs, were conservative in their views,

154 men with whom successful and powerful agricultural business leaders could be comfortable. Hutchison, a strong believer in the free market and states' rights, disapproved of the "socialistic tendencies" of the Roosevelt administration; Crocheron shared Hutchison's concern about the federal interventions of the New Deal as well as his view of the communist threat.

Though his sympathies were in tune with the right-wing views of many in California agriculture, Hutchison occasionally disagreed with their more extreme statements. Longtime editor of the *Pacific Rural Press* John Pickett, for example, was prone to reactionary outbursts—as in his editorial on the Imperial Valley struggles in April 1934: "The main danger . . . is from the socially-minded busybodies and public sobsisters . . . harder to deal with than the Communist leaders."[75] But when Pickett in 1938 attacked student political activities at the University, Hutchison defended freedom of speech. Conceding that students had criticized him for his connections with captains of industry, Hutchison nevertheless wrote Pickett that "all shades of opinion" should be represented within the University. "The worst thing that could happen to America would be to destroy the freedom of its universities" and have them become "propagandists for the reigning order," he wrote, reminding Picket of what was happening in Europe.[76]

In the charged political atmosphere of the New Deal years Hutchison had to be wary of offending his supporters, many of whom were also his friends. His ambivalence about research in rural sociology was not only a matter of unease about the methodology and personnel available in this field, it also stemmed from his desire to keep the College from offending the farm community. Yet he recognized limitations in the thinking of farm people and regretted that his own education had been lacking in breadth. In his presidential address to the Association of Land-Grant Colleges and Universities in 1944, Hutchison described the needs of agricultural students for broader exposure to social and political thought:

> Graduates of our agricultural, engineering and home economics curricula need to be more than good technicians—more than competent, skilled, professional men and women. They need to be educated individuals capable of thinking and acting intelligently as citizens in a free society. They need to be informed—intelligently informed, on national and international matters as well as upon the affairs which concern their own immediate community and state; above all they need to be capable of exercising cool, deliberate and critical judgment. . . . The complexity of modern civilization demands that every agricultural student have some understanding of man's economic, political and social institutions, the interplay of the factors which have led . . . to their change and historical development, and problems concerning the organization of human society.

He granted too that "Few agricultural curricula afford any opportunity whatever for exploration . . . into the fields of the humanities, or for an . . . appreciation of the great literary, artistic and philosophical expressions of human experience and reflective appraisal of their meaning and value."[77]

Such thoughts may have stemmed from Hutchison's observations of his colleagues during depression and war. They may also have been an expression of his own concerns regarding the role of the College of Agriculture; but they did not lead him to embrace sociology as a desirable addition to college work.

## THE COLLEGE WITH TWO MASTERS

Administration in a public university has always been a political balancing act. With the mission to serve the public, the institution is dependent upon the public will for its own support; with the need to be free of political control in pursuit of truth, the institution must rely on political approval to be maintained. The land-grant institution also serves diverse public interests and must interpret those interests broadly, in the context of many competing needs, rather than from a narrow or short-term point of view. But when a particular part of the institution has a well-defined clientele, its staff must inevitably experience a certain tension between the demands of that clientele and the overall mission of the University itself. Thus the dilemma of the College of Agriculture: the College has a particular body of clients for subject-oriented education and research. How the College fulfills its obligations to that body of clients has sometimes been a source of controversy.

In a lucid analysis of the relationship between science and society, historian Charles Rosenberg has described the "endemic ambiguity" of the agricultural sciences: the tension between the pursuit of knowledge for its own sake and the pressure to apply knowledge for purposes of economic growth or private profit; the sometimes uneasy strain between the internal allegiance of scientists to an intellectual discipline and the external demands from a clientele anxious to solve problems.[78] The ambiguity of which Rosenberg wrote lies in the mismatch between the ultimate goals of science itself—to pursue truth, to extend the frontiers of knowledge, to recognize and work on enduring issues of importance, and to practice the highest standards of free inquiry without fear of reprisals—and society's need for practical and useful research in the name of national productivity and well-being.

The agricultural experiment stations were created to develop scientific knowledge to help farmers improve their lot. As the institutions matured, however, they began to build a culture of their own, the requirements of which coexisted with the earlier conception of service to a particular community.

As Rosenberg points out,

> Interest-group politics created the American experiment stations; once created, the men who staffed these new institutions, motivated by their own values and institutional needs, became an interest group of their own, forging pragmatic alliances and a research policy based on a shared interest in the growth of productivity through the rational application of technology.[79]

In earlier decades the partnership between science and agriculture was advantageous to both and widely accepted as deserving of public support. As long as more than a quarter of the population relied on farming for a living—and the Jeffersonian notion of the virtuous yeoman as democracy's backbone lingered on—colleges of agriculture could depend on fairly widespread approval for their work. Developments of the 1930s, however, at least in California, shrank the farming population, changed its image in the public mind, and helped define it as powerful minority special-interest group. Because agricultural scientists continued to need political support, the trend pushed agricultural college administrators ever more closely into the arms of farm organizations and business leaders. Ultimately, the agricultural science establishment became a kind of "island empire," a world of its own too far removed from the concerns of the larger world to recognize how fast it was changing.[80]

Hutchison was a capable administrator, a man of integrity, and a dedicated builder of his institution. His view of the College of Agriculture, however, was very traditional—witness his choice of title for California's 1939–40 biennial experiment station report: *Science, Servant of Agriculture*. The implications of this title, on close examination, are not altogether reassuring: servants are expected to be competent, but not to take a philosophically inquiring approach to their work.

# NOTES

1. "Economic Problems of California Agriculture: A Report to the Governor of California," Agricultural Experiment Station *Bulletin 504* (Dec. 1930), p. 5.

2. "The Agricultural Situation in California," Agricultural Extension Service *Circular 18*, pp. 3–6 (included in *Report of the Work of the Agricultural Experiment Station of the University of California, July 1, 1927, to June 30, 1928*).

3. See Walton Bean, *California: An Interpretive History* (New York: McGraw-Hill, 1988), pp. 409–24; Carey McWilliams, *Southern California Country: An Island on the Land* (New York: Duell, Sloan and Pearce, 1946), pp. 294–312; Walter J. Stein, *California and the Dust Bowl Migration* (Westport, Conn.: Greenwood Press, 1973); James N. Gregory, *American Exodus: The Dust Bowl Migration and Okie Culture in California* (New York: Oxford University Press, 1989).

4. California Department of Water Resources, "California Rainfall Summary: Monthly Total Precipitation, 1849–1980" (Sacramento: State GPO, July 1981), p. 13, fig. 2, Long Term Precipitation Trends.

5. See Erwin Cooper, *Aqueduct Empire* (Glendale: Arthur H. Clark, 1968), pp. 147–66; Robert de Roos, *The Thirsty Land: The Story of the Central Valley Project* (Stanford: Stanford University Press, 1948), pp. 36–45.

6. U.S. Bureau of the Census, *Historical Statistics of the United States, Colonial Times to 1970, Pt. 1* (Washington, D.C.: Department of Commerce, 1975).

7. Ellen Liebman, *California Farmland: A History of Large Agricultural Landholdings* (Montclair, N.J.: Rowman & Allanheld, 1983), pp. 95–97.

8. See Murray Benedict, *Farm Policies of the United States, 1790–1950* (New York: The Twentieth Century Fund, 1953), pp. 276–348, on New Deal agricultural programs.

9. Irving Bernstein, *The Turbulent Years: A History of the American Worker, 1933–1941* (Boston: Houghton Mifflin, 1970), pp. 252–98.

10. Stuart Jamieson, "Labor Unionism in American Agriculture," U.S. Bureau of Labor Statistics *Bulletin 836* (Washington, D.C.: 1945), pp. 72–79; Howard De Witt, *Violence in the Fields: California Filipino Farm Labor Unionization During the Great Depression* (Saratoga, Calif.: Century Twenty One Publishing, 1980), pp. 79–81.

11. See Bernstein, *Turbulent Years*, pp. 160–68, on the Imperial Valley episode; also Cletus Daniel, *Bitter Harvest: A History of California Farmworkers, 1870–1941* (Berkeley: UC Press, 1982), pp. 222–57.

12. Stein, *California and the Dust Bowl Migration*, pp. 157–60.

13. U.S. Senate, Committee on Education and Labor, *Violations of Free Speech and Rights of Labor. Hearings before a Subcommittee*, 76th Cong. (Washington, D.C.: U.S. GPO, 1940–43).

14. See Verne A. Stadtman, *The University of California, 1868–1968* (New York: McGraw-Hill, 1970), pp. 257–80 and passim, on Sproul. Hutchison's oral history, *The College of Agriculture, University of California, 1922–1952* (Berkeley: UC Regional Cultural History Project, 1961), describes his career. The quote on Hutchison is from John Kenneth Galbraith, "Berkeley in the Age of Innocence," *The Atlantic* 223:6 (June 1969): 62–68.

15. Stadtman, *University of California, 1868–1968*, pp. 259–60.

16. Descriptions of the Agricultural Legislative Committee, which later became the Agricultural Council of California, and of the San Andreas Canyon Club are from oral histories: Hutchison, *College of Agriculture*, pp. 60–63; Ryerson, The world is my campus, pp. 127–29; and James B. Kendrick, Jr., *From Plant Pathologist to Vice President for Agriculture and Natural Resources, University of California, 1947–1986* (Berkeley: UC Regional Oral History Office, 1989), pp. 58–59. The Executive Bulls are mentioned in J. Earl Coke, *Reminiscences on People and Change in California Agriculture, 1900–1975* (Davis: UC Oral History Office, 1975), pp. 217–20.

17. Stadtman, *University of California, 1868–1968*, pp. 261–73; C. B. Hutchison, *Science, Servant of Agriculture–The Director's Biennial Report from July 1, 1938, to June 30, 1940* (included in *Report of the Work of the Agricultural Experiment Station of the University of California from July 1, 1939, to June 30, 1940*), p. 178.

18. See Celeste Turner Wright, *University Woman: The memoir of Celeste Turner Wright, Professor of English, Emeritus* (Davis: UC Oral History Center, 1981) for descriptions of Davis in the 1920s and 1930s.

19. Agnes Fay Morgan, "The History of Nutrition and Home Economics in the University of California, Berkeley, 1914–1962," unpublished manuscript; also Hutchison, *College of Agriculture*, pp. 306–23.

20. Historical facts about the Davis campus are recorded in five issues of *UC Davis Magazine*: Fall 1983, Winter 1984, Spring 1984, Summer 1984, and Summer 1987.

21. Horticultural material regarding the UCLA College of Agriculture was provided to the author by Professor Emeritus Charles A. Schroeder, March 1990.

22. Harry W. Lawton and Lewis G. Weathers, "The Origins of Citrus Research in California and the Founding of the Citrus Research Center and Agricultural Experiment Station," in Walter Reuther, E. Clair Calavan, and Glenn E. Carman, eds., *The Citrus Industry*. 281–335 (Oakland: UC Division of Agriculture and Natural Resources, 1989), vol. 5, p. 322–25.

23. See Experiment Station *Reports* during the 1930s; for the first time, each biennial *Director's Report* was given a unique title: *New Facts for California Farmers* (1932–34), *Partners in Progress* (1934–36), *Toward Better Agriculture* (1936–38), *Science, Servant of Agriculture* (1938–1940). Another rich source of information is Claude B. Hutchison, ed., *California Agriculture* (Berkeley: UC Press, 1946).

24. Hans Jenny, "Exploring the Soils," in Hutchison, ed., *California Agriculture*, 325–30; R. Earl Storie, "An Index for Rating the Agricultural Value of Soils," Agricultural Experiment Station *Bulletin 556* (1933).

25. George S. Wells, *Garden in the West: A Dramatic Account of Science in Agriculture* (New York: Dodd, Mead, 1969), pp. 21–39; Frank Adams, "History of the Irrigation Division, 1910–1954" (Davis: UC Department of Water Science and Engineering, 1969).

26. See Frank G. Parsons, *The Story of Seed Certification in California, 1937–1976: Recollections of Frank G. Parsons* (Davis: UC Oral History Center, 1979).

27. Wells, *Garden in the West*, pp. 89–105.

28. Harold H. Cole, *Adventurer in Animal Science: Harold H. Cole* (Davis: UC Oral History Center, 1977), pp. 97–105.

29. UC Archives, College of Agriculture Files, Box 1180 ("Old Dormant Special Problems"); Hutchison, *College of Agriculture*, pp. 216–20.

30. Roy Bainer, *The Engineering of Abundance: An Oral History Memoir of Roy Bainer* (Davis: UC Oral History Center, 1975), pp. 106–66.

31. See William V. Cruess, *A Half Century in Food and Wine Technology* (Berkeley: UC Regional Oral History Office, 1967); *Emil M. Mrak, A Journey Through Three Epochs: Food Prophet, Creative Chancellor, Senior Statesman of Science* (Davis: UC Oral History Program, 1974).

32. Clifford B. Anderson, "The Metamorphosis of American Agrarian Idealism in the 1920s and 1930s," *Agricultural History* 35 (Oct. 1961): 182–88.

33. H. R. Tolley, *How California Agriculture Profits by Economic Research: Accomplishments of the Giannini Foundation of Agricultural Economics* (Berkeley: UC Press, 1934); also Emmett Fiske, "The College and Its Constituency: Research and Community Development at the University of California, 1875–1978" (UC Davis, Ph.D. thesis, 1979) pp. 213–22.

158    34. Richard S. Kirkendall, "Howard Tolley and Agricultural Planning in the 1930s," *Agricultural History* 39 (Jan. 1965): 25–33.

35. See E. C. Voorhies, F. E. Todd, and J. K. Galbraith, "Honey Marketing in California" and "Economic Aspects of the Bee Industry," Agricultural Experiment Station *Bulletins 554* and *555* (1933); "California County Expenditures," *Bulletin 582* (1934).

36. R. L. Adams and T. R. Kelly, "A Study of Farm Labor in California," Agricultural Experiment Station *Circular 193* (1918), pp. 8–9, 11.

37. California Mexican Fact-finding Committee, *Mexicans in California* (Sacramento: State GPO, 1930), part II.

38. UC Archives, *Presidents' Papers*, Folder 439:2 (1934).

39. "Seasonal Labor Requirements for California Crops," Agricultural Experiment Station *Bulletin 623* (1938); "Composition and Characteristics of the Agricultural Population in California," *Bulletin 630* (1939).

40. See Richard Steven Street, "The Economist as Humanist: The Career of Paul S. Taylor," *California History* 58 (Winter 1979–80): 350–61. Also Paul S. Taylor, *Paul Schuster Taylor, California Social Scientist* (Berkeley: UC Regional Oral History Office, 1973).

41. Bean, *California: An Interpretive History*, p. 498.

42. Hutchison, *College of Agriculture*, pp. 116–17.

43. Hutchison, *Toward Better Agriculture (Director's Biennial Report)*, p. ix.

44. UC Archives, *Presidents' Papers*, Folder 240 (1938).

45. See Richard Kirkendall, *Social Scientists and Farm Politics in the Age of Roosevelt* (Columbia: University of Missouri Press, 1966).

46. UC Archives, *Grether Papers*, Box 1, "CVP Studies," contains minutes of Problem 24 committee meetings. Fiske, "The College and Its Constituency," pp. 257–72, discusses the CVP studies.

47. See Walter Goldschmidt, *As You Sow: Three Studies in the Social Consequences of Agribusiness* (Montclair, N.J.: Allanheld, Osmun, 1978; Richard S. Kirkendall, "Social Science in the Central Valley of California: An Episode," *California Historical Society Quarterly* 43 (Sept. 1964): 195–218; Sheridan Downey, *They Would Rule the Valley* (San Francisco: privately printed, 1947); Michael N. Hayes and Alan L. Olmstead, "The Arvin and Dinuba Controversy Reex-

amined" (Davis: Agricultural History Center Working Paper No. 8, December 1981).

48. Charles M. Hardin, "The Bureau of Agricultural Economics Under Fire: A Study in Valuation Conflicts," *Journal of Farm Economics* 28 (Aug. 1946): 635–68.

49. UC Archives, *Presidents' Papers*, Folder 255, "Alsberg to Hutchison" (Sept. 27, 1939).

50. The three-volume documentary project was titled *Japanese-American Evacuation and Resettlement* (Berkeley: University of California Press, 1946–54). Individual volumes include *The Spoilage*, by Dorothy Swaine Thomas and Richard S. Nishimoto (1946); *The Salvage*, by Dorothy Swaine Thomas with Charles Kikuchi and James Sakoda (1952); and *Prejudice, War, and the Constitution*, by Jacobus ten Broek, Edward N. Barnhart, and Floyd W. Matson (1954). Thomas objected to graduate student Morton Grodzins's use of the research material in his book *Americans Betrayed* (University of Chicago Press, 1946). See UC Archives, *Presidents' Papers*, "Grodzins Affair."

51. Orville E. Thompson had this title at Davis in 1964.

52. Gladys L. Baker, "County Agent Work Under the Roosevelt Administration," in *The County Agent* (Chicago: University of Chicago Press, 1939), pp. 69–70, 94–96.

53. UC Archives, *Presidents' Papers*, Folder 240:1 (1935).

54. Wayne Rasmussen, *Agriculture in the United States: A Documentary History* (New York: Random House, 1975), vol. 3, pp. 2538–41. Since the funding allocation formula was based on percentage of farm population, the Bankhead-Jones Act did not help California as much as it did more rural states.

55. "Land Use Planning in California?" *Transactions of the Commonwealth Club of California, 1938–39*, vol. 33, pp. 191–231.

56. Hutchison, *Science, Servant of Agriculture*, pp. 3–4.

57. UC Archives, *Presidents' Papers*, Folder 240, "Letter from L. A. Nichols to Harold Ellis" (1935).

58. Clarke A. Chambers, *California Farm Organizations: A Historical Study of the Grange, the Farm Bureau and the Associated Farmers, 1929–1941* (Berkeley: UC Press, 1952), pp. 57–59.

59. Quotes are from subpoenaed letters in the La Follette hearings: U.S. Senate Committee on Education and Labor, *Violations of Free Speech and Rights of Labor*, 76th Cong., Pt. 68, Supp. Exhibits, pp. 24,958–24,963.

60. UC Archives, *Presidents' Papers*, Folder 240 (1938).

61. Hutchison, *The College of Agriculture*, pp. 394–96.

62. UC Archives, *Presidents' Papers*, Folder 402–1 (1942).

63. Extension's role during World War II is described in one of B. H. Crocheron's speeches, "The Years Between," reproduced in *Bertram Hanford Crocheron: Architect and Builder of the California Agricultural Extension Service* (Berkeley: UC Agricultural Extension Service, 1967).

64. Otey M. Scruggs, "Evolution of the Mexican Farm Labor Agreement of 1942," *Agricultural History* 34 (July 1960): 140–49.

65. UC Archives, *Presidents' Papers*, Folder 402–B (1943).

66. California Agricultural Extension Service, A *Report of the Emergency Farm Labor Project, 1943–1945* (Berkeley: UC Office of the Director of the Extension Service, n.d.).

67. Stadtman, *University of California, 1868–1968*, pp. 305–19. Morgan, "History of Nutrition and Home Economics," pp. 11–13.

68. *Proceedings of the Association of Land-Grant Colleges and Universities, 58th Annual Convention, 1944* (Chicago: ALGCU, 1944), pp. 233–76.

69. See Benedict, *Farm Policies of the United States, 1790–1950*, pp. 469–70; California State Reconstruction and Reemployment Commission, *Suggested Agricultural Policies for California* (Sacramento: State GPO, 1947); *Transactions of the Commonwealth Club*, 40 (1946), 41 (1947), 42 (1948).

70. UC College of Agriculture, *The Agricultural Extension Service: A Postwar Reappraisal.* Confidential Report. (Berkeley: UC Agricultural Extension Service, September 1, 1945.)

71. Agricultural Research Study Committee, *Report on Agricultural Research in California, Presented to the Governor of California and the Fifty-Seventh Regular Session of the California Legislature in Accordance with the Provisions of S.B. 124, Chapter 144, Statutes of 1945* (Sacramento: State GPO, November 29, 1946).

72. Ibid.

73. Agricultural Research Study Committee, *Report . . . 1947.*

74. Agricultural Research Study Committee, *Report . . . 1948.*

75. Pickett, "Farm Labor and the Agitators," April 21, 1934.

76. UC Archives, *Presidents' Papers*, 1938, Folder 240.

77. Hutchison, "The Liberal Education of the 'Industrial Classes,'" in *Proceedings ALGCU 1944*, pp. 24–32.

78. Charles E. Rosenberg, *No Other Gods: On Science and American Social Thought* (Baltimore, Md.: Johns Hopkins Press, 1976), p. 145.

79. Ibid., pp. 171–72.

80. See Andre Mayer and Jean Mayer, "Agriculture: the Island Empire," *Daedalus* 103 (Summer 1974): 83–96.

# 6

# Prosperity and Problems

## 1948–1968

*Students and faculty in the field. Agricultural field trips offer significant learning experiences, supplementing classroom instruction.*

Science and technology transformed American agriculture after World War II, and in California the diversity and value of agricultural production grew enormously as hundreds of thousands of acres came under irrigation from new federal and state projects. As the University decentralized with growth, Davis and Riverside became general campuses. College of Agriculture academic programs became increasingly sophisticated, and research and extension staff, facilities, and activities multiplied. By the 1960s, however, recognition of the societal impacts of technological change had created new public environmental and social concerns. Outside and inside the Division of Agricultural Sciences there began a critical re-examination of its traditional roles.

# 6

# Prosperity and Problems   1948–1968

## GREAT LEAPS FORWARD

Demobilization and the return to peace after World War II brought not only major new international political alignments but also a period of intense economic development, enthusiasm for scientific and technological change, and domestic social reaction. People wanted to turn their thoughts toward a better future. They were eager for restored order and tranquillity at home; they poured their energies into building families and careers and developing a new prosperity based on progress in science and technology. They were not, during the 1950s, in a mood for political activism or controversy. Such proclivities were moreover discouraged in those years of McCarthyism and House Un-American Activities Committee investigations. The generation then growing up would later be called the "silent generation"—concerned with shaping life in a rapidly changing environment, but not inclined to argue the consequences of change.

The scientific community, much bolstered in some fields by federal investments during the war, again took up the research that had been placed on hold while the nation fought. Major scientific and technical developments emerged from the war years for peacetime applications. The nation established a new reliance on the airplane, antibiotic drugs to fight infection, and chemical "miracles" like DDT that could be used against pests and disease. Other advances in engineering and transportation, food production and processing, and public health and medicine found ready application in a society eager to take advantage of new solutions to old problems.

While all sectors of society saw rapid technical progress, particularly pronounced were the gains in agriculture. The years from 1941 through 1973 have been termed "the second American agricultural revolution" by historians of science and technology. The factors that made up this revolution included greater use of soil conditioners, fertilizers, and cover crops; adoption of more productive crop varieties and livestock breeds; more efficient crop production and livestock feeding regimes; widespread advances in mechanization; better control of insects and diseases; and more careful conservation practices. Many of these advancements were results of agricultural research that had been carried on for years before the war but whose adoption had been delayed by the stringencies of the Depression.[1]

For example, farmers facing wartime labor shortages had mechanized many standard operations. Some adopted tractors for the first time; others began to use power take-off devices to add tractor engine energy to trailed or mounted machinery. Engineers developed hydraulic power to ease many tasks requiring heavy lifting or pulling. Mechanical planters and harvesters began to be used for important commodities like corn, sugar beets, and cotton.[2] A significant impact of mechanization was the release of millions of acres of land formerly used for feeding work animals that could now be used to produce marketable crops and commodities. Less recognized was the growing dependence of agriculture—like the rest of society—on the use of fossil fuels.

Another great boost was given agriculture by the synthetic organic pesticides developed during World War II to fight insect-vectored diseases such as malaria, typhus, and sleeping sickness. One of these was DDT (dichloro-diphenyl-trichloroethane), originally developed in Switzerland. DDT proved a boon for the eradication of vermin, as did development of the chlorinated hydrocarbons by the Allies and the organophosphates by the Germans. The use of these new chemicals in agriculture brought cheap, effective control of pest problems that had long hindered productivity. Large corporations began to manufacture and market the new products, and the pesticide industry boomed. Selective herbicides also came into common use in the 1940s.[3]

FARM MECHANICS STUDENTS, 1948. THE USE OF TRACTORS AND OTHER FARM MACHINERY INCREASED EXPONENTIALLY AFTER WORLD WAR II.

Other scientific developments from war-related research proved useful to farmers, food processors, and distributors. For example, the use of penicillin as a therapeutic agent enhanced animal weight gain, and radioactive isotopes (by-products of atomic research) made excellent tracers for studying elements in plant and animal life. Rapid development and refinement of scientific precision instruments made laboratory research both easier and more determinate, and expanded options for scientists who had previously had to build their own equipment.[4]

Bumper crops in 1948 pushed total U.S. farm output to 150 percent of the average between 1935 and 1939, and the trend upward continued. Higher production in the 1950s was met by demand for farm products during the Korean War, and the 1954 Agricultural Trade Development and Assistance Act provided another outlet for surplus commodities by channeling food aid to needy nations. Across the country agriculture changed rapidly, becoming more productive, more efficient, more scientifically grounded and technically sophisticated. Its practice demanded more skills and more capital. Marginal farmers were squeezed by more competitive neighbors, retiring older farmers sold out, and farm numbers dropped steadily while average farm size got bigger. The trend paralleled general industrialization, and though some worried about the future of the family farm, the advantages of progress seemed clearly to outweigh their concerns.[5]

## *166* POSTWAR TRENDS
## IN CALIFORNIA

### POPULATION AND LAND USE

The overwhelming fact of life in California after the war was growth. In 1940 California's population was 6.9 million; by 1950 it was 10.6 million. Military duty and wartime industries brought many newcomers, thousands of whom opted to stay after the war was over, attracting still others. New residential subdivisions, especially in the south, sprouted across California, supplanting crops. School districts strained to house new hordes of children. While the nation's general migration pattern continued to be rural-to-urban, in California the trend was even stronger. Concentrated largely along the coast, the boom spread across the Los Angeles basin and around San Francisco Bay. By 1950 only about 5 percent of the population lived on farms, down from nearly 10 percent before the war. In 1960 farm residents accounted for only about 2 percent of California's 15.7 million citizens.[6]

FARMLAND BEING CONVERTED TO A SHOPPING MALL. THOUSANDS OF ACRES NEAR CITIES BECAME SUBURBS DURING THE 1950S.

The cities continued to swallow up large tracts of land formerly in agriculture. In 1950 Los Angeles County was still one of the most agriculturally productive counties in the nation, with a diversified farming economy taking full advantage of the mild year-round climate and proximity of urban markets. By 1960 rapid suburban growth and accompanying air pollution had diminished the basin's productivity, and agriculture became steadily less important as other industries grew. The tidy orchards and garden farms of Santa Clara County, south of San Francisco, shared a similar fate. In the late 1930s the county had 100,000 acres in orchard and 20,000 in vegetables; by 1955 nearly one-third of this acreage had been converted to urban uses. Ten years later only 52,000 acres of farmland remained, and as "high-tech" industries proliferated, urban development continued to shoulder agriculture aside.[7]

Nevertheless, even though some of the state's oldest and best farmland was disappearing under asphalt and concrete, its agricultural industry was thriving. Around 1950, the growth of irrigated farming in the Central Valley and in the southern desert valleys watered by the Colorado River lifted California to first place among all states in value of agricultural products. By 1960 its total agricultural production was valued at more than $3 billion—nearly 9 percent of total U.S. gross farm income, earned on about 3 percent of its cropland. The state produced almost half the national output of all fruits and nuts and about a third of all vegetables, on a declining number of farms (99,274 in 1959). California farms continued to be distributed between very large and very small holdings, with relatively fewer middle-size farms than in the country at large. While farms of 1,000 acres or more accounted for about 6 percent of California holdings compared with 3.5 percent in the nationas a whole, nearly 60 percent were less than 50 acres, compared with 33 percent overall.[8]

In 1962 California became the most populous state in the union. By this time it was clear that new land use patterns were radically altering the native landscape and that population growth was spawning a plethora of problems. Schools felt great pressure to expand; water delivery systems were stretched to serve more customers and water quality problems emerged; highway construction snaked through new areas as traffic clogged old roadways; and smog, first reported in the Los Angeles basin in the early 1940s, began to threaten other metropolitan areas.

Educators and policymakers, concerned about the implications of growth for all sectors of society, convened in a 1963 series of University conferences entitled "California and the Challenge of Growth."[9] Land use and environmental matters began to loom larger in the public mind. State government passed a pathbreaking series of laws aimed at protecting natural resources, including the California Land Conservation Act (1965), the Mulford-Carrell Air Resources Act (1967), and the California Environmental Quality Act (1970). Other legislation helped bring about organization of local planning agencies and monitoring programs for pesticides.

## WATER AND POLITICS: THE CVP AND THE SWP

Phase I of the Central Valley Project (CVP), mandated under federal authority during the Depression and constructed starting in 1937, took nearly 30 years to complete. In 1944 the U.S. Bureau of Reclamation completed Shasta Dam, the CVP's linchpin in

AERIAL VIEW OF THE CALIFORNIA AQUEDUCT, SLICING THROUGH ORCHARDS IN BLOOM IN THE SAN JOAQUIN VALLEY.

the foothills at the head of the Sacramento Valley, and its many-fingered reservoir began impounding waters from California's far northern mountains. In the immediate postwar years other segments of the CVP system were activated. In 1951 the first water flowed directly south from Shasta Dam almost 500 miles to the San Joaquin Valley through connected waterways and pumping stations. Its delivery made possible the expansion of irrigated agriculture on hundreds of thousands of acres. In hot, dry Kern County, at the southern end of the valley, cultivated land soared from 200,000 acres in the mid-1930s to more than 700,000 in 1960. By the project's twenty-fifth anniversary in 1961, the bureau had in operation seven dams and reservoirs, 390 miles of canals, eight pumping complexes, and several large electrical power plants.[10]

The successes of the CVP were not achieved without controversy. The federal acreage limitation (160 acres per person) on subsidized irrigation water deliveries remained a source of impassioned debate. In the early 1950s rural representatives mounted a determined effort to "buy back" the CVP from the federal government, but their lobbying came to naught. In 1958 the U.S. Supreme Court ruled to uphold the acreage limitation on water benefits. The ruling allowed water contractors who had infringed on the limit several years to comply with its stipulations.[11]

168     Not all of California's water needs were met by the CVP. In the late 1940s proposals were made for another statewide aqueduct system to divert waters from the Feather River in northeastern California down across the Delta, the San Joaquin Valley, and the Tehachapi Mountains into southern California. In 1959 the Burns-Porter Act authorized the State Water Project (SWP), which was narrowly approved by voters in 1960. The centerpiece of this system was the massive earth-fill dam at Oroville. Eventually the SWP provided water for the arid west side of the San Joaquin and the state's south-lands; however, the proposed San Joaquin Drain, intended to cope with increasing salinity problems, was not completed.[12]

In the twenty-some years of intensive water development in California after the war, the euphoria of progress largely overwhelmed the caveats. Enormous projects produced exciting opportunities for both agricultural and urban interests. As the years passed, however, ominous signs began to appear: shifting water tables; concentration of nitrates, salts, and toxic elements in groundwater and surface drainage basins; and wildlife kills. By the late 1960s many environmentalists, scientists, and policymakers recognized the dilemmas created by California's monumental commitment to water engineering.

## THE REAPPORTIONMENT OF THE LEGISLATURE

Another significant event of the period was the 1965 reorganization of the California legislature. With increasing concentration of population in urban areas it became obvious that senators from the rural districts exercised a disproportionate share of political power. By the mid-1950s just one-quarter of the population was electing three-quarters of the state senators. The views of rural voters, particularly the views of organized agriculture, were thus far better represented in the legislature than those of city voters. Although several initiatives seeking to modify the system were defeated, the U.S. Supreme Court in 1964 ruled that in the election of state legislators each person's vote must be approximately equal, and seats in both houses must be distributed according to population rather than geography. Accordingly, the 1965 reapportionment had senatorial districts that did not deviate by more than 15 percent in population. In the next year's election, control of the Senate passed to urbanized southern California, which for years had already dominated the Assembly.[13]

The implications of legislative reapportionment were far-reaching for California agriculture as an industry and as a political force—and for the University of California. No longer would there be a key group of senators traditionally rural in outlook, committed to support of the farming community. Given the relatively weak political party system in California, interest-group politics would become increasingly dominant, and the old agricultural lobbies would lose power as many politically active special interests proliferated. Agricultural activities at the land-grant University, traditionally supported by loyal farm interests, would also come under much more skeptical scrutiny from urban legislators.

## REASSEMBLING THE UNIVERSITY

### GROWTH AND CHANGE IN THE UNIVERSITY

Like colleges and universities everywhere, the University of California scrambled to provide facilities and services for returning veterans after World War II. With the aid and encouragement of the G.I. Bill providing benefits for higher education, young men and women opted for college and university work in numbers far higher than before the war. Their arrival on campuses in the late 1940s and again after the Korean conflict sent a series of tremors through academic life. Temporary buildings went up in haste, and the legislature authorized many permanent new buildings to serve the needs of a projected later wave of enrollments that would hit the colleges and universities from the postwar "baby boom." All of the University's campuses were strained to their limits. Admissions pressures brought further development of the smaller campuses and the creation of three entirely new ones.[14] By 1950 the UCLA student body was nearly as large as Berkeley's; a UC campus at Santa Barbara, created by absorbing the Santa Barbara State College in 1944, was going up at a former Marine Corps air station at Goleta; and a plan for expansion at Davis and Riverside had been drawn up by a committee of thirteen headed by Harry B. Walker, professor of agricultural engineering at Davis.[15]

In 1951 the Regents approved the opening of a College of Letters and Sciences at Davis, beginning a long-range metamorphosis of that campus with new majors in chemistry, zoology, botany, history, and English. Stanley B. Freeborn, a medical entomologist and former assistant to Dean Hutchison at Berkeley, became provost at Davis in 1952. In 1958 he was named chancellor, and the next year the Regents declared UC Davis a general campus with authority to add new majors, schools, and colleges and to expand its graduate programs. In announcing the reorganization the Regents stated that the Davis campus would continue to be the University's "major center for research and teaching in agriculture, which will remain a dominant emphasis."

On Freeborn's retirement in 1959, Emil M. Mrak, chair of the department of food science and technology, became chancellor, serving until 1969. Mrak, a rotund and friendly man with a deep interest in people, became a superb lobbyist and chief for the Davis campus, building its capacities and prestige and maintaining calm even through the difficult 1960s. An avowed friend of agriculture, he used his close ties with agribusiness to strengthen the campus in myriad ways.[16]

In 1953 the University also established a College of Letters and Science at Riverside, transforming the Citrus Exper-

iment Station there into a college campus (though members of the Experiment Station staff did not then participate in instruction). In 1959 the Regents declared Riverside, like Davis, to be a general campus, emphasizing "distinction in undergraduate instruction," especially in the liberal arts. The scholarly zoologist Herman Spieth, named provost at Riverside in 1956, served as chancellor from 1959 to 1964.[17]

Having shepherded the University through depression, war, and postwar expansion, University President Sproul was a well-loved benevolent patriarch when he retired in 1958, at the age of sixty-seven. His successor was Clark Kerr, professor in industrial labor relations and first chancellor (1952) of the Berkeley campus.

Planning for growth—and the future of a changing institution—dominated Kerr's career as president. Under his leadership the University not only designated Davis and Riverside as general campuses but established entirely new campuses at San Diego, Irvine, and Santa Cruz. Enrollments soared, and huge infusions of state and federal money during the 1960s helped construct new facilities and implement new programs. Increases in biology, health, and physical sciences research were especially marked, with many grants from the National Science Foundation, the National Institutes of Health, and the U.S. Public Health Service flowing into departments on the several campuses.

Designs for expansion of the University were not the only planning consideration. By the late 1950s legislative concerns about overlap and competition among institutions of higher learning culminated in development of a Master Plan for Higher Education. This landmark document delineated the roles and functions of California's three-tiered system, reserving to the University major responsibility for doctoral programs and designating it the state's primary state-supported academic agency for both basic and applied research. The state and community colleges were given a broader role in undergraduate and some kinds of graduate instruction.[18]

170     Kerr, a brilliant analyst and student of management, became nationally known in 1963 through his presentation of the annual Godkin Lectures on higher education at Harvard University. Published as *The Uses of the University*, Kerr's analysis of the modern American "multiversity" described its profound differences from earlier medieval and later nineteenth-century academies by reviewing its current functions and competing influences, including the impact of vastly increased federal spending for research on university governance and priorities.

> [W]ith the exception of the comparatively restricted area of agriculture and military training, there was no continuing federal involvement with higher education until World War II. . . . [F]ederal support has [now] become a major factor in the total performance of many universities, and the sums involved are substantial. Higher education in 1960 received about $1.5 billion from the federal government—a hundred-fold increase in twenty years. . . . Clearly the shape and nature of university research are profoundly affected.[19]

He also spoke of the pluralistic components and clientele of the University and the need to balance the expectations and needs of faculty, students, alumni, government, industry, and the public.

Kerr's articulate statements about the "uses of the University" had significant implications for agriculture. As the land-grant university evolved in this period of growth and change, reconfiguring its structure and orienting itself toward new social and economic priorities, new constituencies and influences became increasingly important. The prominence of others—agriculture among them—began to decline.

## REBELLION AND REACTION AT BERKELEY

Despite new managerial sophistication and steady progress on reorganizing the state's system of higher education, all was not well at the University of California in the early 1960s. The "silent generation" of college students had moved on, and the idealism of the civil rights movement and confidence encouraged by the accession of the youthful new Kennedy administration engendered student militance in the form of protests of a number of perceived societal problems. Much of the idealism turned to frustration and anger after President Kennedy's assassination in November 1963, but the militance remained. Many young people adopted unconventional styles of dress and behavior.

Students who were alienated by some of the problems in the University identified by Clark Kerr himself—impersonality, teaching made subordinate to research, the seeming irrelevance of some academic work—determined to push for change. They mounted a series of startling public demonstrations in Berkeley beginning in September 1964. Potentially volatile situations on the Berkeley campus, not resolved in attempted negotiations, were met with force that alienated some nonparticipants even while others approved. Before the eyes of a national television audience, student eruptions turned into ugly street scenes and rude confrontations with police, including teargassing episodes. For several years "Berkeley" became synonymous with student protest, polarizing generations and provoking both widespread social disapproval and further demonstrations in other parts of the country, especially against the escalating war in Vietnam.

For gubernatorial candidates in California's 1966 election, events at the University became a hot political issue. Ronald Reagan campaigned with the promise that, if elected, he would initiate a thorough investigation of the University. Backed by conservatives and others concerned about current trends—including the ability of government to sustain its financial commitments to education and social programs—Reagan won the governorship. Many of his supporters came from the state's agribusiness community. In his drive for governmental economy, Reagan targeted the University, along with other state agencies and programs, for substantial budget cuts. Nor was this the only blow struck in reaction to the disorder at Berkeley: at Governor Reagan's first meeting with the Board of Regents in January 1967, Clark Kerr was dismissed.[20]

# CHANGES IN THE COLLEGE OF AGRICULTURE

## ADMINISTRATIVE REORGANIZATION

Although decentralization away from Berkeley was clearly the trend as the university system grew after the war, the College of Agriculture, with its statewide network of facilities and activities, presented a unique case in administration. Before his retirement Dean Hutchison—also serving as Vice President of the University—had begun to shift the headquarters of several agricultural programs from Berkeley to Davis. Hutchison intended that all agricultural activities of the University eventually be moved to Davis.[21] Blocky new buildings went up there in the 1950s to house the departments of food science and technology, soils and plant nutrition, and poultry husbandry, and shifts in staff brought innovative approaches to the study of some of the agricultural sciences.[22]

However, the trend toward decentralization was not fully completed for the agricultural programs. Instead, an overarching structure was established at Berkeley to administer all instruction, research, and extension work in agriculture, and within the University this separatist structure formed a kind of statewide campus of its own.

DEDICATION OF HARING HALL, NEW HOME OF THE SCHOOL OF VETERINARY MEDICINE AT DAVIS, 1949. FROM LEFT TO RIGHT ARE COLLEGE OF AGRICULTURE DEAN AND UNIVERSITY VICE PRESIDENT CLAUDE HUTCHISON; GEORGE HART, NEW DEAN OF THE SCHOOL; PROMINENT DAIRYMAN JOHN WATSON, LATER PRESIDENT OF THE STATE BOARD OF AGRICULTURE AND A REGENT OF THE UNIVERSITY; UC PRESIDENT ROBERT GORDON SPROUL; AND DEAN EMERITUS CLARENCE HARING, FOR WHOM THE BUILDING WAS NAMED.

In June 1952, when Hutchison retired after more than 22 years as an administrator, the College of Agriculture was officially reorganized and renamed the Division of Agricultural Sciences under the direction of a new Vice President–Agricultural Sciences. Harry R. Wellman, director of the Giannini Foundation from 1942 to 1952, was appointed to the position, taking responsibility for all agricultural activities within the University. Included under the umbrella of the Division in 1952 were the Colleges of Agriculture on three campuses, the Agriculture Experiment Station, the Agricultural Extension Service, the Giannini Foundation of Agricultural Economics, the School of Veterinary Medicine at Davis (established in 1941 but not in operation until 1948), and the School of Forestry at Berkeley (established in 1947).[23] Teaching programs in agriculture at Berkeley, Davis, and Los Angeles were now headed by their own semiautonomous deans: Knowles Ryerson, who moved somewhat reluctantly from Davis to become dean at Berkeley; Fred N. Briggs at Davis, a renowned plant breeder who became a quietly effective administrator; and Robert W. Hodgson at Los Angeles, leader of the successful program in subtropical horticulture. The deans reported to Wellman as head of the Division rather than to their respective chancellors.

172 Wellman, an agricultural economist, was highly respected for his constructive approach and calming influence in difficult situations—qualities that some years later would help steady the University when Wellman became Acting President after the dismissal of Kerr. Wellman's administrative style included wide consultation. To strengthen his connections with the agricultural community outside the University, Wellman appointed an Agricultural Advisory Council consisting of 21 members representing various agricultural organizations, areas, and commodities groups across the state. The council met twice a year to discuss matters of mutual interest including the research agenda. Wellman used it as a sounding board for new initiatives and at times invited its recommendations for Division action. The group may have influenced his decision not to move Division headquarters to Davis but to maintain it close to the Office of the University President.[24]

Wellman headed the Division until 1958, when he became Vice President of the University under Kerr. That year the title Vice President–Agricultural Sciences was changed to University Dean of Agriculture, and 40-year-old Berkeley soil scientist Daniel G. Aldrich was appointed to the position. Aldrich, an extraordinarily handsome and energetic individual, initiated several changes in the Division, but his tenure was relatively brief, for in 1963 he was tapped to become chancellor of the new Irvine campus. His successor as University Dean of Agriculture was Davis agronomist Maurice

HONORED FOR "OUTSTANDING CONTRIBUTIONS TO AMERICAN AGRICULTURE" BY THE FEDERAL LAND BANK OF BERKELEY, 1967: DAVIS CHANCELLOR EMIL MRAK, IRVINE CHANCELLOR DANIEL ALDRICH, AND ACTING UNIVERSITY PRESIDENT HARRY WELLMAN. BEFORE ENTERING ADMINISTRATION, MRAK WAS A FOOD TECHNOLOGIST, ALDRICH A PLANT AND SOIL SCIENTIST, AND WELLMAN AN AGRICULTURAL ECONOMIST.

L. Peterson. Peterson also assumed the title of Director of the Agricultural Experiment Station after the retirement of Paul F. Sharp (1949 to 1962), until Clarence F. Kelly (1965 to 1971) was appointed. Peterson was a good and conscientious administrator, but unprepared for the turmoil of the mid-1960s; struggling to maintain the strength of the Division while accepting Kerr's mandate for campus decentralization, he experienced his five years as Dean as difficult and frustrating. He resigned the position to return to research and teaching in the fall of 1967, and Kelly became Acting Dean until James B. Kendrick was appointed to lead the Division in 1968.[25]

It had become increasingly clear that administration of a centralized College of Agriculture was cumbersome at best and perhaps even inhibiting to innovation and change. The 1961 University-wide Academic Plan called for the diversification of the college on three campuses and the total elimination of agriculture from UCLA. During Peterson's tenure, therefore, while administration of the Agricultural Experiment Station and Extension Service remained headquartered at Berkeley, authority for final approval of campus deans' decisions on teaching curricula, operational budgets, and faculty recruitment and promotion passed to their respective chancellors. As part of the process of differentiating into distinctive programs building on the unique advantages of each campus, each college would eventually assume a new name.

## TEACHING PROGRAMS: THE CAMPUSES

Campus teaching programs evolved with postwar changes. The immediate flood of returning veterans, many of whom opted to study agriculture, was met with temporary classroom buildings and dormitory housing. Soon the two branches of the College of Agriculture at Davis and Los Angeles were offering more specialization and new opportunities for graduate work reflecting the advances in science. By the mid-1950s, however, in line with diminishing career opportunities in farming and greater alternatives in other fields, student interest in traditional agricultural subjects began to decline at the university level. Academic programs reflected not only shifts in student interest but the personality of each campus.

"FUTURE OF AGRICULTURE" FLOAT IN PICNIC DAY PARADE ON DAVIS CAMPUS, 1948. THE DESIGN OF THE FLOAT REFLECTS THE UNIVERSITY'S INCREASING EMPHASIS ON SCIENCE AND SCIENTIFIC CAREERS IN AGRICULTURE.

At Davis the establishment of a College of Letters and Science in 1951 brought broader academic opportunities, and the growing student body gradually became less rural in outlook. In 1956 the Regents reviewed a master campus development plan, which set a goal of 5,000 students and emphasized graduate work in the sciences; the Regents' Committee on Educational Policy affirmed that agriculture should continue to be the primary focus at Davis. During Briggs's tenure as dean, new academic breadth requirements diversified the undergraduate curricula in the College of Agriculture to include more classes in the social sciences and humanities, but graduate work in these fields was carried on in closer association with Berkeley because of superior library facilities there.

By 1959, when Davis became a full-fledged independent campus, its departments were developing important new thrusts in the biological sciences. Graduate training in all fields became increasingly important. With the introduction and refinement of instruments such as the centrifuge, the mass spectrometer, the respirometer, and later the electron microscope, research made quantum leaps forward, particularly in biochemistry, microbiology, and virology. The great strength of the campus in the basic sciences contributed to the renown of its departments of botany, enology, and genetics. Year by year faculty and graduate researchers contributed to better scientific understanding of basic biological processes—for example, the intricacies of metabolic pathways and the role of natural regulators like hormones in the physiology of plants and animals. The relatively small size of the campus during these years contributed to the cross-fertilization of ideas between members of many disciplines, and the innovative concept of the "graduate group" linked scientific specialists working in several departments.

One such group was the soil and plant nutrition group, which made many significant interdisciplinary contributions

174 to the study of soil and plant relationships. With the completion of Hoagland Hall, named for Dennis R. Hoagland, the pioneering architect of the group at Berkeley, the Kearney Foundation headquarters moved to Davis. The foundation's endowment came from the sale in 1948 of the Kearney Ranch, which the University had run for profit since 1910 (but with an average return of only 1.8 percent over the years, despite capable management). The University sold the property in 43 separate transfers for nearly $2 million, which, along with accumulated profits, endowed the M. Theo. Kearney Foundation of Soil Sciences, approved by the Regents in 1951 to pursue "the study of the relations of soil and water to plants through basic physical, chemical, biological, and hydrological research, with particular reference to arid and semi-arid environments." Under soil scientist Perry Stout, Kearney staff addressed a variety of issues bearing not only on agricultural production but also on animal and human health,

EXPERIMENT STATION RESEARCHERS MEASURING SOIL EROSION IN FARMED FIELDS. SOIL STUDIES CONTINUE TO BE AN IMPORTANT PART OF UC RESEARCH.

including the generation of radon by soils, the importance of cobalt and molybdenum in nitrogen fixation, and magnesium's toxicity (grass tetany) to grazing animals. They also developed new techniques such as selenium determination by X-ray fluorescence and helped to develop atomic absorption spectrophotometry.[26]

The changes in a general orientation toward science were made plain when, after nearly 40 years in existence, the Davis two-year nondegree program in agricultural production was phased out in 1960. The "University Farm" was no more; the Davis campus was no longer a rural outpost where students focused mainly on management practices, but an independent university campus with a growing reputation for its strengths in the agricultural and biological sciences. That year the Davis enrollment projection in President Kerr's UC Growth Plan was tripled, to 15,000.

In 1962 Dean Briggs retired and was succeeded by animal scientist James H. Meyer. In October 1964, at about the same time that rebellion at Berkeley was making headlines, faculty in the College of Agriculture at Davis under the leadership of Dean Meyer convened at a special conference at Lake Tahoe to discuss needs for reorganization in the teaching curriculum.

As in many agricultural colleges across the country, undergraduate enrollment figures showed a marked drop in the crop production majors while interest had picked up in agricultural economics, landscape horticulture, and the professional scientific fields. A report on Davis student interests showed that those opting for traditional agricultural or home economics majors tended to be utilitarian, conservative, and less intellectually adventurous than students in the College of Letters and Science.[27] Meyer and many of the faculty agreed that the College needed to take steps to avoid "organizational dry rot" and revitalize its programs to attract new kinds of students and provide new kinds of service to society. One such program had already begun (in 1962) under the auspices of the Kellogg Foundation, offering a B.S. in International Agricultural Development.

Following the Tahoe conference, in 1965 the faculty voted to reduce the number of curricula from 13 to 7 and majors from 43 to 19, allowing students more flexibility in planning their course work. The seven new general curricula were in agricultural science and management (to prepare students for careers in production, processing, and marketing), agricultural economics and business management, agricultural biosciences, agricultural education and international development, consumer and family sciences, food science and technology, and soil and water science. A report prepared for the Regents claimed that the Davis reorganization was the most far-reaching of any agricultural institution in the United States.[28]

The curricula development conference was followed in 1966 by another Tahoe conference on research, at which Meyer candidly presented the challenge of changing the College of Agriculture to cope with changes in society since World War II:

JAMES MYER, CHANCELLOR OF THE DAVIS CAMPUS FROM 1969 TO 1987.

Colleges of Agriculture . . . stand at the threshold of a new era that calls for a fresh outlook on teaching and research. This era should have started at the end of World War II, but because the academic community is slow to change, because the change in the traditional role of the agricultural industry has not been well recognized, and because an attitude of complacency has prevailed, we are groping for the form best suited to this second era. . . .

For the last 75 years . . . faculty . . . have trained their own successors; but while an effective team resulted, it was a group interested in maintaining the status quo. . . . Agricultural fac-

ulties may have tended to lose touch with the natural sciences not pertaining directly to agriculture, the social sciences, and the humanities. It is to be hoped that this will be recognized and corrected because exposure and reflection on a wide range of ideas more easily results in creativity. . . .

[W]e need to realize that farming, important as it is, is only part of . . . food production and use, and that it employs only a fraction of the labor force. . . . We should widen our horizons and think in international terms. The renewal and use of natural resources should be studied intensively . . . [and] should include the entire public interest. . . . [We must] broaden our vision and reshape the fundamental approach.[29]

The ferment encouraged by Meyer's two Tahoe conferences eventually brought about significant new strategies for the College—and a change in its title to the College of Agricultural and Environmental Sciences in 1967. Departmental majors were reorganized. The names of several departments were changed to reflect new priorities. Poultry husbandry became avian science; animal husbandry became animal science; agronomy became agronomy and range science; and landscape horticulture became environmental horticulture. Interdepartmental programs were encouraged, and groundwork was laid for new departments and combinations of programs, including consumer sciences, environmental studies, environmental toxicology, atmospheric sciences, wildlife biology, nutrition, and "applied behavioral sciences" (formerly the department of agricultural education), in which sociologically oriented community studies provided an organizing focus. Although Meyer moved on to become chancellor at Davis in 1969, the renaissance that he began within the College continued to unfold through the 1970s.

176     At Berkeley, meanwhile, the College of Agricultural Sciences developed a new academic plan in 1961 that emphasized the basic sciences, restructuring departments and strengthening graduate work in such fields as entomology, genetics, molecular biology, and nutrition. Eventually, with campus reorganization in 1973, the College dropped the word "agriculture" from its title completely, becoming the College of Natural Resources. Although some departments continued work relating to agriculture, its overall focus shifted increasingly toward conservation and resource studies and toward ever more fundamental and theoretical work in the natural sciences. In Berkeley's highly urbanized, intellectual milieu, relatively little understanding or sympathy remained for production agriculture, and in fact some of the most stinging criticisms of California's agricultural system would eventually emerge from there.

    At UCLA the fate of agricultural programs paralleled the postwar fate of agriculture in the Los Angeles basin. The number of agricultural majors dropped from a high of 131 in 1949 to less than 50 in 1956. As the booming UCLA campus began to need more space for new students and programs, administrators looked covetously at the more than 40 acres reserved for agricultural research, beginning a series of land use reviews that eventually spelled doom for the experimental orchard and greenhouses. In 1958 President Kerr announced the reassignment of most of UCLA's agricultural program to the Riverside campus, and after more than twenty years in operation the College of Agriculture at Los Angeles was gradually phased out. Faculty had the choice of moving to other campuses or into other departments on the Westwood campus, where appropriate. UCLA's unique small orchard, with its excellent collection of subtropical varieties, went the way of other agricultural land in the Los Angeles area when it was paved over to provide parking spaces. By 1965, with all agricultural programs officially transferred or discontinued, the urbanization of UCLA was complete.[30]

At Riverside the old Citrus Experiment Station coexisted with the new small liberal arts college (called by some the "Amherst of the West") until a graduate division was formed in 1960. At that time Experiment Station staff assumed professorial titles, and in 1961 undergraduate instruction began in the newly organized College of Agricultural Sciences under the direction of Dean Alfred M. Boyce. (Boyce also continued to serve as director of the renamed Citrus Research Center and Agricultural Experiment Station.) The Riverside instructional program was especially strong in plant pathology, with steadily advancing faculty competencies in microbiology, biochemistry, virology, and entomology, and special interests in nematology and biological control.[31]

## AGRICULTURAL RESEARCH AT MIDCENTURY

The U.S. agricultural science establishment as a whole enjoyed generous support in the years following World War II. "With the war won and the Great Depression behind it," wrote one observer, "America faced the future with renewed optimism, secure in its belief that many of the world's problems could be solved or at least lessened by scientists and the technological miracles which streamed forth from their laboratories."[32] Federal and state legislation provided handsome appropriations for the agricultural sciences until well into the 1960s. Through the new Hatch Act (1955), for example, Congress increased funding for the state experiment stations by 66 percent between 1955 and 1961.[33]

    The California legislature responded generously to the recommendations of the Agricultural Research Study Committee (see chapter 5), and research facilities expanded enormously statewide. The Regents acquired nearly 3,000 acres around the Davis campus between 1945 and 1954, and the field station network begun years earlier underwent great expansion. As the number of farm advisors and Extension specialists increased, so did their arrangements for "test plots" with cooperating farmers; scattered across the state in any given year were several thousand Extension-directed field trials. The University's resources for agricultural research also included many new campus and county buildings and laboratories and several organized research units funded for particular purposes.

## THE FIELD STATION NETWORK AND OTHER RESEARCH FACILITIES

Between 1951 and 1968 the official agricultural field stations expanded from five to ten, dotted strategically across the length and breadth of California to serve regional research needs.[34]

The *Imperial Valley Field Station* at Meloland near the Mexican border, begun in 1912 on 40 acres with one agronomist, expanded to 250 acres in 1945. This field station, dedicated to research on agriculture under desert conditions, supported work on a number of field and truck crops as well as on livestock management, including experiments in modifying high-temperature environments for plant and animal health.

THE SIERRA FOOTHILL RANGE AGRICULTURAL FIELD STATION. THE VARIED TERRAIN IS TYPICAL OF MUCH OF CALIFORNIA'S FOOTHILL RANGELANDS.

In 1946 the *Tulelake Field Station* opened on 18 acres in Siskiyou County next to the Oregon border. Situated at 4,000 feet, with very cold winters and a short growing season, the Tulelake station concentrated mainly on field and row crops suitable to the area such as barley and potatoes, vegetable crops for cold climates, and weather studies.

The *Antelope Valley Field Station* near Lancaster in southern California opened in 1949 on 60 acres. At an elevation of 2,400 feet, with a short, hot growing season, moderately cold winters, and a shortage of irrigation water, the station was dedicated to agronomic crop research under both dryland and irrigated conditions, and to studies of water use efficiency. This station closed in 1969.

The *Deciduous Fruit Field Station* in San Jose, in operation since the 1920s, continued to provide facilities for fruit crop research on about 15 acres. Work there consisted primarily of strawberry-breeding trials and the study of disease control methods for strawberries, tree fruits, and walnuts.

The *Hopland Field Station*, established in 1951 on 4,637 acres in southern Mendocino County, began a long-term series of range and livestock management studies whose goal was to improve the state's millions of acres of rangeland

178 for productive purposes. Wildlife management and hydrological experiments on watershed units were also major research areas.

The *South Coast Field Station*, established in 1956 on 200 acres of the Irvine Ranch southeast of Santa Ana in Orange County, supported interdisciplinary research on avocados, citrus, ornamental horticulture, turfgrass, strawberries, and vegetables.

The *West Side Field Station* opened in 1959 south of Five Points in the San Joaquin Valley to conduct wide-ranging crop research directed at the problems of Central Valley agriculture. Researchers at this station also participated in cotton investigations with the USDA Cotton Field Station at Shafter.

The *Lindcove Field Station* in Tulare County east of Visalia opened in 1959 to develop and evaluate new varieties and better cultural practices for the citrus industry then moving into the southern San Joaquin Valley. Researchers there also cooperated with the USDA Date and Citrus Station at Indio.

The *Sierra Foothill Range Field Station*, purchased in 1960 and consisting of 5,700 acres in Yuba County near Brown's Valley, became a center for studies on management of range cattle, brush conversion, range improvement, and watershed enhancement.

The *Kearney Horticultural Field Station*, on 230 acres south of Fresno and west of Reedley, was purchased in 1961 and 1965 partly through a grant from the Kearney Foundation fund, with matching funds raised under the auspices of the San Joaquin Valley Fruit and Grape Station Trust. At this site, better located and more productive than the original Kearney Ranch, the University started many permanent plantings, including grapes, olives,

FORESTRY STUDENT CONDUCTING CONTROLLED POLLINATION STUDIES IN REDWOODS.

walnuts, and fruit crops, and many departments as well as the USDA Crops Research Division at Fresno began studies.

Other University research facilities were also expanded during this period. In 1962 the Citrus Experiment Station at Riverside acquired 840 acres in nearby Moreno Valley for field and vegetable crops research. The same year the School of Forestry purchased 160 acres to complete the experimental tract known as Blodgett Forest, a grant of 2,680 acres of mixed conifer forest near Georgetown in El Dorado County donated by a lumber company in 1933. (The School's second research tract, Whitaker's Forest, was 320 acres of sequoia forest in Tulare County, given to the University in 1914.)

Another field station supporting UC research but administered by industry was located at Biggs in the Sacramento Valley. Originally a USDA rice research station, the facility came briefly under UC control in the early 1950s but later was transferred to the California Cooperative Rice Research Foundation.

The Regents also authorized two unique new natural resource research centers at Riverside. The Air Pollution Research Center, first organized within the experiment station in 1957, became a Universitywide facility in 1961 (and will be discussed in more detail later). The Dry Lands Research Institute was established in 1963, through Rockefeller Foundation grants, to study the resources and problems of arid lands around the world. Researchers used the 10,000-acre Philip L. Boyd Desert Research Center in Deep Canyon (75 miles from Riverside and 15 miles south of Palm Springs) as a living laboratory for the study of desert plants and animals.

## HIGHLIGHTS OF EXPERIMENT STATION RESEARCH

The enormous growth and diversity of California's physical research facilities in this period was reflected in a proliferation of research projects. Not surprisingly, the increasing complexity of the enterprise had a kind of centrifugal effect on record keeping. With the consent of President Sproul, Claude Hutchison had discontinued the College and Experiment Station's long series of unified public reports in 1940. Thereafter, sequential reports were filed primarily within the administrative units or sent on perfunctorily in response to USDA regulations.

To some degree public reporting took place in the monthly *California Agriculture: Reports of Progress in Research*, published by the Experiment Station beginning in December 1946 and available free to individuals, libraries, and governmental agencies. In 1960 University Dean Dan Aldrich

SUCCESSFUL STRAWBERRY GROWER, 1960S. UC VARIETY TRIALS SUPPORTED A GREAT EXPANSION OF CALIFORNIA'S COMMERCIAL STRAWBERRY PRODUCTION.

organized an agricultural publications and communications unit within Extension, with the goal of reaching nonfarm as well as farm audiences. This group of professional writers and media specialists greatly increased the Division's ability to extend information and also served a public relations function. Newspaper and radio outreach increased, brochures and pamphlets were produced at frequent intervals, and an award-winning television program documenting University agricultural research successes aired through NBC for several years. "Success stories" were also highlighted in a celebratory book commissioned for the University's 1968 centennial: *Garden in the West: A Dramatic Account of Science in Agriculture*.[35]

Agricultural research success stories abounded during these years. For example, soil scientists published an 800-page major reference book on soil nutrition that came to be considered the subject's bible. Crop specialists revitalized the state's $50 million strawberry industry through development of higher-producing varieties adaptable to longer growing seasons, dramatically improved cotton yields, helped the state's citrus industry relocate to the San Joaquin Valley as older orchard areas in southern California were lost to urbanization, and developed a new safflower industry for marginal lands. Plant pathologists and pest specialists successfully fought epidemics of citrus tristez and pear blight, controlled the spotted alfalfa aphid devastating California fields in the 1950s, identified pheromones as a new means of controlling insect infestations, and determined better ways of controlling public health pests like mosquitoes and starlings. Animal scientists developed vaccines for control of ram epididymitis and other serious diseases, nearly eliminated brucellosis in the state's dairy herds, and helped expand poultry production through better management and feeding practices. Range specialists conducted burning and revegetation studies on rangeland watersheds to improve management practices for

180 animal production and wildlife habitat. Food technologists developed clearer understanding of the enzymatic changes in fruits and vegetables during storage, processing, and distribution. Nutritional scientists studied astronauts' dietary needs in space under the aegis of the National Aeronautics and Space Administration. Agricultural economists tackled thorny problems in marketing and agricultural policy, such as the significance of tariffs in worldwide commodity trade, the likely impacts on California of the European Common Market, and California farm size efficiency.

Administrators and researchers in the Division of Agricultural Sciences were justly proud of their collective ability to unravel complex problems and find potential solutions. Their team efforts on a number of occasions saved parts of the agricultural industry severely threatened by outbreaks of pests or disease; their studies of production, marketing, and distribution practices helped lower food costs and make available more discretionary income for consumers. National economic studies in the 1970s showed very high rates of social return to investment in agricultural research.[36] Nevertheless, the Division's own descriptions of its research work tended to consistently overlook the downside of technological change

ENOLOGIST DINSMORE WEBB INSPECTING THE
UC DAVIS WINE COLLECTION, 1960S.

in agriculture—the accompanying environmental and social costs. Most agricultural scientists were focused chiefly on fairly narrow problem solving, often in response to organized interests, and paid little attention to the side effects of their work. That attitude was about to be challenged.

## THE CASE OF THE TOMATO HARVESTER

One of the most dramatic—and trumpeted—successes of the period eventually brought this issue into focus: the case of the tomato harvesting machine. In this episode UC scientists and engineers brought a remarkable combination of skills to the service of a major industry facing labor shortages, but not until after the tomato industry had been radically transformed did anyone question the social consequences of their work. By that time the tomato harvester had become symbolic of much of the change in American agriculture generally. The machine's success came to represent the paradox of the land-grant colleges of agriculture themselves: technical triumphs suddenly became subjects of controversy.

Mechanization in agriculture had already proceeded in some crops for decades, and for the most part the innovations of agricultural engineers had been well received. Like other industries, agriculture became more productive as its labor needs were minimized and fewer persons were required to perform the tedious, backbreaking work of earlier days. Mechanical reapers and threshers changed the nature of American grain farming before the turn of the century. As the twentieth century wore on, tractors and power take-off devices revolutionized fieldwork. Forklifts raised and hauled heavy loads of boxes and bags in orchard, vineyard, and shed. Mechanical shakers and catchers began to replace men with poles and mallets knocking nuts or prunes from trees to the ground, and other machines did the work of thousands of sugar beet thinners and cotton pickers. Mechanization reduced not only labor needs but the physical strain associated with many menial jobs. Managerial anxieties and the risks associated with bad weather during harvest were lessened. Though these advantages primarily accrued to the farmer, they served national purposes as well, for agricultural productivity was obviously increased.

Agricultural engineers didn't ordinarily think about the farmers who couldn't afford the new machines, nor about the farmworkers displaced—but others did. In earlier days the machines that replaced labor during the industrial revolution in England had inspired the Luddite riots, and job-replacing machinery became a focal point in industrial labor union negotiations in twentieth-century America. In agriculture, however, no vocal group paid much attention to the impacts of mechanization on small farmers or farmworkers until after the tomato harvester revolutionized the processing tomato industry in the mid-1960s. Then the social consequences of farm mechanization became a cause célèbre, the rallying cry of a persistent set of critics of the land-grant colleges and of the University of California in particular. The story combines history, technology, and politics in one complex, fascinating issue.

When the wartime federal farm labor agreement with Mexico expired, farm interests negotiated annual extensions of the *bracero* program until 1949. In 1950, however, the Mexican government refused to extend the arrangement without

BACKBREAKING TRADITIONAL METHODS OF HAND HARVESTING. HERE, 1930S WORKERS GRUB OUT SUGAR BEET CROP FOR PROCESSING. THE SUGAR BEET INDUSTRY WAS HIGHLY LABOR-INTENSIVE UNTIL UC AGRICULTURAL ENGINEERS DEVELOPED MECHANIZED PLANTING AND HARVESTING TECHNIQUES.

some reforms. That year the President's Commission on Migratory Labor, for whom UC agricultural economist Varden Fuller served as executive secretary, made several dozen detailed recommendations for changes in federal and state farm labor regulations, only a few of which were adopted.[37] Despite the commission's emphatic recommendation against further dependence on foreign labor, agricultural pressure groups, largely from the South, Arizona, and California, persuaded a Congress preoccupied with the Korean War to pass Public Law 78, which became the basis for the *bracero* program of the next fourteen years. Although *braceros* accounted for only about 30 percent of the total seasonal work force in California in the peak year 1959, they contributed more than 80 percent of the labor for the tomato harvest. Their presence angered critics of agribusiness, who claimed that without the *braceros* domestic farmworker wages and working conditions would be forced to improve.

By the early 1960s a growing reform bloc of urban liberals was bringing about the decline of rural influence in Congress, while the promise of mechanization was offering alternatives to hand labor for peak periods of cultivation and harvest in many crops. In a climate of struggle for the civil rights of minorities, the Johnson administration directed the Department of Labor to terminate the *bracero* program in 1965. At about the same time Cesar Chavez's efforts to organize California's farmworkers took off dramatically, and for the next several years the unionizing activities of the United Farm

182 Workers dominated the scene in the state's fields, aided by widespread press coverage.[38]

As it became clear that the *bracero* program was on its way out, there was talk in California of the processing tomato industry moving into Mexico, where a labor supply could be assured for the six to eight weeks of hand harvesting required. Obviously such a move would be a disaster for California tomato growers and the communities dependent on them. To help "save" the tomato industry, the 1964-65 state legislature put $150,000 into the University's agricultural research budget to accelerate research on the mechanized production of horticultural crops. Meanwhile, some research already under way was nearing a real breakthrough.

For almost twenty years researchers at Davis had been experimenting with mechanical harvesting of processing tomatoes. The main figures were Coby Lorenzen and Istvan Janos Szluka, agricultural engineers, and Fred "Jack" Hanna, a plant breeder. The problems were formidable: Tomatoes are by nature a soft fruit, non-uniform in set and ripening over a period of time—certainly not suitable for once-over mechanical harvesting, nor able to withstand hard mechanical parts and rough handling. To accommodate the crop to machinery, the engineers worked with the plant breeder, a collaboration that had already proved successful in sugar beet mechanization. Hanna set about breeding a processing tomato that would withstand bumping and be more

MECHANIZED TOMATO HARVESTING. INSTEAD OF PICKING TOMATOES INTO HAND-CARRIED BUCKETS, WORKERS ON A SHADED PLATFORM SORT FRUIT THAT IS MECHANICALLY CUT AND CONVEYED UP TO THEM, AS THE MACHINE MOVES THEM ACROSS THE FIELD.

conveniently shaped for machine pickup, would set fruit uniformly across the plant, would ripen more or less at the same time, and could be parted easily from the vine. Years of patient work produced a firm, small, elongated, and uniformly ripening tomato by the early 1960s. Meanwhile Lorenzen was devising machines that could sever the tomato plants at ground level and lift them to a separating mechanism where fruit could be stripped undamaged from the vines. Other scientists began to develop improved cultural practices to maximize the yield and quality of the new varieties.

With the end of the *bracero* program in sight, trials of a prototype machine took place in several cooperating farmers' tomato fields. Problems were ironed out, and 262 mechanical tomato harvesters—picking an estimated quarter of the state's tomato crop—were in commercial use by 1965, the "year of transition."[39] By 1968, 95 percent of the state's processing tomato acreage was being harvested by 1,400 machines, and by 1970 California's entire crop was machine picked.[40]

During these years a marked change in the industry took place. While many tomato growers invested in the new machines, others dropped out of the business entirely. The number of California tomato growers declined from about 4,000 in the 1950s to around 800 by 1978. The harvest work force, though varying from year to year, declined from about 40,000 in 1960 to about 23,000 in 1970. Meanwhile, according to grower reports, "An industry which had been threatened with annihilation in California, embarked instead on an era of expansion."[41] Not only was the processing tomato industry "saved" from departure to Mexico, but California now had a competitive advantage over other states, where mechanized harvesting was less feasible because of weather conditions.

By this time the Agricultural Experiment Station had under way some 80 other mechanization projects involving twenty crops, including cucumbers, lettuce, grapes, prunes, and orchard crops. UC publicists celebrated these new engineering achievements, but at a time when farm labor unionization struggles were being dramatized by the news media, farm mechanization was becoming controversial. The tomato harvester became a convenient metaphor for the whole equity issue, so long disregarded in agriculture's single-minded drive toward production efficiency.

Few at Davis had foreseen the attacks that would center around the tomato harvester. Although proposals had been made to use some of the legislature's 1964 appropriation to research the impacts of mechanization on farm labor, they had not been funded. Researchers in the emerging department of applied behavioral sciences conducted several ethnographic surveys to identify ways in which migrant farmworkers might be helped, but their reports did not attract much attention. The departments of agricultural engineering and agricultural education tried a training program

A PROTOTYPE MECHANIZED PEACH HARVESTER, DEVELOPED IN THE 1960S AT UC DAVIS. THE OPERATOR SITS UNDER A PROTECTIVE SHIELD WHILE THE MACHINE EMPLOYS THE SHAKE-CATCH METHOD TO HARVEST PEACHES FOR PROCESSING.

to teach former farmworkers mechanical skills, but the project fizzled from lack of participation by the workers selected for the project.[42]

Agricultural economists meanwhile worked out calculations showing that the net social gain from increased production and lower consumer costs easily outstripped the costs of research and development of the tomato harvester; but they conceded that all social costs were not factored in:

Our study of the development of the mechanical tomato harvester provides a microscopic look at a general social dilemma. The talents of science and industry combine to create economically productive innovations, but the very success of these sectors . . . creates consequences which bear unfavorably . . . on less organized and therefore more vulnerable sectors. . . . If a fraction of the great economies generated by such technical innovations as the harvester could be allocated out of general taxes and applied to destroying the "vicious cycles of poverty" that afflict society, immobilities [of workers]—and thus the social costs accompanying such innovations as the tomato harvester—would be substantially reduced.[43]

California's tomato harvester controversy was perhaps but the tip of the iceberg in the broader issue of the evolving role of the land-grant colleges of agriculture. By 1970 land-grant agricultural research nationally was coming under scrutiny and attack. *Hard Tomatoes, Hard Times* was, in fact, the evocative title given a 1972 book highly critical of the research establishment (see chapter 7).[44]

## 184 CONTINUITY AND CHANGE
## IN EXTENSION WORK

In July 1948, on the eve of his retirement as director of the California Agricultural Extension Service, B. H. Crocheron died suddenly. His 35-year career had spanned Extension's beginnings before World War I through decades of change. With agriculture on the verge of a great leap forward and generous amounts of federal and state money flowing into institution building for the future, his successor would need to be both capable and foresighted.

J. Earl Coke, chosen as the state's second Extension director in 1949, was a true representative of California agriculture. Raised on a small California farm and winner of a boys' agricultural club transcontinental trip in 1916, Coke entered the College of Agriculture at Berkeley, taking two semesters at the University Farm. After graduation in 1923, he became a traveling farm advisor. Appointed the first Extension specialist in agronomy in 1928, Coke organized grain variety trials and helped establish the UC seed certification program. His work and his pleasing personality caught the eye of the sugar beet industry, which hired him away from the University in 1934. He had risen to become vice president of the Spreckels Sugar Company when he was invited back to the University to lead the Extension Service.

Coke initiated a number of changes in Extension. Although a lifelong admirer of Crocheron, he recognized that his predecessor's autocratic leadership style was no longer appropriate, and among his early actions were decentralization and delegation of more responsibility to the local level. The chief farm advisor in each county became "county extension director," and the title of "assistant" farm advisor was dropped. Local program planning was encouraged, and "top-down" administration changed to a more collaborative approach.

He encouraged the broadening of Extension subject matter and its clientele base. In late 1949 he assigned a home economics specialist to work with the destitute families of farm laborers in Kern County. After the widely publicized deaths of two migrant children from malnutrition, Coke put two more home economists to work in early 1950 to educate low-income families about health, nutrition, home management, and child care. For the next two years this program was underwritten by the Rosenberg Foundation of San Francisco. Later, in 1955, Smith-Lever "special needs" funds provided for three full-time specialists to work with migrant families in Kings and Fresno counties, in addition to several part-time aides working in Los Angeles, San Bernardino, Madera, Tulare, and Kern counties. Meanwhile, the 4-H program was redesigned to include nonfarm youth and nonagricultural projects such as electricity, small-engine repair and maintenance, and entomology.[45] Extension staff more than doubled between 1945 and 1955, from 269 to 549, and a large number of specialists was added in such areas as range management, ornamental horticulture, vegetable crops, marketing, and youth counseling.

While these changes were under way, Coke was called to Washington to serve as Assistant Secretary in the U.S. Department of Agriculture under Ezra Taft Benson in the Eisenhower administration. Responsible for the research, extension, and land-use activities of the department, Coke took nearly two years' leave of absence from Extension while acting Director Wayne Weeks continued the reorganization in California. In 1955, tired and drained after the death of his wife, Coke returned to California but almost immediately decided to leave Extension for a position as vice president of the Bank of America in San Francisco.

Succeeding Coke as third director of the California Agricultural Extension Service was George B. Alcorn, an Extension agricultural economist since 1937 and specialist in marketing. Alcorn was an engaging, kindly man who had gained the support of many farm advisors disaffected by Coke's long absence. As an in-house candidate he reflected both the strengths and deficiencies of his background. Praised for his integrity and his down-to-earth approach, Alcorn was highly supportive of both his staff and his traditional agricultural constituency, but he believed in consensual management rather than in bold leadership, and his view of Extension work reflected his training as an economist: "Our real business is specialized education for certain segments of the population. . . . [T]he business outlook in that market is bright. . . . The demand for our merchandise is almost unlimited."[46]

In Alcorn's 19 years as director, Extension programs stressed farm and business efficiency, market expansion, and information on public policies relating to agriculture: taxation, zoning, and other governmental regulations. As the number of commercial farmers kept declining, Extension established working relationships with other sectors of agribusiness—processors, shippers, and suppliers that benefited from Extension training and analysis of their business operations.

Specialization within Extension continued to increase. Because the multiplicity of California's agricultural enterprises and problems demanded greater technical expertise, and because so many California farmers were now college graduates, farm advisors were encouraged to take graduate training, and specialists increasingly had doctoral degrees. By 1960 Extension's more than 500-person academic staff included new specialists in apiculture, biometrics, climatology, crop processing, dairy prod-

GEORGE B. ALCORN, DIRECTOR OF THE CALIFORNIA AGRICULTURAL EXTENSION SERVICE FROM 1956 TO 1975.

ucts, soils and water salinity, forest products, nematology, parasitology, enology, pesticide safety, consumer marketing, wildlife management, and public affairs. As experiment station staff turned toward more basic research in their disciplines, Extension specialists conducted more applied research. Many of them began producing newsletters to reach wider audiences, and home economists started general newspaper columns. Extension expertise was extended toward part-time farmers, public lands officials, turf growers, floriculturalists, golf course managers, and landscapers.

In continuation of Coke's initiatives, Extension's traditional 4-H program was gradually transformed. Youth work by the agricultural colleges had been conceived as a way to demonstrate new practices to adults, but by 1920 it had evolved into a form of vocational preparation supplementing education in the schools. During the 1950s young suburban families began to seek 4-H involvement as a "value shelter" where their children could be exposed to traditional values about work and achievement. 4-H specialists designed increasingly diverse projects to teach rational thought and decision-making processes. By the end of the 1960s, under federal pressure to extend the benefits of 4-H membership to low-income and urban youth, the California Extension Service reported about 20 percent of its 50,000 club members from these new groups.[47]

Despite these efforts to diversify programs and clientele, Extension's administrative bureaucracy was not especially adept at handling the challenges presented by rapid political and economic change. The 1960s brought a new kind of

186 political activism, and Extension's lagging response eventually made it vulnerable to criticism. In 1964 Extension celebrated its fiftieth anniversary—and coincidentally that of the Farm Bureau—with a number of special events and promotional publications. Well before this, however, a national reexamination of the Agricultural Extension Service had begun to take place, focusing on its changing role in a society vastly different from that in 1914.

In 1955, to encourage new programs with a broader application to nonfarm audiences, Congress authorized special appropriations—the so-called 3(d) monies—to augment federal formula funding under the Smith-Lever Act, and in 1957 the national Extension Committee on Organization and Policy commissioned a report on Extension's future. This publication, titled "Statement of Scope and Responsibility" and popularly known as the Scope Report, concluded that the organization needed to broaden its vision and shift program priorities and methods to meet new societal needs.[48]

URBAN YOUTH PARTICIPATING IN A 4-H-SPONSORED RECYCLING DRIVE. THE NATURE OF 4-H ACTIVITIES HAD BROADENED BY THE 1960S, FROM TRADITIONAL FARM-BASED PROJECTS TO THOSE THAT WOULD ALSO BE MEANINGFUL TO CITY YOUTH.

Although this had begun to happen in a small way in California, without a clearer mandate for change institutional inertia slowed program alterations, and there was little interest in more rapid change when the traditional agricultural production programs were so successful.

Coupled with institutional inertia were some hard cuts made by Governor Reagan in the 1967 University budget. The traditional political support of agribusiness for the University, especially the Division of Agriculture, did not intervene this time, for many rural conservatives were deeply offended by the disorders at Berkeley. Support for Extension work was cut more than 10 percent, and 22 staff members were encouraged to retire early or resign, the cutbacks hitting hardest in home economics.

With this kind of budgetary stress, despite federal directives, the kind of work the Scope Report called for did not get off the ground in California until the 1970s. In 1969, however, Extension was required to accept the Expanded Federal Nutrition Education Program (EFNEP), which mandated outreach to nonfarm, nonrural clients in providing dietary counseling for low-income families. To some degree this work revitalized the home economics program; staff began to work directly with public health officials, welfare caseworkers, schoolteachers, farmworkers' camps, and federal housing projects. EFNEP was Extension's first big step toward meeting the needs of urban minorities and other disadvantaged adults.

# NATIONAL CONCERNS AND CALIFORNIA CONNECTIONS

## ENVIRONMENTAL AWARENESS

Undeniably the seminal document in raising midcentury environmental awareness was Rachel Carson's *Silent Spring*. Published in 1962, this eloquent book by a well-known writer-scientist galvanized public concern by describing the mounting threat of indiscriminate pesticide use. Although the volume was criticized by some scientists for inaccuracies, its message about toxic residues influenced government agencies to implement new regulations and eventually ban some pesticides entirely.[49] Long before Carson's book climbed the best-seller lists, however, scientists at the University of California were well aware of pesticide problems (and Carson had cited some UC studies in support of her arguments).

Pest control measures had been studied through the Agricultural Experiment Station since the nineteenth century; some of the early measures used to control perennial pests such as codling moth (lead arsenate, for example) were known to be highly dangerous for humans. The "miracle" compound DDT, first reported on in the February 1947 issue of *California Agriculture*, appeared to offer both more effective pest control and less threatening side effects, and subsequent work led to the introduction of dozens of improved sprays or dusts and the dropping of older measures. These new agents effectively dealt with many serious pest infestations, increasing agricultural productivity and in most cases evincing few or no adverse effects on crops, human beings, or the environment—at least in the short term. But as the amount of land treated with the new chemicals in California grew—aerial coverage alone soared from about 300,000 acres in 1946 to almost 5,000,000 in 1955—Experiment Station scientists began to observe that the synthetics could harm nontarget species.

Until the mid-1950s, research on such subjects was carried out by individuals in various departments on the several campuses; many of their short reports began to appear in *California Agriculture* and other research periodicals. In 1956 Robert L. Rudd and Richard E. Genelly, research zoologists at UC Davis working on a grant from the California Department of Fish and Game, published a painstaking monograph on the effects of five major pesticides on California wildlife.[50] Other researchers, aware that developing insect resistance to some compounds made it necessary to apply ever higher concentrations, began documenting their observations. By this time more than 300 chemical compounds—fungicides, herbicides, insecticides, nematicides, growth regulators, and all their siblings—were being used in U.S. agriculture, and an estimated 20 percent of all usage took place in California. As pesticide usage continued to grow, driven by the engine of economic advantage, it became evident that a more unified approach toward investigation of impacts was needed.[51]

In 1957, partly because of public concern about pesticide residues in milk, the legislature appropriated special funds to the University for research on the health aspects of pesticide use. The Davis campus used its share of these funds to establish a Pesticide Residue Research Laboratory in the department of entomology, at first housed in an old garage with basic analytic equipment secured through the National Institutes of Health. In 1962, the year Carson's book was published, the laboratory became an official research unit known as the Agricultural Toxicology and Residue Research Laboratory, dedicated to studies of human and environmental health problems arising from the use of agricultural chemicals. Two years later—in a new building at Davis financed through a National Science Foundation grant, matching state funds, and a gift from Regent Norton Simon—a laboratory staff of four scientists with 25 technicians and support personnel analyzed pesticide residues in plant and animal

188 products, soil, and water. Their instrumentation included spectrophotometers, colorimeters, fluorometers, gas chromatographs, and other advanced equipment for chemical manipulations. The laboratory rapidly gained recognition for its toxicological research, and in 1968, after six years of ad hoc teaching and graduate work, the research unit became a full-fledged department of environmental toxicology, with responsibility for a wide range of instructional, research, and public service activities.[52]

As the chemical industry continued to expand through the early 1960s, University researchers field-tested new compounds at the request of companies that contributed sample materials and small grants of money to support investigations. Some entomologists and others were skeptical, however, about the cumulative effects of the potent new compounds, and a vocal minority rejected the chemical approach to focus on biological control research at Riverside and Berkeley. At times viewed by their peers as ecological radicals, they found relatively little funding for their work, for the research system of the time did not have the means to aggressively pursue long-range, more environmentally sensitive control measures.[53]

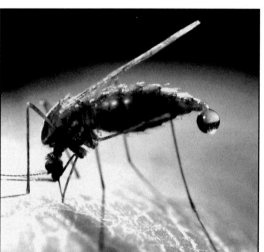

CLOSE-UP OF MOSQUITO POISED ON HUMAN FLESH. MOSQUITO CONTROL RESEARCH WAS ONE OF THE EARLIEST ARENAS FOR TESTING THE PRINCIPLES OF INTEGRATED PEST MANAGEMENT AT THE UNIVERSITY. BIOLOGICAL CONTROL IN THE FORM OF FUNGAL PARASITES OF MOSQUITO LARVAE IS ONE OF THE BEST-KNOWN OUTCOMES OF SUCH RESEARCH.

Synthetic agricultural chemicals had significant pragmatic value, and a powerful clientele supported their use. Nevertheless, many in the Experiment Station and some outside it realized that a broader view of pest and disease control was needed. Integrated control—combining biological and cultural practices with the use of chemicals—was a standard technique employed by competent farmers and researchers long before it got its name. UC scientists A. E. Michelbacher and Oscar Bacon were the first to use the term *integrated control* formally in their 1952 article on walnut pests. In 1959 other Berkeley researchers published a paper in *Hilgardia* describing the integrated control concept and defining economic thresholds for injury levels as the basis for decision making.[54] Following years saw experimentation with combinations of parasites or other biological controls along with cultural practices, resistant varieties, and chemical insecticides as needed to minimize pest outbreaks. A noteworthy success of this approach was the project that eventually regulated the population of the spotted alfalfa aphid, which wreaked havoc in alfalfa stands in the 1950s. Later, in 1964, the Cling Peach Advisory Board supported an Experiment Station project to develop a similar integrated control program for pests of peaches, and the grape industry funded another for control of grape pests.[55]

Thus by the late 1960s many scientists along with like-minded farmers were examining the ecology of pest control and moving away from an unquestioning reliance on chemical pesticides. The traditional academic approach to research tended to yield fragmental knowledge rather than understanding of total agricultural and environmental systems, however, and most farmers continued to use chemicals routinely because they seemed indispensable in protecting their crops. Despite evolving regulations, the political will to develop alternative technologies was not evident before the 1970s.

During the 1950s the University initiated two other environmental research facilities. In 1956 the Regents approved organization of the Water Resources Center (WRC) at UCLA, and in 1957 the Air Pollution Research Center opened at Riverside.

The Water Resources Center was established as an independent unit to encourage and coordinate research and education on California water problems. Through the WRC, research allocations could be granted to departments for individual and group studies on various aspects of the state's water resources. Subjects of inquiry might include law, economics, and political science as well as engineering, irrigation, drainage, watershed management, hydrology, meteorology, and geophysics. Water quality studies and saline water treatment were to be given particular attention. Seawater conversion research was assigned to the center in 1958. The WRC was also designated an archival deposit for historical material and given authority to sponsor publications and conferences.[56]

The Air Pollution Research Center was organized under the leadership of John T. Middleton and other researchers at the Citrus Experiment Station who had recognized the dangers of air pollution in the Los Angeles basin before the end of World War II. As mounting evidence accumulated on damage to agricultural crops and forest trees from auto and industrial emissions, researchers monitored the effects of

AIR POLLUTION RESEARCH AT UC RIVERSIDE, 1967. LEMON TREES IN PLASTIC ENCLOSURES ARE MONITORED TO DETERMINE THE EXTENT OF INJURY FROM CONTROLLED EXPOSURE TO PHOTOCHEMICAL ELEMENTS IN SMOG.

carbon monoxide and other gases on plant growth in controlled environmental chamber studies. In time they identified more than 100 different elements and mechanisms in smog having adverse effects on crops, animals, and human beings. In 1961 the center became a systemwide facility whose mission was to support and stimulate research, instruction, and public service on all aspects of air pollution and potential control measures. Researchers undertook new studies on how to detect and control emissions before the accumulation of damaging concentrations. They also began to examine patterns of land use and transportation that might help alleviate air pollution.[57]

### THE "WAR ON POVERTY" IN RURAL CALIFORNIA

As the land-grant colleges approached their centennials, subsidized technical assistance for "agribusiness" was becoming a debatable question. The land-grant system, originally conceived as a kind of developmental agency for nudging backward farmers into the industrial age, had obviously accomplished its mission: American agriculture had become a giant, productive industry, in some ways the envy of the world. Now, even as the Extension Service celebrated its fiftieth anniversary in 1964, its relationship with commercial farmers was undergoing re-examination in the halls of Congress, the U.S. Department of Agriculture, and the land-grant colleges themselves.

190     Key to the debate was the awareness that enclaves of backwardness and farm poverty still existed despite all previous efforts to extend aid. Particularly in Appalachia, the Deep South, and the Ozarks, pockets of rural squalor remained nearly untouched. From places like these had come the influx of job seekers to California during the Depression; a generation later, poverty in the more remote areas was still endemic. And, in fact, much urban poverty was a result of the migration of the rural poor from areas where they had been squeezed out of farming even on the subsistence level. In the ongoing consolidation of farms during the 1950s, the problems of the rural poor had received scant attention, but in the activist 1960s the issue re-emerged, with a new twist.

The Scope Report of 1958 recommended that "community improvement and resource development" be an area for focused attention by the Extension Service, the details of which were left up to the individual states. Although some state extensions set up community development units, others assigned the responsibility to staff in existing units, primarily in agricultural economics. Shortly after publication of the report, President Eisenhower issued Executive Order 10847 establishing a U.S. Committee for Rural Development, which began a pilot "economic development" program, enlisting Extension among involved agencies in 100 counties across the country. The Kennedy administration also put funds into these programs and expanded the number of counties eligible to receive assistance. Earmarked monies, along with Smith-Lever "special needs" funds, were to be used to help low-income rural people achieve better lives.[58]

The money proved less than effective in alleviating the problem. Even the Economic Opportunity Act of 1964, which made it federal policy to eliminate poverty in the United States, had little apparent impact on rural America. In September 1966 President Johnson issued Executive Order 11306 establishing a National Advisory Commission on Rural Poverty charged with appraising conditions in substandard rural areas in order to develop a design for action programs. The commission's 1967 report, *The People Left Behind*, described the problem:

> [R]ural poverty affects some 14 million Americans. . . . [It] is so widespread, and so acute, as to be a national disgrace, and its consequences have swept into our cities, violently. . . . Some of our rural programs, especially farm and vocational agriculture programs, are relics from an earlier era. They were developed in a period during which the welfare of farm families was equated with the well-being of rural communities and of all rural people. This is no longer so. . . . They were developed without anticipating the vast changes in technology, and the consequences. . . . [T]hese programs have helped to create wealthy landowners while largely bypassing the rural poor. . . . We have not yet adjusted to the fact that . . . from 1950 to 1965, new machines and new methods increased farm output in the United States by 46 percent—and reduced farm employment by 45 percent.[59]

The next year another government publication, *A People and a Spirit*, enunciated a broader conception of Extension's role in disseminating information from throughout the University to a wide range of clients:

> In its infancy, the Cooperative Extension Service was dedicated to improving the lot of a class of people who were in fact disadvantaged compared to the rest of society. The emergence of the Extension function and the response by innovative and concerned individuals has led to an increased involvement with people in the middle- and upper-income levels. The current urgent problems of the United States have refocused attention on the problems of those who are alienated by race, income, or other factors. For these reasons, the Joint Study Committee recommends that:
>
> "The Cooperative Extension Service should increase its emphasis on programs designed to motivate and otherwise assist the disadvantaged and the alienated. . ."[60]

Much of the concern about the disadvantaged was aimed at the states in which poverty was most obvious. But who were the rural poor in California, and where did they live? The great variability across California made it difficult to generalize: subsistence farmers had never been common here; part-time farmers usually had other jobs; and small farms by the 1960s were more often "hobby" farms or rural residences than serious attempts at making a living.[61] Leasing or rental arrangements in California agriculture did not fit the pattern of the "tenant farmer" in many other states. Here, too, a wide array of educational and employment opportunities offered alternatives to most rural poor people willing to change location or alter their lifestyles.

Nonetheless, on a national map drawn up to illustrate the economic status of rural populations by county, the San Joaquin Valley stood out.[62] There many farmworkers, especially the seasonal migrants moving among the varied crops of California's heartland, continued to live on the fringes of society in obscurity and semidestitution—no longer the "Okies" of the Depression, but Mexican immigrants. The farm labor unionizing efforts of the decade brought this group to public attention, and the civil rights movement endorsed their cause. The 1965 Delano strike

against grape growers by the United Farm Workers won widespread public sympathy.

The change in perspective recommended by the several reports was not mirrored within the UC Division of Agricultural Sciences. Efforts by a few Experiment Station staff and Extension specialists in the 1950s to improve working conditions and employment standards in Central Valley dairies had met with little success. Most later UC research and Extension activities on farm labor were limited to data collection, with the exception of those modest projects at Davis described previously. Up through the end of the 1960s, University work focused almost exclusively on improvements in food production or advances in basic science. Lacking a clear plan and decisive leadership to articulate new goals, members of the Division found it difficult to move beyond "tunnel vision" while struggling through budget crises. In the throes of widespread social change, the institution moved toward the 1970s with a "general feeling of treading water and waiting for positions to be filled."[63] For a while, as a series of leadership shifts took place between 1967 and 1969, simple momentum carried the ship forward.

MIGRANT FARMWORKER HOUSING. POOR HOUSING, LOW PAY, AND INVOLUNTARY EXPOSURE TO DANGEROUS PESTICIDES WERE THE FOCUS OF THE 1960S MOVEMENT TO BETTER THE LIVES OF SEASONAL FARMWORKERS.

192 By 1968, however, the Regents were beginning to question what the University was doing to meet the social and political crises of the day. At their May meeting, new University President Charles J. Hitch presented a special report on "The University and the Urban Crisis," calling for research and Extension efforts similar to those in agriculture to meet the needs of cities, along with affirmative action programs in student recruitment and university employment. A year later, in May 1969, the Regents questioned the new Vice President–Agricultural Sciences, James B. Kendrick, on what, if any, efforts were being made by the Division to improve the lives of farmworkers and the disadvantaged rural population. Not much could be recounted.[64]

## CRITICISM AND SELF-EXAMINATION: A NEED FOR CHANGE

In 1968 the Independent Socialist Clubs of America published a 32-page pamphlet titled "The Dirt on California: Agribusiness and the University," attacking the University of California's connections with commercial agriculture. The authors declared that Agricultural Experiment Station research was a great windfall for the agricultural industry:

> There is no other big industry in the United States which has its money-making research done for it, free, by a government agency on such a scale. . . . The free "tax-paid clinic" for this industry . . . is not mainly going to help the Joad family or somebody's kitchen garden, but rather is service-oriented toward the big agri-corporations of the state.[65]

Furthermore, they wrote, the University had tacitly supported the union-busting activities of the Associated Farmers in the 1930s; even in the 1960s California growers continued to exploit farmworkers while some University staff endorsed extension of the *bracero* program. Accusing the Regents of a conflict of interest in reviewing agricultural

research policy, the authors stated that mechanization research served growers but jeopardized the livelihoods of workers, without any concomitant effort to help them achieve better working conditions or alternative occupations.

The publication was strident, distorted, and ideologically driven in its Marxist analysis of the "university's integration into the power structure of capitalist society." In some ways the pamphlet was hardly more than a gnat's attack on an elephant; in retrospect, however, it was the opening salvo in the battles of the 1970s over the role of agricultural research and Extension within the University. And its rhetoric touched on real and significant issues—issues that were also beginning to be discussed by some within the Division.

In November 1967 Acting University President Wellman, recognizing the gathering tensions between organized agriculture and its critics, appointed a twelve-person long-range planning committee for the Division, chaired by Clarence F. Kelly. The committee's deliberations were completed by June 1968. Its report conceptualized the mission of the Division in new ways:

> The University must be responsive to the needs of all the people of California. A most significant trend in the state is the rapidly increasing pressure of people on a limited resource supply. This pressure makes it essential to use land and other limited resources so that they best serve the long term needs of the people. Some aspects of this overall problem—for instance, haphazard allocation of cropland to non-farm uses—are immediately important in California. Other aspects—for instance, food scarcity—may threaten other areas of the world. . . . But they cannot realistically be ignored as only a remote threat. The total problem created by the pressure of people on agricultural and other renewable natural resources is of vital importance to all. . . .

> The division should focus primarily on the development and use of knowledge to deal with all phases of the pressure of people on resources. The division can do this best in its areas of special competence—agriculture, family and consumer sciences, and renewable natural resources.

Recommendation: Research and teaching programs aimed at maintaining the quality of the California environment should be clearly designated as an essential part of the mission of the division.

The report also specifically identified a need for research and Extension work in areas heretofore largely ignored:

[C]onsidering the increased need for solutions to "people problems," there is need (1) to strengthen the division in the social sciences such as sociology and psychology, and (2) to involve the division more directly in programs to solve problems of poverty, hunger, and lack of skills and motivation. Such programs should be designed to benefit disadvantaged consumers in both rural and urban areas.

The division, with its traditional orientation to problem-solving and its history of involvement in rural community problems, has a unique capability within the University to undertake this mission. . . .

Recommendation: the division should strengthen its capability for dealing with population pressure problems and the displacement of people by technological change. Research teams should include social scientists who can foresee the social impact of the accomplishments of other members of the team. . . .

Recommendation: In cooperation with other agencies . . . the division should organize community development programs for disadvantaged areas of our cities. These programs should be designed to motivate and train people for self-help community improvement.[66]

Despite this thoughtful appraisal, little would come of the committee's recommendations. In the shifts of leadership then going on, the document had no quarterback to carry it. Incoming administrators, walking into managerial brush-fires, had not been part of the process of creating the report, and they did not take it seriously enough to pursue its recommendations.[67] Traditional conceptions of the Division's role—with primary emphases on production efficiency and basic science—would remain in place until events of later years forced painful reassessments.

## EVOLUTION OF THE DIVISION OF AGRICULTURAL SCIENCES

The twenty-year postwar period—an era of rapid, almost revolutionary change for American agriculture—was largely a period of confidence and satisfaction for the nation's colleges of agriculture. The heady "can-do" attitude that permeated public thought after the successes of World War II and the development of apparent miracles like nuclear energy, penicillin, and DDT and other chemical compounds also shaped thinking in academic circles. The social, economic, and environmental consequences of some of these wonders could not easily be foreseen, and only as realities emerged did scientific thought take a chastened turn. By the mid-1960s, however, the nation's changed political climate and the coalescing crises within society began to force re-examination of certain basic issues embedded in the land-grant university's traditional relationship between science and agriculture.[68]

The University of California felt these shifts and strains in its own unique way. The great expansion of the Division of Agricultural Sciences through the 1940s and 1950s brought many new facilities and talented people to the service of California agriculture, and the state and nation benefited through substantially improved agricultural productivity and marketing. Yet some of the apparent triumphs of the times had side effects that eventually sparked public criticism. Few of the Division's administrators were inclined, by either temperament or training, to reflect on the long-range implications of rapid societal change, however, and budget cuts made institutional response to changed circumstances difficult at best. Shifts in leadership as several top administrators retired or were promoted in the late 1960s slowed even the normally sluggish pace of the bureaucracy. Even the long-range 1968 review of the Division's goals and programs ended up on the shelf, ignored and then forgotten.

194     Several emerging issues that bore on Division activities, ranging from purely pragmatic matters to questions of value and philosophy, were hardly recognized at the time. These included changes in basic funding sources, the shift from client- to discipline-centered research, the difficulty of reallocating permanent positions in a bureaucratic structure, the decline of agrarianism and the growth of agribusiness, the equity impacts of technological change on society as a whole, and, not least, the disjunction between science and social values.

Changes in funding had unexpected but undeniable effects on planning. Until the 1960s basic institutional support supplied most of the Division's funding needs, and most research was programmatically planned to accomplish certain goals. As expenses grew but support did not, researchers—who often supported graduate students as assistants—developed a more entrepreneurial mentality. "Project funding" had been a part of the college research budget since its earliest days, but with state and federal budget cutbacks came a growing search for extramural competitive research grants. One result was that project priorities tended to coincide with the agenda of the funding organizations. Although federal and state formula funds supported salaries, research itself often was directed toward projects supported by special appropriations or by industry. Earmarked money for stipulated projects thus sometimes became "the tail that wagged the dog." While grant funding may have made the institution more responsive to specific goals, an unintended effect was to hamstring the Division's ability to set its own agenda. Even when there was interest in new kinds of research, some projects never got off the ground because there was no way to pay for them.

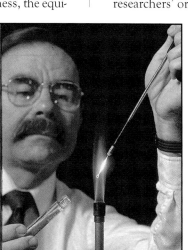

MICROBIOLOGIST RALPH KUNKEE STERILIZING INSTRUMENTS FOR ENOLOGICAL RESEARCH.

The explosion of science in the postwar era also shaped new aspirations and goals among researchers. Rapidly expanding scientific fields divided into subspecialties, and sophisticated new equipment made it possible to pursue laboratory research into ever more finely focused directions. Advances in transportation and communication shifted researchers' orientation from local or regional needs toward those of their national or international peer groups. Experiment Station scientists tended to do less applied, problem-solving work and more discipline-centered technical and theoretical work; this trend further diluted their connection with local constituencies.

Another issue was simple bureaucratic inertia—the problem of bringing about change in a large and cumbersome institution. Immediately after the war the Division hired a large number of new career employees; twenty years later, those institutional commitments continued. As time passed, some teaching and research areas within the Division began to seem less important, others more so; but until senior faculty retired, their positions were assigned. Institutional stability sometimes came at the price of flexibility.

While scientific research increasingly took place in the laboratory, farming continued its gradual shift from a way of life to a highly competitive business. Reflecting national priorities, efficient production became farmers' overriding goal, and the agrarianism of earlier years came to seem simply irrelevant. In the drive for efficiency, technological change was inevitable, and questions of equity were largely dismissed. Technological progress in general was assumed to bring improvements in the average standard of living—and so it did; but policymakers paid scant attention to the people left behind—those who, for whatever reasons, do not benefit from the general prosperity—until the political climate forced them to do so.

The dilemmas presented by technological change, which have become clear in many venues besides agriculture, are problems apparently inherent in the disjunction between science and social values. Scientists try to be value-free in their pursuit of objective fact; they narrowly define their goals in order to concentrate on accuracy; and they employ reductionist methods to clarify goals and results. But their narrow focus can reduce their overall vision, and problems having multiple dimensions can turn out to have been inadequately conceptualized. The obvious advantages of technological progress are sometimes counterweighed by unforeseen correlatives, and scientists alone cannot predict or plan for them.

Who, then, is to determine what levels of risk from new technology are acceptable? Who is to decide whether labor-saving machinery or cancer-causing substances should be used in industry? Who is to weigh the pros and cons of business consolidation, or to construct a wise economic or environmental policy? Who, for that matter, is to evaluate the merits of building an atomic bomb? The ethical questions raised by scientific research when it is translated into technological change may be beyond the responsibility of individual scientists. But they are surely within the purview of the University.

At its best the University is both marketplace and monastery, where society is served through the development of science and technology but where intellectual debate may clarify the meaning of change in the context of perennial human values. In the fall of 1960 Regents Professor Sir Charles P. Snow, an eminent British physicist and novelist, lectured at Berkeley on the danger of academic specialization, making a plea for "cross-cultural" understanding between the sciences and the humanities.[69] His thoughtful arguments for cross-disciplinary connections were applicable to a wide range of activities within the University, but perhaps nowhere more clearly than in the Division of Agricultural Sciences, the "island empire." Though Claude Hutchison perhaps interpreted the need for connections less broadly, he too understood the importance of the relationship between parts of the University when he stated, "You can have a great University without a college of agriculture . . . but you cannot have a great college of agriculture without a great University."[70]

As the nation's colleges of agriculture stood at the beginning of their second century, a Carnegie Foundation study reflected on the paradoxes of their success in transforming American agriculture, commenting:

> The American colleges of agriculture face some hard choices. They have had a hundred years of distinguished public service to agriculture. Yet the understanding and respect of each generation must be earned anew. Each college needs highly competent staff that includes men and women with the skills to project its forward look as much as an uncertain world allows.[71]

In a century of change, Eugene Hilgard's eloquent plea for regarding the practice of agriculture as "a learned profession" had been fulfilled. The centennial celebration of the University of California brought recognition of its agricultural programs as among the finest in the world, unparalleled in their scientific sophistication and ability to marshal team effort to solve complex challenges. The land-grant colleges themselves had moved far from their origins as places of "practical" education for the "industrial classes"; in the process, however, American society had been transformed and political balances had shifted. Because democratic institutions must be continually renewed, the traditional partnership between the land-grant complex and society—between the University of California's Division of Agricultural Sciences and its varied constituencies—was now ready for reinterpretation.

# NOTES

1. See Sherman E. Johnson, "Changes in American Farming during World War II," in Wayne Rasmussen, ed., *Readings in the History of American Agriculture* (Urbana: University of Illinois Press, 1960), pp. 275–86; also, "Introduction," in Wayne D. Rasmussen, ed., *Agriculture in the United States: A Documentary History* (New York: Random House, 1975), vol. 4, pp. 2917–21.

2. On the history of mechanization in California, see Roy Bainer, *The Engineering of Abundance: An Oral History Memoir of Roy Bainer* (Davis: UC Oral History Center, 1975), pp. 268–73.

3. Mary Louise Flint and Robert van den Bosch, *A Source Book on Integrated Pest Management* (a limited distribution report produced in 1977 by UC's Center for Integrated and Biological Control), pp. 108–9.

4. Clarence Kelly, "*California Agriculture . . . 20 Years Later*," *California Agriculture*, 20 (Dec. 1966): 3–6.

5. See Kenneth L. Bachman and Jackson V. McElveen, "The Family Farm, 1958," in Rasmussen, *Agriculture in the United States*, vol. 4, pp. 2922–28.

6. U.S. Bureau of the Census, *Historical Statistics of the United States, Colonial Times to 1970* (Washington, D.C.: U.S. Department of Commerce, 1975); also, Elmer W. Learn, James M. Lyons, and James Meyers, "Strategic Planning: Phase I—Background Information" (unpublished report of UC Division of Agriculture and Natural Resources, Sept. 1987), p. 5.

7. See Richard G. Lillard, *Eden in Jeopardy: Man's Prodigal Meddling with His Environment: The Southern California Experience* (Westport, Conn.: Greenwood Press, 1976), pp. 78–89; Yvonne Jacobson, *Passing Farms, Enduring Values: California's Santa Clara Valley* (Los Altos, Calif.: William Kaufmann, 1984), pp. 230, 231, 233.

8. U.S. Bureau of the Census, *Historical Statistics*, vol. 1, p. 464; Philip S. Parsons and C. O. McCorkle, Jr., "A Statistical Picture of California's Agriculture," *Circular 459* (Berkeley: UC Division of Agricultural Sciences, revised May 1963).

9. Seven conferences were held between March and November 1963 on the subjects of education, the arts, agriculture, the impact of science, the metropolitan future, natural resources, and "man under stress." Their proceedings were published under the general title *California and the Challenge of Growth*.

10. Erwin Cooper, *Aqueduct Empire* (Glendale, Calif.: Arthur H. Clark, 1968), pp. 147–66.

11. Walton Bean, *California: An Interpretive History* (New York: McGraw-Hill, 1988), pp. 405–7. Later critics eyeing compliance methods continued to complain that large agricultural firms were circumventing the intent of the 1902 Newlands Act.

12. Cooper, *Aqueduct Empire*, pp. 199–241.

13. Bean, *California: An Interpretive History*, pp. 528–30; Learn, Lyons, and Meyers, "Strategic Planning," pp. 31–32.

14. Verne A. Stadtman, ed., *The Centennial Record of the University of California* (Berkeley: UC Printing, 1967), pp. 349–52.

15. Ibid., pp. 353–55.

16. Ibid., pp. 404–6.

17. Ibid.; Harry W. Lawton and Lewis G. Weathers, "The Origins of Citrus Research in California and the Founding of the Citrus Research Center and Agricultural Experiment Station," in Walter Reuther, E. Clair Calavan, and Glenn E. Carman, eds., *The Citrus Industry*, (Oakland: UC Division of Agriculture and Natural Resources, 1989), vol. 5, p. 325.

18. California Liaison Committee of the State Board of Education and the Regents of the University of California, *A Master Plan for Higher Education in California, 1960–1975* (Sacramento: State Department of Education, 1960).

19. Clark Kerr, *The Uses of the University: With a "Postscript–1972"* (Cambridge, Mass.: Harvard University Press, 1972), pp. 52–53.

20. Stadtman, *Centennial Record*, pp. 487, 489–92.

21. See Harry R. Wellman, *Teaching, Research and Administration, University of California, 1925–1968* (Berkeley: UC Regional Oral History Office, 1976), pp. 77–80, on the 1949 Hutchison plan.

22. A 1958 decision to form a "graduate group" of biochemists in all departments led to the great strength of the biochemistry program at Davis. See "History of the Department of Biochemistry," unpublished manuscript, UC Davis Department of Biochemistry.

23. Space does not permit a description of the formation and history of the School of Veterinary Medicine and the School of Forestry, but see D. E. Jasper, *A Short History of the School of Veterinary Medicine, University of California* (Davis: Simmons Publishing, 1964) and Paul Casamajor, ed., *Forestry Education at the University of California: The First Fifty Years* (Berkeley: California Alumni Foresters, 1965).

24. Wellman, *Teaching, Research and Administration*, pp. 86–88; Emmett Fiske, "The College and Its Constituency: Research and Community Development at the University of California, 1875–1978" (Ph.D. diss., University of California, Davis, 1979), pp. 322–25.

25. Learn, Lyons, and Meyer, "Strategic Planning"; in an interview with this author, Peterson called his years in Berkeley "the five worst years of my life."

26. UC Archives, *Regents' Records*, special folder, "Kearney Vineyard"; "Prospectus and First Year Annual Report of the 1986–91 Mission on Water Penetration Problems in Irrigated Soils," (Davis: UC Kearney Foundation of Soil Science, Dec. 1987).

27. Tahoe Curricula Development Conference, UC Davis College of Agriculture, October 23–25, 1964: *Background Material*, "Preliminary Analysis of Agricultural Student Profiles," M. C. Regan, pp. 54–61 (unpublished conference materials lent to author by Chancellor Emeritus James H. Meyer).

28. UC Office of the Regents, *Regents' Minutes* (Oct. 1965).

29. J. H. Meyer, "Will There Be A Second Era?" (paper delivered at the Conference on Undergraduate Education in the Biological Sciences for Students in Agriculture and Natural Resources, Washington, D.C., November 11, 1966). Included in background document for the Tahoe Research and Organization Conference, November 3–5, 1966, pp. 57–65. Another contribution to this document was "Research–Tomorrow, 1965–1995," comprising results of a campuswide questionnaire sent to all faculty and staff in the College and Experiment Station at Davis to develop information for the conference.

30. Historical material on the UCLA College of Agriculture was provided by Professor Emeritus Charles A. Schroeder, March 1990.

31. On Riverside in the 1950s and 1960s, see Herman T. Spieth, *From Farm Boy to Evolutionist: The Memoir of Herman T. Spieth* (Davis: UC Oral History Center, 1978), pp. 114–82; and James B. Kendrick, Jr., *From Plant Pathologist to Vice President for Agriculture and Natural Resources, University of California, 1947–1986* (Berkeley: UC Regional Oral History Office, 1989), pp. 82–89. Also, Ansel Adams and Nancy Newhall, *Fiat Lux: The University of California* (New York: McGraw-Hill, 1967), pp. 41–45, 142–43, 150; and Albert G. Pickerell and May Dornin, *The University of California: A Pictorial History* (Berkeley: UC Printing, 1968), pp. 164–97.

32. Norwood A. Kerr, *The Legacy: A Centennial History of the State Agricultural Experiment Stations, 1887–1987* (Columbia: Missouri Agricultural Experiment Station, Mar. 1987), p. 94.

33. Ibid., p. 100.

34. Information on the agricultural field stations is from Stadtman, *Centennial Record*, pp. 23–24, and from occasional descriptive articles in *California Agriculture* between 1962 and 1965. By 1964 the University was also making plans for a Land and Water Natural Reserve System, reflecting the ecological diversity of the state.

35. George S. Wells, *Garden in the West: A Dramatic Account of Science in Agriculture* (New York: Dodd, Mead, 1969). See also Henry Schacht, *Henry Schacht and the Art of Agricultural Communication* (Davis: UC Oral History Center, 1977), pp. 139–58.

36. See R. E. Evenson, P. E. Waggoner, and V. W. Ruttan, "Economic Benefits from Research: An Example from Agriculture,"

198    *Science* 205 (Sept. 14, 1979): 1101–7; and Vernon W. Ruttan, *Agricultural Research Policy* (Minneapolis: University of Minnesota Press, 1982), chap. 10, pp. 237–61.

37. See U.S. President's Commission on Migratory Labor, *Migratory Labor in American Agriculture* (Washington, D.C.: U.S. GPO, 1951).

38. Ellis W. Hawley, "The Politics of the Mexican Labor Issue, 1950–1965," *Agricultural History* 40 (July 1966): 157–76; Ernesto Galarza, *Merchants of Labor: The Mexican Bracero Story* (Santa Barbara: McNally and Loftin, 1964); Ernesto Galarza, *Farm Workers and Agri-Business in California, 1947–1960* (Notre Dame, Ill.: University of Notre Dame Press, 1977).

39. See U.S. Department of Labor, *Year of Transition: Seasonal Farm Labor 1965, Report from the Secretary of Labor* (Washington, D.C.: USDL, 1965), p. 1: "Predictions that California's agricultural industry could not function without the massive importation of foreign farm labor proved inaccurate."

40. "The Great Tomato Machine," *California Tomato Grower* 22(6):4–12.

41. Ibid.

42. A 122–page progress report, "Research on Agricultural Mechanization, 1966," was produced by the Agricultural Experiment Station in 1967. The unfunded research proposals were mentioned in a personal communication to the author by J. H. Meyer, May 8, 1990. Information on research by the department of Applied Behavioral Sciences is from California Aggie Alumni Association, "UCD and the Migrant Farm Workers," *UCD Dimensions* (Fall 1968), pp. 3–6. The abortive farm worker training project planned through the Sacramento Single Men's Self-Help Group was mentioned in an author's interview with Roger Garrett, October 1990.

43. Andrew Schmitz and David Seckler, "Mechanized Agriculture and Social Welfare: The Case of the Tomato Harvester," *American Journal of Agricultural Economics* 52 (Nov. 1970): 575–76.

44. Jim Hightower, *Hard Tomatoes, Hard Times: A Report of the Agribusiness Accountability Project on the Failure of America's Land Grant College Complex* (Cambridge, Mass.: Schenckman, 1973); for other descriptions and analyses of the mechanization issue, see Wayne Rasmussen, "Advances in American Agriculture: The Mechanical Tomato Harvester as a Case Study," *Technology and Culture* 9 (Oct. 1968): 531–43; William F. Friedland and Amy Barton, *Destalking the Wily Tomato: A Case Study in Social Consequences in California Agricultural Research* (Davis: UC Davis Department of Applied Behavioral Sciences, 1975); A. I. Dickman, *Interviews with Persons Involved in the Development of the Mechanical Tomato Harvester, the Compatible Processing Tomato and the New Agricultural Systems That Evolved* (Davis: UC Oral History Center, 1978); Paul Barnett, *Labor's Dwindling Harvest: The Impact of Mechanization on California's Fruit and Vegetable Workers* (Davis: California Institute for Rural Studies, 1978); papers in *Technological Change, Farm Mechanization, and Agricultural Employment* (Davis: UC Davis Department of Agricultural Economics, 1978); Orville E. Thompson and Ann F. Scheuring, *From Lug Boxes to Electronics* (Davis: UC Davis Department of Applied Behavioral Sciences, 1979); Philip L. Martin and Alan L. Olmstead, "The Agricultural Mechanization Controversy," *Science* 227 (Feb. 1985): 601–6.

45. J. Earl Coke, *Reminiscences on People and Change in California Agriculture, 1900–1975* (Davis: UC Oral History Center, 1975), pp. 66–90.

46. Alcorn's introductory remarks at the Extension Biennial Conference at Asilomar on January 13, 1959.

47. On Extension in the 1960s, see Ann F. Scheuring, *A Sustaining Comradeship: A Brief History of University of California Cooperative Extension, 1913–1988* (Berkeley: UC Division of Agriculture and Natural Resources, 1988), pp. 38–49; also Learn, Lyons, and Meyers, "Strategic Planning," pp. 110–13.

48. 1957 Extension Committee on Organization and Policy, Subcommittee on Scope and Responsibility, "The Cooperative Extension Service . . . Today: A Statement of Scope and Responsibility" (April 1958). See Fiske, "The College and Its Constituency," pp. 337–46, for a description of the aftermath of the Scope Report in California.

49. Rachel Carson, *Silent Spring* (Boston: Houghton Mifflin, 1962); see also Frank Graham, Jr., *Since Silent Spring* (Boston: Houghton Mifflin, 1970).

50. Robert L. Rudd and Richard E. Genelly, "Pesticides: Their Use and Toxicity in Relation to Wildlife," California Department of Fish and Game, *Game Bulletin* 7 (Sacramento: State GPO, 1956). Rudd held an appointment from 1957 to 1964 in the Agricultural

Experiment Station. In 1964 the University of Wisconsin Press published his book *Pesticides and the Living Landscape*, a scientific counterpart to Carson's work that Rudd had actually completed earlier.

51. Pest resistance and other issues are discussed in UC entomologist Robert van den Bosch's angry *The Pesticide Conspiracy* (Garden City, N.J.: Doubleday, 1978). The 20 percent estimate is from a report on the Agricultural Toxicology and Pesticide Residue Laborary prepared for the Regents' October 1963 meeting.

52. "Academic Plan for the Department of Environmental Toxicology, 1989–1994," departmental files.

53. These recollections were expressed in the author's interviews with H. Lange, J. Lyons, R. Rudd, and M. Stimmann, April 1990.

54. A. E. Michelbacher and O. G. Bacon, "Walnut Insect and Spider-Mite Control in Northern California," *Journal of Economic Entomology* 45 (Dec. 1952): 1020–27; V. M. Stern, R. F. Smith, R. van den Bosch, and K. S. Hagen, "The Integrated Control Concept," *Hilgardia* 29 (Oct. 1959): 81–101. The forerunner of IPM control procedures was probably the 1946 supervised control developed by Ray F. Smith of Berkeley, in which investigators sampled commercial fields for pests and natural enemies on a routine basis and relayed the information to the grower to help make management decisions (Harry Lange, "Historical Notes: Prepared for the Pacific Branch, Entomological Society of America," unpublished manuscript, c. 1985).

55. Kelly, "California Agriculture . . . 20 Years Later," *California Agriculture*, 20 (Dec. 1966): 3–6.

56. Stadtman, *Centennial Record*, p. 522.

57. Ibid., p. 25.

58. Donald L. Nelson, "Silver Threads Among the Gold: The First 25 Years of Community and Rural Development Programs," Joint Planning and Evaluation Staff Paper Series 80–PPS-08 (Washington, D.C.: U.S. Department of Agriculture, Nov. 1980), pp. 5–6; other information is from author's interview with Clair Christensen, April 1990.

59. U.S. National Advisory Commission on Rural Poverty, *The People Left Behind* (Washington, D.C.: U.S. GPO, Sept. 1967), p. ix.

60. Joint USDA/NASULGC Extension Study Committee, *A People and a Spirit*, (Fort Collins: Colorado State University, 1968), p. 93.

61. See Varden Fuller, "Farm Population of California," Parts 1–3, *California Agriculture*, 8 (Nov., Dec. 1954) and 9 (Jan. 1955): entire issues.

62. U.S. National Advisory Commission, *The People Left Behind*, p. 4.

63. Kendrick, *From Plant Pathologist to Vice President*, p. 150.

64. UC Archives, *Regents' Minutes* (May 1968, May 1969).

65. Anne Draper and Hal Draper, *The Dirt on California: Agribusiness and the University* (Berkeley: Independent Socialist Clubs of America, 1968), pp. 5, 6.

66. Division of Agricultural Sciences Long-Range Plan (June 28, 1968), pp. 32, 34.

67. Learn, Lyons, and Meyers, "Strategic Planning," p. 68; Kendrick, *From Plant Pathologist to Vice President*, pp. 149–53. Kendrick stated that he was "somewhat disappointed" in the report and found no enthusiasm for it among the several deans. He paid more attention to the 1967 report of the Agricultural Advisory Council, chaired by Robert W. Long of the Bank of America, which concentrated on the need for a specialized research and extension center for the San Joaquin Valley. Another, shorter, ad hoc report was released privately in October 1967, titled "Agricultural Round Table Subcommittee Interim Report on Agriculture Within the University of California." It expressed distress about the "erosion" of agricultural work in the University, which the committee viewed as a "fine progress machine" for industry.

68. Thanks are due to Constant C. Delwiche, professor emeritus in Land, Air, and Water Resources at UC Davis, for his contributions to this section.

69. See C. P. Snow, *The Two Cultures: A Second Look* (New York: Mentor Books, 1964).

70. Quoted in *In Memoriam, University of California* (Berkeley: University of California Academic Senate, September 1980), p. 125.

71. Charles E. Kellogg and David C. Knapp, *The College of Agriculture: Science in the Public Service* (New York: McGraw-Hill, 1966), p. 214.

# 7

# New Directions

## 1969–1989

*Oak woodlands in northern California. During the 1980s the renamed Division of Agriculture and Natural Resources augmented its environmental activities and took on responsibility for the University's Natural Reserve System.*

THE 1970S AND 1980S WERE WATERSHED YEARS FOR THE NATION AS WELL AS FOR CALIFORNIA AND ITS UNIVERSITY. NEW INTERNATIONAL RELATIONSHIPS AND DOMESTIC CONDITIONS BEGAN TO RESHAPE GOVERNMENTAL AGENDAS AND POPULAR OPINION. UNIVERSITY TEACHING CURRICULA EVOLVED TO MEET STUDENT NEEDS, BUT CRITICISM OF THE TRADITIONAL LAND-GRANT AGRICULTURAL RESEARCH AND EXTENSION SYSTEM MOUNTED. THE SYSTEM CONTINUED TO PRODUCE SIGNIFICANT ACHIEVEMENTS, BUT ADAPTATIONS TO SOME CHALLENGES WERE SLOWED BY ORGANIZATIONAL PROBLEMS. BY THE END OF THE 1980S THE DIVISION OF AGRICULTURE AND NATURAL RESOURCES WAS MOVING IN SEVERAL NEW DIRECTIONS WITH A BROADENED SENSE OF MISSION AND A MORE DIVERSE STAFF; YET SERIOUS QUESTIONS CLOUDED ITS FUTURE.

# 7

# New Directions   1969–1989

## THE BACKGROUND FOR CHANGE

### NATIONAL PREOCCUPATIONS

The tumultuous decade of the 1970s brought painful rifts in American assumptions. New technological advances and societal influences pushed the nation into a future it did not anticipate or understand, while unresolved international conflicts darkened the nation's mood and caused dissension at home. The undeclared war in Vietnam was finally brought to a close in April 1975 when helicopters lifted the last remaining Americans off the roof of the U.S. Embassy in Saigon, but not until public frustration, growing costs in human suffering, and the increasing drain on the American economy had taken a high toll. The conflict in Southeast Asia and the continuing U.S.–Soviet military standoff were largely accountable for the political and economic malaise that characterized the years following.

Widespread domestic dissatisfaction revealed itself in a general questioning of many economic and social practices. Perhaps the two outstanding trends of the decade were the embracing of a new environmental ethic, particularly among the young, and the rising power struggle between the "estab-lishment" and groups that felt they had too long been ignored or discriminated against. The passage of the Civil Rights Act of 1972 brought increased hope and new opportunities for women and minorities. Popular disillusionment with politics after the Vietnam War and the Watergate affair brought about attempts to return to a more idealistic agenda for the federal government under President Carter. Ultimately, however, his administration proved too inexperienced politically to complete many of his initiatives.

The 1970s were largely a good decade for American agriculture. A combination of events, including change in international capital markets and a series of bad crop years in other countries, encouraged a surge in American agricultural exports. American farm income went up as surpluses were eliminated, and farmers hastened to plant more acres to meet demand. Many, buoyed by optimism, went deeply into debt to expand their holdings.

At about the same time, however, there emerged some serious public criticism of the land-grant university system of agricultural research and extension. In 1972 James Hightower's *Hard Tomatoes, Hard Times*, subtitled *A Report of the Agribusiness Accountability Project on the Failure of America's Land Grant College Complex*, charged that the system had, by its heavy emphasis on production technology, favored the development of large, capital-intensive farming corporations ("agribusiness") over the needs of small farmers and rural communities. Along with other criticisms of the nation's agricultural research system, the book influenced policymakers. The 1977 National Agricultural Research, Extension and Teaching Act emphasized Congressional interest in directing more research toward such matters as alternative energy sources, human nutrition, conservation of natural resources, and the needs of the "family farm." Minnesota populist Bob Bergland, Carter's Secretary of Agriculture, mounted an effort to reorganize the Department of Agriculture to reflect new priorities.[1]

In 1980 another burst of national discontent brought Ronald Reagan to the presidency. Reagan's personal charm helped promote a reversal of the "new agenda," both economically and environmentally. Weary and resentful of the years of turmoil, Americans for a time turned inward, seeking personal goals and "privatization." America was said to be moving into a "postindustrial" era, in which services overshadowed manufacturing industries, and the widespread use of computer technology expanded information networks. The shift of domestic priorities in the 1980s was reflected in sharp debates over national economic policy, international competition, balance of payments, and rising federal deficits. The Reagan administration attempted to dismantle or reduce a number of established governmental programs, to rearm the nation, to cut taxes in order to stimulate investment, and to curb trends toward greater environmental regulation. Deadlocks between a Democratic Congress and the Republican executive branch hindered full accomplishment of this agenda. Special interest groups, aware of their potential power at the ballot box and in the courtroom, became increasingly influential in politics.

The prosperity of 1970s agriculture vanished due to shifts in the world economy and new agricultural competition from abroad. In the mid-1980s, farmers bore their worst depression in 50 years. Land values declined, overextended farm borrowers lost equity, and a rash of foreclosures hit some areas hard. Public scrutiny focused on conventional agriculture's contribution to environmental degradation. Consumer groups expressed rising concern about the safety of the food supply. Late in the decade, dire warnings of environmental catastrophe surfaced with scientific projections of widespread global climate changes caused by buildup of the "greenhouse gas" carbon dioxide in the earth's atmosphere.

## CALIFORNIA AT THE CROSSROADS

By the mid-1970s, 90 percent of California's population lived in urban areas, two-thirds of them south of the Tehachapis. The proportion of Hispanics, blacks, and Asians in the general population grew through immigration and relatively high birth rates, and it was predicted that by the year 2000 white Californians would no longer be the majority. These demographic factors, coupled with developments from the state legislative reapportionment of 1965, brought about a marked shift in legislative attitudes toward traditional agricultural and rural interests. In 1975 the legislature, in concert with Governor Jerry Brown's administration, passed the California Agricultural Labor Relations Act, viewed at the time as pathbreaking legislation enabling farm workers to unionize. Though farm organizations were not pleased, they were relatively unable to oppose the public's wave of sympathy for disadvantaged farm laborers led by union organizer Cesar Chavez. A decade later, unionization of farmworkers had gained little ground because of the continuing influx of workers from Mexico, but agriculture's longtime influence in politics continued to shrink. Late in the Brown administration, the Mediterranean fruit fly controversy pitted anxious city residents against farm interests

206 desperate to stop a potential infestation and crop loss by the aerial spraying of pesticides in urban areas.

While urban growth meant more demand for food, it also increased pressure on the state's natural resources. Residential and industrial development encroached on farmland along the coast and in the interior valleys. Mainly urban-based environmentalists resisted further development of water supplies, and tensions over allocation of existing supplies between agriculture and municipal-industrial uses were exacerbated by the droughts of the mid-1970s and the late 1980s. In 1982 voters repudiated bonds for construction of the Peripheral Canal to move water from northern California around the Delta to the San Joaquin Valley—a defeat popularly construed as an environmentalists' triumph over big agricultural and southern California water interests. Critics also attacked various forms of subsidies available to farmers and ranchers through federal water projects, commodity price supports, and low grazing fees on public lands.

Rising farm management costs along with financial overextension helped bring about attrition of some California farm operations during these two decades. California recorded a historic low of 67,674 farms in

the 1974 agricultural census; but then a new trend developed. As Californians migrated from urban to rural areas in search of a better life in the countryside, the number of small farms again began to grow. Many of these small operations were "hobby" or part-time farms supported in part by external earnings, and few were intended to be self-sustaining entities, but their increase contributed to a two-tiered kind of agriculture in which, by 1987, the top 7 percent of California farms accounted for 75 percent of the value of sales, while the bottom 70 percent accounted for less than 5 percent. The term "dual farm economy" was coined to describe the growing disparity between those science-driven, highly capitalized businesses that now supplied most of the nation's supermarkets and the small, less industrial farms more oriented toward local consumers and often interested in "alternative" farming practices. This marked heterogeneity of interests and constituents had significant implications for land-grant research and Extension nationally; in California it led to the restructuring of some programs and the creation of new ones.[2]

NEW HOUSES OVERLOOKING CROPS IN SAN DIEGO COUNTY. SOME OF THE STATE'S MOST PRODUCTIVE FARMLANDS HAVE BEEN REPLACED BY PROLIFERATING RESIDENTIAL SUBDIVISIONS.

# A NEW GENERATION AT THE UNIVERSITY

The decade of the sixties had introduced unprecedented challenges to the University of California. Continuing student unrest, especially at Berkeley, eroded public support, and the legislature began to take a more critical view of the institution. Curricular and administrative reorganizations eventually reshaped many University programs, including those in agriculture. Changing political circumstances also affected the relative influence of agriculture within the University.

## CHANGING STUDENT INTERESTS

Some observers blamed the mood of disaffected students in the late 1960s and early 1970s on the Vietnam war, but young activists expressed other serious concerns that ran to the heart of the University. Many expressed frustration with the increasing scale and impersonality of higher education and its lack of opportunity for individual expression. They deplored a lack of "relevancy" in their classes and the University's seeming reluctance to reallocate teaching and research resources to programs addressing current issues. These issues included apparently intransigent poverty at some levels of society, apartheid (at home and abroad) in policy and practice, lack of political power among young people and ethnic minorities, sometimes corrupt corporate ethics and skewed governmental priorities, and the continuing deterioration of the environment. While many of these issues were national or international in their implications, students used their local campuses as platforms from which to press for social change; achieving the right to vote at age eighteen, in 1971, greatly increased their political strength.

Individual members of the faculty at all levels shared many of these views. Except for a small minority of predominantly younger, nontenured members, however, the faculty in general was not sympathetic with the militant tactics some student groups adopted. Nor was the faculty willing to embrace uncritically the solutions being proposed, particularly with respect to course and curricular matters. Nevertheless, student and faculty agreements brought about important changes in undergraduate programs. Internship programs were developed to tie classroom learning and supervised external work together into a coherent learning experience. Academic leaves of absence were easier to get. Enrollment was liberalized in many courses, new courses were introduced to encourage student exploration, and opportunities to create individual majors were expanded.

## ADMINISTRATIVE MATTERS

The end of the 1960s brought wholesale shifts in the University's administration. A new generation of administrators faced difficult tasks: how to rally the financial support of alumni angered by events on campus; how to maintain relationships with agricultural and other historically important constituencies; how to relate to other sectors of higher education; how to withstand assaults on traditional University funding; and how to deal with conflicting pressures being brought to bear on the University. Despite the difficulty of breaking through the defensive mentality exhibited by some faculty and staff, administrators of the 1970s tried hard to adjust to new trends in the legislature and to recover the respect of a changing and more critical public.

Legislative attitudes toward the University were to some extent linked with statewide fiscal retrenchment. Student unrest provided a convenient opportunity to check the rapid expansion in funding for higher education that had resulted from the state's economic growth and historically accepted formula-based appropriations. Some legislators, pressing for academic and administrative changes in the University, were frustrated by the institution's constitutional autonomy.

208 Hence they adopted several new strategies: re-examination of the autonomy concept, pressure to shorten Regents' terms (ultimately achieved), interruption of the formula-driven block budget funding so long enjoyed by the University, restrictive budgetary language and specific program cuts and appropriations through "line items," and requests for exhaustive reports on various matters.

Fiscal problems were not the whole story. University personnel practices came under fire by legislators insisting that the University review its faculty and staff recruitment, retention, and advancement rates to provide greater service to groups historically underrepresented in the student body. Under some duress, the institution eventually mobilized affirmative action programs to address the student body's ethnic mix and the problems of preferential admission, remedial education, and financial aid.

ENTOMOLOGY PROFESSOR TOM BELLOWS, A SPECIALIST IN THE BIOLOGICAL CONTROL OF PESTS AND IN TESTING FOR PESTICIDE RESIDUES, IN HIS LAB AT UC RIVERSIDE.

**AGRICULTURAL TEACHING PROGRAMS**

The College of Agriculture at Davis led the way in trying to accommodate legitimate student concerns, which helped it retain student enrollments while comparable colleges across the nation suffered declines. Dean James Meyer's initiatives in the mid-1960s led to substantial ferment within the College. During 1969-70, when Meyer became chancellor at UC Davis, incoming Dean Chester McCorkle presided over a series of intensive workshops, retreats, and meetings to create consensus for a plan to form several teaching divisions; these took control of production-oriented departmental undergraduate programs and shifted curricular decision making to cross-departmental faculty committees. Succeeding Deans Alex McCalla and Charles Hess carried curricular reform forward in the 1970s.

While Davis continued to be the only UC campus offering a full agricultural curriculum, the basic thrust of its programs changed. Courses were strengthened in scientific rigor, and, where appropriate, faculty introduced more current topical subject matter. Traditional courses in livestock judging and majors in home economics were gradually phased out. Fields lumped within the home economics curriculum, including human nutrition, design, and child development, eventually emerged as separate areas of study. Agricultural production undergraduate majors continued to decline, particularly in the plant sciences.[3] On the other hand, reorganized programs in agricultural economics and applied behavioral sciences attracted many new majors and course enrollments. Progress in scientific method and research technology, along with new grants for research, encouraged students to opt for master's and doctoral degrees in many fields. Because of the recognized high quality of their academic training, many UC Davis graduates in the agricultural sciences found good positions in business and government as well as in agriculture-related occupations.

At Berkeley enrollments in the agricultural sciences recovered from their decline in the 1960s. The 1973 reorganization of the College of Agriculture, creating the College of Natural Resources, contributed to the turnaround in student interest at both graduate and undergraduate levels. Berkeley programs continued to be strong in plant pathology, entomology, genetics, soils and plant nutrition, and resource economics and management.

At Riverside the increase in undergraduate enrollments during the 1960s took place almost entirely in the biological sciences.[4] Riverside graduate programs were recognized for their strength in the fields of soil science, entomology, plant pathology, and citrus production. With the reorganization of the College of Natural and Agricultural Sciences in 1974, enrollment of graduate and undergraduate students almost doubled.

## AGRICULTURE'S DECLINING INFLUENCE IN THE UNIVERSITY

To some degree agriculture's political position within the University changed when seats on the Board of Regents were reorganized by constitutional amendment in 1974 and the chair of the State Board of Agriculture no longer served as an ex officio member. While representing but one vote, this member had always been a spokesperson for the University's agricultural activities. Now no designated voice existed among the Regents on such matters. Nor was the same priority assumed for agricultural programs, given that the University had diversified dramatically in the postwar years and that an ever smaller proportion of the state's population was engaged in farming and related activities.

Agricultural research funding suffered in several ways. While the University continued to grow in enrollments and number of programs, proportional state funding did not. Administrators had to grapple with serious resource allocation issues, both on individual campuses and between campuses. Medical school and other development siphoned off large amounts of money, at the expense of long-sacrosanct programs like the Agricultural Experiment Station. Appointments in the Experiment Station were affected as campus administrators juggled the funds assigned for agriculture: some research positions were transferred to teaching programs, and some nonagricultural faculty received Experiment Station appointments.

When enrollments in the agricultural sciences grew in the late 1970s and early 1980s, student-to-faculty ratios rose above campus averages. Since most agricultural faculty also held part-time Experiment Station appointments, there was some erosion during this period of time spent on research, leading to concern for future research productivity. Because graduate students play a vital role in agricultural research, decline in student support in the mid- to late 1980s contributed to the problem.

Division administrators had to contend with the difficulties inherent in a two-tiered research and extension bureaucracy. Campus officers assumed greater authority over faculty appointments and research funding allocations; Extension retained its own separate administration; and coordinated planning languished for lack of strong central authority. During the 1980s faculty turnover rose significantly, especially in the Experiment Station, as postwar hirees began to retire. While the transition theoretically offered the Division as well as the campuses an opportunity to shift resources toward new programs, it also coincided with systemwide requirements that vacated positions, salary money, and overhead support be returned to the University's central administration in order to meet overall savings goals and other funding needs.

210

# CHALLENGES FOR AGRICULTURAL RESEARCH

The turbulence of the 1960s seemed at first to have little relevance to the Division of Agricultural Sciences (as it was known then); by the decade's end, however, social critics were beginning to focus on the agricultural research and extension establishment. Special-interest advocates and legislative committees began to question the goals and practices of the land-grant system; some countered the system's triumphs of enhanced agricultural productivity with evidence of associated costs to the environment. Others brought up issues of food safety and the changing structure of American agriculture. Criticism buffeted the University of California's agricultural programs until some adjustments were made; but because the institution was slow to change, some years of controversy tarnished its splendid reputation.

## PRODUCTION VERSUS ENVIRONMENTAL QUALITY ISSUES

By the 1970s evidence was accumulating that America's food production system was beginning to threaten environmental quality. For example, it was known even before Rachel Carson's *Silent Spring* that some pesticide residues persisted in the environment and accumulated in food chains, killing nontarget organisms and contaminating soil and water. Scientists had observed that some residues actually decreased the effectiveness of pest control by destroying beneficial

ORGANIC FARMER SELLING HIS CROP OF STRAWBERRIES IN AN OUTDOOR FARMER'S MARKET. MANY SUCH SMALL-SCALE GROWERS BEGAN DIRECT MARKETING IN THE 1980S, ENCOURAGED BY POPULAR INTEREST IN PESTICIDE-FREE FOODS.

organisms and developing resistance in target species. There were reports of fertilizer residues contributing to excessive nitrate buildup in drainage ponds and groundwater. Some large-scale beef and poultry production facilities had demonstrated monumental waste disposal problems; wastes from industrial-scale food processing also created problems. Other agricultural practices contributed to air and water pollution, soil erosion, and loss of wildlife.

The impact of high-technology agriculture on the environment attracted considerable public attention, and some legislative action, during the 1970s. UC scientists predicted this trend would increase:

> In California, restrictions on agricultural production have resulted from controls on land use, solid waste disposal, use of crop-protection chemicals, air quality, and water quality. It seems likely U.S. and California agriculture will operate within an increasingly complex framework of policies and procedures designed to achieve two goals simultaneously—protect the environment and increase food production.[5]

Some in the national agricultural arena began to examine potential strategies for minimizing the side effects of current farm practices. Interest in the "organic" movement became mainstream when, in April 1979, Anson Bertrand, Director of Science and Education at the U.S. Department of Agriculture, appointed a national team of scientists to conduct a study of organic farming practices in the United States and Europe. The USDA study was initiated after numerous requests for information had revealed widespread public unease about energy shortages, food safety, and environmental matters. The most frequently expressed concerns included sharply rising costs and uncertain availability of energy and chemical fertilizers (including heavy reliance on international suppliers), steady decline in soil tilth and productivity from erosion and loss of organic matter, pollution of waterways by agricultural drainage, hazards to human and animal health from indiscriminate use of pesticides, and deterioration of regional family farm and local marketing systems. Many believed that a shift, at least to some degree, toward organic farming techniques might alleviate some of these problems and in the long term ensure a more stable and sustainable domestic agriculture.

Released in July 1980, the USDA report was a milestone for the federal and land-grant research institutions, for it legitimized academic discussion about organic farming techniques.[6] At a time when increasing apprehensions about the adverse effects of America's current system of agriculture were being aired—particularly with regard to the intensive, continuous production of cash grains and the extensive, sometimes excessive use of agricultural chemicals—the USDA report brought "alternative" approaches closer to the conventional food production system.

Only a few months later, however, another report on organic farming took a more skeptical view. In October 1980 the Council for Agricultural Science and Technology (CAST), a council of the professional societies, organizations, and individuals most often associated with "conventional" agriculture, issued its own report, "Organic and Conventional Farming Compared." Its authors pointed out that the word *organic* was commonly used as a synonym for "natural," and that believers in the movement regarded organically grown food as nutritionally superior to conventionally grown food; that, except for natural products such as rock phosphate and limestone, organic growers considered use of plant nutrients from off the farm for application to the soil as undesirable; and that so-called natural chemicals were

regarded as safe while manufactured chemicals were condemned as hazardous. CAST representatives took issue with some of these stands as being unrealistic.[7]

While not all agreed that organic farming was the agriculture of the future, nor that the nation's public research institutions had failed to serve the needs of organic farmers, the legacy of the USDA study, at least, was that discussion of the fundamental nature of the food production system was now a legitimate issue to be considered by research institutions.

## PESTICIDE RESIDUE AND FOOD SAFETY ISSUES

A review of national and regional surveys conducted in 1987 showed that fears among consumers regarding the effects of pesticide residues on public health grew in the years after 1965.[8] The discovery of high levels of ethylene dibromide in cake and muffin mixes in 1984 and of the illegal use of aldicarb on watermelons in 1985 heightened public concern about the potential for unsafe pesticide residues in food. When specifically queried about food safety, 77 percent of respondents in a 1984 survey of more than 1,000 U.S. households conducted by the Food Marketing Institute considered pesticide residues on produce to be a serious health hazard; more than 60 percent also regarded the use of antibiotics and hormones in animal production as a hazard. Apparently even small levels of exposure to chemicals in food troubled many consumers, explaining in part the preference for the "zero risk" policy called for by some consumer advocates.

Many agricultural scientists believed that public concern regarding food safety was exaggerated. Pest control specialists pointed to stiff federal requirements for testing and regulating pesticides and to some twenty years of regulatory legislation in the state of California. By the mid-1980s California had passed laws that (1) controlled the use of chemicals having the potential to contaminate groundwater; (2) called for the state

212 to review federal standards governing the pesticide residue levels allowable in food; (3) required chemicals currently in use to be re-examined for potential birth defect and cancer-causing effects; and (4) mandated that clear warnings be provided to persons exposed to hazardous substances, creating a "bounty" for whistle-blowers on chemical use violators. Nevertheless, opponents of pesticides continued to believe that current rules were deficient in safeguarding human health and the environment. In 1988 the California Assembly Office of Research published a report entitled "The Invisible Diet: Gaps in California's Pesticide Residue Detection Program," which questioned the state's monitoring ability as well as current tolerance standards for pesticide residues.[9]

## THE FARM SIZE ISSUE

The changing structure of American agriculture became another subject of controversy. Hightower's *Hard Tomatoes, Hard Times* contended that rural America was in crisis, its land-grant institutions having helped create "an automated, integrated and corporatized agriculture," the primary beneficiaries of which were agribusiness corporations. Similar arguments appeared in *The Politics of Land: Ralph Nader's Study Group Report on Land Use in California* (New York, 1973). Called the Fellmeth Report after its project director, this 700-page book exhaustively examined California land ownership patterns, agricultural practices, university research support, commercial and industrial threats to wild areas, trends in urban expansion, and "power politics." The authors maintained that large land holdings had historically resulted in "unjust enrichment" and that ongoing concentration of land resources represented a threat to democracy:

> Almost by definition, highly concentrated ownership and control of land mean more political and economic power and greater ability to oppose contrary interests than do widely diffused ownership or control. Large landholders direct a greater portion of their earnings toward political ends than do smaller holders. And the large owner's land-use decisions have a greater public impact, thus giving him greater bargaining power with officials.[10]

A few years later a less ambitious but equally pointed report called *Getting Bigger: Large Scale Farming in California* laid out a "directory" of the state's 211 largest farms, listing all operations of more than 5,000 acres of cropland. The author reported that the largest 3.7 percent of California farms controlled 59 percent of the state's cropland, and that the ten leading landowners held an aggregate of 520,700 acres. Calculating that these 211 large-farm operators averaged about 11,460 acres each, he concluded that "This scale size is significantly greater than any previous work has suggested."[11]

These publications had a decidedly polemical cast, a fact that disturbed and polarized many associated with the state's agriculture even while they recognized the ongoing farm size trends. Up to this point, few postwar UC agricultural researchers had exhibited much concern about ownership trends in California agriculture. On the contrary, the working partnership between the College and the industry grew stronger as both scientific and commercial enterprises flourished, and the size issue was eclipsed by greater interest in productivity and marketing. Now, in an effort to shed light on the issue, a group of agricultural economists mobilized to produce a set of papers on cost-size relationships in agriculture. The resulting multiauthor publication was objective in analysis, moderate in tone, and less conclusive than the Fellmeth Report.

> One may conclude from this review that there is no single simple explanation for the trend toward ever-larger farms. While considerable evidence exists that there is a significant technical basis for economies of scale in farming . . . cost-savings tend to level off at a "medium size" unit, with the least-cost point varying widely for different type farms. Explanations of expansion beyond this point involve [many

influences]: government policies, tax structure, the product marketing system, the risk environment, changes in labor costs and in energy costs and availability. . . .

There is considerable difference of opinion about the effects of concentration of American agriculture in fewer hands. Increased efficiency on farms has freed all but three percent of our population from growing food and fiber. Yet, if most cost economies can be achieved, say, on farms with gross sales of $75,000 to $100,000, why should there be farms with gross sales of $500,000 or more? Is the rural community worse off when surrounded by a few large farms rather than many smaller ones? Agricultural economists, rural sociologists, and policy makers continue to wrestle with this question.[12]

These general concerns permeated many public discussions about agriculture, both nationally and in California; but as the 1970s and 1980s progressed other challenges confronted the Division, ranging from lawsuits to legislation, policy debates to personnel actions. Three particularly public events brought unwelcome publicity to the Division and reaffirmed the need for at least some change in the way it went about its business.

## PUBLIC DEBATES ON RESEARCH PRIORITIES

### THE MECHANIZATION LAWSUIT

On January 17, 1979, suit was filed against the University of California in Alameda County Superior Court by attorneys for California Rural Legal Assistance, directed against agricultural mechanization research and development undertaken by the University. Plaintiffs were the California Agrarian Action Project, Inc., described as a nonprofit corporation organized to aid small-scale family farmers and the disadvantaged people of rural California, and nineteen farmworkers from various counties who contended that their livelihoods

were threatened by agricultural mechanization projects sponsored by the University. Named defendants were six Regents of the University, three administrators, and 300 unnamed "Doe" defendants described as being "Regents, administrators, faculty members, researchers, employees or agents of the University."

The complaint alleged improprieties on the part of the named defendants resulting from conflicts of interest stemming from their associations with or ownership interests in agricultural business concerns. It went on to recite several adverse social impacts of mechanization research, including the loss of jobs, the undermining of collective bargaining efforts by farmworkers, increased financial pressures forcing the small farmer out of business, creation of inferior produce along with high prices, and deterioration of the quality of life in rural California. The plaintiffs charged that the defendants were utilizing public tax funds to convey a private benefit to a select group of agribusiness interests, in violation of the California Constitution, the Political Reform Act, the Hatch and Bankhead Jones acts, and the Smith-Lever Act.

The plaintiffs' summary of what they desired from the court process was as follows:

Plaintiffs by this action seek, inter alia, the following remedies: (a) an injunction prohibiting the University from engaging in mechanization projects conveying a special economic benefit to narrow, private agribusiness interests at the expense of farmworkers, small family farmers, consumers, taxpayers and the quality of rural life; and (b) an injunction prohibiting the University Regents and other University officials and employees from participating in or influencing decisions concerning agricultural mechanization research and development in which they are financially interested contrary to conflict of interest laws; and (c) an order prohibiting any individual defendant who was financially interested in any contract made in his or her official capacity concerning agricultural mechanization from ever holding office in California, and declaring all such contracts null and void; and (d) an order prohibiting the University's State Cooperative

Extension Service from engaging in agricultural mechanization research and development in violation of the federal statute creating the Service; and (e) an order requiring those defendants who have, with respect to University agricultural mechanization research and development, knowingly provided a gift of public funds to a private interest or entered into contracts in which they were financially interested, to repay those public monies to the State of California; and (f) an order requiring the University to use the patent royalties received from agricultural machines developed previously by the University to provide retraining and relief to farmworkers replaced by those machines.[13]

The case was assigned to Judge Spurgeon Avakian of the Alameda Superior Court. In a July hearing University attorneys objected to the lawsuit on the grounds that its allegations were so broad and loose that the University could not adequately respond. When the judge sustained these objections, plaintiffs filed a revised complaint identifying 69 research projects to which they objected and the acts or omissions of the defendants which they claimed to be improper. After another lengthy hearing in January 1980, Judge Avakian permitted the lawsuit to go forward but significantly narrowed the scope of the case, expressing his opinion that evaluation of research as "good" or "bad" for society was not a matter for judicial resolution.

> Whether a particular research project is beneficial or harmful to the public interest . . . will still be the University's decision to make. The results and ultimate consequences of research (whether "basic" or "applied") can hardly be known in advance, and even in historical perspective the question . . . . often remains a matter of opinion. . . . It is not a matter of judicial decision in this case whether agricultural mechanization is good or bad for society.[14]

Following this decision, the plaintiffs' attorneys made extensive use of the Public Records Act, over time taking some 70 depositions of University personnel throughout the state and filing more than two dozen detailed demands for documents. In spring 1984 the case went to trial for

about five weeks. The plaintiffs called forth a series of witnesses who testified about the improper influence of corporate money in determining research priorities, the generally undesirable social consequences of mechanization research, and the desirability of making research decisions based upon a social impact analysis. Before plaintiffs had concluded their case, however, Judge Avakian became ill, and a mistrial was declared.

The case was reassigned to Judge Raymond Marsh, who in 1986 restructured the issues to be tried, dismissing all but two of the previous claims. Marsh declared his intention to determine whether the federal Hatch Act required a process of evaluation of research from the standpoint of its presumed beneficiaries, "primarily small and family farmers," and whether "public purposes predominated over private benefits" in particular University research projects. CRLA and the University agreed to shorten the new trial by relying primarily upon documentary evidence. After two days of hearings as well as submission of voluminous declarations and exhibits, CRLA withdrew its complaint about claimed gifts of public funds. Thus the case came down to one remaining issue, whether the Hatch Act and related acts implied a process of evaluation to determine whether agricultural experiment station research would benefit small family farmers. In November 1987 Judge Marsh issued his opinion that the Hatch Act did imply such a process, and that the University was required to establish appropriate procedures; nor could this requirement be construed as an abridgment of academic freedom.

The decision made the front pages of major newspapers. A Los Angeles Times editorial called it a "setback for research," commenting that the Hatch Act is a "broad and potentially contradictory mandate" and that no definition of "small family farms" ever actually appeared in the court proceedings—perhaps in "tacit appreciation of the radical changes that have taken place in agriculture and the problem of discriminating between part-time and hobbyist farmers . . . and small full-time farmers."[15]

After considerable internal discussion, the University filed an appeal. Subsequently the First District Court of Appeal in San Francisco overruled Judge Marsh's opinion, concluding that nothing in the Hatch Act or Experiment Station mandate required the University to develop a process for evaluating the impact of research on "legislatively intended beneficiaries, with primary consideration for the small family farmer." The California Supreme Court denied a request for review. Thus, after eleven years of litigation, the case of *California Agrarian Action Project* v. *Regents* was laid to rest in 1989, with all substantive issues finally decided in the University's favor.

This protracted and expensive lawsuit revolved around several significant issues: the definition of public benefit as applied to publicly funded research, the University's procedures for choosing research personnel and projects, and the desirability and feasibility of formal social impact analysis for projects likely to contribute to technological change.

The general stance of the University with regard to public benefit was that all technological developments have the potential of harming some people and helping others, and that at bottom such evaluations become a question of values. As for procedures for choosing University personnel and projects, while they agreed that research analyzing the social impacts of technological change might be a legitimate subject of scholarly inquiry, administrators believed that to override the University's established planning and budgetary processes in response to litigation undertaken by special interest groups would set a dangerous precedent. They also stated their emphatic opposition to any requirement for social impact analysis as a precondition to undertaking research projects. In 1979 the Academic Senate reported its views on this subject to the Regents by giving a variety of reasons why it deemed such a requirement undesirable: It might be necessary to know the actual outcome of research before its impacts could be assessed; scientists and engineers are not equipped to do sociological and economic analysis; even if social impacts could be successfully determined in advance, an impact analysis might not be particularly useful as a guide to decision making about research; and, finally, new knowledge should not be discouraged because of fear of what might be learned.[16]

Despite the outcome, the plaintiffs believed that their suit had an impact on the University's behavior, if only by publicizing the needs expressed in the complaint. In fact, agricultural economists and others at Davis had already tried to grapple with the mechanization issue, though not to the satisfaction of farmworker advocates.[17] Even while the suit was moving through the courts, several activities addressing some of the same concerns were already under way in the Division.

## THE "ICE-MINUS" EPISODE

Another aspect of agricultural technology drew public fire during the 1980s—the release of genetically engineered organisms into the environment. Controversy over this resulted in a multistep environmental impact review for experiments conducted by Berkeley faculty member Steven Lindow.[18]

As a graduate student in plant pathology, Lindow had discovered that a common bacterium, *Pseudomonas syringae*, causes the formation of damaging ice crystals on plant leaves when the temperature drops a few degrees below freezing. He reasoned that, if the normal bacterial population of leaves could be replaced by bacteria lacking the genes to produce the ice-nucleation protein, frost damage to plants might be significantly reduced. (Such bacteria occur naturally, but not in sufficient numbers to replace their ice-forming counterparts.)

With his colleague Nickolas Panopoulos, Lindow developed a technique using recombinant DNA technology to

216 genetically alter the ice-forming bacteria—not by adding any new genetic information, but by deleting the genetic code necessary to produce the ice-nucleating protein: hence the development of "ice-minus" bacteria. Extensive greenhouse and laboratory experiments with potatoes demonstrated the effectiveness of these recombinant organisms in providing a significant measure of protection from frost damage. The next and logical extension of these experiments was to field-test the organisms to determine whether preplanting treatment of seed pieces or the spraying of genetically altered bacteria on potato plants could prevent or reduce frost damage. Lindow decided to conduct tests on a half-acre plot at the University's Tulelake Field Station, which often experiences late-spring frosts. Because the research involved the use of recombinant DNA molecules, Lindow and Panopoulos asked for approval by the National Institute of Health (NIH). The NIH granted permission for the field tests in June 1983.

SCIENTISTS APPLYING ICE-MINUS BACTERIA TO THE EXPERIMENTAL POTATO PLOT IN TULELAKE.

The experiment did not proceed smoothly. Members of a wary public did not support the NIH approval, and on September 14, 1983, public-interest advocate Jeremy Rifkin, president of the Foundation on Economic Trends, filed a lawsuit claiming that the approval violated the National Environmental Policy Act. Subsequently the NIH prepared an Environmental Impact Assessment and a "Finding of No Significant Impact (FONSI)" on the proposed field test, issued the document in January 1985 for public comment, and duly certified it in July. The Environmental Protection Agency (EPA) reviewed the FONSI and sought comments from several federal agencies and the general public. EPA representatives examined Lindow's records pertaining to the experiment, visited the Tulelake station in April 1986, and attended a University-sponsored community meeting about the proposed field test. This review ended with the EPA granting an Experimental Use Permit on May 13, 1986, authorizing Lindow to conduct small-scale field tests. In granting the permit, the EPA stated that the extensive scientific review process had indicated that "these experiments pose minimal risk to public health and the environment."

Again, a public-interest group challenged the project. In August 1986 Californians for Responsible Toxics Management of Tulelake applied for a restraining order to prevent the University from planting ice-minus-treated seed potatoes. Although it was not required, the University agreed to prepare an environmental impact report (EIR) conforming to state guidelines. The researchers and interested biotechnology companies disagreed with the decision because they believed that it would set a precedent, but the action was taken to allay public concern about the experiment and to mollify those who felt that the University was running roughshod over a powerless local community. The Draft EIR, issued in December 1986, was made available for public review and discussed in a public hearing. After detailed responses had been made on all questions raised, the EIR was certified and the experiments were allowed to proceed.[18]

On April 19, 1987—early enough for frosts still to occur in Tulelake—potatoes were planted in the experimental plot in preparation for the treatment. Vandals almost immediately destroyed approximately 3,000 of the seedlings. The researchers replanted most of these, and on the morning of May 28, after some four years of litigation and meetings, Lindow sprayed the ice-minus bacteria onto the seedlings—and into the environment. During the two killing frosts that followed the applications, the treatment proved to reduce frost damage by 80 percent on average.

The experiment contributed to a better understanding of the diversity of ice-nucleating species and the dynamics of bacterial colonization; but probably more significant was its demonstration of the complexity of biotechnology research under field conditions. One writer, commenting on the conflict between scientists' and the public's perceptions of risk, summarized the ice-minus episode as follows:

> Perhaps the most ironic aspect of this long-running and unfinished controversy is that the brilliant minds that figured out this world-tranforming technology in the first place have yet to figure out a way to ease public fears about it. Until they can make that one-percent risk appear vanishingly small rather than parlously large, science and society will continue to be at odds as they walk awkwardly, at arm's length, toward the 21st century.[19]

## TOWARD A SUSTAINABLE AGRICULTURE: SAREP

In 1986 the Division undertook a pioneering program called the Sustainable Agriculture Research and Education Program (SAREP)—but not until it was more or less thrust upon the institution by legislators who shared some of the public's concerns about the long-term effects of current agricultural practices. By this time, "sustainable agriculture" had become the popular term for an environmentally responsive food production system, relying less on artificial inputs and highly mechanized operations and more on an understanding of natural biological processes that could be continued indefinitely.

As in other land-grant institutions, UC agricultural research and extension programs after World War II emphasized the use of high-input technologies—mechanization, pesticides, and chemical fertilizers. The concerns of farmers interested in alternative practices were given little if any attention. During the early 1980s, because of the apparent indifference exhibited by the Division toward these alternatives, State Senator Nick Petris, who was keenly interested in the subject, spearheaded the criticism directed toward the University on this issue. As a result, three events occurred more or less concurrently in 1985.

First, Division Vice President Kendrick appointed a University Committee on the Sustainability of California Agriculture, charged with defining a Division research and extension agenda focusing on more resource-conserving, energy-efficient, sustainable farming systems. Second, at the suggestion of legislators, the Division conducted hearings throughout the state to determine the need for such a program. Third, Senator Petris's office began to draft the text of SB 872, the Sustainable Agriculture Research and Education Act of 1986.

In fall 1985, after notices had been mailed to hundreds of interested parties and media advisories sent to all local news organizations, public hearings took place in Watsonville, Riverside, Oceanside, Fresno, and Sacramento. At these five meetings approximately 110 speakers gave testimony about their views of UC research and extension activities. The transcripts and additional comments by the committee contributed to the language being drafted for SB 872.

Meanwhile, the committee sponsored a Sustainability of California Agriculture Symposium in Sacramento (January

218 1986), in collaboration with staff from the Agroecology Program at UC Santa Cruz. The Santa Cruz entity was not part of the Division, and in fact represented views strongly opposed to much traditional divisional activity. The conference bought together a broad spectrum of growers, scientists, and people active in sustainable movements in other states to explore the issue of long-term agricultural sustainability in California. Some media observers were impressed:

> The University of California, long accused of a farm research strategy that favors big landowners and the chemical industry, has lent its prestige for the first time to a rival concept. The concept, called "sustainable ag," uses terms like "organic," "natural," "holistic" and "biotechnology," a vocabulary that in some UC units would have meant exile, loss of tenure or a scientific assignment to count tumbleweeds in Modoc County.[20]

The University initially opposed SB 872, not because of the program itself but because the language proposed would have placed decision making in the hands of public members of an advisory committee. After the Division negotiated with staff members working on the bill and a number of drafts were exchanged, mutually agreeable language was developed. The Sustainable Agriculture Research and Education Act passed the legislature and was approved by the governor on September 26, 1986.

SAREP's three major areas of responsibility were defined as the administration of competitive research grants, the development and distribution of information, and the estab-

SAREP RESEARCHER'S LABORATORY, SHOWING HOT WATER DIP ALTERNATIVE TO FUNGICIDE SPRAYS FOR THE PRESERVATION OF FRUIT CROPS.

lishment of long-term farmland research sites—much in the mode of traditional field stations, but dedicated specifically to "sustainable" research. The Office of the President of the University along with the Division allocated $300,000 of existing funds for startup costs, a director was appointed, and the program took up headquarters at UC Davis. To advise on program goals and priorities and to make recommendations on award of competitive grants, SAREP was given two advisory groups: a technical review panel and a public advisory board including some twenty persons actively involved in agricultural production (large-, medium-, and small-sized conventional and organic growers), as well as representatives from government, public organizations, and other institutions of higher education. Because it would be directly involved in decision making for a Division program, the advisory committee was a compromise viewed as pathbreaking by administrators.

Early in SAREP's life, considerable discussion among staff and the advisory committee led up to a "position paper," which laid out the goals of the program:

> Sustainable agriculture integrates three main goals—environmental health, economic profitability, and social and economic equity. . . . Sustainability rests on the principle that we must meet the needs of the present without compromising the ability of future generations to meet their own needs. Therefore stewardship of both natural and human resources is of prime importance. . . . A systems perspective is essential, [implying] interdisciplinary efforts in research and education.[21]

In its first four years, SAREP provided $1.2 million for 51 research projects, ranging from postharvest fungicide alternatives, controlled-grazing studies, and an investigation of the effects of legume cover crops to a dairy waste management survey and a study of urban gardening.

Why did it take litigation and legislation to persuade the Division to revamp some of its traditional practices and priorities? Part of the answer lies in the hidebound attitude exhibited by some agricultural scientists early in the period. ("Ecology is the new theology," scoffed one Experiment Station administrator in 1970.) This attitude was slow to change, but gradually the Division's vice president and his colleagues began to realize the need for better communication with nonagricultural audiences. In 1979 Kendrick conceded that "Agricultural research, education and extension have too long been a citadel of isolation on campuses and in society in general. We are now experiencing the consequences of that isolationism. The challenge is clear."[22]

A stepped-up public relations effort to communicate the real accomplishments of the land-grant system was not the only need, however. A major hindrance in adapting to necessary change was the nature of the agricultural research establishment itself. As one mid-1970s observer wrote,

> [The national agricultural research establishment] is an amorphous hulk of disjointed and often competitive components, each of which is being tugged and pulled by myriads of special interests. It does not have a unified program but rather is influenced by annual budget decisions at the macro level and the project level while the whole complicated bureaucratic superstructure that separates the two levels moves along unchanged. As such, the establishment in its totality is largely impervious to political manipulation in the short run.[23]

This general description of the national scene fit the state level as well. In California, underlying administrative problems were demonstrated in terms of "paper" and practical lines of authority, basic funding changes, and conflicting perceptions of appropriate clientele, program, and staffing.

## ADMINISTRATIVE REORGANIZATION EFFORTS

In 1968, when UC Riverside plant pathologist James B. Kendrick became Vice President of the Division of Agricultural Sciences, it was the last Universitywide academic unit to survive the decentralization directed by President Kerr. For the next twenty or more years, as the campuses exerted more authority over programs and staffing, this administrative arrangement would present difficulties. Much of the Division's history during this period was in fact made on the campuses rather than in the offices of the Berkeley administration, yet the uneasy relationship between levels prevailed throughout the political squalls of the period, frustrating some decision making and discouraging even the most energetic efforts to revitalize the organization.

New University President Charles J. Hitch issued a "Statement of Policy" dated April 4, 1968, which described the duties and responsibilities of the Vice President–Agricultural Sciences:

> He will be responsible for developing a Master Plan for the Division, for reviewing its plans and programs on a continuing basis and for overall budgetary planning. . . . In order to facilitate such decisions, vacated academic positions in the Agricultural Experiment Station and the Agricultural Extension Services shall be filled only with the approval of the Vice President. . . . Proposals for transferring a vacated academic position and related support from one department to another on the same campus or from one campus to another, shall be considered in the regular budgetary process. Close coordination with campus administrations will be necessary.[24]

Charged with the responsibility for centralized planning, Kendrick distributed Division's *Long-Range Plan* prepared by the Kelly committee (see chapter 6) to each campus dean in July 1968, with copies for each department chair, asking for comments to be returned by October 1 so that there could be full discussion of the recommendations. But essentially no

220 comments were received and little interest shown in action on the report, for several reasons. The entire administration was in transition; within one year the University greeted a new president, a new executive vice president, a new vice president for agricultural sciences, a new director/dean on the Riverside campus, and a new chancellor and dean at Davis. Kendrick himself had little enthusiasm for the document.[25] And the natural forces of the University's now-decentralized administration, with campuses each seeking their own character and direction, were almost designed to impede any centralized grand strategy for the Division.

The Kelly plan having been shelved, several further efforts at coordinated planning were undertaken; none achieved any notable success. Several years of sorting out a functional set of operational policies to accommodate University decentralization began in 1971–72, at a time when budget reductions were the order of the day. Hence the focus of all administrative units was on preserving existing resources, and there was little interest in statewide planning that might result in further losses through transfers or reallocations.

To develop some processes by which to deal with the problem of shared authority between the campuses and the Division, the Vice President appointed a committee in 1971, chaired by Experiment Station Director Boysie E. Day, to develop a "Five-Year Plan for the California Agricultural Experiment Station." One of this plan's goals was to specify research roles for the three campus branches of the Experi-

JAMES B. KENDRICK, VICE PRESIDENT OF THE DIVISION OF AGRICULTURAL SCIENCES FROM 1968 TO 1986.

ment Station. Another was to categorize research efforts into the nine broad research program goals of the federal classification system established in the 1960s.[26] A third was to delineate the organization and functional responsibilities of the station's directorate (composed of the Vice President, Director, and campus Associate Directors). The Five-Year Plan was released for review in May 1972. On governance, the report spelled out lines of authority:

The Vice President–Agricultural Sciences has overall responsibility for the Division . . . for coordination of programs between the Agricultural Experiment Station and Agricultural Extension Service. He is responsible to the President of the University . . . and advises the president on all matters relating to the agricultural sciences. . . . He is responsible for the annual allocation of noncampus special funds.

Campus chancellors had functional responsibility for

implementation of the campus role in the overall divisional plan and coordination and implementation of the Agricultural Experiment Station campus role with the campus academic plan . . . provision of administrative services relating to campus structure, organization, budget, personnel, and related matters . . . [and] preparation and forwarding of the annual budget, including the campus Agricultural Experiment Station budget and staffing plan.[27]

To counterweight this apparent dichotomy of responsibility, chancellors and representatives, along with the directorate, were to perform an annual review of the pertinence of campus programs and budgets to the statewide plan. In practice, however, these budgets were essentially a "pass-through" at the Vice President's office; only special items or increments above the previous year's budget were examined. Although the Vice President did discuss staffing with campus officers and had nominal authority to transfer positions between campuses, he exercised that authority only once.

In early 1972 recently appointed University Vice President McCorkle (formerly Dean of Agriculture at Davis) proposed the preparation of a master plan on instructional programs within the Division. This planning group included Chancellors Bowker from Berkeley, Meyer from Davis, and Hinderaker from Riverside; the two Vice Presidents McCorkle (chairman of the committee) and Kendrick; senior advisor Dan Aldrich from Irvine; and Harry O. Walker of the Davis campus, who served as staff to prepare the committee's report (later often referred to as the "Walker report"). Recognizing that the nature of needed instruction and research in agriculture was being changed by outside trends in society as a whole, this report included suggestions for revisions in the descriptive titles of the schools and colleges as well as a more appropriate title for the Division. The report also reaffirmed the responsibility of the Vice President for systemwide planning as well as the authority of the chancellors for campus budgets and programs.[28]

Despite these efforts, the inevitable issue that dogged the "shared governance" arrangement was whether the relationship was one of equal partners or only of a benign formality. The Walker report drew criticism from the statewide Academic Planning and Program Review Board that "the proposals on personnel appointments are ambiguous and even contradictory." Even though lines of authority were defined, the tenuous relationship between the Vice President–Agricultural Sciences and the chancellors remained a persistent bureaucratic problem.

One notable attempt to bring research and extension activities into closer coordination was the 1973 decision to combine the directorships of both the Experiment Station and the Extension Service with the vice presidency. In 1973 Kendrick became Director of the Experiment Station, appointing an associate director to carry out operational activities. On George Alcorn's retirement as Director of Extension (renamed Cooperative Extension in 1974 to reflect its wider scope of activities and clientele), the Vice President also assumed his responsibilities in 1975. The change was more difficult in the case of Extension, since this organization had a long-standing tradition of separatism, stemming partly from the legacy of its first director, B. H. Crocheron, and partly from the fact that county-based personnel had more local than institutional orientations. Hence there was only reluctant agreement within Extension to the new administrative structure. While an associate director was appointed for operational activities, as with the Experiment Station, many Extension personnel felt that they had lost a full-time director.[29]

Dissatisfaction with the new arrangements simmered. Many staff thought that the Vice President had too many other responsibilities to pay close attention to their needs. By 1981, acceding to pressures, Kendrick agreed to return to separate directorships. He then appointed plant physiologist Lowell Lewis Director of the Agricultural Experiment Station and agricultural economist Jerome Siebert Director of Cooperative Extension.

In 1986 Kendrick announced his retirement after eighteen years as chief administrator for the agricultural sciences. His successor, appointed in January 1987, was Kenneth R. Farrell, a former UC agricultural economist who had gone on to Washington, eventually becoming director of the

222    National Center for Food and Agricultural Policy, a unit of Resources for the Future.

## A NEW ADMINISTRATION

The incoming Vice President immediately launched a three-part process of strategic planning. In the first phase staff gathered information and analyzed various characteristics of the Division's environment, emphasizing changes of the previous twenty-five years and identifying issues likely to become important. The Phase I report emphasized the need to address the lingering problems of decentralization.[30]

After thorough discussion of these issues, Farrell directed three administrative changes. First, he again combined the directorships of the Experiment Station and Cooperative Extension with the vice presidency, effective January 1, 1988. This move was intended to provide authority to combine all Division resources into a single cohesive program planning entity, with the Vice President responsible for establishing intermediate and long-term goals and priorities for both research and extension. His next step was to fully decentralize Extension by delegating line authority for program operations to four regional directors. This administrative structure paralleled that of the agricultural deans on campuses with respect to Experiment Station research activities. Third, on July 1, 1988, Cooperative Extension specialists, historically housed with campus disciplinary departments

KENNETH R. FARRELL, VICE PRESIDENT OF
THE DIVISION FROM 1987.

but in fact reporting to the statewide director, were transferred to the authority of department chairs and campus deans. This step was a historic change (for California) in bringing department-based Experiment Station and Extension scientists together for more effective coordination in the execution of Division programs.

The Division was now positioned to take up the task of Phase II: defining its mission, goals, and priorities for the next decade or more. With thousands of academic staff members and a multimillion-dollar budget under its umbrella, the Division faced a daunting array of public expectations. Yet its resources were under siege.

## THE NEW HUNT FOR MONEY

Between the mid-1960s and mid-1980s a marked transition in agricultural research and extension funding took place.[31] In 1963 the postwar period of almost routine annual increases in general funding came to an end. In 1967-68 the base budget for the Experiment Station was cut 3 percent, then slashed a further 8 percent three years later. These cuts, along with the growing fraction of resources committed to salaries and the nearly uninterrupted inflation in operating costs, left less money available for discretionary purposes. Thus two significant changes came about during the 1970s and 1980s: government increasingly earmarked funds for special programs perceived as high priority (often referred to as "line item" or categorical appropriations), and an entrepreneurial spirit intensified within the institution and among faculty members as they engaged in extramural fund-raising.

The first significant federal mandate of the period was the assignment of the Expanded Food and Nutrition Education Program (EFNEP) to the Extension Service in 1968-69, followed in the 1970s by special funds for work on farm safety, integrated pest management, and urban youth development. State categorical appropriations included, in 1969, $100,000 to enhance research activities in the San Joaquin Valley and $280,000 to address critical needs in agricultural research. These items were followed over the next two decades with special funding for a small-farms program, an agricultural personnel management program, an integrated pest management program, an agricultural issues center, a gene resources conservation program, a sustainable agriculture program, and an integrated hardwood range management program. While these program mandates did much to supplement the overall budget, "targeted" funding also eroded the Division's decision-making authority.

## INSTITUTIONAL AND FACULTY ENTREPRENEURSHIP

With general funds shrinking, agricultural faculty sought other sources of money to underwrite projects, including foundations, nonagricultural federal agencies, and private companies. Preparing grant applications took up an increasing share of faculty time. Budget builders, administrators, and enterprising faculty members became adept at tapping new funding. Their program and project goals were often framed in terms of public and legislative concerns, industry advisory group recommendations, or federal agency priorities. Overhead costs were written into many contracts and grants and helped support personnel in many departments. This kind of entrepreneurship had some disadvantages—it did not help long-term program building, for example—but it also encouraged responsiveness to popular interests and contributed to "accountability" for funds spent.

The trend inevitably influenced the choice of some research projects as well as faculty loyalties and expenditures of core support funds. To help compensate for the loss of state general funds in the early 1970s, deans and directors encouraged staff to work with commodity groups to increase private contributions for research. By 1989 some 37 state and federal marketing order boards, commissions, and councils were taxing themselves to develop funds for research benefiting their industries. Although critics contended that commercial farm groups had too much influence on the direction of research, reductions in state funding actually tightened that relationship.

A FRESNO EFNEP STAFF MEMBER TRAINING FUTURE AIDES IN PRINCIPLES OF GOOD NUTRITION.

The entrepreneurial search for extramural funding had other consequences as well. Businesses researching new products could buy help and offer advanced equipment, and many faculty were happy to engage in applied work supported by private industry. But this flow of corporate money created a new problem by raising major questions about patent, license, and royalty arrangements. This problem was especially troublesome in biotechnology, where corporations and venture capitalists were willing to fund research programs—provided the University would promise them exclusive licensing of any commercially feasible results.[32] Furthermore, some faculty formed their own companies to commercialize the new technologies. Conflict of interest became a new and difficult matter for concern.

## PROPOSITION 13 AND COUNTY EXTENSION OFFICES

Traditionally supported by a three-part arrangement among federal, state, and local governments, Extension suffered a blow to its base funding in June 1978 when Proposition 13, a popular initiative passed by disgruntled taxpayers, limited the power of local governments to fund programs through increased property taxes. Though the true effects of this initiative would not show up for several more years, by the mid-1980s it was becoming clear that county governments were less able to continue unquestioned support of Extension work. And even when local allocations were maintained or increased, funding did not keep up with inflation. With fewer resources, Extension strove to perform its traditional roles and even to assume some new ones, but in various areas local staffing and services had to be cut. The organization tried to adapt to new budget stringencies in other ways by charging fees for publications, computer software, conferences, and services, and by developing endowment and foundation programs for gifts and grants.

## NEW PERCEPTIONS OF CLIENTELE AND STAFFING

### URBAN PROGRAMS

California's continuing urbanization posed a challenge to the Division's traditional operating philosophy and procedures, especially for community-based Cooperative Extension. Though Extension had begun in the 1960s to move toward engaging groups other than its farm-centered constituency, not until 1969 did it have an explicit mandate, through EFNEP, to work with urban audiences. For nearly two decades Extension debated the appropriate level of its commitment to urban work. Recommendations were made, plans formulated, and regional efforts mounted—but no coherent "urban program" emerged.

By the late 1980s, California's urban extension efforts fell into three categories. First was EFNEP, which tallied in its first ten years some 100,000 low-income homemakers helped by nutritional education work in 17 counties.[33] Federal funding cuts in the 1980s created a need to reorganize this program, which by USDA mandate had relied on direct-contact methods with individuals and small groups. Second, following the Youth EFNEP funding that put new professional youth advisors in the most urban counties, Extension's traditional 4-H program steadily, if slowly, explored new subjects and forms of involvement for inner-city youth. Third, the "urban horticulture" program successfully brought the University's expertise to landscapers and gardeners in metropolitan areas. Most "public service" advisors in urban counties developed local educational activities related to commercial and home ornamental horticulture; the Master Gardener volunteer program became an accepted part of Extension activity; and mass media outreach expanded to disseminate information about such topics as drought-tolerant plantings and pest management for home gardens.

Significant organizational problems impeded urban extension work. First was the difficulty of sponsoring public programs not perceived as relevant to 90 percent of the public. Extension did not seem able to gain political support from urban interest groups as it had done with traditional agricultural interests. Not even the nutrition, 4-H, and urban horticulture services enjoyed effective support beyond the local level; in fact, there were no really successful examples of such support nationwide. No organized or even reflexive "urban" interest seemed to exist in state politics to support Extension efforts, and the size and diversity of the urban audience itself created a planning problem. Most program proposals tended to minimize any research problem-solving role and to maximize "contact" numbers. In contrast, Extension practice until the 1960s had emphasized research application and technology transfer to individuals and small groups rather than the distribution of popular information. Extension's strongest support traditionally came from those receiving technical problem-solving and consulting educational services, not from those receiving general information. Some analysts thought that urban programs, like agricultural ones, ought to relate to specific technical problems for which interest support groups existed or could be developed—similar, for example, to the local farm bureaus organized before World War I. One such problem, they suggested, might be the toxic waste disposal difficulties faced by local governments.[34]

URBAN CHILDREN ENJOYING AN EDUCATIONAL OUTING TO A FARM. BRIDGING THE GAP BETWEEN CITY AND COUNTRY WAS A NEW GOAL AS EXTENSION BEGAN TO REDEFINE ITS ROLE IN MODERN TIMES.

## AFFIRMATIVE ACTION

In the late 1970s another administrative issue emerged—controversy about Extension's deficiencies in both program outreach to minorities and its own personnel practices.

Legislators charged that the University-sponsored 4-H program made inadequate efforts to reach urban low-income families, while its agricultural program gave little attention to farmworkers, small farms, or rural minority, low-income populations.[35] At least some Extension staff agreed. Within 4-H, friction developed between new youth advisors hired with EFNEP monies, who concentrated almost exclusively on urban low-income residents, and youth advisors with pre-existing appointments, who continued serving voluntarily enrolled rural and suburban clients.

Both inside and outside the organization, disagreements continued over Extension's general mission, specific objectives, and outreach obligation. Three factors contributed to the tensions. First was some confusion between the concepts of nondiscrimination and affirmative action. Many Extension staff felt that they were fulfilling their affirmative action obligations by forwarding evidence of nondiscriminatory behavior. Second, the organization had long held the view that its programs were offered for voluntary embrace or rejection by its clients; the concept of holding it responsible for minority participation obviously conflicted with that philosophy. Third, Extension as a whole never clearly resolved how staff should define

226 appropriate potential clients. Until the 1980s only the 4-H and Family and Consumer Science programs ever engaged in serious clientele analysis. Program accountability, too, was hampered by inconsistent record keeping.[36]

With respect to personnel issues, a few years after passage of the 1972 Civil Rights Act several staff members filed complaints alleging discriminatory behavior by the Extension administration in hiring, promotion, and disciplinary practices. Although the first woman to serve as a county director was appointed in Contra Costa County in 1974, little progress was made toward hiring blacks or Hispanics until publicly aired complaints led to legislative scrutiny. In February 1979 President David Saxon appointed a task force, chaired by Assistant Vice President Walter Strong, to "determine if there is any truth to . . . allegations . . . about patterns of racial discrimination in the Cooperative Extension Service." The task force recommended appointment of a full-time affirmative action officer and increased involvement of minorities in all phases of program and policy development.[37]

The affirmative action office established for Cooperative Extension in 1979 was reviewed by a federal audit team in 1982, reorganized in 1985, and audited again in 1987. By this time Extension had made substantial progress: although several job categories still showed ethnic or gender imbalance, by 1987 ten women were serving as county directors and 22 as farm advisors, and minority academic appointments had risen from 43 to 64. The following year Vice President Farrell initiated a major review culminating in "Planning for Diversity: An Affirmative Action Plan," which was intended to be a major turning point for the organization.

In retrospect Extension appears to have been more successful in achieving affirmative action within its staff than in its programs. The core issues in programming—clientele definition, outreach obligations and goals, and even subject matter identification—have remained topics of debate as Extension has continued efforts to redefine its historical mission and meet the needs of a changing world.

STAFF MEMBER OF THE RURAL DEVELOPMENT CENTER IN SALINAS INDICATING POINTS OF INTEREST AT DEMONSTRATION PLOT. DOZENS OF WOMEN JOINED EXTENSION IN THE 1980S, FILLING ROLES LONG HELD BY MEN.

## CONTINUITY AND CHANGE IN RESEARCH AND EXTENSION

Compared with the changes in teaching curricula that took place during the 1970s, changes in general UC agricultural research and extension priorities came more slowly. Dedicated to enhancing agricultural production, long considered a laudable goal, many staff felt confusion and resentment when critics attacked that traditional orientation. They also differed among themselves over whether the "mission" of the Experiment Station was primarily to develop scientific knowledge or to serve the agricultural industry—an old theme in station history—and whether their primary clientele were the firms that produced the most food for the nation or the people who still viewed farming as a way of life, though their contributions to overall production might be minor. The development of the "dual farm economy" in the postwar period complicated these questions, for even though most scientists and engineers believed that their discoveries were applicable to any size of operation, it was true that new technology was most rapidly adopted by the larger farms that could afford it.

The debate over "mission" was not the only source of tension. Advocates inside and outside the Division urged that it tackle social issues with the same competence and verve that it employed in science and technology research. But there were barriers to change in this direction. Given the evolution of California agriculture and of the institution, "social" efforts were difficult for many faculty and administrators to contemplate, let alone pursue. Political, sci-

IPM ADVISOR RELEASING VIAL OF WESTERN PREDATORY MITES ONTO GRAPEVINES IN SONOMA COUNTY. THESE MITES HAVE PROVIDED EFFECTIVE CONTROL OF CERTAIN GRAPE PESTS.

entific, and pragmatic considerations all contributed to this attitude. In the mid-1930s Dean Hutchison had expressed his discomfort with social science research as compared with "hard" or experimental science; the same bias had since favored quantitative studies in economics rather than development of methodologies in other social sciences. Critics pointed out the inadequacies of this approach—"Too much analysis of economic activity is restricted to the symbols of wealth. As a result, the analysis has been highly abstract, excessively aggregate with its data, and devoid of focus on the . . . players."[38] But administrators were reluctant to undertake new, untried directions at the cost of established successful programs.

Continuity in long-term major UC agricultural research programs in fact produced significant achievements during this period. Yet new program initiatives and emerging technologies also began to change the agenda.

### SOME RESEARCH ACHIEVEMENTS OF THE PERIOD

Even while squalls blew over the Division, its usual work in laboratories and fields continued. Some of the major achievements of the times were linked with contemporaneous political or economic events; others were the outgrowth of long years of consistent, though undramatic, effort.

The Integrated Pest Management (IPM) Program was one of the latter. In 1979 a formal proposal for this program—a full-scale multidisciplinary effort to protect California crops with minimal use of pesticides—was approved by the legisla-

228 ture for $1.2 million. Research on pest management already stretched back for a century in California; what was new about this effort was its broad, "integrated" approach. The statewide IPM program was to bring together all pertinent disciplines in research and extension activities, aimed not at the *elimination* of pests but at their *management*. This meant developing the concept of "economic thresholds" as a guide to control tactics, in preference to blanket applications of pesticides at regular intervals; it also meant developing knowledge about many old and new techniques for controlling pest populations, including the use of weather data, natural predators, and cultivation practices, with recourse to chemical control only when necessary. As the program grew, it developed a permanent staff of IPM farm advisors and specialists, a computer facility, and a manuals group to produce high-quality technical publications for a variety of crops; it also earned widespread national and international respect for its excellence.[39]

Other continuing long-range work in the Experiment Station included the Mosquito Research Program, first funded in 1965 and augmented in 1973 and 1974; joint efforts with government agencies on salinity and drainage problems in the San Joaquin Valley; forestry research under the McIntire-Stennis Cooperative Forestry Research Act of 1962; environmental studies in the San Joaquin-Sacramento Delta; studies of surface and groundwater quality and supply, including efficient irrigation; and the internationally known program in viticulture and enology, honored on its centennial in 1980 by a special resolution of the California legislature. Many of these projects and programs were highlighted in occasional special issues of *California Agriculture*, a bimonthly, nationally distributed magazine of research reports.

Another significant long-range program began with public interest in genetic resource conservation during the late 1970s. In 1981 the University made two proposals for germ plasm conservation projects to the California Department of Food and Agriculture, but neither was funded. Subsequent work by the U.S. Department of Agriculture and the State Senate Office of Research led to a major symposium on genetic resource conservation for California, held in the Napa Valley in 1984; one of its major recommendations was to establish a UC Genetic Resources Conservation Program (GCRP) within the Division. The University then made a budget request for $1 million annually, beginning with the 1985-86 fiscal year; Governor George Deukmejian supported the program but reduced the funding to $250,000. The GRCP was established on the Davis campus to identify imperiled resources, sponsor conservation research, develop a conservation plan for California, and foster its adoption through education and outreach activities.[40]

Some Division activities were inspired by crisis. In the early 1970s, after bad crop years in several countries resulted in a temporary world food crisis that seriously depleted American grain reserves, a Division task force examined short- and long-range demands on U.S. food supplies and the factors that might affect the ability to meet those demands. More than 100 staff members reviewed human nutritional requirements, world population demographics, agricultural productivity in various parts of the world, the economics of food distribution, and the need for farsighted food policies. The task force report, titled *A Hungry World: The Challenge to Agriculture*, recommended institutional reforms and better planning, technical aid to developing countries, enlightened world trade policies, strengthened efforts at resource conservation, and a world food reserve program.

The early 1970s also produced a short-term but threatening "energy crisis." After volatile prices in international oil markets convinced policymakers that more had to be done to develop alternative sources of energy, state and federal incentives spurred research on conservation and renewable energy sources. Accordingly, UC agricultural engineers conducted major energy audits and proposed conservation plans for agricultural operations, and Extension specialists analyzed energy use in cultivation practices, irrigation, greenhouse production, transportation, and processing. In cooperation with the California Energy Commission and the Public Utilities Commission, farm advisors distributed information on biomass conversion, wind and solar installations, and methane gas production from livestock manure.

Other timely research focused on emerging situations. The Division sponsored many new studies on environmental problems—air pollution, waste disposal, acidity in Sierra lakes, and lead levels in soils along highways. Scientists pursued work on potential threats to agriculture, from environmental degradation to poor land use planning and competition for limited water supplies. Economists (and a few sociologists) completed "people-oriented" projects, including compilation of farm labor statistics and analysis of the impact of various legislative actions; research on the problems of small-town governments; and collection of data on women in agriculture. Although not all these projects were "successful" in the sense of accomplishing change, they contributed to a better understanding of some of California's long-standing problems.[41]

In 1983 the name of the Division was changed from Agricultural Sciences to Agriculture and Natural Resources, part-

SPANISH-SPEAKING EXTENSION STAFF MEMBER DEMONSTRATES PEST IDENTIFICATION ON GRAPE LEAVES TO HISPANIC VINEYARD WORKERS, COLUSA COUNTY.

ly to reflect the transfer of authority for the University's Natural Reserve System to the Division. By this time the reserve system consisted of 26 mostly undisturbed natural areas representing different types of California habitat, acquired by gift, purchase, lease, or use agreements and administered by the University as living laboratories for the study of ecological diversity. The system was established to serve as a kind of "ecosystem library" available for research purposes to any qualified student or researcher worldwide.

## NEW PROGRAM THRUSTS FOR EXTENSION

While the major efforts of Extension specialists and farm advisors continued to be directed toward the agricultural industry, several new program thrusts gradually emerged. In the early 1970s, federal "War on Poverty" funds had reached some mainly Hispanic farming cooperatives in the Central Valley and along the central coast. These groups hoped to establish themselves in the intensive strawberry or other specialty market crops; their group efforts lasted only a few years, but some people gained enough from their experience to carry on as independent producers.[42] An Extension community development specialist at Davis, with funds from the Rural Development Act of 1972, employed two Spanish-speaking research associates to work with low-income farmers in the San Joaquin Valley; these temporary staff members later became full-fledged permanent farm advisors, and subsequently the legislature appropriated funds to hire four more advisors to work with "limited-resource" farmers.

In 1977 an interagency committee (representing the state's Employee Development Department, the nonprofit Central Coast Counties Development Corporation, and Cooperative Extension) was formed to oversee research on a "Small Farm Viability Project." Its report, produced at the Davis campus, recommended a number of policies to promote the small family farm as "indispensable to a sound agriculture and a prosperous rural society."[43] The following year, federal funds underwrote the founding of a Small Farm Center at UC Davis, its mission to provide access to the kinds of information most needed by small agricultural producers. The center filled a special niche: its staff participated in and coordinated conferences and workshops, maintained a clearinghouse for publications on topics ranging from specialty crops to direct marketing, and acted as liaison among UC personnel, public and private organizations, and small-scale farmers.[44]

Also in 1977 designated state funds established the nation's first extension program in farm personnel management. The first advisor worked with Fresno County employers to develop more progressive labor practices, including safety programs. By 1981 there were five such advisors, as well as a statewide specialist in Berkeley.

A new arena in food production opened when, in 1970, the University became the Sea Grant institution for California and shortly thereafter rose to Sea Grant College status in recognition of its strong marine research activities. In 1972, with the hiring of a specialist in marine fisheries, Extension began a marine advisory program for the commercial seafood industry. The next year a statewide seafood technology specialist began work. Marine

SUCCESSFUL LAOTIAN FARMER NEAR FRESNO SHOWING OFF ONE OF HER SPECIALTY CROPS OF ORIENTAL VEGETABLES AND HERBS. MANY SOUTHEAST ASIAN REFUGEES BECAME SMALL-SCALE FARMERS IN THE CENTRAL VALLEY DURING THE 1980S.

advisors—"farm advisors in hip boots"—were subsequently stationed to serve most of the counties along California's coastline. In 1977 an aquaculture specialist was headquartered at Davis to consult with California's growing number of freshwater catfish and trout growers as well as with commercial oyster and abalone operations. [45]

Public concern over declining native oak populations in California was the impetus for the University's 1986 proposal for an Integrated Hardwood Range Management Program. The legislature provided funds for five Extension specialists to work on long-range management of native hardwood and rangeland vegetation species. In cooperation with the State Board of Forestry, other state institutions, and private firms, the new group began to develop strategies for encouraging oak regeneration and restoring overgrazed rangeland.

## THE EFFECTS OF EMERGING SCIENTIFIC TECHNOLOGIES

Major advances in the 1970s and 1980s affected the apparatus and nature of scientific inquiry almost as much as they promised to change daily lives. With the advent of computerized data storage and manipulation systems as well as of biotechnology, agricultural scientists anticipated breakthroughs in tackling old and new agricultural problems.[46]

The first central computers were brought to university campuses in the early 1960s. Expressed as millions of ordinary instructions per second (MIPS), computing power grew exponentially from around 0.25 MIPS executed by a single central processing unit in 1960 to 10 MIPS by late 1985, with 100

MIPS projected for 1990.[47] Similarly, the memory of a single integrated circuit chip showed steady growth from around 4 kilobytes (4 "binary thousand" or 4,096 bytes) in 1973 to 256 kilobytes in 1983 and to over 2 megabytes in 1990. With computer graphic capabilities greatly aiding data analysis and word-processing software facilitating reporting, personal computers and workstations became essential desktop tools of the professional staff researcher.

Computer technology brought about the automated collection, manipulation, and processing of information for agricultural research. In livestock production, for example, computers came to be used for electronic animal identification, estrus detection, fertility monitoring and pregnancy data collection, and disease control and prevention via animal temperature monitoring and medical histories. In the plant sciences, computers assisted in identification of pests, monitoring of stages of crop growth and weather interactions, retrieval of growth and production data, construction of predictive models for analyzing pest-crop interactions, and development of strategies for insect control. New uses for information processing steadily emerged.

The second major technology advance of the period was biotechnology, the use of technologies based on living systems to develop useful processes and products. It includes the techniques of recombinant DNA, gene transfer, embryo

POMOLOGIST GAIL MCGRANAHAN CHECKING HER EXPERIMENTAL WALNUT PLANTINGS, WHICH WERE GENETICALLY MANIPULATED TO ACHIEVE INCREASED VIGOR AND PRODUCTIVITY.

manipulation and transfer, plant regeneration, cell culture, monoclonal antibodies, and bioprocessing engineering. During the 1980s biotechnology began to offer great potential for developing higher-yielding, more nutritious crop varieties having a longer shelf life, better resistance to disease and adverse conditions, and less need for fertilizers and other chemical inputs. In animal agriculture, biotechnology's greatest immediate potential lay in therapeutics and vaccines for disease control. Bioprocessing—the use of living systems or their components to create useful products—began to offer new ways to manufacture food products, to treat wastes, and to convert renewable resources into fuel.[48]

In the 1980s much basic research in biotechnology by UC agricultural scientists sought to understand the mechanisms of gene expression and to explore methods of genetic manipulation. A special issue of *California Agriculture* in August 1982 reported on studies of the regeneration of protoplasts and plants through somatic cell genetics. Some agronomists and pomologists worked on integrating conventional and molecular genetics to add disease resistance and salt tolerance to field and orchard crops; others attempted to enhance nitrogen fixation in legumes and other crops. With the scientific groundwork being laid for later applications in farming and food processing, the nation's first biotechnology Extension specialist was appointed at Berkeley in 1990.

Although it had great potential to improve the efficiency and quality of agricultural production, biotechnology research raised concerns about its potentially complex secondary and tertiary effects. Public debate on animal biotechnology, for example, focused on the use of the growth hormone bovine somatotropin (BST) to increase milk production and feed efficiency and to accelerate animal growth. PST, the equivalent of BST in swine, was shown to stimulate growth rate and feed efficiency and to dramatically alter hog carcass composition, decreasing fat and increasing protein content. Consumer groups raised serious concerns about pass-through effects on humans ingesting these products, however, and others questioned whether small-scale producers would be able to compete in a marketplace altered by a new jump in production.[49] Many agricultural scientists maintained that biotechnology would not necessarily lead to new biological hazards, and that the risks associated with transgenic plants or animals would be no different from those of classical breeding programs. Others did not agree. UC scientists were involved in some of these discussions early on, through the Agricultural Issues Center.[50]

## THE DIVISION'S RESPONSE TO COMPLEX PUBLIC ISSUES

By definition, the agricultural research and extension establishment is a problem-solving organization. Research personnel seek solutions for real-world problems related to the agricultural production system; extension agents spread the word by education. One difference between earlier years and the 1970s was that *problems* had often turned into *issues*—they involved complex, interrelated factors, many different disciplines, and, often, political processes not subject to technical manipulation. Hence the Division began during this decade

to organize a new kind of problem-solving entity, the interdisciplinary task force. On several issues, agricultural specialists, economists, and others from outside the Division collaborated in efforts to clarify issues and make recommendations on policy choices.

The first such major effort was the task force convened in 1973 to study the implications of the worldwide food crisis of that year. The second was a 1977 task force mobilized for a nearly year-long exercise in agricultural policy analysis. This massive exercise, engaging nearly 200 people, was divided into eleven study group subject areas. In a series of meetings University staff from many departments joined representatives of government, public-interest groups, and the private sector. Ultimately the task force report identified crucial questions underlying agricultural policy issues in California for the next decade and the information needed to help meet their resolution.[51] Shortly after the report's appearance, Vice President Kendrick reflected on its significance:

> The report was not intended to provide answers and make recommendations. Its value lies in the fact that for the first time major policy issues facing agriculture in the years ahead are identified and assembled in one place, making clearer than ever that these problems interrelate with each other and must be approached systematically.... The report may well be of greater value to those outside of agriculture than to those of us within because it shows unmistakably that some issues long thought to be solely in the domain of agriculture are in fact of concern to nearly everyone.... The University's Division of Agricultural Sciences can perform its most useful service if it participates fully in understanding the issues, analyzes and researches them, and establishes a new relationship with those elements of society that are concerned about California's agricultural future.[52]

The idea for a formal agricultural policy research center was conceived a few years later, when key faculty and administrators proposed a permanent, interdisciplinary academic center for focusing the University's expertise on the long-term problems facing California agriculture. Not everyone was enthusiastic: because they feared "advocacy" in public policy formulation, some believed that the University should stay out of the policy arena. "The proposal to establish an agricultural policy center has created apprehension," wrote Kendrick. "Policy proposals involve strong emotions, because when imposed, they affect people's lives, livelihoods, and well-being." But he went on to explain that such a center would focus on research and training of future policy professionals rather than on policy formulation per se, and its governance would "ensure independence and impartiality."[53]

The name of the new center, the Center for the Analysis of Western Agricultural Issues (rather than Agricultural Policy Center), reflected that distinction. A formal proposal for a systemwide center was included in the University's 1985-86 budget request and approved by the legislature. On April 29, 1985, the California Assembly endorsed the Center's proposed six priority areas of concentration: (1) international trade, with an emphasis on Pacific Rim nations; (2) the effects of advances in productivity and technology on agriculture, with attention to social and economic impacts; (3) natural resources, with an emphasis on water, land use, and energy policies; (4) heightened awareness of the role of various minority groups in agriculture and allied industries; (5) the impacts of national agricultural policies and of fiscal, tax, and monetary policies on Western agriculture; and (6) the implications of changing food consumption patterns.

The Center was charged with conducting applied research and analysis of issues and with extending its findings to agricultural organizations, government agencies, interest groups active in the policy process, and the general public. Through these efforts the Center was expected to improve public understanding of agricultural issues and to facilitate policy decision making. An advisory board made up of leaders from the agricultural community and the public sector was to select issues for study, and faculty from UC and other institutions and representatives from government and industry would be recruited for project activities.

In 1986 the Center undertook its first major project, "Marketing California Specialty Crops: Worldwide Competition and Constraints." This started what evolved into a standard format for addressing large multidisciplinary issues. A steering committee designed the approach, topical study groups focused on specific aspects of the project, and the Center provided research support. These activities led up to a large public symposium, with subsequent publication of semitechnical reports written for policymakers and the interested public.

The Center's second major project, "Chemicals in the Human Food Chain" (1987-88), drew dozens of participants from three UC campuses and Stanford University, representing veterinary medicine, crop sciences, agricultural economics, philosophy, and law. This project also concluded with a major symposium and a book-length report. The Center's next major study examined the loss of farmland to urbanization in the Central Valley. Study groups spent nearly two years examining natural resources, population growth, land use patterns, transportation networks, and institutional factors. Symposia in Sacramento and Fresno drew more than 250 participants each.[54]

Other activities of the Center included specially commissioned studies, usually at the request of a state agency. Two such projects were a series of "white papers" requested by the California Department of Food and Agriculture on critical agricultural and resource issues in the first decade of the next century, and a report on the status of the Williamson Act (California Land Conservation Act of 1965). Another special project examined agricultural drainage problems in the San Joaquin Valley.

234

## TOWARD THE
## TWENTY-FIRST CENTURY

After more than 100 years of land-grant education and research, the United States is an immensely different place from what it was in the days of the Morrill Act (1862) and the Hatch Act (1887). The frontier is long gone: continental resources have been mapped and exploited, the hinterlands settled; cities are the power centers of our society, and farmers account for less than 2 percent of our population. Science has transformed agriculture. In the last quarter of the twentieth century scientific sophistication in laboratory and field has grown enormously, and new heights of agricultural productivity have been achieved—with concomitant impacts on the structure of agriculture. Like the rest of our complex economy, food production is big business,

LAKE SHASTA, THE PRIMARY RESERVOIR OF THE CENTRAL VALLEY PROJECT, AT A LOW POINT IN DROUGHT. EVEN WITHOUT DROUGHT, POPULATION GROWTH AND ENVIRONMENTAL NEEDS ARE STRAINING THE STATE'S WATER DELIVERY SYSTEMS.

dominated by marketing giants and factorylike production systems. Agricultural production and processing, packaging, and marketing are integrated into the national and international economies. Multinational firms and international monetary policies increasingly affect, directly or indirectly,

agricultural decisions at home. Influences from far beyond the farm gate affect local farm economies in ways both dramatic and subtle. Higher prices in international oil markets and greater competition for local water exert immediate effects on farming practices, while changes in national food preferences or availability of seasonal labor gradually shift cropping patterns. Technological change brings new opportunities as well as new problems.

While the nation today enjoys an abundant variety of agricultural products, the lawsuits and the legislative mandates described in this chapter illustrate public concern about some of the directions in which modern agriculture has moved. Environmental issues surround the use of high-input technologies as well as the release of genetically altered organisms. Equity issues arise from the impacts of technological change—who benefits and who loses. Critics question the role of the land-grant complex in promoting societal change and call for new priorities in agricultural research, including sustainability of practices and wider distribution of benefits. Inevitably some are impatient with the slowness of the complex to adapt to these challenges.

In the 1970s the University of California's Division of Agricultural Sciences was caught in the crossfire of special interest politics. Despite the institution's achievements, some groups called for an overhaul of its goals and procedures. Others in the agricultural establishment found any change threatening. These were not easy years for the Division, as it began to accommodate diverse viewpoints in its programs. Its slowness to respond was a matter partly of diminished discretionary funding, partly of the lag inherent in a cumbersome bureaucracy; but more significant was the increased politicization of the agricultural issues being debated. Many research, teaching, and extension activities related to the "new" problems of the 1970s and 1980s were fraught with controversy because they involved opinions and values as well as statistics and experiments. Since solutions to complex problems also frequently required political action, it became difficult or impossible to measure the relative "success" of (or societal benefit received from) University efforts. Frustration grew among both public-interest advocates and agricultural scientists who had always thought of their work as being outside the political arena.

FARM ADVISOR LOUIE VALENZUELA EXAMINING STRAWBERRY VARIETY TRIALS IN SAN LUIS OBISPO COUNTY. VARIETY TESTING IS STILL IMPORTANT IN UNIVERSITY RESEARCH.

The mission, goals, and procedures of the land-grant system of agricultural research and extension will doubtless be debated even more in the future. What *should* be the continuing focus of the land-grant system? It has achieved many of its early goals: most Americans eat well, and the nation's food production system functions smoothly. Some have said that the agricultural industry now can and should support more

of its own research and development needs. But new and threatening problems continue to emerge: pests, diseases, degradation of soil, water, and air resources, competing pressures on limited resources. Because agriculture is an essential component in the nation's physical and economic health, protecting and improving the industry would seem to warrant continued dedicated public assistance. Today, however, the future of agriculture and of the nation's well-being also depends on many interrelating factors off the farm, such as changing demographics, water and land use policy, and national and international marketing and distribution patterns. Though the need continues for better technical knowledge, the problems to be studied are now much more varied, and agricultural teaching, research, and extension work must now consider much nonproduction-related subject matter. Effective use of research results also calls for decisions of a different type than those relating solely to technology transfer. It is not enough to develop knowledge useful to the individual producer, who will decide whether to plant hybrid corn and whether to buy a new harvester; the industry as a whole has even greater needs for knowledge about social, economic, and political issues. And wise use of that knowledge, in the forging of intelligent policy choices, frequently requires group action, often governmental intervention.

In view of shrinking budgets, California's land-grant university will surely have to define clearer priorities for its agricultural research and extension efforts. One choice might be to forgo its claim to serve the entire population, as it did in

236 earlier, rural days, and to hew strictly to production-related matters. Another might be to continue broadening its scope of work to include the conservation of natural resources as well as emphasis on human health, food distribution, and food safety. Still another, even more ambitious, choice might be to encourage the spread of the Cooperative Extension model into other schools and colleges within the University, and to enlist other fields' expertise (such as that of public health, education, sociology, and political science) to help solve critical societal problems in depressed rural communities and inner cities.

Thoughtful and sympathetic critics of the land-grant system have recognized its needs for firm focus and farsighted leadership. They have encouraged the kind of soul-searching, rigorous analysis necessary to the future survival of a time-honored system rich with accomplishments. "Dedicated action . . . must occur now if the Land-Grant Colleges . . . are to be known as other than a historical phenomenon of the nineteenth-to-twentieth century—a good idea that was lost with the dawning of the year 2000."[55] And they have reaffirmed its value as a resilient system:

> No one can argue that the United States agricultural research "establishment" has not yielded results. It has produced research that has created the most technologically efficient agriculture in the world. It has participated in many fundamental research developments which have had wider application than just agriculture. And it has provided an environment for training superb scientists who work all over the world. It has accomplished this . . . for three principal reasons. First, it has been sufficiently well supported that overlap, competition, and, yes, nonproductive research could be afforded. In other words, it has not prevented a good deal of exploration and chancy research as a "well-planned" bureaucratic system might. Second, it has preserved to a considerable extent, given all the potential pressures, sufficient intellectual freedom to allow first-rate scientsts to be productive. And third, it has been very adept at fitting itself into the political and social fabric of the United States. Its survival and growth over the last century, while still maintaining control of its own destiny, attest to this.[56]

The last quarter century has brought a recapitulation of themes in California land-grant history. The land-grant university has a unique role to perform in society. Its teaching helps shape productive citizens, its research achieves better understanding of the natural world, and its extension work improves people's daily lives. Activities and clientele—even short- and intermediate-term goals—have changed, but the land-grant system has endured for more than a century. How will it endure into the next?[57]

# NOTES

1. See "The New Agenda Institutionalized," pp. 149–68, in Norwood Allen Kerr, *The Legacy: A Centennial History of the State Agricultural Experiment Stations, 1887–1987* (Columbia: University of Missouri–Columbia Agricultural Experiment Station, 1987).

2. U.S. Bureau of the Census, *1987 Census of Agriculture*, Vol. 1: *Geographic Area Series*, part 5, *California: State and County Data* (Washington, D.C.: U.S. Department of Commerce, 1989); Kenneth R. Farrell, "Redefining Goals and Priorities," *California Agriculture*, 41 (Mar.-Apr. 1987), p. 2.

3. More vocationally oriented production agriculture programs at other state institutions (the California Polytechnic Colleges at San Luis Obispo and Pomona; and Fresno State and Chico State Colleges, later State Universities) tended to attract undergraduates preparing for farming careers.

4. In the 1960s Vice President Harry Wellman and Riverside Chancellor Herman Spieth agreed to develop a modest program in production agriculture at Riverside, tailored to southern coastal and inland valley agriculture. Although program recommendations were developed, other demands and a lukewarm response from other agricultural campuses thwarted the idea.

5. University of California Food Task Force, *A Hungry World: The Challenge to Agriculture*, Summary Report (Berkeley: UC Division of Agricultural Sciences, July 1974), pp. 34–35.

6. USDA Study Team on Organic Farming, *Report and Recommendations on Organic Farming* (Washington, D.C.: U.S. Department of Agriculture, July 1980).

7. Council for Agricultural Science and Technology, Report No. 84, *Organic and Conventional Farming Compared* (Ames, Iowa: CAST, Oct. 1980).

8. C. Bruhn, S. Lane, and L. Walton, "Perspective of Consumers," in Harold O. Carter and Carole F. Nuckton, eds., *Chemicals in the Human Food Chain: Sources, Options, and Public Policy* (Davis: UC Agricultural Issues Center, 1988), pp. 9–13.

9. J. M. Lyons, "Options and Alternatives," in Harold O. Carter and Carole F. Nuckton, eds., *Chemicals in the Human Food Chain: Sources, Options, and Public Policy* (Davis: UC Agricultural Issues Center, 1988), pp. 57–60.

10. Robert C. Fellmeth et al., *Politics of Land: Ralph Nader's Study Group Report on Land Use in California* (New York: Grossman, 1973), p. 16.

11. Don Villarejo, *Getting Bigger: Large Scale Farming in California* (Davis: California Institute for Rural Studies, 1980).

12. Harold O. Carter, Warren E. Johnston, and Carole Frank Nuckton, eds., *Farm-Size Relationships, with an Emphasis on California: A Review of What Is Known about the Diverse Forces Affecting Farm Size, and Additional Research Considerations* (Davis: UC Department of Agricultural Economics, December 1980).

13. Descriptions of the trial and quotes from legal documents are taken from the UC General Counsel's several reports to the Regents between 1979 and 1989. (Oakland: UC Office of the General Counsel).

14. Ibid.

15. *Los Angeles Times* (Nov. 21, 1987), Pt. II, p. 8.

16. Personal communication from George Marchand, Special University Counsel, May 1992.

17. Refugio Rochin offered a tentative approach to gauging the worth of mechanization research in "Farm Mechanization

238 Research: Assessing the Consequences," *California Agriculture*, 32 (Aug. 1978): 8–10; and Philip L. Martin and Stanley S. Johnson discussed the economic and legal implications in "Agricultural Mechanization and Public Policy," *California Agriculture*, 32 (June 1978): 4–5, commenting, "If the concept of culpability were exorcised from farm mechanization discussions, the issue could be seen as one in which society is pursuing incompatible social goals. Society strives for both full employment and increased agricultural productivity. These goals inevitably collide."

18. The following narrative of events is derived from the author's interview with Robert Payton, who served as coordinator for the ice-minus hearings. For the reports themselves, see UC Division of Agriculture and Natural Resources, "Ice Nucleating Minus Research Field Test," Draft Environmental Impact Report, December 1986, State Clearinghouse No. 86093001, with Appendices; Final Impact Report, February 1987.

19. Stephen Hall, "One Potato Patch That Is Making Genetic History," *Smithsonian*, 18 (Aug. 1987): 125–36.

20. L. Ludlow, "UC's Farming Switch–It's All Ears for Getting Off 'Pesticide Treadmill.'" *San Francisco Examiner* (Feb. 2, 1986), p. B-1.

21. Gail Feenstra et al., "What Is Sustainable Agriculture?" (Davis: UC Sustainable Agriculture Research Education Program, Dec. 1991).

22. J. B. Kendrick, "Publicly Funded Agricultural Research–An Anachronism or a Challenge?" *California Agriculture*, 33 (Mar. 1979): 2.

23. Alex F. McCalla, "Politics of the Agricultural Research Establishment," in Don F. Hadwiger and William P. Browne, eds., *The New Politics of Food* (Lexington, Mass.: D.C. Heath, 1978), pp. 77–91.

24. C. J. Hitch, "Statement of Policy for the Division of Agricultural Sciences" (Berkeley: UC Berkeley Division of Agricultural Sciences, April 4, 1968).

25. "It was something I had no part in initiating, so I didn't feel any particular ownership of what was produced, and since it contained what I thought were some deficiencies, it wound up being a nice exercise without much impact." From James B. Kendrick, Jr., *From Plant Pathologist to Vice President for Agriculture and Natural Resources, University of California, 1947–1986* (Berkeley: UC Regional Oral History Office, 1989), p. 153.

26. The USDA established the Classified Research Information System (CRIS) to facilitate annual reporting on Experiment Station projects. The nine CRIS categories are (1) resource conservation and management, (2) environmental enhancement, (3) production capacity and efficiency, (4) product improvement and marketing, (5) protection of plants and animals, (6) family and consumer welfare, (7) community and economic development, (8) disciplinary research, and (9) youth development (4–H). In 1973 the University of California reported 2,670 projects in these nine categories.

27. B. Day, "A Five-Year Plan for the California Agricultural Experiment Station" (Berkeley: UC Division of Agricultural Sciences, 1972).

28. C. O. McCorkle, "Report and Recommendations of the Task Force on Agricultural Instructional and Related Programs to the Academic Planning and Program Review Board" (Berkeley: UC Office of the President, Dec. 5, 1972).

29. Kendrick, *From Plant Pathologist to Vice President*, pp. 290–91.

30. Elmer W. Learn, James M. Lyons, and James Meyers, "Strategic Planning: Phase I–Background and Information" (Berkeley: UC Division of Agriculture and Natural Resources, November 1987).

31. Ibid. The Learn, Lyons, and Meyers analysis of funding for UC agricultural research over 25 years showed that the federal share of the Agricultural Experiment Station (AES) budget declined after the 1960s, while the private sector shouldered an increasing share. State general appropriations provided a much larger share of the base funding for AES (62 to 65 percent) than for all University research (18 to 23 percent). While the absolute level of total expenditures for both research and extension grew almost fourfold during the period, much of this increase was accounted for by salary increases as well as inflationary price jumps for equipment and supplies.

32. The farm community perceives that paying royalties and fees for the products of technologies developed at publicly supported universities is in effect paying twice. The key issue debated within the university context is whether patents should be viewed primarily as an instrument for an orderly process in technology transfer

or as a source of funding to compensate for the decline in public funding.

33. See Gaylord Whitlock, "EFNEP Helps Low-Income Families Improve Diets," *California Agriculture*, 30 (Dec. 1976): 6–8.

34. This discussion is condensed from Learn, Lyons, and Meyers, "Strategic Planning."

35. Assemblyman John Vasconcellos raised these issues, among others, in a letter to UC President David Saxon on December 23, 1977. (Sacramento: California State Assembly Ways and Means Committee).

36. This discussion is condensed from Learn, Lyons, and Meyers, "Strategic Planning."

37. Walter Strong et al., "Report of the Task Force on Affirmative Action Issues in the University's Cooperative Extension Service" (Berkeley: UC Office of the President, June 1979). In July 1979 President Saxon also directed Vice President Kendrick to review and report on Extension program services.

38. Fellmeth et al., *Politics of Land*, p. viii.

39. See the special issue on Integrated Pest Management in *California Agriculture*, 32 (Feb. 1978). IPM photographers developed a very high-quality collection of insect photos as an aid to precise pest identification, and manuals gradually became available for most of California's leading crops.

40. The historical development of the program is described in the Genetic Resources Conservation Program's *Annual Report, 1985–1986*.

41. The regular, varied research reports appearing in *California Agriculture* provide a fairly good chronological record of Experiment Station work over time.

42. See Refugio I. Rochin and Steven Huffstutlar, "California's Low-Income Producer Cooperatives," *California Agriculture*, 37 (Mar.-Apr. 1983): 21–23.

43. See *The Family Farm in California: Final Report of the Small Farm Viability Project, Submitted to the State Legislature* (Sacramento: State GPO, 1977).

44. UC Small Farm Center, "The Small Farm Program: the First Fifteen Years" (Davis: UC Davis Small Farm Center, Jan. 1990).

45. See G. A. Beall, "Developing the Sea's Resources: The Marine Advisory Program," *California Agriculture*, 30 (Oct. 1976): 8–13.

46. See M. J. Phillips, "Implications of Evolving Technology for American Agriculture" (Washington, D.C.: U.S. Congress Office of Technology Assessment, 1986).

47. H. Gerola and R. E. Gomory, "Computers in Science and Technology: Early Indications," *Science* 225 (July 6, 1984): 11–18.

48. Committee on a National Strategy for Biotechnology in Agriculture, "Agricultural Biotechnology: Strategies for National Competitiveness" (Washington, D.C.: Board of Agriculture, National Research Council, 1987).

49. M. Hansen et al., "Plant Breeding and Biotechnology: New Technologies Raise Important Social Questions," *BioScience* 36 (Jan. 1986): 29–39.

50. See M. L. Hayenga, "Biotechnology in the Food and Agricultural Sector: Issues and Implications for the 1990s" (Davis: UC Davis Agricultural Issues Center Paper No. 88–5, 1988).

51. *Agricultural Policy Challenges for California in the 1980's: The Report of the University of California Agricultural Issues Task Force, 1978*. (Berkeley: UC Division of Agricultural Sciences *Special Publication 3250*, Oct. 1978).

52. J. B. Kendrick, "The Next Step," *California Agriculture*, 32 (Dec. 1978): 2.

53. J. B. Kendrick, "Agricultural Policy Center–Friend or Foe?" *California Agriculture*, 39 (Mar.-Apr. 1985): 2.

54. See Harold O. Carter and Carole Frank Nuckton, eds., *California's Central Valley–Confluence of Change* (Davis: UC Agricultural Issues Center, 1990).

55. James H. Meyer, "Rethinking the Outlook of Colleges Whose Roots Have Been in Agriculture" (Davis: UC Office of the Chancellor Emeritus, March 1992), p. 15.

56. McCalla, "Politics," pp. 77–91.

57. Thanks to Elmer Learn, Alex McCalla, and Robert Peyton for their contributions to nuancing this discussion.

# Literature Cited

Academic plan for the Department of Environmental Toxicology, 1989–1994. Unpublished manuscript. Davis: UC Davis Department of Environmental Toxicology.

Adams, Ansel, and Nancy Newhall. 1967. *Fiat lux: The University of California.* New York: McGraw-Hill.

Adams, Frank. 1959. *Frank Adams, University of California, on irrigation, reclamation, and water administration.* An oral history. Berkeley: UC Regional Cultural History Project.

——. 1969. History of the irrigation division, 1910–1954. Unpublished manuscript, UC Davis Department of Water Science and Engineering.

——. 1987. *Edward F. Adams, 1839–1929.* Berkeley: privately printed.

Adams, R. L. 1921. *The marvel of irrigation: A record of a quarter century in the Turlock and Modesto irrigation districts, California.* San Francisco: Bond Department of The Anglo and London Paris National Bank.

*Agricultural policy challenges for California in the 1980s: The report of the University of California Agricultural Issues Task Force, 1978.* 1978. Berkeley: UC Division of Agricultural Sciences Special Publication 3250.

Amerine, Maynard. 1962. Hilgard and California viticulture. *Hilgardia* 33(1):1–23.

Anderson, Clifford B. 1961. The metamorphosis of American agrarian idealism in the 1920s and 1930s. *Agricultural History* 35 (Oct.):182–88.

Bachman, Kenneth L., and Jackson V. McElveen. 1975. The family farm, 1958. In *Agriculture in the United States: A documentary history,* ed. Wayne D. Rasmussen, 2922–28 (New York: Random House.

Bailey, Liberty Hyde. 1911. *The country-life movement in the United States.* New York: Macmillan.

Bainer, Roy. 1975. *The engineering of abundance: An oral history memoir of Roy Bainer.* Interviews conducted by A. I. Dickman. Davis: UC Oral History Center.

Baker, Gladys L. 1939. *The county agent.* Chicago: University of Chicago Press.

Barnett, Paul. 1978. *Labor's dwindling harvest: The impact of mechanization on California's fruit and vegetable workers.* Davis: California Institute for Rural Studies.

Baur, E. John. 1966. California crops that failed. *California Historical Quarterly* 45:41–68.

Bean, Walton. 1944. James Warren and the beginnings of agricultural institutions in California. *Pacific Historical Review* 13:361–75.

——. 1988. *California: An interpretive history,* 5th ed. New York: McGraw-Hill.

242 Benedict, Murray. 1953. *Farm policies of the United States, 1790–1950.* New York: The Twentieth Century Fund.

Bernstein, Irving. 1970. *The turbulent years: A history of the American worker, 1933–1941.* Boston: Houghton Mifflin.

*Bertram Hanford Crocheron, architect and builder of the California Agricultural Extension Service.* 1967. Berkeley: UC Agricultural Extension Service.

Blackford, Mansel. 1977. *The politics of business in California, 1890–1920.* Columbus: Ohio State University Press.

Borg, Axel. 1987. *Bibliography of California Agricultural Experiment Station publications, 1877 to 1975.* Unpublished reference manuscript in Shields Library, Bio-Ag section.

Bowers, William L. 1974. *The country life movement in America, 1900–1920.* New York: Kennikat Press.

Bruhn, C., S. Lane, and L. Walton. 1988. Perspective of consumers. In Harold O. Carter and Carole Frank Nuckton, eds., *Chemicals in the human food chain: Sources, options, and public policy.* Davis: UC Agricultural Issues Center, pp. 9–13.

Brunner, Edmund de S., and Mary V. Brunner. 1922. *Irrigation and religion: A study of religion and social conditions in two California counties.* New York: Doran.

Buck, Solon Justus. 1913. *The Granger movement: A study of agricultural organization and its political, economic, and social manifestations, 1870–1880.* Harvard Historical Studies, Vol. 19. Cambridge, Mass.: Harvard University Press.

California Aggie Alumni Association. 1968. UCD and the migrant farm workers. *UCD Dimensions* (Fall):3–6.

California Agricultural Extension Service. n.d. *A report of the emergency farm labor project, 1943–45.* Berkeley: UC College of Agriculture, Office of the Director of the Extension Service.

California Agricultural Research Study Committee. 1946, 1947, 1948. *Reports on agricultural research in California, presented to the governor of California and the California legislature in accordance with the provisions of S.B. 124, Chapter 144, Statutes of 1945.* Sacramento: State Government Printing Office.

*California and the challenge of growth: A series of statewide conferences on problems arising from California's great population increase–1963.* 1964. Berkeley: UC Printing Dept.

California Department of Water Resources. 1981. California rainfall summary: Monthly total precipitation, 1849–1980. Sacramento: State Government Printing Office.

California Liaison Committee of the State Board of Education and the Regents of the University of California. 1960. *A master plan for higher education in California, 1960–1975.* Sacramento: California State Department of Education.

California Mexican Fact-Finding Committee. 1930. *Mexicans in California, a report of Governor C. C. Young's Mexican Fact-Finding Committee.* Sacramento: State Government Printing Office.

California Special Legislative Commission on Agricultural Education. 1923. *Report as authorized by A. B. 1335, 44th Session of the Legislature of California.* Sacramento: State Government Printing Office.

California State Board of Control. 1920. *California and the Oriental: Japanese, Chinese, and Hindus, report . . . to Governor Wm. D. Stephens, June 19, 1920.* Sacramento: State Government Printing Office.

California State Reconstruction and Reemployment Commission. 1947. *Suggested agricultural policies for California.* Sacramento: State Government Printing Office.

Carr, Ezra Slocum. 1875. *The patrons of husbandry on the Pacific coast.* San Francisco: Bancroft.

Carson, Rachel. 1962. *Silent spring.* Boston: Houghton Mifflin.

Carter, Harold O., and Carole Frank Nuckton, eds. 1988. *Chemicals in the human food chain: Sources, options, and public policy.* Davis: UC Agricultural Issues Center.

———. 1990. *California's Central Valley–confluence of change.* Davis: UC Agricultural Issues Center.

Carter, Harold O., Warren E. Johnston, and Carole Frank Nuckton, eds. 1980. *Farm-size relationships, with an emphasis on California: A review of what is known about the diverse forces affecting farm size, and additional research considerations.* Davis: UC Department of Agricultural Economics.

Chambers, Clarke A. 1952. *California farm organizations: A historical study of the Grange, the Farm Bureau and the Associated Farmers, 1929–1941.* Berkeley: UC Press.

Chan, Sucheng. 1986. *This bittersweet soil: The Chinese in California agriculture.* Berkeley: UC Press.

Chinn, Thomas W., ed. 1969. *A history of the Chinese in California: A syllabus.* San Francisco: Chinese Historical Society of America.

Cleland, Robert Glass. 1969. *From wilderness to empire: A history of California.* New York: Knopf.

Cleland, Robert Glass, and Osgood Hardy. 1929. *The march of industry.* Los Angeles: Powell.

Cohen, Michael P. *The history of the Sierra Club, 1892–1970.* San Francisco: Sierra Club Books.

Coke, J. Earl. 1975. *Reminiscences on people and change in California agriculture, 1900–1975.* Interviews conducted by Ann Foley Scheuring. Davis: UC Oral History Center.

Cole, Harold H. 1977. *Adventurer in animal science: Harold H. Cole.* Interviews conducted by Reuben Albaugh, Irving I. Geschwind, and Hubert Heitman. Davis: UC Oral History Center.

Committee on a National Strategy for Biotechnology in Agriculture. 1987. *Agricultural biotechnology: Strategies for national competitiveness.* Washington, D.C.: Board of Agriculture, National Research Council.

Conkin, Paul. 1960. The vision of Elwood Mead. *Agricultural History* 34 (Apr.):88–97.

Cooper, Erwin. 1968. *Aqueduct empire.* Glendale, Calif.: Arthur H. Clark.

Cordasco, Francesco. 1960. *Daniel Coit Gilman and the protean Ph.D.: The shaping of American graduate education.* Leiden, The Netherlands: Brill.

Council for Agricultural Science and Technology. 1980. *Organic and conventional farming compared.* Ames, Ia.: CAST Report No. 84.

Crissey, Forrest. 1914. *Where opportunity knocks twice.* Chicago: Reilly & Britton.

Crouchett, Lorraine Jacobs. 1982. *Filipinos in California.* El Cerrito, Calif.: Downey Place Publishing.

Cruess, William V. 1967. *A half century in food and wine technology.* An interview conducted by Ruth Teiser. Berkeley: UC Regional Oral History Office.

Curti, Merle, and Vernon Carstensen. 1949. *The University of Wisconsin: A history, 1848–1925.* Madison: University of Wisconsin Press.

Danbom, David B. 1979. *The resisted revolution: Urban America and the industrialization of agriculture, 1900–1930.* Ames: Iowa State University Press.

Daniel, Cletus E. 1982. *Bitter harvest: A history of California farmworkers, 1870–1941.* Berkeley: UC Press.

Daniels, Roger. 1962. *The politics of prejudice: The anti-Japanese movement in California and the struggle for Japanese exclusion.* Berkeley: UC Press.

Das, Rajani Kanta. 1923. *Hindustani workers on the Pacific coast.* Berlin: Walter de Gruyter.

Davison, Stanley R. 1979. *The leadership of the reclamation movement, 1875–1902.* New York: Arno Press.

Day, B. 1972. A five-year plan for the California Agricultural Experiment Station. Berkeley: UC Division of Agricultural Sciences.

De Witt, Howard. 1980. *Violence in the fields: California Filipino farm labor unionization during the Great Depression.* Saratoga, Calif.: Century Twenty One Publishing.

de Roos, Robert. 1948. *The thirsty land: The story of the Central Valley Project.* Stanford, Calif.: Stanford University Press.

Deutsch, Monroe, ed. 1926. *The abundant life.* Berkeley: UC Press.

Dickman, A. I. 1978. *Interviews with persons involved in the development of the mechanical tomato harvester, the compatible processing tomato and the new agricultural systems that evolved.* Davis: UC Oral History Center.

Downey, Sheridan. 1947. *They would rule the valley.* San Francisco: privately printed.

Draper, Anne, and Hal Draper. 1968. *The dirt on California: agribusiness and the university.* Berkeley: Independent Socialist Clubs of America.

Duffy, William J. 1972. *The Sutter Basin and its people.* Davis: privately printed.

Eddy, Edward Danforth, Jr. 1956. *Colleges for our land and time: The land-grant idea in American education.* New York: Harper.

244

Edwards, Everett E. 1940. American agriculture—The first 300 years. In *Yearbook of Agriculture 1940*, 171–276. Washington, D.C.: U.S. Department of Agriculture.

Ellsworth, Clayton. 1960. Theodore Roosevelt's Country Life Commission. *Agricultural History* 34 (Oct.):155–72.

Erdman, Henry E. 1958. The development and significance of California cooperatives, 1900–1915. *Agricultural History* 32 (July):179–84.

———. 1971. *Agricultural economics: Teaching, research and writing, University of California, Berkeley, 1922–1969.* An interview conducted by Malca Chall. Berkeley: UC Regional Oral History Office.

Evenson, R. E., P. E. Waggoner, and V. W. Ruttan. 1979. Economic benefits from research: An example from agriculture. *Science* 205:1101–7.

1957 Extension Committee on Organization and Policy, Subcommittee on Scope and Responsibility. 1958. *The Cooperative Extension Service . . . today: A statement of scope and responsibility.* Washington, D.C.: USDA.

*Family farm in California, the: Final report of the Small Farm Viability Project, submitted to the California state legislature.* 1977. Sacramento: State Government Printing Office.

Feenstra, Gail, et al. 1991. What is sustainable agriculture? Davis: UC Sustainable Agriculture Research and Education Program.

Fellmeth, Robert, et al. 1973. *Politics of land: Ralph Nader's study group report on land use in California.* New York: Grossman.

Ferrier, William Warren. 1930. *Origin and development of the University of California.* Berkeley: Sather Gate Book Shop.

———. 1937. *Ninety years of education in California, 1846–1936.* Berkeley: Sather Gate Book Shop.

Fiske, Emmett. 1979. The college and its constituency: Research and community development at the University of California, 1875–1978. Ph.D. diss., University of California, Davis.

Flint, Mary Louise, and Robert van den Bosch. 1977. *A source book on integrated pest management.* Berkeley: UC International Center for Integrated and Biological Control.

Frakes, George E., and Curtis B. Solberg, eds. 1971. *Minorities in California history.* New York: Random House.

Friedland, William F., and Amy Barton. 1975. *Destalking the wily tomato: A case study in social consequences in California agricultural research.* Davis: UC Department of Applied Behavioral Sciences Research Monograph 15.

Fuller, Varden. 1939. The supply of agricultural labor as a factor in the evolution of farm organization in California. Ph.D. diss., University of California, Berkeley.

Galarza, Ernesto. 1964. *Merchants of labor: The Mexican bracero story.* Santa Barbara, Calif.: McNally and Loftin.

———. 1977. *Farm workers and agri-business in California, 1947–1960.* Notre Dame, Ill.: University of Notre Dame Press.

Galbraith, John Kenneth. 1969. Berkeley in the age of innocence. *The Atlantic* 223(6):62–68.

———. 1988. *The great crash, 1929.* 1954. Reprint, Boston: Houghton Mifflin.

Gerola, H., and R. E. Gomory. 1984. Computers in science and technology: Early indications. *Science* 225:11–18.

Goldschmidt, Walter. 1978. *As you sow: Three studies in the social consequences of agribusiness.* Montclair, N.J.: Allanheld, Osmun.

Graham, Frank, Jr. 1970. *Since silent spring.* Boston: Houghton Mifflin.

Great tomato machine, the. 1979. *California Tomato Grower* 22(6):4–12.

Gregory, James N. 1989. *American exodus: The dust bowl migration and Okie culture in California.* New York: Oxford University Press.

Grodzin, Morton. 1946. *Americans betrayed.* Chicago: University of Chicago Press.

Haber, Samuel. 1964. *Efficiency and uplift: Scientific management in the Progressive Era, 1890–1920.* Chicago: University of Chicago Press.

Hall, Stephen. 1987. One potato patch that is making genetic history. *Smithsonian* 18 (Aug.):125–36.

Hansen, M., et al. 1986. Plant breeding and biotechnology: New technologies raise important social questions. *BioScience* 36 (Jan.):29–39.

Hardin, Charles M. 1946. The Bureau of Agricultural Economics under fire: A study in valuation conflicts. *Journal of Farm Economics* 28(3):635–68.

Hawley, Ellis W. 1966. The politics of the Mexican labor issue, 1950–1965. *Agricultural History* 40 (July):157–76.

Hayenga, M. L., Biotechnology in the food and agriculture sector: Issues and implications for the 1990s. 1988. Davis: UC Agricultural Issues Center Paper No. 88-5.

Hayes, Michael N., and Alan L. Olmstead. 1981. The Arvin and Dinuba controversy reexamined. Davis: UC Agricultural History Center Working Paper 8.

Hays, Samuel P. 1959. *Conservation and the gospel of efficiency: The Progressive Conservation Movement, 1890–1920.* Cambridge, Mass.: Harvard University Press.

Heizer, Robert F., and Alan F. Almquist. 1971. *The other Californians: Prejudice and discrimination under Spain, Mexico, and the United States to 1920.* Berkeley: UC Press.

Hewitt, William B. 1987. R. E. Smith: Pioneer in phytopathology. *Annual Review of Phytopathology* 25:41–50.

Hightower, Jim. 1973. *Hard tomatoes, hard times: A report of the Agribusiness Accountability Project on the failure of America's land grant college complex.* Cambridge, Mass.: Schenckman.

Hilgard, Eugene W. 1882. Progress in agriculture by education and government aid. Parts 1 and 2. *Atlantic Monthly* (Apr.):531–42; (May): 651–61.

———. 1884. *Report on the physical and agricultural features of the state of California, with a discussion of the present and future of cotton production in the state.* Washington, D.C.: U.S. Department of the Interior, Census Office.

Hine, Robert V. 1953. *California's utopian colonies.* New York: Norton.

Hitch, C. J. 1968. Statement of policy for the Division of Agricultural Sciences. Berkeley: UC Dvision of Agricultural Sciences.

Hodgson, Robert W. 1917. Hilgard Hall: A gift of the citizens of California. Berkeley: UC Printing Dept.

Hofstadter, Richard, and Wilson Smith, eds. 1961. *American higher education: A documentary history.* Chicago: University of Chicago Press.

Holliday, J. S. 1981. *The world rushed in: The California gold rush experience.* New York: Simon and Schuster.

Hutchison, Claude B., ed. 1946. *California agriculture.* Berkeley: UC Press.

———. 1961. *The College of Agriculture, University of California, 1922–1952.* An interview conducted by Willa Klug Baum. Berkeley: UC Regional Cultural History Project.

*In memoriam: Benjamin Ide Wheeler.* 1928. Berkeley: UC Press.

*In memoriam: Edward James Wickson. Addresses delivered at a memorial service October 14, 1923.* 1924. Berkeley: UC Printing Dept.

*In memoriam: University of California.* 1980. Berkeley: UC Academic Senate.

*In memoriam: Eugene Woldemar Hilgard.* 1916. Berkeley: UC Press.

Iwata, Masakazu. 1962. The Japanese immigrants in California agriculture. *Agricultural History* 36 (Jan.):25–37.

Jacobson, Yvonne. 1984. *Passing farms, enduring values: California's Santa Clara Valley.* Los Altos, Calif.: William Kaufmann.

James, Marquis, and Bessie R. James. 1954. *Biography of a bank: The story of Bank of America NT & SA.* New York: Harper & Row.

Jamieson, Stuart. 1945. Labor unionism in American agriculture. *Bulletin 836.* Washington, D.C.: U.S. Bureau of Labor Statistics.

*Japanese farmers in California, the.* circa 1918. San Francisco: The Japanese Agricultural Association.

Jenny, Hans. 1946. Exploring the soils. In Claude B. Hutchison, ed., *California Agriculture,* 325–30. Berkeley: UC Press.

———. 1961. *E. W. Hilgard and the birth of modern soil science.* Pisa, Italy: Collana della Rivista Agrochimica.

Jewett, Alyce Williams. 1982. *Saga of UCD.* Davis: privately printed.

Johnson, Sherman E. 1960. Changes in American farming during World War II. In Wayne Rasmussen, ed., *Readings in the history of American agriculture,* 275–86. Urbana: University of Illinois Press.

Johnstone, Paul H. 1940. Old ideals versus new ideas in farm life. In *Yearbook of agriculture 1940,* 111–69. Washington, D.C.: Department of Agriculture.

246

Joint USDA/NASULGC Extension Study Committee. 1968. *A people and a spirit.* Fort Collins: Colorado State University.

Kanzaki, Kuchi. 1921. *California and the Japanese.* San Francisco: Japanese Association of America.

Kellogg, Charles E., and David C. Knapp. 1966. *The College of Agriculture: Science in the public service.* New York: McGraw-Hill.

Kendrick, James B., Jr. 1989. *From plant pathologist to Vice President for Agriculture and Natural Resources, University of California, 1947–1986.* An interview conducted by Ann Lage in 1987. Berkeley: UC Regional Oral History Office.

Kerr, Clark. 1972. *The uses of the university: With a "postscript–1972."* Cambridge, Mass.: Harvard University Press.

Kerr, Norwood Allen. 1987. *The legacy: A centennial history of the state Agricultural Experiment Stations, 1887–1987.* Columbia: University of Missouri–Columbia Agricultural Experiment Station.

Kershner, Frederick D., Jr. 1953. George Chaffey and the irrigation frontier. *Agricultural History* 27 (Oct.):115–22.

Kirkendall, Richard S. 1964. Social science in the Central Valley of California: An episode. *California Historical Society Quarterly* 43(3):195–218.

——. 1965. Howard Tolley and agricultural planning in the 1930s. *Agricultural History* 39 (Jan.):25–33.

——. 1966. *Social scientists and farm politics in the age of Roosevelt.* Columbia, Mo.: University of Missouri Press.

Kroeber, Theodora. 1962. *Ishi in two worlds: A biography of the last wild Indian in North America.* Berkeley: UC Press.

Lange, Harry. circa 1985. Historical notes. Manuscript prepared for the Pacific branch of the Entomological Society of America.

Lawton, Harry W., and Lewis G. Weathers. 1989. The origins of citrus research in California and the founding of the Citrus Research Center and Agricultural Experiment Station. In Walter Reuther, E. Clair Calavan, and Glenn E. Carman, eds., *The citrus industry,* Vol. 5, 281–335. Oakland:UC Division of Agriculture and Natural Resources.

Learn, Elmer W., James M. Lyons, and James Meyers. 1987. Strategic planning: Phase I–Background information. Berkeley: UC Division of Agriculture and Natural Resources.

Leonard, Karen. 1985. Punjabi farmers and California's alien land law. *Agricultural History* 59 (Oct.):549–62.

Leung, Peter C. Y., with L. Even Armentrout Ma, ed. 1984. *One day, one dollar: Locke, California, and the Chinese farming experience in the Sacramento Delta.* El Cerrito, Calif.: Chinese American History Project.

Liebman, Ellen. 1983. *California farmland: A history of large agricultural landholdings.* Montclair, N.J.: Rowman & Allanheld.

Lillard, Richard G. 1976. *Eden in jeopardy: Man's prodigal meddling with his environment: The Southern California experience.* 1966. Reprint, Westport, Conn.: Greenwood Press.

Lyons, J. M. 1988. Options and alternatives. In Harold O. Carter and Carole Frank Nuckton, eds., *Chemicals in the human food chain: Sources, options, and public policy,* 57–60. Davis: UC Agricultural Issues Center.

Malin, James C. 1947. *The grassland of North America: Prolegomena to its history.* Lawrence, Kans.: privately printed.

Martin, Philip L., and Alan L. Olmstead. 1985. The agricultural mechanization controversy. *Science* 227 (Feb.): 601–6.

Mayer, Andre, and Jean Mayer. 1974. Agriculture: The island empire. *Daedalus* 103: 83–96.

McCalla, Alex F. 1978. Politics of the agricultural research establishment. In Don F. Hadwiger and William P. Browne, eds., *The new politics of food,* 77–91. Lexington, Mass.: D. C. Heath.

McConnell, Grant. 1953. *The decline of agrarian democracy.* Berkeley: UC Press.

McCorkle, C. O. 1972. Report and recommendations of the task force on agricultural instructional and related programs to the Academic Planning and Program Review Board. Berkeley: UC Office of the President.

McElvaine, Robert S. 1984. *The Great Depression: America 1929–1941.* New York: Random House.

McGowan, Joseph A. 1961. *History of the Sacramento Valley.* New York: Lewis Historical Publishing.

McWilliams, Carey. 1939. *Factories in the fields: The story of migratory farm labor in California.* Boston: Little, Brown.

——. 1946. *Southern California country: An island on the land.* New York: Duell, Sloan and Pearce.

Mead, Elwood. 1903. *Irrigation institutions: A discussion of the economic and legal questions created by the growth of irrigated agriculture in the west.* New York: Macmillan.

———. 1920. *Helping men own farms: A practical discussion of government aid in land settlement.* New York: Macmillan.

Metcalf, Woodbridge. 1969. *Woodbridge Metcalf, Extension forester, 1926–1956.* An interview conducted by Evelyn Bonnie Fairburn. Berkeley: UC Regional Oral History Office.

Meyer, James H. 1966. Will there be a second era? Paper delivered at the Conference on Undergraduate Education in the Biological Sciences for Students in Agriculture and Natural Resources, Washington, D.C., 11 November; also included in the background document for the UC Davis Research and Organization Conference at Lake Tahoe, 3–5 November.

———. 1992. Rethinking the outlook of colleges whose roots have been in agriculture. Davis: UC Office of the Chancellor Emeritus.

Michelbacher, A. E., and O. G. Bacon. 1952. Walnut insect and spider-mite control in northern California. *Journal of Economic Entomology* 45:1020–27.

Morgan, Agnes Fay. n.d. The history of nutrition and home economics in the University of California, Berkeley, 1914–1962. Unpublished manuscript in Bancroft Library, Berkeley.

Mrak, Emil H. 1974. *Emil M. Mrak, a journey through three epochs: Food prophet, creative chancellor, senior statesman of science.* Interviews conducted by A. I. Dickman. Davis: UC Oral History Program.

Nelson, Donald L. 1980. Silver threads among the gold: The first 25 years of community and rural development programs. Joint Planning and Evaluation Staff Paper Series 80–PPS-08. Washington, D.C.: U.S. Department of Agriculture.

Nelson, Lowry. 1969. *Rural sociology: Its origin and growth in the United States.* Minneapolis: University of Minnesota Press.

Noda, Kesa. 1981. *Yamato Colony, 1906–1960: Livingston, California.* Livingston, Calif.: Livingston-Merced JACL chapter.

Nordhoff, Charles. 1883. *California for immigrants.* San Francisco: Southern Pacific Railroad.

Nordin, D. Sven. 1974. *Rich harvest: A history of the Grange, 1867–1900,* 62–83. Jackson: University Press of Mississippi.

Nye, Ronald L. 1983. Federal versus state agricultural research policy: The case of California's Tulare Experiment Station, 1888–1909. *Agricultural History* 57 (Oct.):436–49.

Orsi, Richard J. 1975. The octopus reconsidered: The Southern Pacific and agricultural modernization in California, 1865–1915. *California Historical Quarterly* 54(3):197–200.

Packard, Walter. 1970. *Land and power development in California, Greece, and Latin America.* An interview conducted by Willa Klug Baum. Berkeley: UC Regional Oral History Office.

Parsons, Frank G. 1979. *The story of seed certification in California, 1937–1976: Recollections of Frank G. Parsons.* Interviews conducted by Harriet Parsons, Burt Ray, and Avrom I. Dickman. Davis: UC Oral History Center.

Parsons, Philip S., and C. O. McCorkle, Jr. 1963. A statistical picture of California's agriculture. Berkeley: UC Division of Agricultural Sciences Circular 459.

Paul, Rodman. 1958. The great California grain war: The Grangers challenge the wheat king. *Pacific Historical Review* 27:331–49.

Pettitt, George A. 1966. *Twenty-eight years in the life of a university president.* Berkeley: UC Printing Dept.

Phillips, M. J. 1986. *Implications of evolving technology for American agriculture.* Washington, D.C.: U.S. Congress Office of Technology Assessment.

Pickerell, Albert G., and May Dornin. 1968. *The University of California: A pictorial history.* Berkeley: UC Printing Dept.

Pisani, Donald J. 1983. Reclamation and social engineering in the Progressive Era. *Agricultural History* 57 (Jan.):46–63.

———. 1984. *From the family farm to agribusiness: The irrigation crusade in California and the west, 1850–1931.* Berkeley: UC Press.

Rasmussen, Wayne, ed. 1960. *Readings in the history of American agriculture.* Urbana: University of Illinois Press.

———. 1968. Advances in American agriculture: The mechanical tomato harvester as a case study. *Technology and Culture* 9(4):531–43.

248 ——, ed. 1975. *Agriculture in the United States: A documentary history*. New York: Random House.

——. 1989. *Taking the university to the people: Seventy-five years of Cooperative Extension*. Ames: Iowa University Press.

Reid, Bill G. 1964. Franklin K. Lane's idea for veterans' colonization, 1918–21. *Pacific Historical Review* 33:447–66.

Reuther, Walter, E. Clair Calavan, and Glenn E. Carman, eds. 1989. *The citrus industry, Vol. 5*. Berkeley: UC Division of Agriculture and Natural Resources.

Robinson, Michael C. 1979. *Water for the west: The Bureau of Reclamation, 1902–1977*. Chicago: Public Works Historical Society.

Rolle, Andrew. 1968. *The immigrant upraised*. Norman: University of Oklahoma Press.

Rosenberg, Charles E. 1976. *No other gods: On science and American social thought*. Baltimore, Md.: The Johns Hopkins Press.

Ross, Earle D. 1942. *Democracy's college: The land-grant movement in the formative stage*. Ames: Iowa State College Press.

Rudd, Robert L. 1964. *Pesticides and the living landscape*. Madison: University of Wisconsin Press.

Rudd, Robert L., and Richard E. Genelly. 1956. Pesticides: Their use and toxicity in relation to wildlife. *Game Bulletin* 7. Sacramento: California State Department of Fish and Game.

Ruttan, Vernon W. 1982. *Agricultural research policy*. Minneapolis: University of Minnesota Press.

Ryerson, Knowles A. 1977. *The world is my campus*. Interviews conducted by Joann Larkey. Davis: UC Oral History Center.

Saloutos, Theodore. 1975. The immigrant in Pacific coast agriculture, 1880–1940. *Agricultural History* 49 (Jan.):182–219.

Schacht, Henry. 1977. *Henry Schacht and the art of agricultural communication*. Interviews conducted by Marvin Brienes. Davis: UC Oral History Center.

Scheuring, Ann Foley. 1987–88. Part 1: From many lands. Part 2: Social climbing. Part 3: Off limits. *California Farmer* 267, no. 8:16–18; no. 9:34–36; 268, no. 1:26–28.

——. 1988. *A sustaining comradeship: A brief history of University of California Cooperative Extension, 1913–1988*. Berkeley: UC Division of Agriculture and Natural Resources.

Schmitz, Andrew, and David Seckler. 1970. Mechanized agriculture and social welfare: The case of the tomato harvester. *American Journal of Agricultural Economics* 52 (Nov.):569–77.

Scott, Roy V. 1970. *The reluctant farmer: The rise of Agricultural Extension to 1914*. Urbana: University of Illinois Press.

Scruggs, Otey M. 1960. Evolution of the Mexican farm labor agreement of 1942. *Agricultural History* 34 (July):140–49.

Shideler, James. 1957. *Farm crisis, 1919–1923*. Berkeley: UC Press.

Shields, Peter J. 1954. *The birth of an institution: The agricultural college at Davis*. Sacramento: privately printed.

*Small farm program, the: The first fifteen years*. 1990. Davis: UC Small Farm Center.

Smith, Michael L. 1987. *Pacific visions: California scientists and the environment, 1850–1915*. New Haven, Conn.: Yale University Press.

Smith, Roy J. 1943. The California land settlements at Durham and Delhi. *Hilgardia* 15(5):399–492.

Smith, Wallace. 1939. *Garden of the sun: A history of the San Joaquin Valley, 1772–1939*. Los Angeles: Lyman House.

Snow, C. P. 1964. *The two cultures: A second look*. New York: Mentor Books.

Spieth, Herman T. 1978. *From farm boy to evolutionist: The memoir of Herman T. Spieth*. Interviews conducted by Marvin Brienes. Davis: UC Oral History Center.

Stadtman, Verne A., ed. 1967. *The centennial record of the University of California*. Berkeley: UC Printing Dept.

——. 1970. *The University of California, 1868–1968*. New York: McGraw-Hill.

Starr, Kevin. 1973. *Americans and the California dream, 1850–1915*. New York: Oxford University Press.

Stein, Walter J. 1973. *California and the dust bowl migration*. Westport, Conn.: Greenwood Press.

Stern, V. M., R. F. Smith, R. van den Bosch, and K. S. Hagen. 1959. The integrated control concept. *Hilgardia* 29(2):81–101.

Street, Richard Steven. 1979–80. The economist as humanist: The career of Paul S. Taylor. *California History* 58(4):350–61.

Strong, Walter, et al. 1979. Report of the task force on affirmative action issues in the University's Cooperative Extension Service. Berkeley: UC Office of the President.

Taylor, Henry C., and Anne Dewees Taylor. 1952. *The story of agricultural economics in the United States, 1840–1932*. Ames: Iowa State College Press.

Taylor, Paul S. 1945. Foundations of California rural society. *California Historical Society Quarterly* 24(3):193–228.

——. 1973. *Paul Schuster Taylor, California social scientist*. An interview conducted by Suzanne B. Riess. Berkeley: UC Regional Oral History Office.

*Technological change, farm mechanization, and agricultural employment*. 1978. Davis: UC Department of Agricultural Economics.

Thomas, Dorothy Swaine. 1946–54. *Japanese-American evacuation and resettlement*, 3 vols. Berkeley: UC Press.

Thompson, Orville E., and Ann F. Scheuring. 1979. From lug boxes to electronics. Davis: UC Department of Applied Behavioral Sciences Agricultural Policy Seminar Monograph 3.

Tolley, H. R. 1934. *How California agriculture profits by economic research: Accomplishments of the Giannini Foundation of Agricultural Economics*. Berkeley: UC Printing Dept.

True, A. C. 1928. *A history of agricultural extension work in the United States, 1785–1923*. Washington, D.C.: U.S. Government Printing Office.

Turner, Frederick Jackson. 1920. *The frontier in American history*. New York: Holt.

UC Food Task Force. 1974. *A hungry world: The challenge to agriculture*. Berkeley: UC Division of Agricultural Sciences.

U.S. Bureau of the Census. 1975. *Historical statistics of the United States, colonial times to 1970*. Washington, D.C.: U.S. Department of Commerce.

U.S. Bureau of the Census. 1989. *1987 census of agriculture*. Vol 1: *Geographic area series*, part 5, *California: State and county data*. Washington, D.C.: U.S. Department of Commerce.

USDA Study Team on Organic Farming. 1980. *Report and recommendations on organic farming*. Washington, D.C.: U.S. Department of Agriculture.

U.S. Department of Labor. 1965. *Year of transition: Seasonal farm labor 1965: A report from the Secretary of Labor*. Washington, D.C.: U.S. Department of Labor.

U.S. National Advisory Commission on Rural Poverty. 1967. *The people left behind*. Washington, D.C.: U.S. Government Printing Office.

U.S. President's Commission on Migratory Labor. 1951. *Migratory labor in American agriculture*. Washington, D.C.: U.S. Government Printing Office.

U.S. Senate, Committee on Education and Labor. 1940–43. 76th Congress. 1940–43. *Violations of free speech and rights of labor: Hearings before a subcommittee*. 76th Congress.

van den Bosch, Robert. 1978. *The pesticide conspiracy*. Garden City, N.J.: Doubleday.

Villarejo, Don. 1980. *Getting bigger: Large scale farming in California*. Davis: California Institute for Rural Studies.

Voorhies, E. C. 1939. The beginnings of agricultural economics at the University of California. Unpublished manuscript in the UC Davis Agricultural Economics Library.

Watkins, T. H. 1983. *California: An illustrated history*. New York: American Legacy Press.

Wellman, Harry R. 1976. *Teaching, research and administration, University of California, 1925–1968*. An interview conducted by Malca Chall. Berkeley: UC Regional Oral History Office.

Wells, A. J. c. 1914. *California for the settler*. San Francisco: Southern Pacific Railroad.

Wells, George S. 1969. *Garden in the west: A dramatic account of science in agriculture*. New York: Dodd, Mead.

Wenzel, Lawrence A. 1968. The rural Punjabis of California: A religio-ethnic group. *Phylon* 29:245–56.

Wickson, Edward J. 1918. Beginnings of agricultural education and research in California. In *Annual report of the College of Agriculture and the Agricultural Experiment Station of the University of California from July 1, 1917, to June 30, 1918*.

Williams, Jerry R. 1982. *And yet they come*. New York: Center for Migration Studies.

Wilson, George E. 1987. *Farmer to farmer around the world*. Stockton, Calif.: University of the Pacific.

250

Wilson, James F. 1976. *James F. Wilson, the oral reminisences of an old sheepherder.* Interviews conducted by A. I. Dickman and G. M. Spurlock. Davis: UC Oral History Program.

Woodbridge, S. M. circa late 1890s. Criticism on the agricultural college at Berkeley. *Herald Bulletin No. 1.* Los Angeles: Los Angeles Herald.

Wright, Celeste Turner. 1981. *University woman: The memoir of Celeste Turner Wright, Professor of English, Emeritus.* Interviews by A. I. Dickman and Robert A. Wiggins. Davis: UC Oral History Center.

## SERIES OF PERIODICALS AND PUBLIC DOCUMENTS

*California Agriculture*

*Los Angeles Times*

*Pacific Rural Press*

*Proceedings of the Association of Land-Grant Colleges and Universities*

*Reports* of the College of Agriculture and the Agricultural Experiment Station of the University of California, 1877–1904, 1913–1940

*Sacramento Union*

*San Francisco Chronicle*

*San Francisco Examiner*

*Sunset Magazine*

*Transactions of the Commonwealth Club*

*UC Davis Magazine*

University of California Agricultural Experiment Station *Bulletins* and *Circulars*

University of California Archives, Bancroft Library, Berkeley

    *College of Agriculture Files*

    *Frederick Slate Papers*

    *Gilman Papers*

    *Grether Papers*

    *Hilgard Papers*

    *Inaugurals, 1872–1899*

    *Land Settlement Papers*

    *Pamphlets Historical, relating to the University of California*

    *Presidents' File, 1966*

    *Presidents' Papers*

    *Presidents' Records*

    *Regents' Records*

    *Wickson Papers*

University of California *Chronicle* (1898–1933)

University of California College of Agriculture miscellaneous publications

USDA *Statistical Bulletins*

USDA *Yearbooks of Agriculture*

## INTERVIEWS

Clair Christensen

Eric Conn

Varden Fuller

Roger Garrett

Glenn Hawkes

Harry Lange

Harry Lawton

Robert Loomis

James Lyons

James Meyer

Milton Miller

Maurice Peterson

Charles Schroeder

Paul Stumpf

Michael Stimmann

Orville Thompson

# Index